Allvoca basic

빅데이터 기반 나에게 필요한 모든 영단어

위편삼절

공자가 주역을 자주 읽어 책을 묶은 가죽끈이 세 번이나 끊어졌다는 뜻으로
한 권의 책을 몇 십 번이나 되풀이해서 읽음을 의미한다

회독 시작일을 기록하세요

1회독	년	월	일
2회독	년	월	일
3회독	년	월	일
4회독	년	월	일
5회독	년	월	일

⟨대한민국 영어 교육의 슬픈 현실⟩

우리는,

수능 시험까지의 학창 시절 12년 동안 무수히 많은 영단어들과 씨름합니다.

성인이 되어 편입 시험을 위한 공부를 이어가기도 하며,

사회 진출을 위해 토익, 공무원 시험, 텝스 시험 등을 준비하고,

유학을 위해 TOEFL, IELTS, GRE, GMAT 등을 준비하기도 합니다.

또, 사회에 나와서는 회화가 부족하여 영어 회화 학원에 등록하기도 합니다.

여기에 슬픈 현실이 있습니다.

학습 자료를 통일하지 않고 매번 새로운 교재를 찾습니다.

그 결과, 학습이 누적되거나 반복되지 않고

우리의 영어 실력은 매번 초기화되다시피 합니다.

만약, 영단어 학습서를 통일하여 암기를 누적 & 반복해왔었다면,

내 영어 실력이 지금보다 더 탄탄하지 않았을까요?

내 인생의 영단어는 『올보카 Basic & Advanced』 속 어휘 7,500개로 충분합니다.

매번 새로운 교재로 어휘력을 초기화하지 마시고, 이 교재만 반복학습하세요.

이것이 어휘 학습의 정석입니다.

저자 송승호

Allvoca
basic

|교재 소개

1. 우선순위 영단어장의 끝판왕

올보카는 빅데이터로 영단어의 우선순위를 정리한 단어장이다.

130억개 영단어 빅데이터를 정제하여 우선순위를 도출하고, 한국 영어학습환경 최적화 작업을
더해 교재를 완성하였다. 총 7,500개의 표제어로 구성된 『올보카 Basic & Advanced』는 주요
영문 텍스트에 99% 이상의 적용률(pg. 10 참조)을 자랑한다. 시험별 높은 적용률은 물론이고, 일
반 영어에도 폭넓게 적용된다.

130억 개 영단어 ⟫⟫⟫⟫⟫ 우선순위 **7,500개**

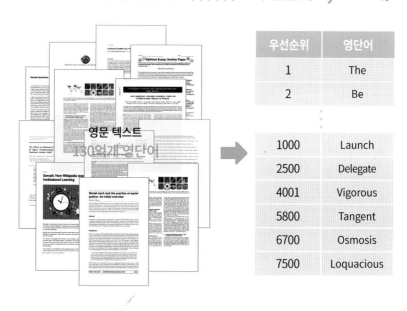

우선순위	영단어
1	The
2	Be
⋮	
1000	Launch
2500	Delegate
4001	Vigorous
5800	Tangent
6700	Osmosis
7500	Loquacious

※ 영문 텍스트 130억 개 출처: 외국 서적, 신문기사, 웹문서 등 방대한 양의 영문 텍스트를
취한한 복수의 말뭉치 데이터베이스(corpus)

8

2. 올보카 제작 과정

첫째, 빅데이터를 활용하여 어휘의 우선순위를 계산했다.

130억 영문 텍스트 속 파생어 및 관련어휘를 표제어와 통합하는 작업을 거쳤고, 통합빈도수를 기준으로 표제어를 정렬했다. 또한, 주요 파생어들은 교재 속 표제어와 함께 표시하였다.

둘째, 특이 사례들은 순위를 조정하였다.

예를들어, 초급 어휘인 'Giraffe(기린)'는 단순 빈도수 기준으로는 최고난도 어휘로 분류된다. 유아용 교재엔 자주 등장하지만 그 외의 텍스트엔 매우 드물게 등장하는 단어이기 때문이다. 올보카는 해당 어휘를 초급 어휘에 해당되도록 순위를 조정하는 등, 난이도 최적화 작업을 진행하였다.

셋째, 외래어는 별도 학습이 가능하도록 필터링하였다.

우리나라에서 유난히 많은 외래어가 사용되는 만큼, 상당수 어휘는 철자만 익히면 단번에 체득 가능하다. 예를들어 Lingerie (란제리), Veranda (베란다), Bourgeois (부르주아) 등의 어휘는 얼핏 보면 생소하지만 발음과 스펠링만 익히면 손쉽게 외워진다. (p.327)

넷째, 일반 학습자 입장에서 불필요한 특수 용어들을 배제하였다.

일례로 'Paraffin' 이란 단어는 'C_nH_{2n+2}의 화학식으로 표현되는 알케인 탄화수소(등유)를 두루 일컫는 표현'인데, 빈도수로는 순위권에 들지만 일반적인 학습자에게 기대되는 어휘가 아니다. 또한, Google nGram 을 활용해 불필요한 고어들도 제거하였다.

다섯째, 교육부 지정 필수 영단어들은 우선순위 산정 시 가중치를 부여했다.

교육부가 공개한 필수 영단어 리스트는 영어 학습의 기초가 되는 어휘들을 담고 있다. 해당 어휘들에 가중치를 부여함과 동시에 교재 내에서 교육부 지정 단어임을 표시하였다. 이는 올보카를 우리나라 영어 학습환경에 최적화하기 위한 작업이었던 만큼 남녀노소 누구나 올보카로 평생 학습이 가능하다.

3. 모든 시험이 대비 가능한 All-in-One 영단어장

올보카 적용률

영어 시험들에 대한 『올보카 Basic & Advanced』의 적용률을 테스트해보았다. 아래 표에서 알 수 있듯이, 사실상 모든 영어 시험은 올보카로 대비 가능하다. 게다가 CNN, TED 강연, 영화, 미드, 유명 연설 등 다양한 영어 콘텐츠에도 높은 적용률을 보이는 만큼 종합 영어 실력 향상에도 매우 효과적이다.

결국 '수능용 단어장', '토익용 단어장' 등 특정 시험 전용 단어장을 따로 살 필요가 없는 것이다. 따지고보면 매우 당연한 것인데, 대부분의 영어 시험은 문제은행식으로 출제되지 않기에 본인의 수준에 적합한 어휘들을 외우는 것이 가장 정직하고 효율적인 학습 방법인 것이다.

시험 영어	적용률	일반 영어	적용률
수능	99.8%	TED 강연	99.0%
공무원	99.4%	CNN	98.0%
TOEIC	99.3%	영화 (타이타닉)	98.9%
TOEFL	99.3%	미드 (프렌즈 시즌1)	99.3%
TEPS	99.2%	오바마 연설	99.8%
SAT	99.1%		

[커버리지 계산 기준] [수능 영어] - 22학년도 문제지 기준, [공무원영어] - '19 서울시 국가공무원 9급 공채 영어 필기시험 기준, [TOEIC] - ETS 공식 토익정기시험 기출문제집 최종회 문제지 기준, [TOEFL] - ETS 공개 공식 기출문제집 Set1 문제지 기준, [TEPS] - 텝스관리위원회 공식 뉴텝스 Sample Test 문제지 기준, [SAT] - College Board 제공 공식 SAT 최종회(8) 문제지 기준, [TED] - Top 4 영상 기준, [CNN] - 홈페이지 기사 제목 기준(5d), [영화] - 타이타닉 transcript 기준, [미드] - Friends Season 1 transcript 기준, [오바마] - 취임 연설 Yes We Can 기준 / 고유명사 제외 (인물명, 도시/국가명, 생소개념, 회사명 등), 의미 유추 가능 합성어 제외 『올보카 Basic & Advanced』 표제어 7,500개 및 파생어 기준 (미표시 확장어 포함) / 전체 확장 리스트는 ALLVOCA.com에서 제공 / 전체 적용률 오차 ±2%

시험별 빈출 어휘

물론, 시험의 특성에 따라 출제 어휘가 특정 분야에 집중될 수는 있다. 예를 들어, 토익은 비즈니스 영어를 중점적으로 출제하여 "broker"이라는 단어의 빈도가 타 시험 대비 상대적으로 높다. 그래서 올보카는 각 시험별 최빈출 표현들을 도출하는 작업까지 진행했다. 시험별 역대 기출문제집, 공식문제집, 시험후기 등을 취합하여(아래 표 참조) 출제 빈도가 높거나 유의미한 단어들을 약 1,000~1,500개씩 추려냈고, 학습 시 참고할 수 있도록 표제어 옆에 해당 시험명을 표기해두었다. (p.12~15 참조)

시험	빈출 어휘 출처(산출 근거)
초중고	교육청 지정 필수 영단어
수능	19개년 기출 주요 어휘
공무원	15개년 기출 빈출 어휘
토익	10개년 기출 어휘
토플	iBT 12개년 기출 및 후기
텝스	10개년 기출 어휘
편입	10개년 전국 편입 기출
GRE, SAT	공식 기출 어휘, 후기 어휘

|시험별 학습 권장량

효과적인 학습을 위해선 명확한 목표 설정이 필수적이다. 아래 표는 학습자가 스스로 계획을 세울 수 있도록 돕는 학습가이드이다. 공식기출문제들의 어휘 및 lexile 지수 분석, 시험 간 점수 환산표, 실제 학생들의 통계 등을 바탕으로 시험 주요 구간 별 학습 권장량이 산정됐다.

올보카는 평생 치를 모든 영어 시험을 대비할 수 있도록 구성돼 있으니 본인의 목표 시험 성적대를 참고하여 학습 계획을 세우도록 하자. 그리고, 매년 어휘 학습을 초기화하지 말고 공부 흔적을 해당 교재에 꾸준히 누적해나가길 추천한다.

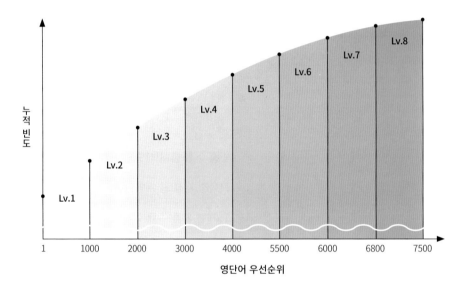

	Lv.1	Lv.2	Lv.3	Lv.4	Lv.5	Lv.6	Lv.7	Lv.8
수능	초등	중등	고등, 3~4등급	고3, 1~2등급	만점			
토익	토익 기초단어		650+	800+	940+	990		
텝스	텝스 기초단어		330+	400+	480+	520+	560+	600
토플	토플 기초단어		85+	95+	105+	110+	115+	120
공무원	공무원 기초단어		70	80	90	95~100		
편입	편입 기초단어			중위권		상위권		최상위
GRE	GRE 기초단어						GRE 빈출 단어	

＊올보카 Basic: Lv.1 ~ Lv.4 / 올보카 Advanced: Lv.5 ~ Lv.8

수능 영어

수능 영어에 출제되는 어휘는 철저히 "빈도수"로 결정된다.

평가원은 수능 출제 매뉴얼에서 다음과 같이 밝히고 있다. *"어휘수를 늘이되 사용 **빈도수가 높은 어휘**를 중심으로 ⋯ (중략) ⋯ 단, **빈도수가 낮은 어휘**를 사용해야하는 경우 주석을 달아주도록 한다."*

그러므로, 수능 어휘는 빈도수를 기준으로 학습해야 한다. 역대 수능 기출문제들을 분석한 결과, 수능 1~2 등급 목표 학생은 빈도수 #4000번(Lv.4)까지, 최상위권 학생은 #5500번(Lv.5)까지 학습하길 권장한다. Lv.6~8 은 일반 수능 수험생이 학습할 필요가 크지 않으며, 시험에 각주로 한글 뜻이 주어지는 단어들이 주로 해당 구간에 속해 있다.

	Lv.1	Lv.2	Lv.3	Lv.4	Lv.5	Lv.6	Lv.7	Lv.8
	~#1000	~#2000	~#3000	~#4000	~#5500	~#6000	~#6800	~#7500
수능	초등	중등	고등, 3~4등급	고3, 1~2등급	만점	✕	✕	✕

토익, 지텔프

ETS(토익 토플 공식 출제기관)의 Test User Guide엔 어휘의 빈도수(word frequency)가 시험 출제 시 활용된다고 명시되어 있다. 하여, 토익은 어휘 빈도수를 기준으로 학습하는 것이 효율적이다. Lv.4(~#4000)로 800점 이상의 안정적 상위권 달성이 가능하고 Lv.6 까지 학습 완료시 어휘 때문에 문제를 틀리는 경우는 없을 것으로 보인다. 토익과 수능은 어휘의 난도 면에서 큰 차이를 보이지 않지만, 각 시험의 주요 어휘는 다소 상이하다. 각 표제어 우측 상단에 추가된 라벨을 참고하면서 학습하자.

	Lv.1	Lv.2	Lv.3	Lv.4	Lv.5	Lv.6	Lv.7	Lv.8
	~#1000	~#2000	~#3000	~#4000	~#5500	~#6000	~#6800	~#7500
토익	토익 기초단어		650+	800+	940+	990	✕	✕
지텔프	지텔프 기초단어		32+	65+	95+	99+	✕	✕

텝스

서울대 언어교육원이 주최한 텝스 20주년 학술대회에서 공개된 자료들에 '어휘 빈도수 (word frequency)'의 개념이 수차례 등장한다. 어휘의 빈도수가 TEPS 출제 시 활용되는 요소임은 틀림없어보인다. 저자도 올보카 영단어 전체를 학습하고 시험에 응시하여 텝스 만점을 달성했다. 만점을 목표로 하는 학생은 Lv.8까지 학습해야겠지만, 아래 표를 참고해 각자의 학습 권장량을 확인하도록 하자. (최빈출 TEPS 어휘들은 토플과 상당 수 겹쳐 교재 내 라벨을 '토플'로 통합명시하였다.)

	Lv.1 ~#1000	Lv.2 ~#2000	Lv.3 ~#3000	Lv.4 ~#4000	Lv.5 ~#5500	Lv.6 ~#6000	Lv.7 ~#6800	Lv.8 ~#7500
텝스	텝스 기초단어		330+	400+	480+	520+	560+	600

토플, 아이엘츠

토익 시험의 주관사인 ETS(Educational Testing Service)는 토플 시험도 관리 및 개발한다. 토익과 마찬가지로, TOEFL 공식 자료에는 "low frequency word"와 "high frequency word"등의 개념이 등장하고, 이를 성적대와 연결지어서 설명을 한다. 공식 기출문제들을 분석한 결과, 95+점이 목표인 학생은 #4000번까지, 115~120점이 목표인 학생은 #7500번까지 학습이 필요하다. 토플은 학생들의 실력 편차가 매우 큰 시험이기에, 본인 성적대에 적합한 어휘부터 암기하는 것이 가장 중요하다.

	Lv.1 ~#1000	Lv.2 ~#2000	Lv.3 ~#3000	Lv.4 ~#4000	Lv.5 ~#5500	Lv.6 ~#6000	Lv.7 ~#6800	Lv.8 ~#7500
토플	토플 기초단어		85+	95+	105+	110+	115+	120
아이엘츠	아이엘츠 기초단어		6	6.5	7~7.5	8	8.5	9

공무원 영어

공무원 영어는 어휘 문제의 비중이 높은데다가 그 출제 범위가 매우 넓다. 따라서, 공무원 수험생은 자신의 목표 성적대까지 학습을 이어나가되 그 과정에서 '공무원' 빈출 라벨이 달린 어휘들은 빠짐없이 암기하도록 해야한다.

또한, '공무원 영단어' 암기 시작 전에 '수능 영단어'부터 끝내야 한다고 알려져있는데, 이는 사실상 올보카의 단계별 학습으로 해결 가능하다. 올보카는 Lv.3까지를 공무원 기초 단어(=수능 단어)로 분류하고 있으며 그 이후 Lv.4 이상부터 목표 성적별 학습량을 제시한다.

	Lv.1 ~#1000	Lv.2 ~#2000	Lv.3 ~#3000	Lv.4 ~#4000	Lv.5 ~#5500	Lv.6 ~#6000	Lv.7 ~#6800	Lv.8 ~#7500
공무원	공무원 기초단어			70	80	90	95~100	

편입, SAT, GRE

편입, SAT, GRE는 어휘 난이도가 가장 높은 시험들이다. 무턱대고 어려운 단어장을 사서 외우지 말고, 자신의 현 실력에 맞는 단어부터 차근차근 외우는 것이 가장 중요하다. 해당 시험들에선 Lv.1~4의 단어들이 '기초 단어'에 해당된다. 『올보카 Basic』은 말그대로 내 기본 실력을 다지고 빈틈이 없는지 체크하는 용도로 활용을 해야하며, 『올보카 Advanced』를 통해 시험용 어휘를 보충하도록 하자. 특히, SAT와 GRE에 빈출되는 최고난도 어휘도 Lv.7~8에 다수 포진되어 있으니 전 범위 학습을 권장한다. (최빈출 SAT 어휘들은 GRE와 상당 수 겹쳐 교재 내 라벨을 'GRE'로 통합명시하였다.)

	Lv.1 ~#1000	Lv.2 ~#2000	Lv.3 ~#3000	Lv.4 ~#4000	Lv.5 ~#5500	Lv.6 ~#6000	Lv.7 ~#6800	Lv.8 ~#7500
편입	편입 기초단어				중위권	상위권		최상위
SAT	SAT 기초단어				650+	720+		780+
GRE	GRE 기초단어						GRE 빈출 단어	

| 구성과 특징

1
순번, 표제어, 발음 기호

130억 빅데이터에 기반한 진정한 우선순위 영단어! 빈도순으로 정렬되어 있다. 복잡한 발음 기호 대신 직관적인 발음 기호를 제공한다.

• Basic: #0001~#4000
• Advanced: #4001~#7500

2
주요 시험

시험별 최중요 어휘들은 표제어 우측 상단에 해당 시험명을 표기하였다. 각 시험마다 약 1,000~1,500개의 최중요 어휘가 표기되어 있다.

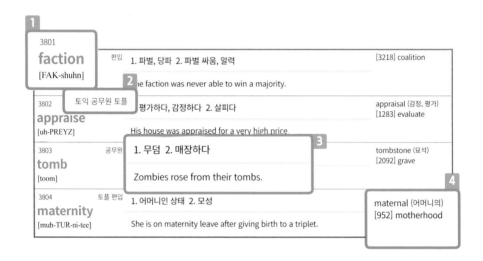

3
뜻, 예문

뜻과 예문이 위아래로 정리되어 있다. 교재 속 예문은 어휘 학습 구간에 적합한 난이도로 구성되어 있다.

(예문 해석 자료 ALLvoca.com 제공)

4
파생어, 관련어

우측열엔 (1) 주요 파생어 와 (2) 관련어가 실려 있다. 관련어들은 순번이 태깅되어 있어 연계 학습이 용이하다.

| 주요 접두사/접미사

접두사와 접미사는 단어의 형태를 확장시켜주고, 교재 속 파생어들을 이해하는데 큰 도움이 된다.
처음부터 모두 외워버리겠다는 생각보단, 여러 번 훑어보면서 몰랐던 표현들만 가볍게 눈으로 익히자.

접두사	의미	예시	예시 뜻
pro, pre	앞에, 미리	predict	예측
re	다시; 뒤로	redo	재도 관리다
in	안에; 아닌	interior	내부
un	아닌	uninterested	관심이 없는
dis	아닌	disadvantage	불이익
non	아닌	nonfiction	논픽션
anti	반대	antisocial	반사회적
counter, contra	반대	contradict	모순
mis	잘못	misunderstanding	오해
a	아닌; 진행 중인	atypical	비정형적인
co, com	함께	co-worker	동료
inter	사이에	interaction	상호 작용
trans	가로질러	transaction	거래
sub	아래에	submarine	잠수함

접미사	예시	뜻
— 명사형 —		
tion, sion	celebration (celebrate)	축하 (축하하다)
ance, ence	existence (exist)	존재 (존재하다)
al	proposal (propose)	제안 (제안하다)
th	strength (strong)	힘 (강한)
ment, ness	movement (move)	움직임 (움직이다)
ity	equality (equal)	평등 (평등한)
sis, ism	socialism (social)	사회주의 (사회적인)
er, or	teacher (teach)	교사 (가르치다)
age	marriage (marry)	결혼 (결혼하다)
hood	childhood (child)	어린시절 (아이)

5 접두사/접미사/어근 (p.18)

어휘 학습의 나비효과를 극대화할 수 있는 주요 접두사/접미사/어근들이 정리되어 있다.

| 외래어 및 기타 표현

무료 MP3 파일 제공 | Allvoca.com

외래어		외래어		외래어	
Accordion	아코디언	Blog	블로그	Chandelier	샹들리에
Adrenalin	아드레날린	Blouse	블라우스	Checkout	체크아웃
Album	앨범	Blu-Ray	블루레이	Cheetah	치타
Algorithm	알고리즘	Bonnet	자동차 본넷	Chef	셰프
Alibi	알리바이	Bouquet	부케	Cherry	체리
Almond	아몬드	Bourgeois	부르주아	Chess	체스
Alphabet	알파벳	Brassiere	브래지어	Chilli	칠리
Alps	알프스	Broccoli	브로콜리	Chimpanzee	침팬지
Aluminum	알루미늄	Brownie	브라우니	Chiropractic	카이로프랙틱
Amateur	아마추어	Brunch	브런치	Chocolate	초콜릿
Amen	아멘	Bulldog	불도그	Cholesterol	콜레스테롤
Ammonia	암모니아	Bulldozer	불도저	Christmas	크리스마스
Antenna	안테나	Burger	햄버거	Cigar	시가
Asparagus	아스파라거스	Burrito	브리토	Circus	서커스
Asphalt	아스팔트	Bus	버스	Clarinet	클라리넷
Aspirin	아스피린	Cafe	카페	Clover	클로버
		Caffeine	카페인	Cobalt	코발트색 (블루)

6 외래어 및 기타 (p.327)

우리나라에서 사용되는 주요 외래어들은 별도 리스트로 제공된다. 발음과 철자 위주로 가볍게 익히도록 하자.

| INDEX

7 INDEX (p.333)

전체 단어를 abc 순으로 정리했다. 모르는 영단어를 접하게 되면, INDEX에서 찾아 학습을 할 수 있다.

ǀ주요 접두사/접미사

접두사와 접미사는 단어의 형태를 확장시켜주고, 교재 속 파생어들을 이해하는데 큰 도움이 된다.

처음부터 모두 외워버리겠다는 생각보단, 여러 번 훑어보면서 몰랐던 표현들만 가볍게 눈으로 익히자.

접두사	의미	예시	예시 뜻
pro, pre	앞에, 미리	predict	예측
re	다시; 뒤로	redo	재도전하다
in	안에; 아닌	interior	내부
un	아닌	uninterested	관심이 없는
dis	아닌	disadvantage	불리한
non	아닌	nonfiction	논픽션
anti	반대	antisocial	반사회적
counter, contra	반대	contradict	모순되다
mis	잘못	misunderstanding	오해
a	아닌; 진행 중인	atypical	비정상의
co, com	함께	co-worker	동료
inter	사이에	interaction	상호 작용
trans	가로질러	transaction	거래
sub	아래에	submarine	잠수함
de	아래로	decrease	감소하다
en	하게 만들다	enlarge	넓히다
be	완전히~하다	befriend	친구가 되다
per	완전히	perfect	완벽
fore	앞에, 미리	forecast	예측
ante	앞에, 이전	anterior	앞쪽의
post	뒤에, 이후	posterior	후방의
bene	좋은	beneficial	이로운
mal	나쁜	malfunction	오작동
auto	자동	automatic	자동
tele	원격	telephone	전화
ambi	두 개	ambiguous	모호한
uni, mono	1	unicorn	유니콘 (뿔 하나)
bi, tri, quad, oct	2, 3, 4, 8	triangle	삼각형
semi	1/2	semifinal	준결승
poly, multi	여러	multitasking	멀티태스킹
super	위, 우위	superior	우월한
bio	생물의	biology	생물학
eco	환경	ecology	생태학
geo	땅	geology	지질학
socio	사회	sociology	사회학

접미사	예시	뜻
– 명사형 –		
tion, sion	celebration (celebrate)	축하 (축하하다)
ance, ence	existence (exist)	존재 (존재하다)
al	proposal (propose)	제안 (제안하다)
th	strength (strong)	힘 (힘 쎈)
ment, ness	movement (move)	움직임 (움직이다)
ity	equality (equal)	평등 (평등하다)
sis, ism	socialism (social)	사회주의 (사회의)
er, or	teacher (teach)	선생님 (가르치다)
age	marriage (marry)	결혼 (결혼하다)
hood	childhood (child)	어린 시절 (아이)
– 형용사형 –		
ant, ent	pleasant (please)	기쁜 (기쁘게 하다)
ful	thankful (thank)	고마운 (고마워하다)
less (-)	hopeless (hope)	희망없는 (희망)
ous	humorous (humor)	유머러스한 (유머)
al, ly, y, ic	original (origin)	기원의 (기원)
ing, ive	excessive (excess)	과도한 (과잉)
able, ible	valuable (value)	가치있는 (가치)
ious	vicious (vice)	악랄한 (악)
– 동사형 –		
en	strengthen (strength)	강화하다 (힘)
ing	walking (walk)	걷는 중 (걷다)
ize, ise	familiarize (familiar)	익히다 (익숙한)
ify	simplify (simple)	단순화하다 (간단한)
– 부사형 –		
ly	simply (simple)	간단히 (간단한)
wise	otherwise (other)	그렇지 않으면 (다른)

| 주요 어근

한글에 한자(漢字)가 있다면 영어엔 어근(word root)이 있다.

최중요 어근들을 반복 학습함으로 어근에 대한 기본 감각을 기르자.

1순위 어근	어근 뜻	예시 1	예시 2
cogn	알다	recognize	cognitive
cred	믿다	credit	credible
dict	말하다	indicate	predict
duc	끌다	introduce	reduce
graph	그리다	calligraphy	autograph
grat	기쁨, 감사	gratitude	gracious
heri	상속	heritage	hereditary
ject	던지다	eject	reject
junct	연결하다	junction	join
just	올바른	justify	justice
leg	법	legal	legislation
medi	중간	medium	intermediate
mit	보내다	commit	emit
par	동등한	compare	parity
para	옆에, 초월	parasite	paranormal
path	느끼다	sympathy	psychopathy
pel	끌어내다	appeal	compel
plic	접다	complicated	replicate
port	운반하다	support	transport
pose	놓다	position	expose
rupt	깨다	corrupt	erupt
sect	자르다	section	segment
sequ	따르다	second	sequence
spec	보다	special	inspect
tain	잡다	contain	obtain
tract	끌다	attract	traction
val	힘 있는	value	prevail
vert	돌리다	advertise	convert
vis	보다	vision	invisible
voc	부르다	voice	vocal

2순위 어근	어근 뜻	예시
alter	다른	alternative
astr	별	astronaut
audi	듣다	audience
cede	가다	procedure
clin	기울이다	decline
fide	믿다	confidence
fort	힘	effort
frag	깨다	fraction
liber	자유	liberty
limin	경계	limit
log	말	dialogue
lumin	빛	illuminate
mand	명령	command
manu	손	manual
medic	의학	medical
mount	오르다	mountain
nom	이름	nomination
norm	규범	normal
ped	발	pedestrian
phon	소리	telephone
scrib	적다	describe
serv	지키다	conserve
spir	숨 쉬다	inspire
stat	서다	statue
terri	대지	territory
test	증언	testimony
vac	비어 있는	vacant
vict	이기다	victory
viv	살아있는	survive

Allvoca.com

#0001~#1000

미국 미취학아동 수준의 어휘력이다.
기초 없이 처음부터 시작하는 학생은 표제어와 예문 중심으로(파생어는 무시) 학습하길
권장한다. 특히, 1~30번 어휘(주로 대명사, 관사, 조동사, 전치사 등)는 가볍게 예문만 읽
고 넘어갈 것을 추천한다. 기초가 어느 정도 갖춰진 학생이라면, 빈틈을 메운다는 자세로
해당 범위를 빠르게 훑으며 다의어와 생소한 파생어를 집중 암기하자.

LEVEL 01

1 **the** [th uh]	초등	1. 그 2. 그만큼	
		The book is interesting.	
2 **be** [bee]	초등	1. ~이다 2. 있다, 존재하다, 위치하다	am (be의 1인칭) being (존재) is (be의 3인칭) was (1,3인칭 과거형)
		Don't be sad.	
3 **to** [too]	초등	1. (방향을 나타낼 때) ~로, ~쪽으로 2. ~까지 3. ~에(게)	
		Let's go to school.	
4 **and** [and]	초등	1. ~와/~과 2. ~하고는, ~한 이후 3. 그래서	
		I like apples and oranges.	
5 **a** [ey]	초등	한 개의	
		I have a pencil.	
6 **of** [uhv]	초등	1. ~의 2. ~에 대한 3. ~을/를	
		She is the mother of three children.	
7 **in** [in]	초등	1. ~안의, ~내의 2. 어떤 기간에 3. (특정한 시간) 후에	inner (내부의) inward (안으로)
		A person is in my house.	
8 **you** [yoo]	초등	1. 너(희들), 당신(들) 2. 여러분	your (너의) yourself (너 자신)
		I love you.	
9 **I** [ahy]	초등	나, 나는	my (나의) me (나) myself (나 자신)
		I am happy.	
10 **that** [that]	초등	1. (먼 것을 가리킬 때)저(것), 그(것) 2. 그만큼, 그 정도	those (그것들, 사람들)
		Is that a rabbit?	
11 **it** [it]	초등	그것, 이것	
		It is a rabbit.	
12 **for** [fawr]	초등	1. ~을 위한 2. ~에 대해 3. 동안 4. 때문에(=because) 5. ~을 향한	
		This cake is for you.	
13 **have** [hav]	초등	1. 가지다, 얻다 2. 겪다 3. 먹다, 마시다	
		I have two cars.	
14 **with** [with]	초등	1. ~와 함께 2. ~에(게)	
		Please come with us.	

15 on [on]	초등	1. ~의 위에 2. ~에 관하여 3. ~(요일)에 4. ~하자마자	
		A pencil is on the desk.	
16 they [they]	초등	1. 그(사람)들, 그것들, 저들	their (그들의) them (그들)
		They are coming to the party.	
17 this [this]	초등	1. (가까운 것을 가리킬 때)이것 2. 지금, 여기	these (이것들)
		This book is very interesting.	
18 we [wee]	초등	우리, 저희	our (우리의) us (우리) ourselves (우리들)
		We like pizza.	
19 as [az]	초등	1. ~만큼, ~한 2. 때문에 3. ~처럼	
		I am as tall as you.	
20 will [wil]	중등 토익	1. ~할 것이다, ~일 것이다 2. 의지 3. 유언	would (will 의 과거형)
		I will study English.	
21 he [hee]	초등	(앞서 언급된 남자를 가리키는) 그, 그 남자	his (그의) him (그를) himself (자신 스스로)
		He is my dad.	
22 do [doo]	초등	하다, 수행하다, 해 나가다	undo (원상태로 되돌리다, 풀다) redo (다시 하다) overdo (지나치게 하다) outdo (능가하다)
		I will do my homework after school.	
23 or [awr]	초등	또는, 혹은, 안 그러면	
		Can you sing or dance?	
24 can [kan]	초등	1. 할 수 있다 2. 해도 된다 3. 캔, 깡통	could (can의 과거형)
		Can I go to the bathroom?	
25 at [at]	초등	1. ~에서(장소) 2. ~에(시간)	
		I met her at a coffee shop.	
26 from [fruhm]	초등	1. ~로부터 2. ~에게서	
		I am from Korea.	
27 not [not]	초등	1. (사건이나 성질이) 아니다, ~하지 않다 2. 부정의 대답	
		He is not stupid.	
28 by [bahy]	초등	1. 옆에, 곁에 2. ~로 인해 3. ~까지는 4. ~만큼 5. ~까지	
		There is a tree by the road.	

29 **but** [buht]	초등	그러나, 하지만, 그렇지만	
		She is not smart but she is kind.	
30 **use** [yooz]	초등 토익	1. 사용하다, 이용하다 2. 용도, 쓸모	user (사용자) useful (유용한)
		Can I use your pen?	
31 **if** [if]	초등	1. 만약, ~라면, ~한다면 2. ~인지 (아닌지) =whether	
		I can help you if you want.	
32 **all** [awl]	초등	모든, 전부	
		She is happy to see all of you.	
33 **some** [suhm]	초등 토익	1. (전체 중의) 일부 2. 조금의, 약간의 3. 어떤	something (어떤 것) someone (어떤 사람) sometimes (때때로) somewhere (어딘가)
		Some people don't like summer.	
34 **one** [wuhn]	초등	1. 하나(의), 일 2. 어느 한 3. 사람, 그것	oneself (자신 스스로)
		Would you like one more slice of cake?	
35 **make** [meyk]	초등	1. 만들다, 제조하다 2. ~하게 하다 3. 벌다, 얻다 4. 판단하다	remake (다시 만들다)
		She made cookies.	
36 **more** [mawr]		1. 더(많은/많이) 2. 더욱	
		I need more time.	
37 **so** [soh]	초등	1. 너무, 그렇게 2. 그래서, 그렇다면, 그러니, 따라서	
		He is so busy.	
38 **get** [get]	초등	1. 받다, 얻다, 구하다 2. 가져오다 3. ~되다 4. 이해하다	got (get의 과거,과거분사)
		Can I get some water?	
39 **she** [shee]	초등	그녀, 그 여자	her (그녀) herself (자신 스스로)
		She is very pretty.	
40 **time** [tahym]	초등 토익	1. 시간(을 맞추다) 2. 시기, 때 3. 시대 4. (-s) 곱하기, 배	timing (타이밍) timely (시기적절한) real-time (실시간) timetable (시간표)
		What time is it?	
41 **when** [hwen]	초등	1. 언제 2. ~때	whenever (언제든지)
		When will you marry me?	
42 **good** [good]	중등 토익	1. 좋은, 기쁜 2. 선	best (최고 좋은) better (보다 좋은) goods (상품)
		He is a good person.	

43 out [out]	초등	1. 밖에(나오다) 2. ~이 다 떨어진	outside (외부) outer (외부의)
		We went out.	
44 there [thair]	초등	그곳에, 거기에	
		The clock is over there.	
45 what [hwuht]	초등	무엇, 어떤	
		What is your name?	
46 about [uh-BOUT]	초등	1. 대략, 약 2. 에 대하여	
		The burger costs about $5.	
47 which [hwich]	중등	어느 것, 어떤 것	whichever (어느 쪽이든)
		Which car is yours?	
48 any [EN-ee]	초등 토익	1. 전혀, 단 하나도 2. 어떤, 아무(것 들 중의)	anything (무엇이든)
		I don't have any friends.	
49 up [uhp]	초등	위로, 위쪽으로	
		The balloon flew up to the sky.	
50 say [sey]	초등	1. 말하다 2. 발언권	said (말했다)
		He said hello.	
51 work [wurk]	초등 토익	1. 일하다 2. 작동되다 3. 효과가 있다 4. 직장	co-worker (동료) workplace (일터) workday (근무일) workforce (노동 인구)
		Work hard and play hard.	
52 also [AWL-soh]	초등	또한, 그리고	
		She is a CEO and also a mother.	
53 like [lahyk]	초등 토익	1. 좋아하다 2. ~와 비슷한, 같은, ~처럼 3. 마치	
		He likes her.	
54 who [hoo]	초등 토익	1. 누구 2. ~한 사람	whose (누구의) whom (누구를) whoever (누구나) whomever (누구나)
		Who are you?	
55 go [goh]	초등	가다, 떠나다, 출발하다	
		Let's go to school.	
56 year [yeer]	초등 토익	1. 해, 연도 2. 학년 3. 나이	yearly (해마다)
		He met her last year.	

57 just [juhst]	초등	1. 그냥, 단지 2. 딱, 적당한 3. 방금, 막 4. 공정한	unjust (부정한)
		I just wanted to say hi.	
58 take [teyk]	초등 토익	1. 가지다, 가지고 가다 2. 시간이 걸리다 3. 사진을 찍다	
		You can take this with you.	
59 other [UHTH-er]	중등	1. 다른, 이 외의 2. 반대의	others (다른 사람들)
		He has no other option.	
60 new [noo]	초등 토익	1. 새로운 2. 색다른	newly (새로이) renewal (갱신)
		She bought new clothes.	
61 see [see]	초등 토익	1. 보다 2. (사람을) 만나다	oversee (감독하다) saw (봤다, 톱) unseen (보이지 않는) foresee (내다보다)
		I can see you.	
62 how [hou]	초등	1. 어떻게 2. 얼마나	
		How can I fix my TV?	
63 need [need]	초등 토익	1. 필요(로 하다) 2. ~해야 한다	needy (궁핍한)
		I need your help.	
64 find [fahynd]	중등 토익	찾다, 발견하다	finding (연구결과)
		She can't find her keys.	
65 know [noh]	초등	1. 알다 2. 친숙하다, 익숙하다	unknown (알려지지 않은) knowingly (알고도) know-how (노하우)
		He knows many things.	
66 than [than]	초등	~보다(비교 상황)	
		She is taller than him.	
67 no [noh]	초등	없다, 아니다, 안된다	
		I have no worries.	
68 into [IN-too]	초등	1. 속으로, 안으로 2. ~을 향해, ~으로	
		They came into the room.	
69 only [OHN-lee]	초등	1. 유일한, 단하나 2. 겨우, 단지 3. 오로지	
		You are the only person that I trust.	
70 day [dey]	초등	1. 날, 하루 2. 낮 3. 시절, 시대	daily (날마다)
		Have a good day.	

71 people [PEE-puhl]	초등	1. 사람들 2. 국민, 대중	
		I don't know these people.	
72 most [mohst]	공무원	1. 가장, 최고/최대로 2. 대부분의, 거의	mostly (대부분)
		She loves him the most.	
73 first [furst]		첫째	
		He finished it first.	
74 look [look]	중등 토익	1. 보다, 바라보다 2. 찾다 3. ~해 보이다, ~인 것 같다 4. 표정, 외모	overlook (간과하다, 내려다보다)
		Stop looking at me.	
75 think [thingk]	초등	1. 생각하다 2. 평가하다 3. 예상하다	thought (생각) thoughtful (사려깊은)
		I will think about it.	
76 then [then]	중등	1. (특정한 시기인) 그 때 2. 이후에 3. 그러면	
		He was only a boy then.	
77 every [EV-ree]	초등	1. 모든 2. 최대의 3. ~마다	everything (모든 것) everyone (모든 사람) everyday (매일) everybody (모든 사람)
		The teacher cares about every student.	
78 may [mey]	초등	1. 해도 된다(허락) 2. ~일지도 모른다 3. 5월	
		You may kiss the bride.	
79 way [wey]	초등	1. 방법, 방식 2. 길 3. 태도 4. 방향	midway (도중에) two-way (양방향의)
		I don't like the way he talks.	
80 after [AF-ter]	초등 토익	1. ~후에, ~뒤에 2. 다음에, 나중에	afterward (이후에)
		She finished after me.	
81 come [kuhm]	초등 토익	오다	incoming (들어오는)
		Will you come to the meeting?	
82 act [akt]	중등 토익	1. 행동(하다), 조치(를 취하다) 2. 연기(하다) 3. 법률	activity (활동) action (행동) active (활동적인) actor (배우)
		Stop acting like a child.	
83 want [wont]	초등	1. 원하다 2. 원하는 것	unwanted (원하지 않는)
		I want some food.	
84 over [OH-ver]	초등 토익	1. 위에 2. ~이상, ~를 넘는 3. ~동안 4. ~에 대해서	overtime (초과근무, 규정 외 시간)
		She put her coat over her dress.	

85 help [help]	초등	1. 돕다, 도와주다 2. 도움, 지원	helpful (도움이 되는)
		May I help you?	
86 include [in-KLOOD]	중등 토익	포함하다, 포함시키다	inclusive (포함하는)
		This course menu includes desserts.	
87 real [REE-uh1]	중등 토익	1. 진짜의 2. 진실된	reality (현실) realistic (현실적인)
		Unicorns are not real animals.	
88 through [throo]	중등	1. ~를 통해, ~사이로 2. 거치다, 지나다	throughout (~내내)
		She walked through the woods.	
89 now [nou]	초등	지금, 당장, 이제	
		I am going to bed now.	
90 very [VER-ee]	초등	1. 매우, 아주 2. 가장	
		She is very kind.	
91 give [giv]	초등	1. 주다 2. 제공하다	given (정해진)
		He gave me a dollar.	
92 student [STOOD-nt]	초등	학생	study (공부하다)
		She is a high school student.	
93 many [MEN-ee]	초등	1. 많은, 여럿의 2. 대부분의, 다수의	
		He has many friends.	
94 well [wel]	초등	1. 잘, 좋게 2. 꽤, 상당히 3. 수월히, 쉽게 4. 우물	
		He sings well.	
95 even [EE-vuhn]	중등 토익	1. 평평하다, 균등한 2. 평평하게 하다, 균등하게 하다 3. 심지어	unevenly (불균등하게)
		The ground is even.	
96 play [pley]	초등	1. 놀다 2. 역할을 하다 3. 경기하다 4. 연극, 극	replay (다시 하다) playful (장난스러운)
		Come play with me.	
97 because [bih-KAWZ]	초등	~때문에, ~라는 이유로	
		I cried because I was sad.	
98 add [ad]	초등 토익	1. 추가하다, 덧붙이다 2. 더하다, 가산하다	additional (추가적인) additive (첨가물) addition (덧셈, 추가)
		Please add more sugar to the coffee.	

99 **provide** [pruh-VAHYD]	중등 토익	1. 제공하다, 공급하다 2. ~에 대비하다, 예방책을 취하다 We will provide you with more information.	
100 **high** [hahy]	중등	1. 높은 2. 값비싼 3. 최고 The price is too high.	height (키) heighten (증폭시키다)
101 **great** [greyt]	초등	1. 위대한, 훌륭한 2. 큰, 많은 You'll do great.	
102 **should** [shood]	초등	~해야 한다, ~할 것이다 We should run.	
103 **long** [LAWNG]	초등 토익	1. 긴, 기다란 2. 오랫동안 3. 간절히 바라다 She has long legs.	length (길이) lengthen (연장하다) longing (열망)
104 **where** [hwair]	초등	어디, 어디에, ~하는 곳 I know where Boston is.	wherever (어디든)
105 **back** [bak]	초등	1. 등 2. 뒤 3. 돌아가다 When will you be back?	backwards (거꾸로)
106 **start** [stahrt]	초등	1. 시작(하다), 출발하다 2. 시작점 The class will start soon.	
107 **thing** [thing]	초등	1. 것, 일 2. 상황 3. 물건 What is this thing?	
108 **while** [hwahyl]	중등	1. ~하는 동안에, 사이에 2. ~에 반하여 We ate dinner while you were sleeping.	whilst (동안)
109 **create** [kree-EYT]	중등 토익	1. 만들다, 창조하다 2. 창립하다 He believes that all men are created equal.	creature (생명체) creativity (창의성)
110 **much** [muhch]	초등	1. 많은, 매우 많이 2. 대부분 I slept too much.	
111 **able** [EY-buhl]	중등 토익	1. 할 수 있는 2. 유능한 She wasn't able to sleep.	ability (능력) enable (가능케 하다) disability (신체 장애)
112 **right** [rahyt]	초등	1. 옳은 2. 정확한 3. 권리, 인권 4. 오른쪽 His answer was right.	

113 set [set]		1. 설정하다 2. 놓다 3. 위치한 4. 세트 Please set the alarm to 4 AM.	reset (재설정) preset (미리 설정된) subset (부분집합, 일부)
114 service [SUR-vis]		1. 서비스 2. 봉사, 근무, 복무 3. 서비스를 제공하다 4. 예배 She complained about the poor service.	
115 such [suhch]	중등	1. 그런, 그러한 2. 매우 I did no such thing.	
116 view [vyoo]	중등 토익	1. 견해, 의견, 관점 2. 보다 3. 전망 What is your view on this matter?	review (리뷰, 평가) interview (인터뷰, 면접) overview (개요) preview (미리보기)
117 different [DIF-er-uhnt]	초등	1. 다른, 별개의 2. 여러가지의 Can we try a different restaurant this time?	difference (차이) differ (다르다) differentiate (차이를 구별하다)
118 own [ohn]	중등	1. 자기 자신의 2. 소유하다 He has never been more proud of his own son.	owner (소유자) ownership (소유권)
119 before [bih-FAWR]	초등	1. 전에 2. 앞에 Finish your homework before bedtime.	
120 information [in-fer-MEY-shuhn]	중등 토익	정보 Can you give me any information on what I should expect?	inform (알리다) informative (정보성) informant (정보원)
121 show [shoh]	초등	1. 보여주다 2. 공연, 전시회 3. 프로그램, 쇼 They have shown much respect for us.	showbiz (연예계, 연예업)
122 try [trahy]	중등	1. 시도(하다), 노력하다 2. 시험해보다 I always try my best.	trial (실험, 재판)
123 change [cheynj]	초등	1. 바꾸다, 변하다 2. 변화 3. (옷을) 갈아 입다 Your house has changed a lot since you moved in.	
124 state [steyt]	중등 토익	1. 상태 2. 국가, 나라 3. 미국 주 4. 말하다 She is in such a good state after losing weight.	statement (성명) statesman (정치인) interstate (고속도로)
125 part [pahrt]	수능 토익	1. 일부, 부분 2. 부품 3. 헤어지다 A single part can represent the whole.	counterpart (비슷한 직위의 상대방) partway (중도에)
126 each [eech]	중등	각각의, 제각기의 I will shake hands with each and every one of you.	

127	초등	여기에, 이곳	
here			
[heer]		Welcome, you've finally arrived here.	

128	수능 토익	1. 장소, 곳 2. 자리 3. 놓다, 두다	placement (배치) misplace (잘못 두다) displace (바꾸어 놓다, 옮겨놓다)
place			
[pleys]		This place is much nicer than your last apartment.	

129	중등 토익	1. 부르다 2. 전화(를 하다)	
call			
[kawl]		Please call me when you are having trouble.	

130	토익	1. 상품, 제품 2. 산물 3. 결과물, 성과물	production (생산) productivity (생산성)
product			
[PROD-uhkt]		My company's new product is selling very well.	

131	중등 토익	1. 안내하다 2. 이끌다 3. 선두 4. 납	leader (지도자, 리더) leadership (리더십) misleading (호도하는)
lead			
[leed]		The green race car is in the lead.	

132		1. 게임, 경기 2. 사냥감	
game			
[geym]		Board games are good for passing time.	

133	토익	1. 삶, 인생 2. 목숨, 생	lifetime (일생) lifecycle (생애 주기) lifelong (평생 동안의)
life			
[lahyf]		Life can be unfair.	

134	중등 토익	사람, 개인	personal (개인적인) personality (성격) personable (매력적인)
person			
[PUR-suhn]		You shouldn't trust a person too easily.	

135	초등	1. 바쁜 2. 통화 중인	
busy			
[BIZ-ee]		I've had a busy week.	

136	초등 토익	세계, 세상	real-world (현실 세상) worldwide (세계적인)
world			
[wurld]		I've been all over the world, but my home is the best.	

137	중등	1. 체제, 체계 2. 시스템	systematic (체계적)
system			
[SIS-tuhm]		She has her own system of doing laundry.	

138	초등	같은(것), 동일한	
same			
[seym]		Please stop asking me the same questions.	

139	초등	1. 만들다, 구축하다 2. 건축하다, 짓다	building (건물)
build			
[bild]		I am working on building a good relationship with my boss.	

140	중등 토익	1. 신청하다 2. 적용하다, 응용하다 3. (약, 크림 등을) 바르다	application (신청서, 적용) applicant (지원자) applicable (적용 가능한)
apply			
[uh-PLAHY]		Which college are you planning to apply to?	

141	토익	1. 프로그램(을 설정하다) 2. 과정	programming (프로그래밍) programmer (개발자)
program [PROH-gram]		This new software program does all the calculations for me.	

142	중등	1. 가만히 있는, 정지한 2. 아직도 3. 그럼에도, 하지만	
still [stil]		Stay still when a bee is flying around you.	

143	초등	1. 마지막의, 끝 2. 지속되다 3. 지난	lasting (지속되는) lastly (마지막으로) everlasting (영원한)
last [last]		I was the last person in the library.	

144	초등	1. 느끼다 2. 기분 3. 만져보다	feeling (느낌) felt (느꼈다)
feel [feel]		He has been feeling healthy lately.	

145	초등 토익	1. 집 2. 고향 3. 고국, 본국	homeless (노숙자) homecoming (동창회)
home [hohm]		Let's go home before it gets too late.	

146	초등	사랑(하다)	lover (사랑하는 사람) lovely (사랑스러운)
love [luhv]		I love the taste of coffee in the morning.	

147	초등	1. ~을 계속하다, 유지하다 2. 가지고 있다	
keep [keep]		She tries to keep it positive even in bad times.	

148	초등	1. 회사 2. 단체, 집단 3. 동료, 일행	
company [KUHM-puh-nee]		Which company do you work for?	

149	중등 토익	1. 개발하다 2. 성장하다, 발달시키다, 발전하다 3. 전개시키다	development (개발) undeveloped (개발되지 않은)
develop [dih-VEL-uh p]		I've developed many skills since I started working here.	

150	초등	1. 아래로, 내려가는, (아래쪽으로)지는 2. 격추하다 3. 우울한	downward (아래로 내려가는)
down [doun]		He walked down the hill.	

151	초등	1. 둘 다(의), 양쪽(의), 쌍방(의) 2. ~뿐만 아니라 ~또한	
both [bohth]		Learn what you can from both sides.	

152	초등 토익	1. 달리다, 뛰다 2. 운영하다 3. 작동하다 4. 유효하다 5. (물이)흐르다	running (달리는) runner-up (2위) outrun (보다 빨리 달리다) runny (흐르는)
run [ruhn]		She is running a marathon next week.	

153	초등	1. 떨어져 있는 2. 꺼진 3. (근무를)쉬는	
off [awf]		I told him to back off.	

154	중등 토익	국가	national (국가의) international (국제적인) nationality (국적)
nation [NEY-shuh n]		We need a president who can unite this nation.	

155 **follow** [FOL-oh]	중등	1. 따르다, ~을 따라가다 2. ~의 결과로 나타나다, 뒤를 잇다 3. 이해하다	following (다음의, 추종세력)
		Just follow his lead.	
156 **point** [point]	초등	1. 요점, 의도하는 바 2. 요소, 점 3. 점수 4. 가리키다	pointer (가르키는 화살표) pointless (의미없는)
		You misunderstood my point.	
157 **end** [end]	초등	1. 끝(내다), 종료(하다) 2. 목표, 목적	endless (끝없는) high-end (최고급의)
		Let's put an end to this conversation.	
158 **mean** [meen]	중등 토익	1. ~의미하다, ~의도하다 2. 못된, 나쁜 3. 평균	meaning (의미) meaningful (의미있는) means (수단,방법,자산)
		She sometimes says things she doesn't mean.	
159 **number** [NUHM-ber]	초등	1. 수, 숫자 2. 번호(를 매기다), 수를 세다	
		There is a small number of people who can do this job.	
160 **pay** [pey]	초등 토익	1. 지불하다, 납부하다 2. 대가를 치르다 3. 임금, 급료	payment (지불) paid (지불된)
		Don't forget to pay your bill.	
161 **around** [uh-ROUND]	초등	1. 주위에, 주변에 2. (빙)돌아 3. 대략, ~쯤	
		Are you from around this neighborhood?	
162 **design** [dih-ZAHYN]	초등 토익	1. 디자인(하다), 설계(하다) 2. 계획(하다), 고안하다 3. 도안	
		He designed his own house.	
163 **school** [skool]	초등	1. 학교 2. 교육하다 3. 학파, 유파	preschool (유치원)
		She schooled me on how to make a pizza.	
164 **offer** [AW-fer]	중등	1. 제의(하다), 제안(하다) 2. 제공하다	
		The offer he made was so good that I couldn't refuse.	
165 **easy** [EE-zee]	초등	1. 쉬운, 만만한 2. 안락한, 편안한	
		The exam was pretty easy.	
166 **require** [ri-KWAHYUHR]	중등	1. 요구하다, 요하다 2. 필요로 하다	
		You are required to take these pills.	
167 **manage** [MAN-ij]	중등 토익	1. ~를 간신히 해내다 2. 운영하다, 관리하다 3. 다루다	management (관리 경영, 기획사) manageable (처리할 수 있는)
		I've managed to escape without a scratch.	
168 **write** [rahyt]	초등 토익	1. 쓰다 2. 기록하다 3. 집필하다	writing (쓰기) writer (작가) written (적힌) handwriting (손글씨)
		She wrote me a sincere letter congratulating me.	

169	초등	1. 읽다, 낭독하다 2. ~라고 적혀있다 3. 이해하다	reader (독자)
read			
[REEd]		I've read this novel many times.	

170	초등	1. 아이, 어린이 2. 자녀, 자식	childhood (유아기)
child			childish (유치한)
[chahyld]		A child tends to be more vulnerable to air pollution than an adult.	

171	중등 토익	1. 경험(하다), 체험(하다) 2. 경력	
experience			
[ik-SPEER-ee-uhns]		I can only recall pleasant experiences from traveling.	

172	중등	1. 지지(하다), 옹호(하다) 2. 지원(하다), 후원(하다)	supporter (지지자)
support		3. 뒷받침하다, 지탱하다	supportive (지지하는)
[suh-PAWRT]		He supports this candidate one hundred percent.	

173	초등	1. 너무, 지나치게 2. 또한	
too			
[too]		You added too much salt to this soup.	

174		팀	
team			
[teem]		Our team won the match.	

175	초등	1. 움직이다, 나아가다 2. 이사가다 3. 행동, 조치, 수 4. 감동시키다	movement
move			(움직임, 사회적 운동)
[moov]		I need some help with moving this table.	unmoved
			(마음이 흔들리지 않는)

176	초등	1. 이름, 성함, 명칭 2. 지명하다, 임명하다 3. 지정하다	namely (즉)
name			
[neym]		Does your dog have a name?	

177	초등	1. 지역 2. 면적 3. 분야, 부문	
area			
[AIR-ee-uh]		It's good to meet someone in this area.	

178	초등	~사이에, ~중간에	
between			
[bih-TWEEN]		She can't decide between vanilla and chocolate.	

179	중등 토익	1. 사무실, 근무처 2. 지위, 공직	officer (장교, 경찰관)
office			
[AW-fis]		I got a new job as an office worker.	

180	초등 토익	1. 주, 일주일 2. 주중	weekly (매주의)
week			weekday (평일)
[week]		How is the week going for you?	weeknight (평일 밤)

181	중등	1. 적은, 별로 없는, 거의 없는 2. (a few로 쓰일 경우) 몇몇(의), 약간의 수	fewer (더 적은)
few			
[fyoo]		I know a few friends who can help me with this.	

182	중등	1. 매우 많이, 대단히 2. 부지	
lot			
[lot]		She has learned a lot from the professor.	

183 **become** [bih-KUHM]	초등	1. ~이 되다 2. 어울리다, 적합하다	
		He has become very friendly with them over the years.	
184 **plan** [plan]	초등 토익	1. 계획(하다) 2. 도면, 지도	
		What is the backup plan in case we fail?	
185 **health** [helth]	중등 토익	1. 건강 2. 의료, 보건	healthy (건강한)
		Your health is the most important thing.	
186 **open** [OH-puhn]	초등 토익	1. 열린, 개방된 2. 솔직한, 개방적인 3. 열다, 개방하다 4. 해결되지 않은	opening (구멍, 개막)
		I am open to trying new activities.	
187 **since** [sins]	중등	1. ~부터, ~이후로 2. ~때문에	
		I've been exercising daily since high school.	
188 **during** [DOOR-ing]	초등	~동안, ~하는 사이에	
		Please do not disturb during working hours.	
189 **live** [liv]	초등	1. 살다, 지내다 2. 생방송의, 생중계의 3. 라이브(공연)	living (살고있는, 생계) lively (생기 넘치는)
		She lives alone.	
190 **another** [uh-NUHTH-er]	초등	1. 또, 더 2. 다른	
		May I please have another cup of water?	
191 **tell** [tel]	초등 토익	1. 말하다 2. 알려주다, 보여주다 3. 판단하다, 식별하다	untold (전해지지 않은) foretell (예견하다)
		You can tell your doctor about the pain.	
192 **relationship** [ri-LEY-shuhn-ship]	중등	관계	relation (관계) relative (친척, 상대적) relate (연관시키다)
		I have a loving relationship with my cat.	
193 **learn** [lurn]	초등	1. 배우다, 익히다 2. 암기하다 3. 깨우치다	learning (학습)
		My daughter finally learned how to ride a bicycle.	
194 **must** [muhst]	초등	1. 반드시 ~해야 한다 2. (추측성) ~일 것이다	
		You must wash your hands after using the toilet.	
195 **direct** [dih-REKT]	중등 토익	1. 직접적인, 직행의, 직통의 2. 지휘하다, 감독하다 3. 지시하다, 명령하다	director (감독) indirectly (간접적으로)
		You can call me on my direct number.	
196 **large** [lahrj]	초등	1. 큰, 대규모의, 대형의 2. 많은	enlarge (확대하다)
		There is a large pile of garbage outside.	

197 **little** [LIT-l]	초등	1. 조금, 약간 2. 작은 3. 어린	
		Can you give me just a little bit more time?	
198 **process** [PROS-es]	중등	1. 과정, 절차 2. 공정 3. 처리하다	
		The transition process went smoothly.	
199 **late** [leyt]	초등 토익	1. 늦은, 늦게 2. 말기의, 말년의 3. 고인이 된	later (나중에) lately (최근에)
		He never came late to a meeting.	
200 **allow** [uh-LOU]	중등	1. 허용하다, 허락하다, 용납하다 2. 가능케하다, ~할 수 있게 하다	allowance (용돈)
		I do not allow that kind of violence.	
201 **power** [POU-er]	초등	1. 힘, 능력 2. 권력, 정권, 강대국 3. (전기)에너지 4. 에너지를 공급하다	powerful (힘있는) overpower (힘으로 압도하다)
		She has a lot of power in her company.	
202 **month** [muhnth]	초등	월, 달, 개월	monthly (매 달)
		I'll be very busy with work next month.	
203 **family** [FAM-uh-lee]	초등	1. 가족, 가정, 식구 2. 가문, 집안 내력	
		Family comes before anything.	
204 **man** [man]	초등 토익	1. 남자 2. 사람, 인간, 인류	manly (남자다운)
		He is a reliable man.	
205 **sure** [shoor]	중등 토익	1. 확신하는, 자신있는 2. 틀림없이, 분명히	surely (확실히) unsure (불확실한)
		I cannot remember for sure.	
206 **put** [poot]	초등	1. 놓다, 넣다 2. 붙이다 3. 쓰다, 기록하다	
		Put the pencil back on the desk.	
207 **complete** [kuhm-PLEET]	중등 토익	1. 완료하다, 끝마치다 2. 완벽한, 모든 것을 갖춘, 완전한 3. 완료된	incomplete (미완성의)
		I can complete what you can't finish.	
208 **market** [MAHR-kit]		1. 시장 2. 시장에서 팔다	marketable (잘 팔리는)
		There is a bubble in the real estate market.	
209 **available** [uh-VEY-luh-buhl]	중등 토익	1. 이용할 수 있는 2. 여유가 있는, 시간이 있는	avail (쓸모, 가치가 있다)
		He is available from 2 to 4 PM.	
210 **big** [big]	초등	1. 큰, 많은 2. 성장한 3. 중요한	
		This deal will give us a big advantage.	

211 **far** [fahr]	초등	1. 먼 곳에, 멀리 2. 오래전, 예전의 3. 훨씬, 대단히	further (더 멀리) farther (더 멀리) afar (멀리서, 떨어져서)
		A coffee shop isn't too far from here.	
212 **level** [LEV-uhl]	중등	1. 수준, 단계 2. 정도 3. 층, 높이 4. 수평의, 평평한 5. 수평이 되게 하다	
		You are ready to move onto the next level.	
213 **without** [with-OUT]	중등	1. ~없이 2. ~하지 않고, ~한 행동을 취하지 않고	
		I cannot live without my computer.	
214 **center** [SEN-ter]		1. 중심 2. 가운데, 중앙 3. 센터, 종합 시설	central (중심의) centralized (중앙화된)
		She loves being at the center of attention.	
215 **problem** [PROB-luhm]	초등	문제	
		You cannot let this problem from making progress.	
216 **free** [FREE]	초등	1. 자유로운, 자주적인 2. 공짜의, 무료의 3. 석방하다, 풀어주다	freedom (자유)
		When are you free?	
217 **post** [pohst]	중등 토익	1. 게시글(을 올리다) 2. 우편(물) 3. 직책 4. 위치, 구역 5. 기둥	poster (포스터) posting (포스팅) postal (우편의)
		I read a positive online post about this bakery.	
218 **case** [keys]	초등	1. 경우, 사례 2. 사건, 소송 건 3. 용기, 통	
		The boss will make an exception for this case.	
219 **small** [smawl]	초등	1. 작은, 소규모의, 소형의 2. 어린 3. 사소한, 중요치 않은	
		Small business owners are competing against corporate giants.	
220 **form** [fawrm]	중등	1. 형태, 모양, 모습 2. 종류, 유형 3. 형성되다 4. 구성하다 5. 서식, 양식	reform (개혁) formation (구조, 형성)
		You have to follow the dance moves in the correct form.	
221 **sign** [sahyn]	중등 토익	1. 징후, 조짐 2. 간판 3. 몸짓, 신호 (하다) 4. 서명하다, 계약하다	signature (서명, 특징) signify (의미하다)
		Weight loss could be a sign of bad health.	
222 **however** [hou-EV-er]	초등	1. 하지만, 그러나 2. 아무리 ~일지라도	
		I can't, however, agree with you.	
223 **group** [groop]	초등	1. 무리, 그룹, 단체 2. 모으다, 모이다 3. 분류하다	
		Can I be part of your group for this presentation?	
224 **water** [WAW-ter]	초등	1. 물 2. 바다, 영해 3. 물을 주다 4. 군침이 돌다	underwater (물속의)
		I try to drink water in the morning.	

225 always [AWL-weyz]	초등	언제나, 늘, 항상	
		I always think about him.	
226 report [ri-PAWRT]	중등	1. 보고서 2. 발표하다, 보고하다, 보도하다 3. 신고하다 4. 성적표	reporter (기자) reportedly (보도된 바에 따르면)
		Have you finished your report yet?	
227 line [lahyn]	초등 토익	1. 선, 줄 2. 전화 3. 줄을 서다	linear (직선의) underline (밑줄을 긋다)
		He drew a straight line with a pencil.	
228 full [fool]	초등	1. 배부른, 가득 찬 2. 완전한 3. 최대의 4. 풍부한	
		I feel so full after dinner.	
229 simple [SIM-puhl]	중등 토익	1. 간단한, 단순한 2. 소박한, 간소한, 평범한	simply (단순히) simplify (간소화)
		She couldn't even answer a simple question.	
230 receive [ri-SEEV]	중등 토익	1. 받다, 받아들이다 2. 환영하다 3. 청취하다, 듣다	recipient (받는 사람) reception (접수데스크)
		You will be receiving a letter soon.	
231 cover [KUHV-er]	중등	1. 덮다, 가리다 (덮개) 2. 다루다, 포함하다 3. 취재하다 4. 보장하다	uncover (발견하다) undercover (위장근무)
		Cover your mouth when you cough.	
232 next [nekst]	초등	1. 다음의, 이후의, 추후의 2. 옆에, 옆의	
		See you next time.	
233 drive [drahyv]	초등	1. 운전(하다) 2. 견인하다, ~하게 하다 3. 욕구 4. 추진력	driven (의욕이 넘치는)
		How long have you been driving?	
234 effect [ih-FEKT]	중등 토익	1. 영향, 효과 2. 느낌, 인상	effective (효과적인)
		This pill had no effect.	
235 result [ri-ZUHLT]	중등	1. 결과, 성과, 결실 2. 생기다, 발생하다	
		Exam results are already out.	
236 under [UHN-der]	초등	1. ~아래에, 밑에 2. ~미만의 3. 종속하여	
		What's under the desk?	
237 important [im-PAWR-tnt]	초등	1. 중요한, 중대한 2. 소중한 3. 영향력이 큰	importance (중요성)
		Your opinion is not that important.	
238 why [hwahy]	초등	1. 왜, 무엇때문에 2. 이유	
		Why are you looking at me?	

239	초등	1. 성장하다, 자라나다 2. 증가하다 3. 키우다, 재배하다	growth (성장)
grow			grown-up (어른)
[groh]		I grew up here.	outgrow (기존 크기 이상 으로 자라다)

240	초등 토익	1. 책, 도서, 저서 2. 장부 3. 예약하다	booking (예약)
book			textbook (교과서)
[book]		He loves reading books.	overbooking (초과 예약)

241	중등	1. 떠나다 2. 두고 오다, (유산으로)남기다 3. 휴가	
leave			
[leev]		Don't leave me alone.	

242	초등	전혀, 결코, 절대	
never			
[NEV-er]		She never lies.	

243	초등	1. 나이가 ~인 2. 늙은, 나이든, 오래된 3. 옛날의, 고대의	
old			
[ohld]		How old is he?	

244	초등	1. 꼭대기, 정상 2. 최고(의) 3. 뚜껑 4. 윗옷 5. 팽이 6. 능가하다	
top			
[top]		She finally climbed up to the top of the mountain.	

245		일원, 구성원, 회원	membership (멤버십)
member			
[MEM-ber]		He became a member of the team.	

246	중등	가능한, 가능성 있는, 할 수 있는	possibility (가능성)
possible			possibly (어쩌면)
[POS-uh-buhl]		It isn't possible to go back.	impossible (불가능)

247	중등 토익	1. 닫다, (눈을)감다 2. 가까운 3. 거의, 곧 4. 친한 5. 종료, 종결, 마감	enclosure (울타리,포함)
close			enclose (둘러싸다, 넣다)
[klohz]		Close the door for me.	

248		1. 이슈, 문제 2. 쟁점, 사안 3. 발행하다, 발부하다 4. 발표하다, 공표하다	
issue			
[ISH-oo]		How many issues are there?	

249	중등	1. 관심, 흥미, 호기심, 감흥 2. 이자 3. 이해관계 4. 관심을 끌다	interesting (흥미로운)
interest			
[IN-ter-ist]		She lost interest in him.	

250	초등	1. 기반, 기초, 토대, 바탕 2. 본부, 본사 3. ~에 근거하다	evidence-based
base			(근거 중심의)
[beys]		He used his own childhood as a base for his novel.	

251		1. 초(시간), 아주 잠시 동안 2. 두 번째(의), 둘째(의)	secondary (이차적인)
second			secondly (둘째로)
[SEK-uhnd]		Wait a second.	

252		데이터, 자료	
data			
[DEY-tuh]		We still need to collect more data.	

253 **value** [VAL-yoo]	중등 토익	1. 가치(있게 생각하다) 2. 값 3. 평가하다	valuation (가치 평가) invaluable (매우 소중한)
		I tend to stick to moral values.	
254 **might** [mahyt]	초등	1. (may의 과거로서)~지도 모른다 2. 힘, 권력	mighty (강력한)
		What he said might be true.	
255 **course** [kawrs]		1. 강의, 과목 2. 방향, 방침 3. 항로	
		How many courses are you taking this semester?	
256 **care** [kair]	초등 토익	1. 상관하다, 신경 쓰다 2. 배려하다 3. 돌봄, 보살핌 4. 걱정, 우려	careful (조심스러운) careless (부주의한)
		She didn't care about the criticism.	
257 **light** [lahyt]	초등 토익	1. 빛, 조명, 전등 2. 밝은, 환한 3. 연한, 옅은 4. 가벼운 5. 불을 붙이다	lighting (조명) lightweight (경량) enlighten (계몽)
		Turn off the light.	
258 **current** [KUR-uhnt]	수능	1. 지금의, 현재의 2. 흐름, 기류 3. 동향, 추세	
		The current plan is not enough.	
259 **list** [list]	중등	1. 목록, 명단(을 작성하다) 2. 상장되다	enlist (입대) listless (열의없는)
		I wrote down a list of things to do.	
260 **continue** [kuhn-TIN-yoo]	중등 토익	계속하다, 지속하다	continuous (계속적인)
		She continued reading.	
261 **city** [SIT-ee]	초등	도시, 시내, 중심지	
		Seoul is a beautiful city.	
262 **idea** [ahy-DEE-uh]	중등 토익	1. 아이디어, 생각, 발상 2. 신념, 사상	ideal (이상적인)
		She has a great idea.	
263 **question** [KWES-chuhn]	수능 토익	1. 질문 2. 의심(하다), 의문 3. 문제	questionable (의심스러운) unquestionably (분명히) questionnaire (설문지)
		Don't ask him any questions.	
264 **ask** [ask]	초등	1. 묻다 2. 요청하다, 부탁하다 3. 초청하다	
		She asked him how old he was.	
265 **hold** [hohld]	초등	1. 잡다 2. 개최하다, 열다 3. 소유하다, 보유하다	
		She is still holding onto her past memories.	
266 **feature** [FEE-cher]	중등	1. 특징, 특성 2. 이목구비, 용모 3. 특집기사, 특종 4. 특별히 특징을 갖다	
		A notable feature of his house is the yellow wallpaper.	

267 **house** [HOUs]	중등	1. 집, 주택 2. 의회 3. 보관하다, 수용하다 4. 거처를 제공하다	household (가족)
		He bought a new house.	
268 **performance** [per-FAWR-muhns]	중등 토익	1. 성능 2. 성과, 실적 3. 공연, 연주회	perform (공연하다)
		This car's performance is great.	
269 **serve** [surv]	중등	1. 제공하다 2. 봉사하다, 기여하다 3. 근무하다, 복무하다 4. (테니스 공 등을)서브하다	servant (하인)
		Dinner will be served soon.	
270 **please** [pleez]	중등 토익	1. 부디, 제발 2. 기쁘게 하다	pleasure (즐거움) pleasant (즐거운)
		Please listen to what I have to say.	
271 **share** [shair]	중등	1. 공유하다, 함께 쓰다, 나눠 갖다 2. 몫, 지분 3. 주식	
		I will share my files with you.	
272 **option** [OP-shuhn]	중등 토익	1. 선택(권) 2. 방안, 방책	optional (선택적인) opt (선택하다)
		There are not too many options for him.	
273 **control** [kuhn-TROHL]	초등	1. 통제하다, 제어하다, 관리하다 2. 지배 3. 규제, 통제, 감독 4. 방지하다, 막다 5. 조절하다	uncontrollable (통제 불가능한)
		I don't know how to control that machine.	
274 **buy** [bahy]	초등	사다, 구입하다, 매수하다	
		I'll buy some clothes tomorrow.	
275 **test** [test]	초등	1. 시험(하다) 2. 검사(하다), 실험(하다)	
		She did well on the test.	
276 **meet** [meet]	초등	1. 만나다 2. 충족시키다, 지키다	
		The couple first met at a store.	
277 **project** [PROJ-ekt]	토익	1. 프로젝트, 사업 2. 예상하다, 추정하다 3. 계획(하다) 4. 비추다, 보여주다	projection (예상)
		His project didn't go well.	
278 **turn** [turn]	초등	1. 돌다, 돌리다, 회전하다 2. 변하다, 바꾸다, 전환하다	
		He turned around to look at me.	
279 **begin** [bih-GIN]	초등 토익	1. 시작하다, 착수하다 2. 출발하다	beginning (시작) beginner (초보)
		She began dancing.	
280 **increase** [in-KREES]	중등	증가(하다), 늘다, 인상(되다)	increasingly (갈수록 더)
		The cost of living keeps on increasing.	

281	초등	1. 유형, 종류 2. 타자 치다	
type			
[tahyp]		He is the type of person you can always talk to.	

282	중등 토익	1. 고려하다, 고찰하다 2. 여기다 3. 감안하다	consideration (고려)
consider			considerate (사려깊은)
[kuhn-SID-er]		He didn't consider the possibility of failure.	considerable (상당한)

283	중등	1. 한 번 2. 한때, 언젠가	
once			
[wuhns]		We only met once.	

284	중등	1. 결정하다, 결심하다 2. 판결하다	decision (결정)
decide			decisive (결정적인, 단호한)
[dih-SAHYD]		She decided not to go.	

285	초등	1. 낮은 2. 아래의 3. 부족한 4. 질 낮은	lower (아래쪽의, 낮추다)
low			
[loh]		He has low blood pressure.	

286	중등	1. 장소, 현장, 부지 2. 웹사이트	on-site (현장의)
site			
[sahyt]		This site would be ideal for our new house.	

287	중등	~것처럼 보이다, ~인 것 같다	seemingly (보이기엔)
seem			
[seem]		She didn't seem that happy to see him.	

288	초등	친구, 동지	friendly (친근한)
friend			friendship (우징)
[frend]		He is a friend of mine.	befriend (친구로 삼다)

289	초등	감사하다, 고마워하다	thankful (고맙게 여기는)
thank			thank-you (고마워)
[thangk]		I'd like to thank all of you for being here today.	Thanksgiving (추수감사절)

290	중등	1. 명령(하다), 지시(하다) 2. 주문하다 3. 순서 4. 질서	disorder (무질서, 장애)
order			orderly (질서있는)
[AWR-der]		The director gave me orders.	

291	초등	1. 손 2. 도움(을 주다) 3. 일손 4. 건네 주다, 넘겨주다, 맡기다	hands-on (직접해보는)
hand			handful
[hand]		My hands are too cold.	(한 움큼, 감당하기 힘든)

292	초등	1. 쪽, 편 2. (옆)면, 측 3. 의견, 입장 4. 편들다	sideways (옆으로)
side			
[sahyd]		I need you by my side.	

293	초등	1. 가지고 오다 2. 초래하다, 일으키다	
bring			
[bring]		Don't forget to bring your wallet.	

294	초등	1. 파일, 정보 2. 보관하다 3. 소송을 제기하다	
file			
[fahyl]		He will be going over that file.	

295 **again** [uh-GEN]	초등	다시, 또, 한 번 더	
		See you again.	
296 **actual** [AK-choo-uhl]	중등	1. 실제의 2. 사실상의	actually (실제로, 사실은)
		The actual cost is lower than the estimate.	
297 **cost** [kawst]	초등 토익	1. 비용, 가격 2. 비용이 들다	costly (값비싼)
		How much will this renovation cost?	
298 **within** [with-IN]	중등	1. ~의 안쪽에, 이내 2. 속으로	
		He returned within 30 minutes.	
299 **note** [noht]	초등	1. 노트, 기록(하다) 2. 주의하다, 유념하다	notable (주목할만한) noteworthy (주목할만한)
		Please take notes on the lecture.	
300 **rate** [reyt]	중등	1. 비율, ~율 2. 속도 3. 평가하다	rating (평가) overrated (과대평가된)
		They traveled at a rate of 55 miles per hour.	
301 **head** [hed]	중등 토익	1. 머리 2. 향하다 3. 우두머리	overhead (머리 위의) forehead (이마)
		He suffered from a head injury.	
302 **event** [ih-VENT]		1. 행사 2. 사건, 경우	eventful (다사다난한)
		The school event begins at 7 pm.	
303 **employee** [em-ploi-EE]	중등 토익	직원, 고용된 자	employ (고용/이용하다) employer (고용주) unemployment (실업)
		The CEO loved all his employees.	
304 **check** [chek]	초등	1. 감시하다, 확인하다 2. 수표 3. 바둑판 무늬	
		Check to make sure the door is locked.	
305 **price** [prahys]	중등	1. 가격 2. 가격을 매기다	pricey (값비싼) priceless (값을 매길 수 없는)
		The price of oil is increasing.	
306 **reason** [REE-zuhn]	중등	1. 이유 2. 이성, 사고력 3. 설명하다 4. 사고하다, 판단하다	reasonable (합리적인) reasoning (논리추론) unreasonably (비이성적으로)
		Pollution is the reason for global warming.	
307 **woman** [WOOM-uhn]	초등	여자	
		The woman was a lawyer.	
308 **hard** [hahrd]	중등	1. 단단한 2. 어려운, 고된 3. 열심히	hardly (거의)
		It takes a long time to complete a hard task.	

309 **believe** [bih-LEEV]	초등	1. 믿다 2. 생각하다 I believe his report.	belief (믿음)
310 **hour** [OUuhr]	초등 토익	시간 The hour is getting late	
311 **train** [treyn]	초등 토익	1. 훈련하다 2. 기차 She is training for the Olympics.	trainer (코치) trainee (코치에게 훈련받는 사람)
312 **special** [SPESH-uhl]	중등 토익	특별한, 예외적인 Today is a special day.	specialist (전문가) specialty (전문성)
313 **present** [PREZ-uhnt]	중등 토익	1. 선물 2. 현재, 현재의 3. 선사하다, 제시하다 I am going to go shopping for a present.	presence (존재) presentation (발표) omnipresent (어디에나 존재하는)
314 **customer** [KUHS-tuh-mer]	초등	고객 The customer was happy with the purchase.	
315 **location** [loh-KEY-shuhn]	중등 토익	위치, 장소 Tell me your location.	locate (위치하다, 위치를 찾아내다) relocate (이전하다) dislocate (탈구시키다)
316 **art** [ahrt]	초등 토익	1. 미술, 예술 2. 기교, 숙련 I'm going to an art exhibition.	artist (예술가) artwork (예술품)
317 **understand** [uhn-der-STAND]	초등	이해하다 She could not understand her husband.	understanding (이해하다) misunderstood (오해된)
318 **account** [uh-KOUNT]	중등 토익	1. 계좌, 계정, 기록 2. 이유(로 여기다) 3. 설명(을 하다) 4. ~의 비율을 차지하다 5. 중요성, 가치 He was old enough to make a bank account.	accounting (회계) accountant (회계사) accountable (책임이 있는)
319 **win** [win]	초등	1. 승리 2. 이기다 I think you will win the game.	winner (승리자)
320 **community** [kuh-MYOO-ni-tee]	중등	공동체 Mark was devoted to helping his community.	communal (공동의)
321 **profession** [pruh-FESH-uhn]	중등 토익	직업, 전문직 Many people want to work in the legal profession.	professional (전문적인) pro (찬성)
322 **store** [stawr]	초등	1. 저장하다, 비축하다 2. 가게, 백화점 Squirrels store food for the winter.	storage (저장, 저장소)

323 cause [kawz]	중등	1. 원인, 이유 2. 초래하다	causation (인과 관계)
		The police will determine the cause of the accident.	
324 research [REE-surch]	중등	연구(하다), 조사(하다)	
		We should search for information.	
325 early [UR-lee]	초등	1. 이른 2. 가까운 미래의 3. 어릴 때의	
		She decided on her career at an early age.	
326 connect [kuh-NEKT]	중등 토익	1. 잇다, 연결하다 2. 접속하다	connection (연결, 관련성) interconnected (서로 관련된)
		Roads and bridges connect one region to another.	
327 less [les]		더 적은, 덜한	lesser (덜한) lessen (줄이다)
		This book is less interesting than I expected.	
328 let [let]	중등	허락하다, 허용하다	
		I will let you watch television.	
329 general [JEN-er-uhl]	중등 토익	1. 전반적인, 보편적인, 일반의 2. (육군) 대장	generalization (일반화) generalize (일반화하다)
		The general opinion is that she is a good person.	
330 color [KUHL-er]	초등 토익	1. 색깔 2. 색칠하다	colorful (다채로운)
		This is a vibrant color.	
331 until [uhn-TIL]	중등	~까지	
		You have until February 9th to finish the project.	
332 food [food]	초등	식품, 음식	
		That country is suffering from a food shortage.	
333 public [PUHB-lik]	중등 토익	공공의	publicity (홍보) publicize (홍보하다) publicist (홍보담당자)
		My neighborhood has a public library.	
334 teach [teech]	초등	가르치다	teacher (선생님) taught (가르쳤다)
		He teaches students art.	
335 body [BOD-ee]	초등	1. 신체 2. 본체 3. 본문	
		The body of the car was rusted.	
336 though [thoh]	중등	그래도, ~에도 불구하고	
		Though young, she is wise.	

337 **access** [AK-ses]	중등 토익	입장(하다), 접속(하다) He gained access to the building.	accessible (접근 가능한)
338 **law** [law]	중등	법, 규칙 We learned about the law of gravity.	lawyer (변호사) unlawful (불법의)
339 **nature** [NEY-cher]	초등	1. 자연 2. 자연의 3. 본성 It is important to preserve nature.	natural (자연스러운) supernatural (초자연의)
340 **often** [AW-fuhn]	초등	자주 He is often late.	
341 **history** [HIS-tuh-ree]	초등	역사 The history of Korea is very long.	historical (역사의)
342 **record** [ri-KAWRD]	중등	1. 기록 2. 기록하다, 녹화하다 3. 경력, 전과 I keep a record of my day through a scheduler.	
343 **term** [turm]	중등	1. 기간 2. 조항 3. 용어, 말 4. 임기 The term of employment is 5 months.	long-term (장기간의)
344 **against** [uh-GENST]	초등	1. 반대하여 2. 대조적으로 3. 불리한 Driving underage is against the law.	
345 **job** [job]	초등	일, 직장 He has a part-time job.	
346 **car** [kahr]	초등	자동차 She got a new car.	
347 **local** [LOH-kuhl]	중등 토익	1. 지방의, 현지의 2. 주민 We should follow local customs.	
348 **country** [KUHN-tree]	초등 토익	1. 국가, 나라 2. 시골, 전원 Africa is not a country.	countryside (시골)
349 **government** [GUHV-ern-muhnt]	중등	1. 정부, 정권 2. 행정, 통치 The government has set out new plans on air pollution.	governor (주지사) govern (통치하다) governance (통치)
350 **organize** [AWR-guh-nahyz]	중등 토익	1. 준비하다 2. 정리하다, 체계를 세우다 I would like to thank you for organizing today's special event.	

351	중등 토익	1. 작전, 활동 2. 수술 3. 기업, 사업체 4. 운용, 작동	operate (운영하다)
operation [op-uh-REY-shuh n]		He directed the operation.	
352	토익 공무원	기술	tech (=technology) biotech (생명공학)
technology [tek-NOL-uh-jee]		Frontier technologies are making our lives much easier.	
353	중등 토익	1. 수업, 강의 2. 학급 3. 계층, 계급 4. 등급	classify (분류하다) classification (분류) classy (고급의) classroom (교실)
class [klas]		I took a class in biology.	
354	중등	교육하다, 가르치다	education (교육) educated (교육 받은)
educate [EJ-oo-keyt]		He was poorly educated.	
355	중등 토익	1. 사진 2. 촬영하다, 사진을 찍다	photo (=photograph)
photograph [FOH-tuh-graf]		Can you take my photograph?	
356	초등	1. 방문(하다) 2. 체류하다, 머물다	visitor (방문자)
visit [VIZ-it]		I visited London.	
357	중등 토익	1. 예상하다, 기대하다 2. 기다리다 3. 요구하다, 바라다	expectation (예상) unexpected (기대치 못한)
expect [ik-SPEKT]		The outcome of the study was as expected.	
358	초등	1. 떨어져 2. 멀리 3. 떠나다	
away [uh-WEY]		Stay away from me.	
359	중등	1. 선발하다, 선정하다 2. 선택하다 3. 엄선된, 고급의	selection (선택) selective (선택적인)
select [si-LEKT]		The president was selected by the people.	
360	중등 토익	1. 마지막의, 최종적인 2. 결정적인 3. 결승전 4. 기말 시험	finally (마침내) finalist (결승 진출자)
final [FAHYN-l]		The decision is final.	
361	중등	1. 보안, 경비 2. 안보 3. 보장 4. 증권	secure (안전한) insecure (불안한)
security [si-KYOOR-i-tee]		He works as a security guard at a hotel.	
362	초등	1. 오늘 2. 오늘날, 현재	
today [tuh-DEY]		What are you doing today?	
363	초등	1. 죽음, 사망 2. ~의 종말	die (죽다)
death [deth]		He wasn't afraid of death.	
364	초등	1. 돌아오다, 복귀하다 2. 돌려주다 3.복귀 4. 수익	
return [ri-TURN]		I'll return at seven.	

365 **enter** [EN-ter]	중등	1. 들어가다 2. 시작하다 3. 입력하다 4. 참가하다	entry (입장) entrance (입구)
		She entered my room.	
366 **treat** [treet]	중등	1. 대우(하다) 2. 여기다, 취급하다 3. 치료하다, 처치하다 4. 선물, 대접	treatment (치료) mistreat (잘못 대하다)
		Don't treat me like a child.	
367 **appear** [uh-PEER]	중등	1. 나타나다 2. ~인 것 같이 보이다 3. 생기다, 발생하다 4. 출연하다	appearance (외모) disappear (사라지다)
		She suddenly appeared amid the crowd.	
368 **money** [MUHN-ee]	초등	돈, 금액, 자금	monetary (화폐의) monetize (현금화하다)
		I have no money left for the month.	
369 **enough** [ih-NUHF]	초등	필요한 만큼의, 충분한	
		It is important to get enough sleep.	
370 **happen** [HAP-uhn]	중등	1. 일어나다, 발생하다 2. 우연히 ~하다	
		Nothing has happened yet.	
371 **season** [SEE-zuhn]	초등 토익	1.계절 2. 철, 시즌 3. 양념하다	seasonal (계절적인) seasoned (숙련된) seasoning (조미료)
		What season do you like the best?	
372 **clear** [kleer]	초등	1. 분명한, 확실한 2. 투명한, 맑은, 깨끗한 3. 치우다 4. 승인하다, 허가하다, 통과시키다	clearance (치우기)
		It is clear that smoking is bad for your health.	
373 **bad** [bad]	초등	1. 나쁜, 좋지 않은 2. 심한, 심각한 3. 잘못된	worsen (악화되다) worst (최악) worse (더 나쁜)
		Here's bad news.	
374 **quality** [KWOL-i-tee]	중등	1. 품질 2. 양질(의) 3. 자질 4. 특성, 특징	qualitative (질적인)
		We prefer quality to quantity.	
375 **sell** [sel]	초등 토익	팔다, 매각하다	best-selling (가장 잘 팔리는) sold (팔렸다)
		I am going to sell my car.	
376 **university** [yoo-nuh-VUR-si-tee]	중등	대학	
		She is a university student.	
377 **story** [STAWR-ee]	초등	1. 이야기 2. 소설 3. 기사	
		Let's hear his story.	
378 **joy** [joi]	초등 토익	1. 기쁨, 즐거움, 환희 2. 만족, 성공	enjoy (즐기다) joyful (즐거운)
		You are the joy of my life.	

379 **hear** [heer]	중등	듣다, 경청하다 Can you hear me?	hearing (공판, 청력) unheard (들어보지 않은) overhear (엿듣다)
380 **word** [wurd]	초등	1. 단어 2. 말, 이야기 3. 말로 표현하다 She knows many words in French.	
381 **step** [step]	중등	1. 단계 2. 걸음 3. 걷다 4. 계단 5. 조치 We are ready for the next step.	footstep (걸음, 발소리, 발자국)
382 **room** [room]	초등 토익	1. 방 2. 자리, 공간 3. 여지 His room is very messy.	restroom (화장실) livingroom (거실)
383 **sense** [sens]	중등	1. 감각 2. 느낌, 감 3. 의미, 뜻 4. 감지하다, 느끼다 She lost her sense of smell.	sensitive (민감한) sensation (전율, 느낌) sensational (엄청난) sensory (감각의)
384 **hope** [hohp]	초등	1. 희망(하다) 2. 바라다, 기대하다 He always hopes for the best.	hopefully (바라건대)
385 **certain** [SUR-tn]	초등	1. 확실한, 틀림없는 2. 특정한, 어떤 We are not so certain about that.	uncertainty (불확실성)
386 **depend** [dih-PEND]	중등 토익	1. 의존하다, 의지하다 2. 신뢰하다 3. ~에 달려 있다 I am depending on you.	depending (의존하는) independent (독립된)
387 **choose** [chooz]	초등	1. 선택하다, 고르다 2. ~하기를 원하다 He chose to stay with me.	chosen (선택된)
388 **night** [nahyt]	중등 토익	밤, 저녁, 야간 Good night everyone.	overnight (하룻밤 동안에) midnight (자정(저녁 12시))
389 **near** [neer]	초등	1. 가까운, 근처(의) 2. 비슷한, 근사한 I live near the school.	nearly (거의) nearby (근처)
390 **save** [seyv]	초등	1. 모으다, 저축하다 2. 구하다 3. 절약하다, 아끼다 She has saved a lot of money.	savings (저축량)
391 **safe** [seyf]	초등 토익	1. 안전한 2. 무사한 3. 신중한 4. 금고 We are safe here.	safety (안전)
392 **talk** [tawk]	초등	1. 말하다, 이야기하다 2. 대화(하다) 3. 회담 4. 연설, 강연 He wants to talk to her.	talkative (수다스러운)

393		성공(작), 성과	successful (성공적인)
success [suhk-SES]		I wish you success in all your future endeavors.	

394	초등	음악, 곡, 노래	musical (뮤지컬)
music [MYOO-zik]		I like pop music.	

395	수능	1. 강요하다 2. 힘, ~력 3. 단체, 집단, 병력	enforce (집행하다) forcibly (강제적으로) forceful (강제적인)
force [fawrs]		He forced her to leave.	

396	초등 토익	보내다	
send [send]		Please send me the mail by tomorrow.	

397		1. 이미지 2. 인상 3. 형태	
image [IM-ij]		Having a good image is important for politicians.	

398	중등	1. (시간 단위의) 분 2. 매우 작은 3. 상세한	
minute [MIN-it]		One hour is 60 minutes.	

399	초등	1.어린, 젊은 2. 신생의	youth (젊은 시절)
young [YUHNG]		Young children need 10 hours of sleep.	

400	중등	1. 최근의, 근래의 2. 근대의	recently (최근에)
recent [REE-suhnt]		Recently, pollution has worsened.	

401	중등	1. 개선하다, 향상시키다 2. 회복하다	improvement (개선)
improve [im-PROOV]		You need to improve your grades.	

402	중등 토익	한계(를 두다), 제한(하다)	limited (제한된) limitation (제약 사항)
limit [LIM-it]		The time limit for this exam is 45 minutes.	

403	초등 토익	1. (어느 장소에 비어 있는) 공간 2. 우주 3. 일정한 간격을 두다	spacious (넓은) spatial (공간적인) spacing (간격) spacecraft (우주선)
space [speys]		There are too many people and not enough space.	

404	초등	1. 얼굴 2. 직면하다	
face [feys]		Wash your face with cold water.	

405	중등	1. 사회의 2. 사교적인, 붙임성 있는	socialism (사회주의) sociable (사교적인) society (사회) sociology (사회과학)
social [SOH-shuh l]		We are facing social problems such as poverty.	

406	초등	1. 이미 2. 벌써	
already [awl-RED-ee]		She has already graduated.	

| 407 **fact** [fakt] | 초등 | 사실 | factual (실제의) |
| | | It is hard to tell fact from fiction! | |

| 408 **ever** [EV-er] | 중등 | 1, 언젠가 2. 이전에 | |
| | | Did you ever smoke? | |

| 409 **bit** [bit] | 중등 | 1. 조금, 약간, 소량의 2. 짧은 공연 | |
| | | She gave me a bit of money. | |

| 410 **kind** [kahynd] | 초등 | 1. 친절한 2. 종류 | |
| | | Being kind is important. | |

| 411 **range** [reynj] | 중등 | 1. 구역, 영역 2. 다양성, 범위 3. 범위로 하다, 분포되어있다 | long-range (장거리) |
| | | The bomb affected a wide range. | |

| 412 **together** [tuh-GETH-er] | 초등 | 1. 함께, 서로 2. 동시에 | |
| | | We graduated together. | |

| 413 **deal** [deel] | 중등 토익 | 1. 거래(하다) 2. 다루다, 관련 있다 | dealer (판매자) |
| | | The deal made a lot of money for the company. | |

| 414 **perfect** [PUR-fekt] | 중등 | 1. 완벽한, 최적의 2. 완벽히하다 | perfection (완벽) imperfect (완벽하지 못한) perfectionist (완벽주의자) |
| | | It was a perfect day. | |

| 415 **charge** [chahrj] | 수능 토익 | 1. 요금(을 청구하다) 2. 충전하다 3. 고소하다 | rechargeable (충전가능한) |
| | | The charge for the service is 10 dollars. | |

| 416 **date** [deyt] | 초등 | 1. 날짜 2. 날짜를 적다, 연대를 예측하다 3. (연인 간의) 데이트(하다) | |
| | | What is the date today? | |

| 417 **size** [sahyz] | 초등 | 1. 크기, 규모 2. 사이즈, 치수 | oversized (너무 큰) downsize (줄이다) |
| | | I wear size 27 pants. | |

| 418 **card** [kahrd] | | 1. 카드, 엽서 2. 카드 놀이 | |
| | | She sent me a card for my birthday. | |

| 419 **least** [leest] | | 1. 최소의 2. 적어도 | |
| | | The garter snake is the least dangerous snake. | |

| 420 **collect** [kuh-LEKT] | 초등 토익 | 1. 모으다, 수집하다 2. 징수하다 | collection (수집품 모음) collective (집단적인) |
| | | I collect post stamps. | |

421	초등	1. 빠른 2. 성급한 3. 이해가 빠른	quickly (빠르게)
quick [kwik]		She was quick to make friends.	

422	중등	1. 몇몇의 2. 여러 가지의	
several [SEV-er-uhl]		Several people were injured in the accident.	

423	중등	1. 주요한 2. 전공(의)	majority (다수의, 과반수 이상의)
major [MEY-jer]		She was assigned a major role in the project.	

424	중등	1. (돈을) 쓰다 2. 보내다	spending (지출) spent (사용한)
spend [spend]		Many people enjoy spending money.	

425	중등	1. 세부, 구체적 내용 2. 상세히 설명하다	
detail [dee-TEYL]		You should add more detail to your essay.	

426	중등 토익	1. 보통의, 일반적인 2. 일상의	usually (보통)
usual [YOO-zhoo-uhl]		As usual, he was right.	

427	중등 토익	동의하다, 합의하다	disagree (동의하지 않다)
agree [uh-GREE]		Do you agree to have the meeting on Monday?	

428	중등 토익	1.이익, 은혜 2. 이익을 주다	beneficial (이로운)
benefit [BEN-uh-fit]		Good grades will benefit your life.	

429	중등 토익	지키다, 보호하다	protection (보호) protectionism (보호주의 무역)
protect [pruh-TEKT]		The strong should protect the weak.	

430	중등	~이든 아니든	
whether [HWETH-er]		Whether or not it rains, let's meet on Sunday.	

431	토익	1. (실물보다 작은) 모형 2. 모범 3. 설계하다 4. (패션)모델	
model [MOD-l]		They made a model of the pyramids.	

432	초등	1. 나이 2. 시대 3. 나이 들다	
age [eyj]		People above the age of 18 can drive.	

433	중등	1. 재정, 재무 2. 금융 3. 자금을 대다	financial (금융의)
finance [fi-NANS]		Understanding finance is important for running a company.	

434	중등 토익	특정한, 분명한	specifically (특히) specify (구체화하다)
specific [spi-SIF-ik]		All regions have specific characteristics.	

435 **lose** [looz]	중등	1. 잃어버리다 2. 지다	lost (잃은) loser (패자)
		He always loses his cellphone.	
436 **industry** [IN-duh-stree]	중등	산업, 사업	industrial (산업의)
		The agricultural industry is suffering from a lack of rain.	
437 **individual** [in-duh-VIJ-oo-uhl]	중등 토익	1. 개인의, 개별적인 2. 개인	
		We all have individual cars.	
438 **release** [ri-LEES]	중등	1. 풀어주다 2. 공개(하다), 발표(하다)	
		Animals should be released from small cages.	
439 **stop** [stop]	초등	1. 멈추다, 중지하다 2. 정류소	nonstop (멈추지 않고) unstoppable (막을 수 없는)
		A red light means that cars should stop.	
440 **speak** [speek]	초등	이야기하다, 연설하다	speaker (화자)
		He doesn't like speaking to a crowd.	
441 **fund** [fuhnd]	중등 토익	1. 투자금, 적립금 2. 투자하다	funding (자금을 지원하다)
		The group is running out of funds.	
442 **press** [pres]	중등	1. 언론 2. 누르다	pressure (압박)
		The press should not report fake news.	
443 **short** [shawrt]	초등 토익	짧은, (키가) 작은	shortage (부족) shorts (반바지)
		He was shorter than his classmates.	
444 **sound** [sound]	초등	1. 소리(를 내다) 2. 들리다 3. 건전한, 건강한	
		Do you hear the sound of a mosquito?	
445 **break** [breyk]	초등	1. 깨뜨리다, 고장내다 2. (관계를) 끊다	broken (고장난) breakdown (무너짐, 해부) outbreak (발발)
		If you break it, you need to pay to replace it.	
446 **condition** [kuhn-DISH-uhn]	초등 토익	1. 상태, 컨디션 2. 조건 3. 컨디션을 잘 조절하다	conditioning (훈련) unconditional (무조건적인)
		She is in good condition because of her regular exercise.	
447 **focus** [FOH-kuhs]	초등	1. 집중(하다) 2. 초점	
		Everyone was focused on the exam.	
448 **pass** [pas]	중등	1. 지나가다 2. 패스하다, 넘기다 3. 허가증 (ex. 프리패스)	passerby (지나가는 사람)
		Two cars passed the school just now.	

449 **along** [uh-LAWNG]	초등	1. ~을 따라, ~을 끼고 2. 함께	
		We walked along the beach.	
450 **standard** [STAN-derd]	중등	1. 표준, 기준 2. 수준	standardized (표준화된)
		The standard class time is 75 minutes in university.	
451 **either** [EE-ther]	중등	1. 또한 2. (둘 중) 하나	
		I don't want dessert either.	
452 **fit** [fit]	중등 토익	1. 꼭 맞는, 적합한 2. 건강한 3. 발작, 격분	fitness (건강)
		The slippers were a perfect fit for Cinderella.	
453 **attend** [uh-TEND]	중등 토익	1. 출석하다, 참석하다 2. 주의하다	attendance (출석)
		She attends class regularly.	
454 **fall** [fawl]	초등	1. 떨어지다 2. (온도가) 내리다 3. 가을 4. 하게 되다	
		The leaves were falling.	
455 **amount** [uh-MOUNT]	중등	1. 양 2. 총합, 총액 (이 ~에 달하다)	
		What is the adequate amount of food for four people?	
456 **per** [pur]	중등	~당, ~마다	
		You should sleep 8 hours per day.	
457 **yet** [yet]	중등	1. 아직 2. 그렇지만	
		Details haven't been worked out yet.	
458 **probably** [PROB-uh-blee]	중등 토익	아마	probability (확률) probable (가능한)
		She was probably right.	
459 **media** [MEE-dee-uh]	중등 토익	(방송) 매체	
		The media plays an important role in politics.	
460 **contact** [KON-takt]	중등	1. 연락하다 2. 접촉(하다) 3. 연락처, 연줄	
		Please don't contact me this weekend.	
461 **science** [SAHY-uhns]	초등	과학	scientist (과학자) scientific (과학적인)
		I have a science quiz tomorrow.	
462 **party** [PAHR-tee]		1. 파티, 잔치 (하다) 2. (정치에서의) 정당	third-party (제 3자)
		You are invited to my birthday party.	

463 **human** [HYOO-muhn]	초등	1. 인간, 사람 2. 인간적인 Humans walk on two legs.	humanity (인류) humanitarian (인도주의자)
464 **million** [MIL-yuhn]	중등	1. 100만 2. 다수 There were millions of flies.	millionaire (백만장자)
465 **opportunity** [op-er-TOO-ni-tee]	중등	기회 Thank you for the opportunity to work here.	opportunistic (기회주의적) inopportune (시기가 좋지 않은)
466 **character** [KAR-ik-ter]	중등	1. 인물 2. 성격, 인격 3. 글자 I like the characters of Alice in Wonderland.	characteristic (특성) uncharacteristic (평소답지 않은)
467 **cut** [kuht]	초등	1. 자르다 2. 삭감하다, 줄이다 3. 베인 상처 Please cut my sandwich in half.	cutback (삭감)
468 **park** [pahrk]	초등	1.공원 2. 주차하다 Shall we go for a walk in the park?	
469 **produce** [pruh-DOOS]	중등	1. 생산하다, 제작하다 2. 농산물 Chickens produce eggs.	producer (제작자) production (생산)
470 **remove** [ri-MOOV]	중등 토익	제거하다, 치우다 Please remove the car that is blocking my door.	removal (제거)
471 **across** [uh-KRAWS]	초등	1. 가로질러 2. 걸쳐서 She walked across the street.	
472 **travel** [TRAV-uhl]	초등 토익	1. 여행(하다) 2. 이동하다 I would like to travel around the world.	
473 **shoot** [shoot]	중등	1. 쏘다, 발사하다 2. 촬영(하다) Shooting a gun is very dangerous.	shot (발사, 촬영) shooting (총격)
474 **below** [bih-LOH]	초등	1. 아래에 2. ~보다 못하여 My book is right below your bag.	
475 **invest** [in-VEST]	중등	투자하다 You should invest carefully.	investment (투자) investor (투자자)
476 **watch** [woch]	초등	1. 보다, 관람하다 2. 시계 Let's watch a baseball game together.	

477	초등	~보다 위에	
above			
[uh-BUHV]		Look above, there are fireworks in the sky.	

478	중등	추천하다	recommendation (추천)
recommend			
[rek-uh-MEND]		I recommend the carrot cake, it is delicious.	

479	수능 토익	1. ~에 의하면 2. ~에 따라	accordance (일치) accord (합의) accordingly (그래서)
according			
[uh-KAWR-ding]		According to the research, cheetahs are the fastest animals.	

480	토익	1. 버튼을 누르다, 클릭하다 2. 딸깍하는 소리	
click			
[klik]		Click the X button to close the advertisement.	

481	중등 토익	1. 알아차리다 2. 공지, 통지	notification (알림) notify (알리다)
notice			
[NOH-tis]		She noticed that I was tired.	

482	초등	1. 들, 밭 2. 경기장	
field			
[feeld]		Cows were eating grass on the field.	

483	중등 토익	구매(하다)	
purchase			
[PUR-chuhs]		I purchased a bag.	

484	중등	1. (짐을) 싸다 2. 가득 채우다 3. (동물) 무리	package (포장)
pack			
[pak]		Can you help me pack the books into the boxes?	

485	토익 공무원	1. 흔한, 보통의 2. 공통의	
common			
[KOM-uhn]		Getting a cold in the winter is very common.	

486	초등	1. 열쇠 2. 핵심적인	
key			
[kee]		She lost the keys to her house.	

487	중등	1. 위치(하다) 2. 자세 3. 신분, 일자리	
position			
[puh-ZISH-uhn]		Do you know the position of the ship?	

488	초등	미래	
future			
[FYOO-cher]		What do you want to be in the future?	

489	초등	1. 판매 2. 세일	sales (영업)
sale			
[seyl]		He has just made his first sale.	

490	중등	1. 암호 2. 규약, 규율	decode (해독하다)
code			
[kohd]		This is a difficult code to solve.	

491 **yes** [yes]	초등	네, 응, 그래	
		Yes, I will marry you.	
492 **practice** [PRAK-tis]	중등	1. 연습(하다) 2. 실행(하다), 실천(하다) 3. 행사하다 4. 관례	practicum (실습 과목)
		If you want to improve your English, you should practice.	
493 **link** [lingk]	중등	연결(하다), 관련성	linkage (연결)
		There is a link between smoking and early death.	
494 **mind** [mahynd]	초등	1. 마음, 정신, 생각 2. 상관하다, 신경쓰다	mind-set (사고방식)
		What is on your mind?	
495 **function** [FUHNGK-shuhn]	중등	1. 기능, 작용 2. (제 기능대로) 작동하다	functionality (기능)
		The function of a broomstick is cleaning.	
496 **due** [doo]	중등 토익	1. 응당, ~할 예정인 2. ~때문에, ~덕분에	overdue (연체된)
		The train is due to arrive in 15 minutes.	
497 **content** [KON-tent]	중등	1. 내용물 2. 만족한	discontent (불만족한)
		The content of this book is very helpful.	
498 **strong** [STRAWNG]	초등	강한	
		The little boy wanted to become strong.	
499 **deliver** [dih-LIV-er]	중등	1. 배달하다 2. 연설을 하다	delivery (배달)
		He delivered pizzas for a living.	
500 **associate** [uh-SOH-shee-eyt]	중등	1. 연관짓다, 연상하다 2. 어울리다 3. 준, 부 (ex. 준회원) 4. 제휴한	association (협회)
		Flowers are associated with love.	
501 **patient** [PEY-shuhnt]	중등 토익	1. 인내심이 있는 2. 환자	patience (인내) impatient (참을성이 없는) outpatient (외래환자) [4024] tolerant
		You need to be more patient.	
502 **property** [PROP-er-tee]	중등	1. 재산, 소유물 2. (고유) 특징, 성질	[374] quality
		He has a lot of property.	
503 **contain** [kuhn-TEYN]	중등 토익	1. 담고있다, 포함하다 2. 억누르다, 저지하다	container (컨테이너) [86] include
		Most brands of coffee contain a lot of sugar.	
504 **refer** [ri-FUR]	중등 토익	1. 참고하다 2. 언급하다, 말하다	reference (참고대상) referral (추천) [876] mention
		When I was doing homework, I referred to this book.	

505	중등	1. 도구 2. 수단	[1541] instrument
tool			
[tool]		Humans are capable of using tools.	

506	초등 토익	문	outdoor (야외)
door			indoor (실내)
			doorstep (문간)
[dawr]		The door was locked.	[2072] gate

507	중등	항목, 품목	[156] point
item			
[AHY-tuhm]		They reduced the price on many items.	

508	중등	1. 합계 2. 전체의	totally (완전히)
total			[207] complete
[TOHT-l]		The total amount I spent shopping was $50.	

509	중등	줄이다	reduction (감소)
reduce			[3435] diminish
[ri-DOOS]		We need to reduce our spending.	

510		1. 최초의 2. 독창적인	originality (독창성)
original			[73] first
[uh-RIJ-uh-nl]		The original Starbucks is in New York.	

511	중등	재료, 원료, 물질	materialize (실현되다)
material			[1432] substantial
[muh-TEER-ee-uhl]		The materials needed for cleaning are soap and water.	

512	중등	있음직한, 가능성이 높은	likelihood (가능성)
likely			[246] possible
[LAHYK-lee]		It is likely to rain tomorrow.	

513	중등	과거의, 지난	[143] last
past			
[PAST]		We cannot change what has happened in the past.	

514	초등	재미있는, 즐거운	funny (웃긴)
fun			[378] enjoyment
[fuhn]		The movie was very fun.	

515	초등	1. 위원회 2. 판자 3. 탑승하다 4. 기숙하다	on-board (배 위에)
board			overboard (배 밖으로)
[bawrd]		The board evaluated his resume.	[1051] council

516	중등	1. 규칙 2. 통치(하다), 통제(하다) 3. 판결을 내리다	ruling (판결, 통치하는)
rule			ruler (자, 지도자)
[rool]		She did not obey the school rules.	[273] control

517	중등	버전, 판	[1685] edition
version			
[VUR-zhuhn]		I liked the first version of the movie more than the second version.	

518	중등	특정한, 각별한	[434] specific
particular			
[per-TIK-yuh-ler]		I like this particular puppy.	

519	초등	대학	collegiate (대학의) [163] school
college [KOL-ij]		Many people choose to work as soon as possible and do not go to college.	
520	중등	솜씨, 기술	skilled (실력있는) skillful (숙련된) [111] ability
skill [skil]		He has amazing artistic skills.	
521	초등	1. 머무르다 2. 특정 상태를 그대로 유지하다 3. 머무름, 방문	[537] remain
stay [stey]		I want you to stay.	
522		1. 부분 2. 절개하다	[125] part
section [SEK-shuhn]		That section of your essay needs to be edited.	
523	중등	1. 신용, 신뢰 2. 공을 주다 3. 칭찬, 인정	[882] trust
credit [KRED-it]		The president got credit for achieving his promises.	
524	초등	1. 서다, 위치하다 2. 입장 3. 스탠드, 가판대 4. 견디다, 버티다	standpoint (입장) [1109] bear
stand [stand]		Stand up and come here.	
525	중등	1. 비평, 해설, 논평 (하다) 2. 댓글	commentary (방송 해설) [1944] remark
comment [KOM-ent]		The professor's comment on her assignment was positive.	
526	중등 토익	묘사하다, 설명하다	description (설명) [630] explain
describe [dih-SKRAHYB]		Can you describe the bag that you lost?	
527	중등	포함하다, 관련되다	[86] include
involve [in-VOLV]		Were you involved in the crime?	
528	중등	상징하다, 대표하다	representative (대표자) misrepresentation (허위 진술) [3139] portray
represent [rep-ri-ZENT]		The bald eagle represents America.	
529		1. 스타일, 양식 2. 방식 3. 스타일링을 하다	stylish (스타일 좋은) [1417] fashion
style [stahyl]		I like this style of clothing.	
530	중등	1. 저지르다 2. 헌신하다	commitment (헌신) [895] engage
commit [kuh-MIT]		She committed murder.	
531	중등	1. 위험 2. 위태롭게 하다	risky (위험한) high-risk (고위험) [2553] hazard
risk [risk]		There is a high risk of cancer if you smoke.	
532	중등 토익	1. 환경 2. 상황	[1346] surroundings
environment [en-VAHY-ruhn-muhnt]		Protecting the environment is important.	

533 **walk** [wawk]	초등	1. 걷다 2. 산책(하다) 3. 길 I enjoy walking around the city.	walk-in (예약 없이 방문가능한) [3456] stroll
534 **source** [sawrs]	중등	원천, 출처 Where is the source of the information?	[1729] origin
535 **whole** [hohl]	중등	전체의, 완전한 The whole pizza is 450 calories.	wholly (완전히) [639] entire
536 **install** [in-STAWL]	중등 토익	설치하다 She is helping me install my television.	installation (설치) [778] establish
537 **remain** [ri-MEYN]	중등	1. 남다, 머무르다 2. (-s) 남은 것 3. (-s) 유적 The question remains unsolved.	[521] stay
538 **phone** [fohn]	초등	전화 David left his phone in the taxi.	telephone (=phone) [129] call
539 **identify** [ahy-DEN-tuh-fahy]	중등 토익	확인하다, 식별하다 Can you identify which person committed the crime?	identity (정체성) identification (신분증) [832] recognize
540 **answer** [AN-ser]	초등	1. 대답(하다) 2. 해답 I waited several days for his answer.	[1666] reply
541 **main** [meyn]	중등	핵심적인 Her main goal in life was to become a lawyer.	mainly (주로) [968] primary
542 **beautiful** [BYOO-tuh-fuhl]	초등	아름다운 Everyone is beautiful in their own way.	beauty (아름다움) [1069] attractive
543 **tax** [taks]	중등	세금 Citizens pay taxes every year.	taxation (과세) tax-free (면세) taxing (아주 힘든) [415] charge
544 **address** [uh-DRES]	초등	1. 주소 2. 어려운 문제를 언급하고 다루다 3. 강연(을 하다) Please write down your address to receive the delivery.	[2240] tackle
545 **period** [PEER-ee-uhd]	중등 토익	1. 기간 2. 단계 3. 생리, 월경 He lost a lot of weight in a short period.	periodically (정기적으로)
546 **series** [SEER-eez]	중등	연속, 일련 A series of unfortunate events occurred in her life.	[1649] succession

547 **energy** [EN-er-jee]	토익	에너지, 힘, 활기 Coffee gives me energy in the morning.	energetic (활기찬) energize (활기를 북돋다) [201] power
548 **single** [SING-guhl]	중등	1. 단 하나의 2. 독신의 A single person can change the world.	singular (단수의) [1183] alone
549 **exist** [ig-ZIST]	중등	존재하다 Cockroaches have existed for thousands of years.	existence (존재) existential (실존의) nonexistent (존재하지않는) [189] live
550 **north** [nawrth]	초등	북쪽 Let's head North.	northern (북쪽의) northwest (북서쪽)
551 **pretty** [PRIT-ee]	초등	1. 예쁜, 아름다운 2. 꽤, 상당히 The flowers are very pretty.	[2366] cute
552 **front** [fruhnt]	초등	1. 정면(의) 2. 정면을 향하다 I read the front page of the newspaper.	forefront (맨 앞의) [404] face
553 **carry** [KAR-ee]	초등 토익	1. 운반하다 2. 휴대하다 He always carries bandaids for his son.	carrier (통신사) carriage (마차) [1109] bear
554 **kid** [kid]	초등	1. 아이 2. 놀리다 Kids need a lot of sleep.	[170] child
555 **air** [air]	초등	1. 공기 2. 대기 The air is very polluted.	midair (공중에서) [2004] atmosphere
556 **black** [blak]	초등	1. 검정, 검은 2. 흑인(의) My favorite color is black.	[941] dark
557 **almost** [AWL-mohst]	초등	거의, 대부분 I am almost there!	[389] nearly
558 **agency** [EY-juhn-see]	중등	1. 기관 2. 대행, 대리점 The agency had too much work to do.	agent (대리인, 첩보원, 행위자) [179] office
559 **clean** [kleen]	초등 토익	1. 깨끗한 2. 청소하다 Her room is very clean.	[372] clear
560 **goal** [gohl]	초등	1. 목표 2. (축구 등 스포츠) 골 My goal is to finish all my homework today.	[1679] objective

561 track [trak]	공무원	1. 추적하다 2. 흔적 3. 경주로 4. 선로, 통로	[2226] trace
		Can you track where my cat went?	
562 device [dih-VAHYS]	중등	장치, 기구	[5017] apparatus
		I have many devices for exercising.	
563 war [wawr]	수능	전쟁	warrior (전사) postwar (전후의) [1214] battle
		Wars should never happen.	
564 picture [PIK-cher]	초등	1. 그림, 사진 2. 상상하다, 머리로 그리다 3. 영화, 작품	pictorial (그림으로 나타낸) picturesque (그림같은) [397] image
		I showed her pictures of my family.	
565 publish [PUHB-lish]	중등 토익	출판하다	publication (출판물) publisher (출판사) [248] issue
		He published a book at the age of 7.	
566 English [ING-glish]		1. 영어 2. 영국의	England (영국)
		English is a great language.	
567 America [uh-MER-i-kuh]		미국	[기타] United States
		America is the world's strongest country.	
568 update [uhp-DEYT]	중등	갱신하다	[1325] upgrade
		You should update your resume.	
569 box [boks]	중등	상자, 함	[218] case
		What's in this box?	
570 although [awl-THOH]	중등	비록 ~일지라도	[336] though
		Although it is late, I still want to meet you.	
571 search [surch]	중등	1. 찾다 2. 검색하다	[910] seek
		I am searching for the perfect home.	
572 compare [kuhm-PAIR]	중등	비교하다	comparison (비교) [688] match
		Do not compare your child to other people.	
573 prepare [pri-PAIR]	중등	준비하다	preparation (준비) prep (준비)
		She's preparing for an exam.	
574 instead [in-STED]	중등	~의 대신에	[581] rather
		Instead of coffee, may I have some tea?	

575 **compute** [kuhm-PYOOT]	공무원	계산하다 I am computing the annual increase in rainfall.	computer (컴퓨터) computation (계산) [1282] calculate
576 **especially** [ih-SPESH-uh-lee]	중등	유별나게, 특히 He is especially shy but considerate.	[518] particularly
577 **solution** [suh-LOO-shuhn]		1. 해결책 2. 용액 I still don't have a solution.	[540] answer
578 **hit** [hit]	초등	1. 때리다, 치다 2. 타격 3. 명중하다 4. 인기 작품, 히트 He hit his friend.	[1226] strike
579 **wide** [wahyd]	중등	1. 넓은 2. 다양하다 I want to live in a house with a wide garden.	width (너비) widen (넓히다) [1630] broad
580 **policy** [POL-uh-see]	중등	정책, 규정 What are the policies of your school?	
581 **rather** [RATH-er]	중등	1. 오히려, 차라리 2. 상당히, 다소 I would rather go swimming than play soccer.	[587] quite
582 **similar** [SIM-uh-ler]	중등 토익	유사한, 비슷한 They look very similar.	similarity (유사성) [138] same
583 **compete** [kuhm-PEET]	중등	경쟁하다, 겨루다 I don't like competing against friends.	competition (경쟁) competitive (경쟁적) competitor (경쟁자) [2787] contend
584 **president** [PREZ-i-duhnt]	중등	1. 대통령 2. 사장 What do you think of the president?	presidential (대통령의) [301] head
585 **fast** [fast]	초등	1. 빠른 2. 단식하다 A rabbit is very fast.	[421] quick
586 **ago** [uh-GOH]	초등	전에 A long time ago, there were dinosaurs.	[105] back
587 **quite** [kwahyt]	중등	상당히, 꽤 The weather is quite hot.	[551] pretty
588 **claim** [kleym]	중등	1. 주장(하다), 요구(하다) 2. 청구하다 3. 차지하다 She claims to be related to a celebrity.	declaim (열변을 토하다) [1022] demand

589 nothing [NUHTH-ing]	초등	아무 것도 아닌, 아무 일도 (아니다) There is nothing special today.	
590 method [METH-uhd]	중등	방식, 방법 I have used this method before.	methodology (방법론) [776] procedure
591 suggest [suhg-JEST]	중등	제안하다, 암시하다 He suggested that we cooperate.	suggestion (제안) [1115] propose
592 finish [FIN-ish]	초등	1. 끝내다, 마치다 2. 마지막, 끝 I can't wait for work to finish!	[207] complete
593 client [KLAHY-uhnt]	중등 토익	고객, 의뢰인 Our store needs to increase the number of clients to make more money.	clientele (전체 고객) [314] customer
594 happy [HAP-ee]	초등 토익	행복한, 유쾌한 Money doesn't make us happy.	happiness (행복) [1886] glad
595 deep [deep]	초등	깊은 Be careful, the water is very deep.	depth (깊이) [3292] profound
596 reach [reech]	중등	1. 도달하다, 도착하다 2. 이루다 3. 영향의 도달 범위 Our advertisements reach millions of consumers.	[748] achieve
597 economy [ih-KON-uh-mee]	중등 토익	경제 The economy is in decline.	economics (경제학) economist (경제학자) [390] saving
598 partner [PAHRT-ner]		1. 협력자 2. 배우자 3. 파트너쉽을 맺다 Having passionate partners is important for success.	[2549] mate
599 piece [pees]	중등	1. 조각, 부분 2. 작품 Could you please cut me a piece of that pie?	apiece (각각) [125] part
600 maintain [meyn-TEYN]	중등	1. 유지하다, 보수하다 2. 계속하다 3. 주장하다 We need to maintain our cultural artifacts.	maintenance (유지보수) [147] keep
601 eat [eet]	초등	먹다 She was eating an apple.	[5375] devour
602 challenge [CHAL-inj]	중등	1. 도전 2. ~에 도전장을 내다 3. 이의를 제기하다 I like a challenge once in a while.	challenging (도전하게 하는) [2329] dispute

603 generate [JEN-uh-reyt]	수능 토익	발생하다, 생성하다 The new manager generated a lot of problems	generator (발전기) [469] produce
604 vary [VAIR-ee]	중등	1. 다르다, 다양하다 2. 바꾸다 His mood varies depending on the weather.	variable (변수) variation (변화) [123] change
605 wonder [WUHN-der]	중등	1. 궁금하다 2. 놀라움 He wondered who had built this beautiful church.	wonderful (아름다운) wondrous (놀라운) [263] question
606 document [DOK-yuh-muhnt]	중등 토익	1. 문서, 서류 2. 기록하다 Do you have the documents to prove your claim?	documentation (서류) documentary (다큐멘터리) [342] record
607 ensure [en-SHOOR]	중등	책임지다, 확보하다 I will ensure the safety of the children.	[1447] guarantee
608 extend [ik-STEND]	중등	연장하다, 넓히다 I will ask the teacher to extend the due date for this assignment.	extension (연장) [995] expand
609 guide [gahyd]	초등 토익	1. 안내자, 가이드 2. 안내하다 The guide knew a lot about the area.	guidance (안내) misguided (잘못 안내된) [195] direct
610 private [PRAHY-vit]	중등	1. 개인의, 개인적인 2. 사립의, 사설의 Could we have a private conversation?	privacy (사생활) [1334] secret
611 road [rohd]	초등	길, 도로 The tree fell over and blocked the road.	[1210] path
612 count [kount]	중등	1. 세다 2. 중요성을 갖다 Can you count how many oranges we have?	countless (셀 수 없이 많은)
613 combine [kuhm-BAHYN]	중등	결합하다, 연합하다 Scientists combined to find a cure for cancer.	combination (조합) [642] join
614 measure [MEZH-er]	중등	1. 측정하다 2. 조치, 대책 Can you measure the temperature for me?	measurement (측정) [1026] assess
615 parent [PAIR-uhnt]	초등	부모 My parents are in Malaysia right now.	parenting (육아) [980] father
616 oil [oil]	초등	기름, 석유 The price of oil is increasing.	[3256] grease

617 white [hwahyt]	초등	흰, 하얀 Snow is cold, white, and beautiful.	whiten (하얗게하다) [3563] pale
618 figure [FIG-yer]	중등	1. 모양, 모습 2. 인물 3. 수치 4. 판단하다 5. 비유 He made a figure of Santa Claus.	figuratively (비유적으로) [159] number
619 heart [hahrt]	초등	1. 심장 2. 마음 His heart was racing quickly because he was nervous.	dishearten (낙심시키다) heartbroken (매우 슬픈) heartache (마음아픔) [1248] core
620 eye [ahy]	초등	1. 눈 2. 보다, 주시하다 There's something in my eye.	[116] view
621 fail [feyl]	초등	실패하다, 실수하다 I won't fail again, I promise.	failure (실패)
622 remember [ri-MEM-ber]	초등	기억하다 Do you remember the party we went to last Christmas?	[129] recall
623 potential [puh-TEN-shuhl]	중등	가능성, 잠재력 She is a smart girl with a lot of potential.	potentially (잠재적으로) potent (강력한) impotence (무기력) [246] possibility
624 print [print]	초등	인쇄하다, 프린트하다 I need to print out my assignment and turn it in.	printer (프린터)
625 wait [weyt]	중등 토익	기다리다 Can you wait 10 minutes for me?	await (=wait for) [357] expect
626 court [kawrt]		1. 법정, 재판소 2. 코트(운동장) 3. 궁정 4. 구애하다 Lawyers spend a lot of time at court.	courtyard (뜰) [122] trial
627 example [ig-ZAM-puhl]	초등	예시, 표본 A cat is an example of an animal.	exemplify (표본이 되다) [431] model
628 bank [bangk]	초등 토익	1. 은행 2. 제방, 둑 3. 쌓이다 If you need to borrow money, please go to a bank.	banking (은행일)
629 film [film]		1. 영화 2. 촬영하다 I enjoy watching old films.	[924] movie
630 explain [ik-SPLEYN]	중등 토익	설명하다 I don't understand this question, can you help me answer it?	explanation (설명) [2184] clarify

631	중등	~의 사이에, ~의 가운데서	amongst (~의 사이에) [178] between
among [uh-MUHNG]		The bees were buzzing among the flowers.	

632	중등	1. 본무, 임무 2. 배역	[125] part
role [rohl]		What is your role on the team?	

633	중등	구성 단위, 한 개	unified (통일된) reunification (재통일) [174] team
unit [YOO-nit]		My apartment has 24 units.	

634		직원	understaffed (인원이 부족한)
staff [staf]		The staff is working hard.	

635	중등 토익	부문, 부서	[179] office
department [dih-PAHRT-muhnt]		Our department is not in charge of that issue, please call the department of education.	

636	중등	1. 돕다, 보조하다 2. (스포츠) 어시스트	assistance (도움) [85] help
assist [uh-SIST]		The money would assist in taking care of her schooling.	

637	중등	그 외에, 그렇지 않으면	elsewhere (다른 곳에서) [1231] otherwise
else [els]		Can someone else do the dishes today?	

638	중등	1. 기사 2. 품목, 물품	[507] item
article [AHR-ti-kuhl]		The newspaper included a photo with the article about the accident.	

639	중등	전체의, 온전한	entirely (전체적으로) [535] whole
entire [en-TAHYUHR]		The entire town was devastated by the earthquake.	

640	중등	1. 식물 2. 심다 3. 공장	plantation (농장) [1911] factory
plant [plant]		Plants make the air fresher.	

641	초등	1. 선택하다, 고르다 2. 선택	picky (까다로운) [359] select
pick [pik]		Can you pick between these two options?	

642	초등	1. 연결하다 2. 참여하다	[1409] unite
join [join]		The two roads join here.	

643	중등	1. 문제, 사안 2. 물질, 물체 3. 중요하다	[248] issue
matter [MAT-er]		This meeting, we have several matters to resolve.	

644	초등	1. 커플 2. 몇, 2개	[1097] pair
couple [KUHP-uhl]		My neighbors are a married couple from Chicago.	

645	초등 토익	1. 가게 2. 쇼핑하다	[322] store
shop [shop]		I bought this shirt from a shop in New York.	

646	중등	1. 경기, 경주 2. 인종 3. 달리다 4. 정치 경쟁	racial (인종의) racist (인종 차별주의자) racism (인종 차별의) [2136] rush
race [reys]		Some people enjoy betting money on horse races.	

647	초등	논의하다, 토론하다	discussion (논의) [392] talk
discuss [dih-SKUHS]		Can we discuss this problem later?	

648	초등	기본적인, 기초적인	[2042] fundamental
basic [BEY-sik]		I have a basic understanding of computer programming.	

649	중등	평범한	abnormal (평범하지 않은) [717] regular
normal [NAWR-muhl]		He is a perfectly normal child.	

650	중등	자원	resourceful (자원이 풍부한) [534] source
resource [REE-sawrs]		The local library is a valuable resource.	

651	중등	책임이 있는	responsibility (책임) [318] accountable
responsible [ri-SPON-suh-buhl]		Children should be responsible for cleaning their rooms.	

652	중등	1. 파악하다, 밝히다 2. 결정짓다 3. 결심하다	determined (결심한) indeterminate (애매한) predetermined (결정난) determinate (확실한)
determine [dih-TUR-min]		She couldn't determine if she'd won this round or not.	

653	초등	1. 입다, 착용하다 2. 의복 3. 닳다 4. 마모, 소모	worn (입던, 해진)
wear [wair]		I don't know what to wear to the party tonight.	

654	중등	~에 관해서	disregard (신경쓰지 않다) [705] concerning
regarding [ri-GAHR-ding]		She sent me an email regarding the employment offer.	

655	초등	1. 불, 화재 2. (총을) 쏘다 3. 해고하다	fiery (불타는) misfire (불발) fireplace (벽난로) [473] shoot
fire [fahyuhr]		A fire burned brightly in the fireplace.	

656	중등	1. 섞다, 혼합하다 2. 혼합	remix (다시 섞다, 리믹스) mixture (혼합) [1620] blend
mix [miks]		Mix two eggs and flour to create the dough.	

657	초등	1. 발, 다리 2. 피트 (약 30cm)	feet (foot의 복수형)
foot [foot]		He hit the soccer ball with his right foot.	

658	중등 토익	필요한, 없어서는 안될	unnecessary (불필요한) [166] required
necessary [NES-uh-ser-ee]		Water is necessary for survival.	

659 ship [ship]	초등 토익	1. 배, 함 2. 배송하다, 운송하다	shipping (배송) [1414] boat
		The ship was sinking at a fast speed.	
660 guy [gahy]	초등	1. 사람 2. 남자	[204] man
		He is a nice guy.	
661 half [haf]	중등	반, 중간, 중도	halve (반으로 줄이다)
		I finished half of my homework.	
662 correct [kuh-REKT]	중등 토익	1. 올바른, 정확한 2. 바로잡다, 고치다	correction (수정) [112] right
		Only tell me correct information.	
663 title [TAHYT-l]	수능	1. 표제, 제목 2. 타이틀, 직함 3. 권리 4. 챔피언인 상태	[176] name
		The title of the book was interesting.	
664 nice [nahys]	초등	좋은, 멋진	
		What a nice car you have!	
665 difficult [DIF-i-kuhlt]	초등	어려운, 힘든	
		This is a difficult task.	
666 choice [chois]		선택, 결정	
		He made the choice to be a moral person.	
667 trade [treyd]	중등	1. 무역 2. 거래, 상업	
		Venice was an important center of trade.	
668 accept [ak-SEPT]	중등 토익	받아들이다, 용인하다	unacceptable (받아들일 수 없는)
		Will you accept their offer?	
669 star [stahr]		1. 별 2. 주연, 인기 배우	stardom (스타의 유명세) starry (별이 많은) [외래어] superstar
		Stars are shining in the night sky.	
670 draw [draw]	중등 토익	1. 그리다 2. 비기다 3. 끌다, 뽑다, 빼다 4. 이동하다	drawing (그림) [912] pull
		He enjoys drawing in his free time.	
671 supply [suh-PLAHY]	중등	1. 공급(하다) 2. 재고품, 지급물	[99] provide
		The company supplies our town with electricity.	
672 defense [dih-FENS]	중등	1. 방어, 수비 2. 변호	defend (방어하다) defensive (방어적인) [429] protection
		Sanitation is the best defense against disease.	

673 **replace** [ri-PLEYS]	중등 토익	대신하다, 대체하다 We need to replace the secretary that left a month ago.	irreplaceable (대체 불가능한) [2386] substitute
674 **previous** [PREE-vee-uhs]	중등	이전의, 앞선 The previous owner didn't take good care of the dog.	[513] past
675 **register** [REJ-uh-ster]	중등	1. 등록하다, 신고하다 2. 나타내다, 표명하다 Let's register our marriage at the city hall.	registration (등록) registrar (등록 담당자) [342] record
676 **drop** [drop]	초등	1. 떨어뜨리다, 떨어지다 2. 방울 The cup shattered because he dropped it.	[454] fall
677 **consumer** [kuhn-SOO-mer]	중등 토익	소비자 Consumers often buy the cheapest product.	consume (소비하다) consumption (소비) [314] customer
678 **degree** [dih-GREE]	중등	1. (온도, 각도 등의) 도 2. 정도 3. 등급, 학위 Water boils at 100 degrees Celsius.	[2124] extent
679 **strategy** [STRAT-i-jee]	중등 토익	전략 The football coach came up with a clever strategy.	strategic (전략적인) strategist (전략가) [1724] scheme
680 **south** [south]	초등	남쪽 We moved south.	southern (남쪽의)
681 **award** [uh-WAWRD]	중등	1. 상 2. 수여하다 Soldiers win an award for bravery.	[1787] prize
682 **kill** [kil]	초등	죽이다 The cat killed the mouse.	overkill (필요 이상의) [1741] murder
683 **screen** [skreen]	중등	1. 화면 2. 가리다 3. 상영하다 I want to buy a television with a big screen.	screening (영화 상영, 검사) [231] cover
684 **street** [street]	초등	거리, 도로 Be careful crossing the street	
685 **fill** [fil]	초등	채우다 The pool slowly filled with water	refill (다시 채우다)
686 **resident** [REZ-i-duhnt]	수능 토익	1. 거주자 2. 거주하는 The residents didn't like the local school.	residence (거주지) reside (거주하다)

687	중등	위에 (on)	
upon [uh-PON]		If you make a wish upon a shooting star, it will come true.	

688	중등	1. 경기 2. 성냥 3. 딱 잘 맞는 (혹은 그런 것) 4. 대등하다, 어울리다	matching (어울리는) unmatched (비교대상이 없는) rematch (재경기)
match [mach]		Did you watch the football match last night?	

689	중등	아마	
maybe [MEY-bee]		Maybe he was right.	

690	초등	1. 땅, 토지 2. 착륙하다	flatland (평지) highland (고지) mainland (본토) [766] ground
land [land]		Farmers use land to grow crops.	

691	초등	앉다	[4654] perch
sit [sit]		Come in and sit down.	

692	초등	내부, 안쪽	[1864] interior
inside [in-SAHYD]		Although it was cold outside, it was warm inside the building.	

693	초등	문화	cultural (문화적인) [3160] cultivation
culture [KUHL-cher]		Korean culture is becoming more popular in other countries.	

694	중등 토익	편안한, 안락한	comfort (편안함) comfy (편안한)
comfortable [KUHMF-tuh-buhl]		This couch is very comfortable to sit on.	

695	중등 토익	1. 나아가게 하다 2. 진출, 전진 3. 미리 (in advance)	advanced (발전된, 고급의) advancement (발전) [1040] progress
advance [ad-VANS]		The soldiers advanced to the capital city.	

696	중등	접근하다, 다가오다	[590] method
approach [uh-PROHCH]		The lion approached the deer silently.	

697	초등	1. 싸우다 2. 전투	[1214] battle
fight [fahyt]		A fight broke out at the hockey game.	

698	중등	1. 소통하다, 통신하다 2. 전달하다	communication (소통) [2902] convey
communicate [kuh-MYOO-ni-keyt]		He and his sons haven't communicated with each other for years.	

699	중등	1. 지열하다 2. 전시	[121] show
display [dih-SPLEY]		The museum had displays of traditional art.	

700	중등	1. 층, 겹 2. 겹을 쌓다	
layer [LEY-er]		The cake had three layers of different flavors.	

701 lay [ley]		1. 놓다, 눕히다 2. 낳다	overlay (덮어씌우다) [206] put
		Can you lay the report on my desk?	
702 brand [brand]	초등	1. 상표, 상품명 2. 낙인을 찍다	[837] mark
		What is the most popular shoe brand these days?	
703 table [TEY-buhl]	초등 토익	1. 테이블, 탁자 2. 표	tabular (표 모양의) [515] board
		It was a sturdy table.	
704 ad [AD]	중등 토익	1. 광고 (advertisement) 2. 서기 (A.D.)	advertise (광고하다)
		There are so many ads in between television programs.	
705 concern [kuhn-SURN]	중등	1. 우려, 걱정(의 대상) 2. 걱정시키다 3. 관계가 있다, 관한	[1133] worry
		He is always concerned about the safety of his son.	
706 career [kuh-REER]	중등	경력, 진로, 직업	[321] profession
		You know how important my career is to me.	
707 request [ri-KWEST]	중등	부탁(하다), 요청(하다)	[1022] demand
		She requested an extra bed in her room.	
708 medical [MED-i-kuhl]	중등	의료의, 의학의	[185] health
		She had a medical problem and needed to see a doctor.	
709 attack [uh-TAK]	중등	1. 공격하다 2. 폭력	[2335] assault
		Some terrorists attacked the neighborhood.	
710 heat [heet]	초등 토익	1. 열 2. 가열하다	[1055] warm
		The evening heat was suffocating.	
711 region [REE-juhn]	중등	지역, 지방	regional (지역적인) [177] area
		This region is famous for its grapes.	
712 prior [PRAHY-er]	수능	이전의, 사전의	priority (우선) prioritize (우선시하다) [119] before
		I have a prior engagement so I cannot be at the meeting.	
713 forward [FAWR-werd]	중등	앞으로	[1280] ahead
		Please take a step forward.	
714 rest [rest]	중등	1. 휴식(하다) 2. 나머지 3. 안정	restless (쉬지 않는) unrest ((특히사회적) 불안) [445] break
		You deserve to rest after working all day.	

715 miss [mis]	초등	1. 놓치다 2. 그리워하다 3. 아가씨 (Ms.) The arrow missed the target	missing (없어진)
716 fine [fahyn]	초등	1. 훌륭한, 괜찮은 2. 벌금 3. 섬세한, 미세한 This wine is very fine.	
717 regular [REG-yuh-ler]	중등 토익	1. 규칙적인, 정기적인 2. 단골 고객 She is a regular customer at our store.	irregular (불규칙적인) [649] normal
718 situation [sich-oo-EY-shuhn]	중등	상황, 사태 I don't know how I got into this situation in the first place.	situate (위치하다) [487] position
719 damage [DAM-ij]	중등	1. 손해, 손상 2. 손해를 끼치다 These delicate china cups damage easily.	[1708] harm
720 subject [SUHB-jikt]	중등	1. 주제, 사안 2. 과목 3. ~되기 쉬운 Please focus, this is an important subject.	[643] matter
721 global [GLOH-buhl]	중등	세계적인 Pollution is a global problem.	globe (지구본) globally (세계적으로) globalization (세계화) [136] worldwide
722 towards [tawrdz]	중등	~쪽으로, ~향하여 The wind is blowing towards your school.	
723 favorite [FEY-ver-it]	초등	1. 가장 좋아하는 2. 우승 후보 Her favorite subject is science.	[1571] favored
724 excellent [EK-suh-luhnt]	중등 토익	우수한, 훌륭한 The little girl gave an excellent speech.	excel (뛰어나다) excellence (우수함)
725 fan [fan]	초등	1. 팬 2. 부채, 선풍기 I am your biggest fan!	[2131] enthusiast
726 soon [soon]	중등	곧, 조만간 The doctor will be here soon.	[443] shortly
727 average [AV-er-ij]	중등	평균의, 보통의 I am of average height.	[2503] ordinary
728 speed [speed]	초등	속도, 빠르기 Driving at excessive speeds causes accidents.	speedy (신속한)

729 **define** [dih-FAHYN]	중등	(의미를) 정의하다, 규정하다	definition (정의) redefine (재정의하다) [652] determine
		What defines a good wine?	
730 **west** [west]	초등	서쪽	western (서양의) westerner (서양인)
		We moved west of Seoul.	
731 **physical** [FIZ-i-kuhl]	중등 토익	신체의	physics (물리학) [335] bodily
		She was physically wounded.	
732 **legal** [LEE-guhl]	중등	1. 합법적인 2. 법적인, 법률과 관련된	illegal (불법적인) [338] lawful
		Don't worry, my plan is all legal.	
733 **chance** [chans]	초등	1. 기회, 가능성 2. 우연	[465] opportunity
		Thank you for the chance to work for your company.	
734 **dog** [dawg]	초등	개	[5107] hound
		Dogs are man's best friend.	
735 **popular** [POP-yuh-ler]	중등 토익	인기 있는, 유행의	popularity (인기) [333] public
		Allen is good looking and popular.	
736 **traditional** [truh-DISH-uh-nl]	중등 토익	전통적인	tradition (전통) [1578] conventional
		Traditional Korean food is very healthy.	
737 **weight** [weyt]	중등	1. 무게 2. 체중 3. 비중, 가중치 4. (헬스) 역기, 무거운 것	weighted (무게를 더한) outweigh (~보다 크다) weigh (무게가 나가다, 무게를 재다)
		The chair broke because of her weight.	
738 **contract** [KON-trackt]	중등 토익	1. 계약 2. 계약서 3. 수축하다 4. (병에) 걸리다	contractor (계약인) contraction (수축) [427] agreement
		Your contract ends in November.	
739 **behind** [bih-HAHYND]	초등	뒤에	[105] back
		His cat was watching him from behind.	
740 **prevent** [pri-VENT]	중등	방지하다, 예방하다	prevention (방지) [439] stop
		We must prevent the cancer from spreading	
741 **exactly** [ig-ZAKT-lee]	중등 GRE	1. 정확히 2. 바로 그렇습니다	exact (정확한) exacting (엄한) [1767] precisely
		You are exactly right.	
742 **score** [skawr]	초등	1. 점수 2. 득점하다 3. 채점하다 4. 20개	[837] mark
		My score is higher than yours.	

743	중등	노력, 수고	
effort			
[EF-ert]		Putting in effort is the key to success.	

744	초등	여자	[307] woman
girl			
[gurl]		The girl was walking to school.	

745	중등	1. ~만큼의 값어치가 있는, ~할 만한 2. 값어치, 가치	worthy (가치 있는) worthless (가치 없는)
worth			[253] value
[wurth]		The good food was worth the long wait.	

746	초등	경찰	policing (감시 활동)
police			[3214] cops
[puh-LEES]		The police kept the town safe.	

747	중등	정치적인	politics (정치) politician (정치인)
political			[580] policy
[puh-LIT-i-kuhl]		There are many political issues on the news.	

748	중등	이루다, 성취하다	achievement (성취) achievable (성취 가능한)
achieve			[596] reach
[uh-CHEEV]		She achieved her dream of getting into Harvard.	

749	초등	1. 피부 2. 가죽 3. 껍질을 벗기다	[3014] peel
skin			
[skin]		His skin was red and itchy.	

750	중등	1. ~할까요 2. ~할 것이다	[194] must
shall			
[shal]		Shall we meet tomorrow?	

751	중등	1. 차량, 탈것 2. ~의 전달 수단	[1775] automobile
vehicle			
[VEE-i-kuhl]		She climbed onto the vehicle and sat on the driver's seat.	

752	초등	준비가 된	readily (손쉽게)
ready			[573] prepared
[RED-ee]		Are you ready to leave?	

753	중등 토익	~를 제외하고	exception (예외) exceptional (특별한)
except			
[ik-SEPT]		I like all fruit except bananas.	

754	중등	독특한, 유일무이한	
unique			
[yoo-NEEK]		He has a unique personality.	

755		1. 인터넷 2. 거미줄	
web			
[web]		I spend a lot of time on the Web.	

756	중등 토익	응답, 대답	respond (반응하다)
response			
[ri-SPONS]		The survey received many responses.	

757	중등 토익	1. 타다 2. 타고 가는 것, 태우고 가는 것 3. 태워주기	override (직권을 이용해 기존 규율을 무시하다)
ride [rahyd]		Can I ride your car?	
758	수능	1. 처형하다 2. 실행하다, 수행하다	execution (실행, 사형)
execute [EK-si-kyoot]		She was sentenced to be executed in three days.	
759		여름	
summer [SUHM-er]		Summer in Korea is very hot.	
760	초등 토익	1. 종이 2. 논문	paperwork (문서 작업) [2179] newspaper
paper [PEY-per]		Wasting paper kills trees.	
761	초등 토익	1. 소개하다 2. 도입하다	introduction (소개) [313] present
introduce [in-truh-DOOS]		I would like to introduce my friend to you.	
762	중등	다양한, 여러 가지의	variety (다양성) [1535] diverse
various [VAIR-ee-uhs]		There are various types of flowers.	
763	중등	1. 다수의, 다양한 2. 배수	multiply (곱하다) multiplication (곱셈) [422] several
multiple [MUHL-tuh-puhl]		There are multiple flavors you can choose from.	
764	초등 토익	1. 멋있는 2. 시원한	[1163] cold
cool [kool]		He is a very cool guy.	
765	초등	1. 동아리, 동호회 2. 클럽 3. 곤봉	[915] stick
club [kluhb]		I am in the school basketball club.	
766	초등 토익	1. 땅, 지면 2. 근거, 이유(로 하다)	foreground (전경) groundless (근거없는) underground (지하) [690] land
ground [ground]		The ground is wet because of the rain.	
767	중등 토익	수정하다, 교정하다	editor (편집자) editorial (사설) [1388] modify
edit [ED-it]		Can you edit my work for me?	
768	중등	목적, 목표, 의도	purposely (일부러) [1679] objective
purpose [PUR-puhs]		What is the purpose of school?	
769	초등 토익	고치다, 해결하다	[1377] repair
fix [fiks]		My computer needs to be fixed.	
770	중등	보험	insure (보장하다) [1808] assurance
insurance [in-SHOOR-uhns]		The Korean national health insurance system is excellent.	

771	토익 편입	1. 권위, 권한 2. 정부 당국	authorize (인가하다) authoritative (권위적인) [201] power
authority [uh-THAWR-i-tee]		He is a respected person with a lot of authority.	
772	토익 편입	지식	knowledgeable (많이 아는) [317] understanding
knowledge [NOL-ij]		Remember to use your knowledge for good and not for evil.	
773	중등	1. 성, 성별 2. 섹스, 성행위	sexy (섹시한) sexism (성차별) [5225] intercourse
sex [seks]		She didn't want to know the sex of the baby.	
774	중등 토익	1. 홍보하다 2. 촉진하다	promotion (승진, 홍보) promotional (홍보의) promo (=promotion) [929] encourage
promote [pruh-MOHT]		I am promoting my product online and offline.	
775	수능	1. 구성하다 2. 작곡하다 3. 침착하게 하다	component (구성품) composer (작곡가) composure (침착함) composition (구성, 작품)
compose [kuhm-POHZ]		Coffee is composed of sugar and milk.	
776	수능	절차	proceed (계속 진행하다, 수익) [198] process
procedure [pruh-SEE-jer]		Divorce is a complicated process.	
777	초등 토익	1. 그리다 2. 페인트(칠하다)	painting (그림) painter (화가) [670] draw
paint [peynt]		Can you paint these flowers for me?	
778	중등	1. 설립하다 2. 확립하다, 확고히 하다	
establish [ih-STAB-lish]		She established a charity for educating children in poverty.	
779	초등 토익	청바지	[2666] pants
jeans [jeenz]		Those jeans have become too tight and I can't wear them anymore.	
780	초등	1. 종, 종소리 2. 벨, 초인종 소리	
bell [bel]		A cracked bell can never sound clear.	
781	초등	1. 암소, 젖소 2. 암컷	
cow [kou]		The cow is considered a sacred animal in India.	
782	초등 토익	축하	congratulate (축하하다)
congratulations [kuhn-grach-uh-LEY-shuhns]		I send you my warmest congratulations on your success.	
783	초등 토익	1. 우리, 새장 2. 새장(우리)에 넣다(가두다)	[2619] jail
cage [keyj]		There is a beautiful bird in the cage.	
784	초등	연필	
pencil [PEN-suhl]		I will get you a pencil and paper.	

785	초등	1. 못생긴, 추한 2. 불쾌한 3. 험악한	[6241] hideous
ugly			
[UHG-lee]		She was frightened by the ugly man.	

786	초등 토익	1. 치과의사 2. 치과	[6396] orthodontist
dentist			
[DEN-tist]		The dentist extracted my wisdom tooth.	

787	초등 토익	동물원	
zoo			
[zoo]		I saw three pandas at the zoo.	

788	초등	1. 열 2. 열병 3. 열풍 4. 흥분	
fever			
[FEE-ver]		The girl's forehead burns with fever.	

789	초등	1. 게으른, 나태한 2. 느긋한	laziness (게으름) [4251] sluggish
lazy			
[LEY-zee]		She got fired because she was lazy.	

790	초등	1. 사촌 2. 친척, 일가	[192] relative
cousin			
[KUHZ-uh n]		I played with my cousins yesterday.	

791	초등	1. 삼촌, 외삼촌, 이모부, 고모부 2. 아저씨	[809] aunt
uncle			
[UHNG-kuh l]		My uncle gave me a birthday present.	

792	초등	토끼	[4368] bunny
rabbit			
[RAB-it]		I saw a rabbit jumping through the fields.	

793	초등	1. 신사, 양반 2. 의원님 3. 귀족 4. 친절한 사람	
gentleman			
[JEN-tl-muhn]		He behaved like a true gentleman.	

794	초등 토익	1. 풍선 2. 열기구 3. 부풀다, 커지다	[2740] swell
balloon			
[buh-LOON]		Can you inflate these balloons for me?	

795	초등	1. 숟가락, 스푼 2. 숟가락을 뜨다	
spoon			
[spoon]		Could you get me a spoon?	

796	초등	1. 수줍은, 부끄러운 2. 내성적인 3. 부족한	[6373] timid
shy			
[shahy]		She is a shy girl.	

797	초등	원숭이	[6102] primate
monkey			
[MUHNG-kee]		Monkeys like bananas.	

798	초등 토익	코끼리	[5584] mammoth
elephant			
[EL-uh-fuh nt]		Elephants have long noses.	

799		1. 나비 2. 접영(수영 동작) 3. 설렘	[4787] flirt
butterfly			
[BUHT-er-flahy]		I saw a butterfly on the wall.	

800	초등	무지개	[2606] spectrum
rainbow			
[REYN-boh]		I saw a beautiful rainbow yesterday.	

801	초등	1. 인형 2. 인형같은 미녀	
doll			
[dol]		She likes to play with her doll.	

802	초등 토익	지우다, 삭제하다	eraser (지우개)
erase			[1740] delete
[ih-REYS]		He erased his hard disk by accident.	

803	초등	포도	[5850] raisin
grape			
[greyp]		Grape juice tastes sweet.	

804	초등	1. 당근, 홍당무 2. 상, 보수	
carrot			
[KAR-uht]		Rabbits like carrots.	

805	초등 토익	1. 안개(로 뒤덮다) 2. 혼란, 당혹 3. 헷갈리게 하다, 당황케 하다	[3900] mist
fog			
[fog]		I can't see anything in this heavy fog.	

806	초등	돌고래	
dolphin			
[DOL-fin]		Dolphins are known to be very smart.	

807	초등	1. 서두르다, 급하게 하다, 빨리하다 2. 재촉하다	[2136] rush
hurry			
[HUR-ee]		You'd better hurry up before the food gets cold.	

808	초등 토익	1. 정오, 낮 12시 2. (한)낮	
noon			
[noon]		Meet me at noon tomorrow.	

809	초등	1. 이모, 고모, (외)숙모 2. 아주머니	
aunt			
[ant]		My aunt and my mother have a close relationship.	

810	초등	1. 일기 2. 수첩	[1806] journal
diary			
[DAHY-uh-ree]		I have kept a diary for 10 years.	

811	초등	개구리	[6549] toad
frog			
[frog]		Frogs eat bugs.	

812	초등	개미	
ant			
[ant]		Ants are small.	

813 **sour** [SOUuhr]	초등	1. 시큼한, 신 2. 짜증난, 화가 난 Lemons are sour.	[3130] bitter
814 **umbrella** [uhm-BREL-uh]	초등 토익	우산 It is raining outside. Please take an umbrella.	
815 **alright** [awl-RAHYT]	초등	알겠어, 괜찮아 It's alright. Anyone can make mistakes.	[외래어] okay
816 **fox** [foks]	초등	여우 Foxes eat rabbits.	foxy (여우 같은, 매력적인)
817 **goodbye** [good-BAHY]	초등 토익	안녕, 작별 인사 Saying goodbye to her best friend made her very sad.	bye (=goodbye) [5200] farewell
818 **handsome** [HAN-suhm]	초등	잘생긴, 훤칠한 Your boyfriend is very handsome.	
819 **thirst** [thurst]	초등 토익	목마름, 갈증 Drinking water resolves thirst.	thirsty (목마른) [1100] desire
820 **supper** [SUHP-er]	초등	저녁 식사 I didn't have supper yet.	[1113] dinner
821 **scissors** [SIZ-erz]	초등	가위 Be careful when using scissors.	[4830] shears
822 **subway** [SUHB-wey]	초등 토익	지하철 Take the subway.	[4631] metro
823 **pear** [pair]	초등	배(과일) This pear tastes so sweet.	
824 **watermelon** [WAW-ter-mel-uhn]	초등	수박 Watermelon is her favorite fruit.	[외래어] melon
825 **clap** [klap]	중등 토익	1. 박수, 손뼉치다 2. (친밀하게)툭 치다 He clapped his hands.	[5073] applaud
826 **frown** [froun]	중등	1. 눈살을 찌푸리다, 얼굴을 찡그리다 2. 탐탁치않아하다 The teacher frowned at the disobedient student.	

827	초등	얼룩말	
zebra			
[ZEE-bruh]		Zebras live in Africa.	

828	초등	기린	
giraffe			
[juh-RAF]		Giraffes have long necks.	

829	중등	꾸짖다, 질책하다	[6362] rebuke
scold			
[skohld]		The child was scolded by his mother.	

830	초등 토익	기억력	memorize (암기하다)
memory			[129] recall
[MEM-uh-ree]		My little sister has great memory.	

831	중등 토익	1. 영향, 효과 2. 영향을 끼치다	[234] effect
impact			
[IM-pakt]		Does the medicine have a clear impact?	

832	중등	1. 알아보다, 인식하다 2. 인정하다	recognition (인식)
recognize			[2025] acknowledge
[REK-uhg-nahyz]		Does your baby recognize you?	

833	중등	1. 감방 2. 세포 3. 휴대폰	[외래어] cellphone
cell			
[sel]		The cells were cold and moldy.	

834	중등	1. ~를 얻다 2. 이익	regain (되찾다)
gain			[1250] obtain
[geyn]		What do you gain from working there?	

835	초등	관광, 투어(하다)	tourist (관광객)
tour			tourism (관광업)
[toor]		I would like to go on a tour around Europe this summer.	[945] trip

836	중등 토익	증가(하다), 상승(하다)	[280] increase
rise			
[rahyz]		The price of water is rising steadily.	

837	중등	표시(하다), 표기(하다)	trademark
mark			(상표,대표상징)
[mahrk]		Can you mark the pages you read?	[702] brand

838	중등	요소, 성분	elementary
element			(초등의, 기초의)
[EL-uh-muh nt]		The element of danger leads many people to try sky diving.	[775] component

839	수능	자치주, 군	[1155] district
county			
[KOUN-tee]		The county has a population of 12,345 people.	

840	초등	1. 창문 2. 컴퓨터 창	[1215] glass
window			
[WIN-doh]		He glanced out the window.	

841 **raise** [reyz]	중등	1. 올리다, 높이다 2. 기르다, 키우다 3. (연봉)인상 4. 불러일으키다 My boss raised my salary by 5%.	[280] increase
842 **construction** [kuhn-STRUHK-shuhn]	중등	건설, 공사 The construction was causing a traffic jam.	constructive (건설적인) deconstruct (해체하다) [854] structure
843 **red** [red]	초등	빨간, 붉은 Roses are red.	redness (붉은 기운) reddish (발그레한) [5511] crimson
844 **load** [lohd]	중등 토익	1. (짐을) 싣다 2. 화물, 짐 She was carrying a heavy load.	overload (과부하) loaded (짐으로 가득찬) unload (짐을 내리다) workload (작업량)
845 **target** [TAHR-git]	중등	1. 과녁, 목표 2. 겨냥하다, 목표로 하다 He focused on the target and threw the ball.	[560] goal
846 **town** [toun]	초등	마을, 도시 The whole town cheered the team.	[261] city
847 **gold** [gohld]	초등	금 Gold is often used to make jewelry.	
848 **avoid** [uh-VOID]	중등	피하다, 회피하다 I am avoiding my ex-girlfriend.	avoidance (회피) [4633] evade
849 **block** [blok]	초등	1. 막다, 차단하다 2. 방해, 차단 3. 사각형 덩어리 4. 도시의 구역, 블록 She blocked me from entering her room.	[3783] obstruct
850 **handle** [HAN-dl]	중등	1. 다루다, 처리하다 2. 감당하다 3. 손잡이 Can you handle the problem?	[167] manage
851 **bar** [bahr]	중등	1. 바, 술집 2. 막대 3. 막다, 금지하다 He bought a hot dog and a coke at the bar.	[849] block
852 **stage** [steyj]	중등	1. 무대 2. 단계 3. 기획하다, 연출하다 We are cleaning the stage for the show tonight.	staged (연출된) [156] point
853 **machine** [muh-SHEEN]	중등 토익	기계 Machines are replacing workers.	[562] device
854 **structure** [STRUHK-cher]	중등	구조 The building has a sturdy structure.	structural (구조적인) restructure (구조 개편) [842] construction

855	중등	1. 개최하다 2. 주인, 숙주 3. 다수, 여럿이 모인 떼	[3974] multitude
host [hohst]		I am hosting a party tonight.	

856	중등	순간, 잠깐	momentarily (일시적으로) momentous (중대한) [398] minute
moment [MOH-muhnt]		For a moment, I was shocked.	

857	중등	발견하다, 찾아내다	discovery (발견)
discover [dih-SKUHV-er]		Who discovered the North Pole?	

858	중등 토익	기관	institute (기관) [778] establishment
institution [in-sti-TOO-shuhn]		She got a job at a financial institution.	

859	초등	1. 초록색(의) 2. 친환경적인	evergreen (상록수) [2155] immature
green [green]		He was wearing a green shirt.	

860	초등	피, 혈액	
blood [bluhd]		We need more blood for the surgery.	

861	수능	동등한, 평등한	equation (공식) inequality (불평등) unequalled (비교대상이 없이 월등한)
equal [EE-kwuhl]		Everyone should be treated in an equal manner.	

862	초등	1. 마시다 2. 음료	drunk (취한)
drink [dringk]		I like drinking water.	

863	중등	아픔, 고통	painful (고통스러운) painkiller (진통제) [1745] hurt
pain [peyn]		She felt a lot of pain from her injury.	

864	중등	영향을 미치다	[1203] influence
affect [uh-FEKT]		The medicine affects my heart rate.	

865	중등	1. 끝부분 2. 조언 3. 기울이다 4. (웨이터에게 주는) 팁	
tip [tip]		The tip of the needle is pointy.	

866	중등 토익	1. 졸업하다 2. 대학교 졸업생	undergraduate (대학 학부) graduation (졸업) postgraduate (대학원)
graduate [GRAJ-oo-it]		I am graduating from university this March.	

867	초등	교회	[2676] temple
church [church]		He goes to church every Sunday.	

868	중등	1. 주식 2. 재고품	[322] store
stock [stok]		You should study economics before trading stock.	

869	중등	1. 추가의, 여분의 2. 특별한	[98] additional
extra [EK-struh]		Can I have some extra fries?	

870	중등 토익	탐험하다	exploration (탐험) [1004] investigate
explore [ik-SPLAWR]		The children ran off to explore the cave.	

871	중등	분석	analyze (분석하다) analyst (분석가) analytical (분석적인) analytics (분석학)
analysis [uh-NAL-uh-sis]		He produced a detailed analysis of the competition.	

872	중등 토익	나타내다	indicator (지표) indication (암시) indicative (암시하는) [121] show
indicate [IN-di-keyt]		The signs indicate our team will win.	

873	공무원	디지털형의	digit (숫자)
digital [DIJ-i-tl]		I use a digital clock.	

874	중등 토익	일어나다, 발생하다	reoccur (다시 발생하다)
occur [uh-KUR]		The accident occurred in Busan.	

875	중등	손실, 상실	[435] losing
loss [laws]		The company experienced a huge loss.	

876	중등	언급하다, 말하다	[191] tell
mention [MEN-shuhn]		He mentioned that you got a promotion.	

877	초등	의사	[1903] physician
doctor [DOK-ter]		You should go and see a doctor about that injury.	

878	중등	1. 본문, 원문 2. 문자	subtext (글자 외의 숨은 의미) [380] wording
text [tekst]		It took me two hours to read the long text.	

879	중등	적당한, 올바른	properly (올바르게) improper (부적절한) [112] right
proper [PROP-er]		Everything is in its proper place.	

880	중등	언어	[1813] speech
language [LANG-gwij]		Language is the most important tool.	

881	중등 토익	1. 지시, 설명 2. 방법	instructor (강사) instruct (지시하다) [1094] direction
instruction [in-STRUHK-shuhn]		I need instructions to bake a brownie.	

882	중등	1. 믿다 2. 신뢰, 신임	trustworthy (신뢰할만한) [1380] faith
trust [truhst]		Do you trust me?	

| 883 slow [sloh] | 초등 | 느린, 더딘 | slowly (느리게) [4251] sluggish |
| | | A snail is slow. | |

| 884 fee [fee] | 중등 | 요금, 금액 | [160] payment |
| | | They charged him a fee for driving too fast. | |

| 885 certificate [ser-TIF-i-kit] | 중등 토익 | 증명서 | certified (공인된) |
| | | Here is my birth certificate. | |

| 886 fair [fair] | 중등 | 공정한, 공평한 | fairly (공평하게, 꽤) |
| | | Fair treatment of all employees is essential. | |

| 887 amazing [uh-MEY-zing] | 중등 | 놀라운 | amaze (놀래다) [4014] astonishing |
| | | New York is an amazing city. | |

| 888 prefer [pri-FUR] | 중등 | 선호하다 | preference (선호) preferable (선호되는) [387] choose |
| | | I prefer chocolate icecream to vanilla icecream. | |

| 889 equipment [ih-KWIP-muhnt] | 중등 토익 | 장비, 설비 | [1406] gear |
| | | The sports team needed more equipment. | |

| 890 earn [urn] | 중등 | 벌다, 얻다, 받다 | earnings (이익, 수입) [834] gain |
| | | I earn $60,000 dollars a year. | |

| 891 hair [hair] | 초등 | 1. 머리카락 2. 털 | hairy (털이 많은) hairdo (헤어스타일) |
| | | There are many ways to prevent hair loss. | |

| 892 separate [SEP-uh-reyt] | 중등 토익 | 1. 분리하다 2. 서로 다른, 개별의 3. 헤어지다 | separation (분리) inseparable (분리할 수 없는) [1800] split |
| | | The teacher tried to separate the fighting students. | |

| 893 extremely [ik-STREEM-lee] | 중등 | 1. 극도로 2. 엄청나게 | extreme (극심한) [1983] exceedingly |
| | | Siberia is known for its extremely cold winters. | |

| 894 via [VAHY-uh] | 중등 | 1. ~ 통해 2. 경유하여, 거쳐 | [88] through |
| | | I turned in my exam via e-mail. | |

| 895 engage [en-GEYJ] | 중등 토익 | 1. 관여하다 2. 사로잡다, 끌다 3. 관계를 맺다 4. 고용하다 | engagement (약혼) [1366] hire |
| | | There is no right or wrong way to engage in political action. | |

| 896 serious [SEER-ee-uhs] | 중등 | 1. 심각한 2. 진지한 | seriously (심각하게) [2092] grave |
| | | Serious issues need to be discussed. | |

897	중등	균형(을 이루다)	imbalance (불균형)
balance [BAL-uhns]		Work-life balance is very important.	

898	중등	1. 중요한 2. 비판적인	critic (비평가) criticism (비난) criticize (비판하다) [2359] crucial
critical [KRIT-i-kuhl]		Clean air is critical to our lives.	

899	중등 토익	1. 발표하다 2. 알리다	announcement (발표) [1714] declare
announce [uh-NOUNS]		The government announced its plan for next year.	

900	초등	1. 건조한, 마른 2. 무미건조한 3. 말리다	[1109] boring
dry [drahy]		Las Vegas is very dry and hot.	

901	중등	1. 기여하다, 공헌하다 2. 기부, 기증하다 3. ~의 원인이 되다	contribution (기여) [91] give
contribute [kuhn-TRIB-yoot]		The CEO contributed to the success of the company.	

902	중등	1. 필수적인 2. 중요한 3. 근본적인, 본질적인	essence (본질) [1927] vital
essential [uh-SEN-shuhl]		Clean water is essential to life.	

903		1. 왼쪽, 좌측 2. 남은 3. 좌파	
left [left]		You need to make a left turn at the intersection.	

904	중등	흥미진진한, 신나는, 흥미로운	excite (신나게하다) excited (신난) [2338] thrilling
exciting [ik-SAHY-ting]		It is exciting to see how things have changed in recent years.	

905	초등	1. 벽 2. 담	wallpaper (벽지) [2584] fence
wall [wawl]		I am going to paint my walls yellow.	

906	초등	1. 틀린, 잘못된 2. 나쁜 행동, 부정	wrongdoing (잘못된 행위) [1513] mistaken
wrong [rawng]		You spelled the word wrong.	

907	초등	동물, 짐승	[2799] beast
animal [AN-uh-muhl]		I am against animal testing.	

908	수능 토익	전문가	expertise (전문 지식) [932] master
expert [EK-spurt]		Many experts are here to share their knowledge.	

909	초등	1. 원하다, 바라다 2. 소원, 바람, 기원	[83] want
wish [wish]		We wish you the best of luck.	

910	중등 토익	1. 추구하다 2. 찾다 3. 청하다	sought (추구되는)
seek [seek]		I always seek for a better life.	

911 east [eest]	초등	1. 동쪽 2. 동방	eastern (동쪽의, 동양의)
		The sun rises in the east.	
912 pull [pool]	중등	1. 당기다 2. 끌다 3. 뽑다	[670] draw
		Try pulling the door if pushing doesn't work.	
913 schedule [SKEJ-ool]	토익	스케줄, 일정(을 잡다)	[184] plan
		I need to check my schedule first.	
914 king [king]	초등	(국)왕	kingdom (왕국) [1082] champion
		The lion is the king of the jungle.	
915 stick [stik]	중등 토익	1. (나무)막대기 2. 찌르다 3. 붙이다 4. 꽂아넣다 5. 끼이다, 갇히다	sticker (스티커) sticky (끈적거리는) stuck (~에 빠져 꼼짝 못하는)
		My dog likes to chew on sticks.	
916 former [FAWR-mer]	중등	1. 이전의, 과거의 2. 전, 전임의 3. 전자의	[674] previous
		She still misses her former husband.	
917 hi [hahy]	초등	인삿말, 안녕	hey (이봐, 안녕) hello (안녕)
		Hi, what have you been up to?	
918 immediately [ih-MEE-dee-it-lee]	중등	1. 즉시, 곧 2. 바로 옆에 3. 직접적으로	immediate (즉각적,직접의) [1752] instantly
		We need to act immediately before it's too late.	
919 stuff [stuhf]	중등	1. 물건 2. (할)일 3. 채우다, (쑤셔) 넣다	[107] things
		I have a closet full of useless stuff.	
920 division [dih-VIZH-uhn]	초등	1. 분배 2. 분열, 분단 3. 분과 4. 나눗셈	divide (나누다) divisive (분열을 조장하는) [1800] split
		The division of labor improves productivity.	
921 regulation [reg-yuh-LEY-shuhn]	수능	1. 규제 2. 규정 3. 법규	regulatory (규제의) regulate (규제하다) [516] rule
		The government is planning to ease regulations.	
922 transfer [trans-FUR]	중등	1. 옮기다, 이송/이전하다 2. 전학을 가다 3. 넘겨주다 4. 환승하다	[175] move
		The doctor transferred his patient to his wife's hospital.	
923 spirit [SPIR-it]	중등	1. 정신, 영혼 2. 기분	spiritual (정신적인) dispirited (낙심한) [1643] soul
		She is sturdy in spirit.	
924 movie [MOO-vee]	초등	영화	[629] film
		What is your favorite movie?	

925 object [OB-jikt]	중등	1. 물체, 물건 2. 목적 3. 대상 4. 반대하다	objection (반대) [768] purpose
		Draw an object near you.	
926 hot [hot]	초등	1. 더운, 뜨거운 2. 매운 3. 치열한, 열띤 4. 인기있는	[773] sexy
		August in Seoul is very hot.	
927 round [round]	중등	1. 둥근, 원형의 2. 어림수의, 대략의 3. ~을 돌아 4. 한 차례, 회	year-round (연중 내내) well-rounded (균형이 잘 잡힌) [278] turn
		The earth is round.	
928 son [suhn]	초등	아들	[170] child
		She has two sons.	
929 encourage [en-KUR-ij]	중등	1. 격려하다, 고무하다 2. 권장하다 3. 조장하다	courage (용기) courageous (용감한) [774] promote
		I encouraged him to become a singer.	
930 factor [FAK-ter]	중등	1. 요인, 요소 2. (수학) 약수 3. 감안하다	[838] element
		What are the factors that drive economic growth?	
931 copy [KOP-ee]	초등 토익	1. 사본 2. 한 부 3. 복사하다 4. 모방하다, 베끼다	[3016] duplicate
		He needs a copy of that document.	
932 master [MAS-ter]	중등	1. 주인 2. 대가, 달인 3. 익히다, 숙달하다	masterful (솜씨가 좋은) [1291] chief
		I am the master of my fate.	
933 definitely [DEF-uh-nit-lee]	중등 토익	확실히, 분명히, 틀림없이	definitive (결정적인) indefinite (무기한의) indefinitely (무기한으로) [385] certainly
		He is definitely wrong about that.	
934 blue [bloo]	초등	1. 파란, 푸른 2. 우울한	[5443] gloomy
		Blue jeans are very trendy.	
935 manufacturer [man-yuh-FAK-cher-er]	중등	1. 제조자, 제조업체 2. 생산업체	manufacture (제조하다) manufacturing (제조업)
		America is one of the largest manufacturers in the world.	
936 vote [voht]	중등	1. 표, 표결 2. 투표권 3. 투표하다	
		A single vote can change the outcome.	
937 mile [mahyl]	토익	마일(약 1.6km)	[외래어] kilometer
		The destination is just a few miles away.	
938 modern [MOD-ern]	중등	1. 현대의, 근대의 2. 최신의	modernize (현대화하다) [2111] contemporary
		Modern technology has made our lives so much easier.	

939	중등	1. 큰, 거대한 2. 막대한, 엄청난	[2777] enormous
huge			
[hyooj]		He made a huge mistake.	

940	중등	1. 점, 반점, 얼룩 2. 장소, 자리 3. 발견하다, 찾다	[128] place
spot			
[spot]		There's a bald spot in my hair.	

941	초등	1. 어두운, 짙은 2. 암흑(의) 3. 음흉한	[5443] gloomy
dark			
[dahrk]		We need to return home before it gets too dark.	

942	중등	1. 더하기 2. 뿐만 아니라, 또한 3. 영상의(기온)	[1876] besides
plus			
[pluhs]		It is 30 dollars plus tax.	

943	초등	1. 편지 2. 글자, 문자	newsletter (소식지)
letter			[299] note
[LET-er]		He wrote her a love letter.	

944	초등	1. 단추, 버튼 2. 단추를 잠그다	[1032] switch
button			
[BUHT-n]		A button came off my shirt.	

945	초등	1. 여행, 수학여행 2. 발을 헛디디다	[1484] journey
trip			
[trip]		They went on a trip to Paris.	

946	중등	등, 기타 등등	
etc			
[et SET-er-uh]		I am planning on buying some apples, bananas, etc.	

947	중등 토익	1. 관습, 풍습 2. 습관 3. 맞춤의	customized (맞춤제작된)
custom			[492] practice
[KUHS-tuhm]		Each culture has its customs and traditions.	

948	중등	1. 휴대폰 2. 이동식의	mobility (이동성)
mobile			immobilize
[MOH-buhl]		What is your mobile number?	(이동하지 못하게 고정하다)
			mobilize (동원하다)

949	중등	1. 모양, 형태 2. 형성하다	[220] form
shape			
[sheyp]		What is the shape of the earth?	

950	초등	1. 도착하다 2. 도래하다, 찾아오다	arrival (도착)
arrive			
[uh-RAHYV]		We arrived on time.	

951	초등	1. 지도, 약도 2. 보여주다 3. (지도를) 그리다	[1273] chart
map			
[map]		I am quite bad at reading maps.	

952	초등	어미, 어머니	motherhood
mother			(어머니인 상황)
[MUHTH-er]		I am a mother of 2 children.	mom (엄마)
			mama (엄마)

953	중등	약(물), 마약	[1402] medicine
drug [druhg]		Drug abuse has become a serious issue recently.	

954	중등	1. 면허(증), 자격증 2. 허가하다	[1061] permit
license [LAHY-suhns]		My driver's license is about to expire.	

955	초등 토익	태양, 해	sunny (화창한) sunlight (햇빛) sunshine (햇빛) sunrise (일출)
sun [suhn]		The sun is a great source of energy.	

956	중등 토익	1. 증거 2. 흔적 3. 근거	[1883] proof
evidence [EV-i-duhns]		DNA evidence plays an important role in solving crimes.	

957	초등	아침, 오전	[3932] dawn
morning [MAWR-ning]		What could be the best morning routine?	

958	초등	나무, 수목	treetop (나무 꼭대기) [1179] wood
tree [tree]		We decorated the Christmas tree with shiny balls.	

959	중등	1. 놀라운/뜻밖의 소식 2. 놀라게하다 3. 기습하다	surprised (놀란) [1728] shock
surprise [ser-PRAHYZ]		It was a surprise to see my old friend.	

960	중등	질병, 질환	diseased (병든) [2113] illness
disease [dih-ZEEZ]		Smoking can cause many diseases.	

961	중등	1. 코치, 지도자 2. 지도하다 3. 대형버스 4. 이등석	[311] train
coach [kohch]		The team's coach is very scary.	

962	중등	1. 주장 2. 논쟁, 말다툼	argue (주장하다) [4678] quarrel
argument [AHR-gyuh-muhnt]		They were arguing for the sake of argument.	

963	수능	개념	conceive (생각하다) conceptual (개념의) misconception (오해) [262] idea
concept [KON-sept]		Understanding concepts could be the hardest part.	

964	중등 토익	1. 영감을 주다 2. 고무하다, 격려하다 3. 고취하다	inspiration (영감) [2297] stimulate
inspire [in-SPAHYUHR]		He inspired her to become an engineer.	

965	초등	1. 잡다, 붙잡다 2. 목격하다, 발견하다 3. (병에, 뾰족한 곳에)걸리다	caught (잡힌) [1757] grab
catch [kach]		I'm going to catch some fish.	

966	초등	1. 만지다 2. 닿다, 접촉하다 3. 마음을 움직이다, 감동시키다 4. 촉각, 촉감, 감촉	untouched (손대지 않은) touching (마음을 움직이는)
touch [tuhch]		Don't touch my hair.	

967 crime [krahym]	중등	범죄, 범행, 죄악	criminal (범인, 범죄의) [1584] offense
		She committed a crime.	
968 primary [PRAHY-mer-ee]	중등	1. 주된 2. 기본적인 3. 초기의 4. 1차의	primarily (주로) [541] main
		Heart disease is one of the primary causes of death.	
969 submit [suhb-MIT]	수능 토익	1. 제출하다 2. 항복하다 3. 복종시키다	submission (복종, 제출) [313] present
		You should submit your college application before the deadline.	
970 baby [BEY-bee]	초등	1. 아기, 새끼 2. 연인을 부르는 애칭	[170] child
		Babies are cute and adorable.	
971 grade [greyd]	중등	1. 품질, 등급 2. 학점, 성적 3. 학년	[353] class
		Grade A eggs are expensive.	
972 typical [TIP-i-kuhl]	중등	전형적인	atypical (이례적인) typically (전형적으로) [649] normal
		Jack was a typical father.	
973 academic [ak-uh-DEM-ik]	초등	학업의, 학문의, 학구적인	academy (학원) [1485] scholarly
		What are the factors that influence the academic performance of students?	
974 scene [seen]	중등 토익	1. 장면, 현장 2. 장(場) 3. 풍경	scenery (경치) scenic (경치가 좋은) [852] stage
		The suspect was caught at the scene.	
975 floor [flawr]	초등	1. 바닥 2. 층 3. 현장, 작업장 4. 청중, 참가자	[766] ground
		Wooden floors make creaky noises.	
976 island [AHY-luhnd]	중등	섬	[3548] isle
		Not all islands are surrounded by the ocean.	
977 express [ik-SPRES]	중등	1. 나타내다, 표현하다 2. 급행의, 신속한, 속달의 3. 급행열차	expression (표현) [1156] voice
		I expressed my feelings for him.	
978 overall [OH-ver-awl]	중등	1. 종합적으로, 전반적으로 2. 작업복	[329] general
		What is the company's overall mission?	
979 appropriate [uh-PROH-pree-it]	중등 토익	1. 적절한, 적합한 2. 도용하다, 차용하다 3. 책정하다	inappropriate (부적합한) appropriation (돈의 책정) [879] proper
		Jeans are not appropriate for an interview.	
980 father [FAH-ther]	초등	1. 아버지, 부친, 아비 2. 조상, 창시자 3. 신부	dad (아빠)
		My father set a curfew.	

981 roll [rohl]	중등	1. 구르다, 굴러가다 2. 말다 3. 통, 두루마리 4. 명부, 명단 He rolled out of bed just before noon.	
982 attempt [uh-TEMPT]	중등	시도(하다), 도전(하다) Even though you failed, it was a good attempt.	[910] seek
983 fish [fish]	초등	1. 물고기, 어류, 생선 2. 낚시하다 3. (손으로 더듬어) 찾다 We prefer meat to fish.	fishing (낚시)
984 gift [gift]	초등	1. 선물(하다) 2. 재능, 재주 He gave her a necklace as a gift.	gifted (탁월한 재능이 있는) [313] present
985 adjust [uh-JUHST]	중등	1. 조정하다, 조절하다, 맞추다 2. 적응하다 I don't know how to adjust that thermostat.	[1415] adapt
986 fly [flahy]	초등 토익	1. 날다, 비행하다 2. 빠르게 가다 3. 파리 4. 바지 지퍼 I am flying to New York tomorrow.	[3148] flee
987 perhaps [per-HAPS]	중등	아마(도), 어쩌면 Perhaps she was right.	[689] maybe
988 suit [soot]	중등	1. 정장, 의복 2. 소송 3. 알맞다, 어울리다 She bought a new suit for that important interview.	suitable (알맞은) [2983] lawsuit
989 song [sawng]	초등	노래, 곡 What is your favorite song?	[1680] tune
990 sleep [sleep]	중등 토익	1. 잠, 수면 2. 자다, 숙면하다 I need at least eight hours of sleep.	sleepy (졸린) sleepless (불면의)
991 advantage [ad-VAN-tij]	중등	1. 이점, 장점 2. 유리한 점 3. 혜택 What are the advantages of globalization?	disadvantage (불리한) advantageous (유리한) [428] benefit
992 fortune [FAWR-chuhn]	중등 토익	1. 운, 행운 2. 재산, 거금 She has good fortune on her side.	fortunately (다행히) unfortunately (불행히도) [1131] luck
993 judge [juhj]	중등	1. 판단하다 2. 심판, 심사위원 3. 판사 4. 재판하다, 판결하다 Don't judge people by their looks.	judgment (판단) judgmental (재판의) [282] consider
994 tend [tend]	중등	1.~하는 경향이 있다 2. 돌보다, 보살피다 I tend to overuse certain words.	tendency (경향) [2304] lean

995 expand [ik-SPAND]	중등	확대하다, 확장하다, 늘어나다, 팽창시키다 He is trying to expand his business.	expansion (확장) expansive (팽창력 있는) [608] extend
996 ought [awt]	고등	1. ~해야 하다 2. 틀림없이 ~일 것이다 3. ~할 필요가 있다 You ought to get your phone repaired.	
997 surface [SUR-fis]	중등	1. 표면, 외관 2. 나타나다, 드러나다, 일어나다 I hate seeing the images of the surface of the moon.	resurface (다시 나타나다) [404] face
998 rely [ri-LAHY]	중등 토익	1. 의지하다, 의존하다 2. 신뢰하다 Work hard, and don't rely on luck.	reliable (신뢰할 만한) reliance (의존) [882] trust
999 bottom [BOT-uhm]	초등	1. 밑바닥, 최하위 2. 하부, 아래쪽 I've hit rock bottom.	[250] base
1000 launch [lawnch]	중등	1. 시작하다, 착수하다 2. 출시(하다), 출범하다 3. 발사(하다) The organization launched a new initiative.	[106] start

#1001~#2000

미국 초등학교 1~2학년 수준의 어휘력이다.
일상 속 단순한 영어 표현들을 이해하기 때문에 최소한의 의사소통은 가능하며 간단한 문장
들도 이해되기 시작한다. 레벨2도 기초 중의 기초이니, 스스로 놓치고 있던 어휘는 없는지
체크하고 감으로 대충 해석해오던 어휘들의 정확한 뜻을 학습하자.

LEVEL **02**

1001	초등	1. 팔 2. 줄기, 갈래 3. 무장하다 4. 무기, 병기	[1467] weapon
arm [ahrm]		His arms are too thin.	

1002	초등	1. 무거운 2. 많은, 빡빡한 3. 심각한	heavily (무겁게) [308] hard
heavy [HEV-ee]		My arms are heavy with shopping bags.	

1003	중등	1. 시설, 설비 2. 기능 3. 재능	facile (쉬운) [111] ability
facility [fuh-SIL-i-tee]		Our apartment has excellent sports facilities.	

1004	중등	수사, 조사, 연구	investigate (수사하다) [2390] inquiry
investigation [in-ves-ti-GEY-shuhn]		The cause of the recent fire is still under investigation.	

1005	중등	비상(사태), 응급	
emergency [ih-MUR-juhn-see]		The government issues an emergency alert in case of heavy rain.	

1006		1. 캠페인, (사회/정치적) 운동 2. 캠페인을 하다 3. 군사 작전	[697] fight
campaign [kam-PEYN]		The national air pollution campaign was launched last year.	

1007		1. 강점, 장점 2. 힘, 내구력, 견고성 3. 용기 4. 세력, 영향력	strengthen (강화하다) [201] power
strength [strengkth]		What could be your strength?	

1008	중등 토익	1. 행동(하다), 수행(하다) 2. 지휘하다 3. (열, 전기를)전도하다	misconduct (잘못된 행동) conductor (지휘자)
conduct [KON-duhkt]		The study was conducted by a group of experts.	

1009	중등 토익	1. 대안 2. 대체의, 대체 가능한	alternate (번갈아가며 하다/하는) [2386] substitute
alternative [awl-TUR-nuh-tiv]		When the plan fails, we need an alternative solution.	

1010	초등	1. 바위, 암석, 돌멩이 2. 록(음악) 3. 보석 4. 흔들리다, 흔든다	rocky (바위가 많은) [1434] stone
rock [rok]		My cat likes to collect rocks.	

1011	중등 토익	1. 상업적인, 영리적인 2. 광고	commerce (상업) [667] trade
commercial [kuh-MUR-shuhl]		Commercial use of my blog posts is not allowed.	

1012	중등	1. 명령(하다), 지휘(하다), 통솔(하다) 2. 능력, (언어)구사력	commander (지휘관) [290] order
command [kuh-MAND]		We are under his command.	

1013	초등	1. 밀다 2. 누르다 3. 강요하다	pushy (강요하며 밀어붙이는) [442] press
push [poosh]		He pushed the door open.	

1014	중등	1. 자리, 좌석, 의석 2. 앉다	[128] place
seat [seet]		Is this seat taken?	

1015 **electric** [ih-LEK-trik]	중등 토익	전기의, 전자의	electricity (전기) electrify (감전시키다,흥분시키다)
		Electric cars are environmentally friendly.	
1016 **hospital** [HOS-pi-tl]	초등	병원	[1154] clinic
		Hospitals are filled with patients during times of epidemics.	
1017 **frequently** [FREE-kwuhnt-lee]	중등	자주, 종종, 흔히	frequent (잦은) frequency (주파수) [340] often
		We frequently go out for dinner.	
1018 **marriage** [MAR-ij]	초등	결혼, 결혼생활, 결혼식	marry (결혼하다) [1336] wedding
		Their marriage didn't work out.	
1019 **realize** [REE-uh-lahyz]	중등	1. 깨닫다, 자각하다 2. 실현하다, 달성하다 3. 현금화하다	realization (깨달음) [317] understand
		She didn't realize how much she loved him.	
1020 **positive** [POZ-i-tiv]	중등	1. 긍정적인 2. 확신하는, 확실한 3. 양성반응	positivity (긍정) [1110] confident
		I'm positive that you will pass the exam.	
1021 **aware** [uh-WAIR]	중등	1. 알고 있는, 인식하는 2. 의식이 높은, 관심이 많은	awareness (인식)
		I am aware of the consequences of failure.	
1022 **demand** [dih-MAND]	중등	1. 수요 2. 요구(사항) 3. 요구하다, 요청하다	on-demand (수요가 있을때 바로) [707] request
		The demand for clean energy keeps on increasing.	
1023 **federal** [FED-er-uhl]	수능	연방 정부의	federation (연방 정부) [154] national
		He is a federal officer.	
1024 **author** [AW-ther]	중등	1. 작가, 저자 2. (책을)쓰다	[168] writer
		Who is the author of this awesome novel?	
1025 **spring** [spring]		1. 봄 2. 용수철 3. 일어나다, 뛰어오르다, 튀다 4. 샘, 샘물	[3114] leap
		Spring usually starts in March.	
1026 **assess** [uh-SES]	중등	평가하다, 감정하다, 측정하다	assessment (평가) [1283] evaluate
		The boss will assess the program's performance.	
1027 **election** [ih-LEK-shuhn]	중등	1. 선거 2. 당선	elect (선출하다, 당선자) [666] choice
		The next presidential election will be held pretty soon.	
1028 **wire** [wahyuhr]	중등 토익	1. 선, 전선 2. 철사 3. 연결하다 4. 송금하다 5. 배선하다	wireless (무선의) wired (유선의) hardwired (내장된, 타고난)
		Can you connect this wire to the television?	

1029	수능	1. 전환하다, 바꾸다 2. 개종하다, 전향하다 3. 개종자, 전향자	conversion (전환)
convert			convertible
[kuhn-VURT]		The heat energy can be converted to electricity.	(전환 가능한)
			[123] change

1030	중등	1. 던지다 2. 내던지다, 버리다 3. 던지기, 투구	[2890] toss
throw			
[throh]		It isn't easy to throw a baseball correctly.	

1031	중등 토익	매년(의), 연간(의), 연례의	biannual (연 2회의)
annual			
[AN-yoo-uhl]		The company is holding its annual party at a nice hotel this year.	

1032	중등	1. 스위치 2. 전환(하다), 바꾸다	[123] change
switch			
[swich]		I flipped the switch to turn on the light.	

1033	중등	1. 먹이다, 먹여 살리다 2. 주다, 공급하다 3. 먹이, 밥	[332] food
feed			
[feed]		You need to feed your dog twice a day.	

1034	초등	듣다, 경청하다	[379] hear
listen			
[LIS-uhn]		We need to listen to people in need of help.	

1035	초등 토익	1. 조언하다, 권고하다 2. 알리다	advisor (고문)
advise			advice (조언)
[ad-VAHYZ]		She advised him not to study abroad.	[120] inform

1036	중등	1. 회사, 기업 2. 딱딱한, 단단한 3. 확고한, 단호한	[308] hard
firm			
[furm]		Large firms and small enterprises should cooperate.	

1037	중등	1. 증명하다, 입증하다 2. 드러나다, 밝혀지다	[121] show
prove			
[proov]		He proved himself wrong.	

1038	수능	1. 시행하다, 실행하다, 이행하다 2. 도입하다	implementation (도입)
implement			
[IM-pluh-muhnt]		New policies will be implemented soon.	

1039	중등	일, 과제, 업무	multitasking
task			(멀티태스킹)
[task]		She successfully carried out the task.	

1040	중등	1. 진전, 진보 2. 진행하다, 앞으로 나아가다	progressive (진보적인)
progress			[695] advance
[PROG-res]		We've achieved great progress in the field of science and technology.	

1041	중등	1. 추정하다, 가정하다 2. 떠맡다, 도맡다	assumption
assume			(추정, 떠맡음)
[uh-SOOM]		I assumed you were busy.	[1312] suppose

1042	토익	기법, 기술	technician (기술자)
technique			[590] method
[tek-NEEK]		The artist is well known for his unique technique.	

1043 **injury** [IN-juh-ree]	중등	1. 부상, 상처 2. 피해	injure (부상을 입히다) [719] damage
		She had a brain injury from a car accident.	
1044 **exercise** [EK-ser-sahyz]	초등	1. 운동(하다) 2. 연습, 훈련 3. 행사(하다), 발휘(하다)	exercisable (행사할 수 있는) [492] practice
		Severe exercise may cause more harm than good.	
1045 **efficient** [ih-FISH-uhnt]	중등 토익	1. 효율적인 2. 유능한	inefficient (비효율적인) [234] effective
		The efficient use of energy is important.	
1046 **maximum** [MAK-suh-muhm]	중등 토익	최대, 최고	maximize (극대화하다) maximal (최대한의) [1868] peak
		What is the maximum number of people allowed in the hotel room?	
1047 **middle** [MID-l]	초등	1. 중앙(의), 가운데, 중간 2. 허리	[214] center
		I'm in the middle of doing something.	
1048 **therefore** [THAIR-fawr]	중등	따라서, 그러므로	[1121] thus
		Their house was bigger and therefore, more comfortable.	
1049 **cycle** [SAHY-kuhl]	초등 토익	1. 순환(하다) 2. 주기 3. 자전거, 오토바이	bicycle (자전거) [1239] bike
		We need to create a virtuous cycle.	
1050 **farm** [fahrm]	초등	1. 농장, 농가, 사육장 2. 경작하다, 사육하다	farmer (농부)
		His family owns a huge farm.	
1051 **council** [KOUN-suhl]	중등	1. 의회 2. 협의회 3. 대책 회의	[515] board
		The council meeting will be held next month.	
1052 **bag** [bag]	토익	가방, 봉투, 주머니	baggage (수화물)
		What's in your bag?	
1053 **corporate** [KAWR-per-it]	중등	1. 기업의, 회사의 2. 법인체(의)	corporation (기업) [148] company
		Adapting to a new corporate culture always takes time.	
1054 **ball** [bawl]	초등 토익	1. 공 2. 무도회	ballroom (무도회장) [1316] dance
		Tennis balls are made of rubber.	
1055 **warm** [wawrm]	초등	1. 따듯한, 따스한 2. 데우다	warmth (온기) [710] heat
		His hands were warm.	
1056 **capital** [KAP-i-tl]	중등	1. 수도 2. 자본금, 자금, 자산 3. 대문자 4. 주요한	capitalism (자본주의) capitalize (대문자로 쓰다) [368] money
		What's the capital of Canada?	

1057	초등	1. 계산서 2. 고지서, 청구서 3. 법안	[1637] legislation
bill [bil]		May I have the bill, please?	

1058	초등	1. 요리하다 2. 요리사	
cook [kook]		He cooked for me.	

1059	중등	1. 존중(하다) 2. 존경(하다), 경의 3. 준수하다 4. 측면	respected (존경받는) respectful (존경하는) respectable (존경할 만한)
respect [ri-SPEKT]		I respect your decision.	

1060	중등	1. 행동, 행실 2. 움직임	misbehave (버릇 없게 행동하다) behave (행동하다) [1008] conduct
behavior [bih-HEYV-yer]		She has been studying animal behavior.	

1061	중등	1. 허용하다, 허락하다 2. 허가증	permission (허가) [200] allow
permit [per-MIT]		Did you permit him to stay up late?	

1062	중등 토익	1. 분포, 분배 2. 유통 3. 배급	distribute (분배하다) [1373] spread
distribution [dis-truh-BYOO-shuhn]		He studies population distributions in particular regions.	

1063	중등	소득, 수입	low-income (저소득) [890] earnings
income [IN-kuhm]		Income inequality is a grave issue.	

1064	초등	1. 지구 2. 땅, 지면 3. 흙	earthly (세속적인) [766] ground
earth [urth]		Earth is the third planet from the sun.	

1065	초등 토익	1. 맛(이 나다) 2. 시식(하다) 3. 감각 4. 취향	tasty (맛있는) tasteful (감각이 있는) [1196] sample
taste [teyst]		Some people don't like the taste of water.	

1066	중등 토익	1. 행정부 2. 관리 3. 집행 4. (약물)투여	administer (관리하다) administrator (행정관) administrative (행정의) [167] management
administration [ad-min-uh-STREY-shuhn]		The new administration took office last year.	

1067	초등	1. 밴드, 악단 2. 무리 3. 띠, 끈	[223] group
band [band]		Who is your favorite member of the band?	

1068	초등 토익	정원, 뜰	[468] park
garden [GAHR-dn]		I want a beautiful garden.	

1069	중등	1. 끌다, 끌어들이다 2. 유치하다 3. 유인하다	attractive (매력적인) [670] draw
attract [uh-TRAKT]		She was successful in attracting attention from the crowd.	

1070	중등	1. 가장자리, 끝, 모서리 2. (칼)날 3. 우위, 유리함	[1823] border
edge [ej]		Beware of sharp edges of an aluminum plate.	

1071 **platform** [PLAT-fawrm]	중등	1. 플랫폼 2. 단상, 연단 3. 발판	[852] stage
		Digital platform businesses are on the rise.	
1072 **approve** [uh-PROOV]	중등	1. 승인하다, 허가하다, 인가하다 2. 찬성하다	approval (승인) [2864] endorse
		The boss approved of my plan.	
1073 **dream** [dreem]	초등	1. 꿈 2. 꿈꾸다	daydream (상상) [1277] fantasy
		Her dream is to become a teacher.	
1074 **cancer** [KAN-ser]	중등	암	[2794] tumor
		Cancer medicines are very expensive.	
1075 **participate** [pahr-TIS-uh-peyt]	중등	참가하다, 참여하다	participation (참여) participant (참가자)
		I would like to thank you for participating in today's event.	
1076 **qualify** [KWOL-uh-fahy]	중등	자격을 갖추다, 자격을 취득하다	qualification (자격요건) disqualify (실격)
		He didn't qualify for the position.	
1077 **lie** [lahy]	수능	1. 거짓말(하다) 2. 누워있다, 눕다, 놓여있다	
		She lies all the time.	
1078 **admit** [ad-MIT]	중등 토익	1. 인정하다, 시인하다 2. (입장, 가입, 입학을)허락하다 3. 받아들이다	admission (입학) admittedly (인정한 것 처럼) [3053] confess
		He admitted his fault.	
1079 **obvious** [OB-vee-uhs]	중등	분명한, 명백한	obviously (당연히) [372] clear
		It was obvious who had eaten the cookie.	
1080 **reveal** [ri-VEEL]	중등	드러내다, 밝히다, 폭로하다	revelation (폭로) [1879] disclose
		He revealed the truth.	
1081 **demonstrate** [DEM-uhn-streyt]	중등	1. 증명하다, 입증하다 2. 보여주다, 설명하다 3. 시위에 참여하다	demonstration (시위) [121] show
		She demonstrated how easy the task was.	
1082 **champion** [CHAM-pee-uhn]	공무원 GRE	1. 챔피언 2. 옹호하다	championship (선수권 대회) [319] winner
		The boxer won the match and became the champion.	
1083 **unless** [uhn-LES]	중등	1.~하지 않는 한 2. ~을 제외하면, ~한 경우 외에는	[213] without
		I am going to leave unless you want me to stay.	
1084 **adult** [uh-DUHLT]	초등	1. 성인(의), 어른 2. 성숙한, 어른다운	adulthood (성년) [2155] mature
		Being an adult isn't easy.	

1085	중등	바다, 해(海)	overseas (해외의) [1950] marine
sea [see]		Sea level rise is known to be caused by climate change.	
1086	초등	1. 두 배의 2. 이중의 3. 2인용의 4. 두 배로하다, 배가하다	[3016] duplicate
double [DUHB-uhl]		The export volume of the country nearly doubled.	
1087	중등 토익	1. 이익, 수익, 이윤 2. 이익을 얻다	nonprofit (비영리적인) profitable (수익이 좋은) [834] gain
profit [PROF-it]		She made a big profit from selling the company.	
1088	중등	1. 복잡한 2. 복합의 3. 건물 단지 4. 콤플렉스	complexity (복잡함) [1817] complicated
complex [kuhm-PLEKS]		Climate change is a complex issue.	
1089	중등	1. 감시하다 2. 추적 관찰하다 3. 화면, 모니터	
monitor [MON-i-ter]		Professional security guards monitor our hotel.	
1090	수능	1. 자취, 흔적 2. 길 3. 루트, 코스 4. 뒤처지다	[561] track
trail [treyl]		The storm left behind a trail of destruction.	
1091	중등	결핍, 부족(하다)	[2193] absence
lack [lak]		A lack of sleep can lead to weight gain.	
1092	초등	실수, 오류	[1513] mistake
error [ER-er]		There are so many grammatical errors in your paper.	
1093	초등	소년, 남아	[4550] lad
boy [boi]		Some boys were playing soccer in our driveway.	
1094		1. 방향 2. 지시, 명령	[131] leadership
direction [dih-REK-shuhn]		We are heading in the right direction.	
1095	초등	1. 잊다, 망각하다 2. 체념하다	unforgettable (잊히지 않는)
forget [fer-GET]		She often forgets how lucky she is.	
1096	중등	인상적인, 감명 깊은	impress (감명을 주다) impression (인상) [1677] grand
impressive [im-PRES-iv]		His piece of artwork is quite impressive.	
1097	중등	1. 한 쌍, 짝 2. 짝을 짓다	[644] couple
pair [pair]		She gave her boyfriend a pair of shoes for his birthday.	
1098	중등	1. 분류(하다), 구분하다 2. 유형, (특정 부류의)사람	[410] kind
sort [sawrt]		He began sorting through a giant stack of papers.	

1099 population [pop-yuh-LEY-shuhn]	중등	인구	populate (거주하다) overpopulation (인구 과잉)
		It is well known that more than half the world's population lives in urban areas.	
1100 desire [dih-ZAHYUHR]	중등 토익	1. 욕구, 욕망, 갈망 2. 바라다, 원하다	desirable (바람직한, 호감가는) [909] wish
		I have no desire to argue with anyone.	
1101 library [LAHY-brer-ee]	초등 토익	1. 도서관, 서재 2. 장서, 수집품, 시리즈	librarian (사서)
		He likes to study in the library.	
1102 station [STEY-shuhn]	중등 토익	1. 역, 정거장 2. 방송국 3. 기지, 주둔지 4. 배치하다, 주둔하다	[487] position
		Meet me at the station later.	
1103 fresh [fresh]	초등	1. 신선한, 산뜻한, 상쾌한 2. 살아있는, 생생한	[1873] novel
		I love eating fresh oranges.	
1104 lock [lok]	중등 토익	1. 잠그다 2. 갇히다 3. 고정시키다 4. 자물쇠, 잠금장치	unlock (잠긴 것을 열다) locker (사물함) interlock (연동하다) [247] close
		Lock the door before you leave the house.	
1105 initial [ih-NISH-uhl]	중등	1. 초기의, 처음의 2. 첫 글자	initially (처음에)
		This is just an initial draft of the plan.	
1106 classic [KLAS-ik]	중등	1. 전형적인 2. 고전적인 3. 일류의, 최고의 4. 고전, 명작 5. 클래식 음악	classical (고전의) [2623] vintage
		He has the classic symptoms of depression.	
1107 beach [beech]	초등	해변, 바닷가, 백사장	[2866] shore
		She enjoys walking on the beach.	
1108 reflect [ri-FLEKT]	중등	1. 반영하다, 나타내다 2. 비추다, 보여주다 3. 반사하다 4. 심사숙고하다	reflection (반사, 성찰) [282] consider
		The government should always reflect the views of the citizens when making policies.	
1109 bear [bair]	중등	1. 참다, 견디다 2. 곰 3. 아이를 낳다, 열매를 피우다 4. 지니다	unbearable (견딜 수 없는) overbearing (고압적인) borne (떠맡은) [553] carry
		I can't bear the pain anymore.	
1110 confidence [KON-fi-duhns]	중등 토익	1. 자신감 2. 신뢰 3. 확신	confident (자신감 넘치는) [2290] conviction
		She is suffering from a lack of confidence.	
1111 welcome [WEL-kuhm]	초등	1. 환영하다, 맞이하다, 환대하다 2. 반가운	welcoming (따뜻하게 맞이하는)
		I'd like to welcome all of you to this beautiful city.	
1112 beyond [bee-OND]	중등	1. ~을 넘어서 2. ~이상으로 3. ~이후에 4. 뛰어넘는	
		The task assigned is beyond his skill and capability.	

1113	수능 토익	1. 저녁 식사 2. 만찬, 정찬	dine (식사를 하다)
dinner			[1359] meal
[DIN-er]		I skipped dinner last night.	

1114	중등 토익	최저(의), 최소한의	minimize (최소화하다)
minimum			minimal (최소의)
[MIN-uh-muhm]		It is tough surviving on minimum wage.	

1115	중등	1. 제안, 제의 2. 청혼, 프러포즈	propose
proposal			(제안하다, 청혼하다)
[pruh-POH-zuhl]		His proposal was rejected.	proposition (제안, 명제)

1116	중등	1. 방식, 방법 2. 기분, 태도 3. 유행	[1417] fashion
mode			
[mohd]		What is your favorite mode of transportation?	

1117	중등	1. 패턴, 양식 2. 무늬	[431] model
pattern			
[PAT-ern]		I've been noticing a certain pattern in horror movies.	

1118	초등	1. 보내다, 부치다, 발송하다 2. 우편(물) 3. 이메일	e-mail (이메일)
mail			mailbox (우편함)
[meyl]		I have mailed you the document.	[217] post

1119	중등	1. 상상하다, 그리다 2. 생각하다	imagination (상상력)
imagine			imaginary (상상 속의)
[ih-MAJ-in]		We all imagine a world free from corruption.	[564] picture

1120	중등	1. 틀, 구조, 뼈대 2. 액자 3. 한 장면 4. 틀에 넣다 5. 누명을 씌우다	[2187] framework
frame			
[freym]		What material is best for window frames?	

1121	중등	따라서, 그러므로, 그렇기 때문에	[1048] therefore
thus			
[thuhs]		We are running out of time. Thus, we need to act now.	

1122	중등	범주, 항목, 카테고리	categorize (분류하다)
category			categorical (절대적인)
[KAT-i-gawr-ee]		The art exhibition has been organized by category.	[353] class

1123	중등	1. 회의, 회기 2. 시간, 기간 3. 연주회	[276] meeting
session			
[SESH-uhn]		If you would take your seats, session 2 will begin soon.	

1124	중등	1. 절대적인 2. 완전한, 완벽한 3. 확실한, 확고한	absolutely (절대적으로)
absolute			[207] complete
[AB-suh-loot]		A dictator is a leader who possesses absolute power.	

1125	중등	1. 손님, 하객, 내빈 2. 게스트 3. 고객	[356] visitor
guest			
[gest]		The guests are on their way.	

1126		화제, 주제	[720] subject
topic			
[TOP-ik]		The topic of my presentation today is taxation.	

1127 accurate [AK-yer-it]	중등 토익	1. 정확한 2. 정밀한 His calculations are not accurate.	accuracy (정확도) inaccurate (부정확한) [1767] precise
1128 gas [gas]	수능 토익	1. 가스, 기체 2. 휘발유 Oxygen is a gas.	gasoline (휘발유) [7124] babble
1129 conference [KON-fer-uhns]	수능 토익	1. 회의, 회담 2. 연맹 The conference will be held next month.	confer (상의하다, 수여하다) [276] meeting
1130 expensive [ik-SPEN-siv]	중등 토익	값비싼, 고가의 She is planning on buying an expensive car.	inexpensive (비싸지 않은) [297] costly
1131 luck [luhk]	초등	행운, 운수 Good luck on your exam.	lucky (운이 좋은) luckily (운 좋게도) [992] fortune
1132 bed [bed]	초등	1. 침대 2. 바닥 3. 지층 Getting out of bed in the morning is too difficult.	
1133 worry [WUR-ee]	초등	1. 걱정(하다) 2. 우려, 걱정거리 Why do I worry so much about everything?	worrisome (걱정스러운) [705] concern
1134 celebrate [SEL-uh-breyt]	중등	1. 기념하다, 축하하다 2. 찬양하다, 기리다 She doesn't celebrate anniversaries.	celebration (축하 행사) [3821] commemorate
1135 weekend [WEEK-end]	초등	주말 I went on a trip during the weekend.	[180] week
1136 airport [AIR-pawrt]	초등 토익	공항 The plane landed at Incheon International Airport.	
1137 feedback [FEED-bak]	토익	피드백, 의견 The speaker asked the audience for feedback.	[756] response
1138 setup [SET-uhp]		1. 설정, 구성 2. 계획된 일, 짜여진 함정 My friends admired my desktop setup.	[2067] trap
1139 bedroom [BED-room]	초등	침실 He did not come out of the bedroom.	[382] room
1140 outstanding [out-STAN-ding]	중등 토익	1. 뛰어난 2. 두드러진, 눈에 띄는 3. 아직 미해결된 The student's work is outstanding.	[724] excellent

1141	초등	영원히	[225] always
forever			
[fawr-EV-er]		I will love you forever.	

1142	토익	1. 탁상(용의) 2. 바탕화면 3. PC	[2152] desk
desktop			
[DESK-top]		Save it anywhere on your desktop.	

1143	토익	배치	[162] design
layout			
[LEY-out]		I did not like the layout.	

1144		주주	
shareholder			
[SHAIR-hohl-der]		The shareholders of the company were upset.	

1145	초등 토익	숙제	[1259] assignment
homework			
[HOHM-wurk]		I have to do my homework.	

1146	토익	고소하다	[2834] petition
sue			
[soo]		Please do not sue me.	

1147	공무원	이정표, 중요한 지점	[3389] landmark
milestone			
[MAHYL-stohn]		Graduating from college was a huge milestone.	

1148	공무원 편입	나머지, 잔여물	[4176] surplus
leftover			
[LEFT-oh-ver]		There is some leftover pizza from the party.	

1149		가축	[3568] cattle
livestock			
[LAHYV-stok]		Many of the livestock on the farm died.	

1150	편입	1. 쾌활하고 사교적인 2. 밖으로 떠나는	[405] sociable
outgoing			
[OUT-goh-ing]		He has a very outgoing personality.	

1151	중등	1. 명예, 영광 2. 존경하다, 예우하다	honorable (명예로운)
honor			
[ON-er]		I am very honored to be invited to speak to you this afternoon.	

1152	초등	아내, 부인, 처	[2742] spouse
wife			
[wahyf]		His wife is 4 years younger than him.	

1153		1. 컵, 잔 2. 한 잔 3. 우승컵 4. ~을 감싸다	[1215] glass
cup			
[kuhp]		Reading a book with a cup of coffee makes me happy.	

1154	중등 토익	1. (전문)병원, 진료소 2. 임상 강의	clinical (임상의) [1016] hospital
clinic			
[KLIN-ik]		He works at a clinic as a dermatologist.	

1155 district [DIS-trikt]	중등	1. 지역, 지구 2. 구역	[177] area
		The storm hit several districts in the region.	
1156 voice [vois]	초등	1. 목소리, 음성 2. 발언권 3. 나타내다, 의견을 표출하다	[440] speak
		Her voice is too loud.	
1157 scale [skeyl]	중등	1. 규모, 범위 2. 눈금, 저울 3. 음계 4. 오르다 5. 크기를 조정하다	scalable (규모 확장이 가능한) [2124] extent
		The scale of the plastic pollution problem is very serious.	
1158 automatic [aw-tuh-MAT-ik]	중등 토익	1. 자동의 2. 무의식적인	[1261] mechanical
		Our company's building has automatic doors.	
1159 famous [FEY-muhs]	중등	유명한, 잘 알려진	fame (명예) defamation (명예 훼손)
		He is a very famous singer.	
1160 ticket [TIK-it]		1. 표, 승차권, 입장권 2. 교통 위반 딱지	[418] card
		All the tickets were sold out yesterday.	
1161 cross [kraws]	초등	1. 건너다, 횡단하다 2. 교차하다, 엇갈리다 3. x 표, 십자가	
		Crossing the streets in Vietnam is difficult.	
1162 restaurant [RES-ter-uhnt]	초등	식당, 레스토랑	
		I will make a reservation at a local restaurant.	
1163 cold [kohld]	초등	1. 추운, 차가운 2. 냉정한 3. 감기	[764] cool
		It's getting cold outside.	
1164 slightly [slahyt-lee]	수능	약간, 조금	slight (약간의) [197] little
		The ground is slightly wet.	
1165 innovate [IN-uh-veyt]	중등 토익	혁신하다, 쇄신하다	innovation (혁신) innovative (혁신적인) [761] introduce
		Companies need to constantly innovate their products.	
1166 loan [lohn]	중등	1. 대출(하다), 융자 2. 대여(하다), 빌려주다	[1857] lend
		He took out a loan to pay off his credit card debt.	
1167 thousand [THOU-zuhnd]	중등	천, 수천의	[1677] grand
		These shoes cost more than two thousand dollars.	
1168 river [RIV-er]	초등	강, 강물	[1470] stream
		I live in a condo with stunning river views.	

1169	중등	1. 상대, 적 2. 반대자	opposition (반대)
opponent			oppose (반대하다)
[uh-POH-nuhnt]		The champion has no opponents.	[2835] adversary

1170	초등 토익	1. 배터리, 건전지 2. 구타, 폭행	[2335] assault
battery			
[BAT-uh-ree]		He needs to replace his watch battery.	

1171	중등	1. 백 년 2. 세기	centenary (백 년의)
century			centennial (백년 마다의)
[SEN-chuh-ree]		He has spent almost half a century studying chemistry.	[기타] hundred

1172	중등	1. 해결하다 2. 다짐하다 3. 의결, 결의하다 4. 결심, 의지	unresolved
resolve			(해결되지 못한)
[ri-ZOLV]		We've resolved the problem.	[1313] solve

1173	초등 토익	1. 가난한, 빈곤한 2. 좋지 못한, 형편없는 3. 빈약한, 부족한	[2096] inadequate
poor			
[poor]		Nobody wants to be poor.	

1174	중등	1. 온도, 기온 2. 체온	[1706] climate
temperature			
[TEM-per-uh-cher]		The global average temperature is increasing.	

1175	중등	1. 관찰하다, 주시하다 2. 준수하다, 지키다	observation (관측)
observe			[476] watch
[uhb-ZURV]		She loves observing the night sky.	

1176	중등	1. 고령자, 연장자 2. 고위의, 상급의, 상위의 3. 졸업반	[2099] superior
senior			
[SEEN-yer]		Many nation-wide benefits are available to senior citizens.	

1177	중등	1. 고통받다, 시달리다 2. 겪다	suffering (고통을 겪는)
suffer			[2516] endure
[SUHF-er]		He suffered from a bad headache.	

1178	중등	1. 흐름 2. 유동성 3. 계속 흘러가다, 흐르다, 이동하다	inflow (유입)
flow			outflow (유출)
			overflow (범람)
[floh]		You should just go with the flow.	[1470] stream

1179	초등	1. 나무, 목재 2. 숲	wooden (나무로 된)
wood			[3688] timber
[wood]		I like plates made out of woods.	

1180	중등	1. 수수료, 커미션 2. 위원회 3. 의뢰(하다), 주문(하다)	commissioner (위원)
commission		4. (장교로)임관시키다	[1051] council
[kuh-MISH-uhn]		He receives 10 percent commission on each sale.	

1181	중등	1. 추정치, 추산(하다) 2. 전망하다	underestimate
estimate			(과소 평가하다)
[ES-tuh-meyt]		Many scientists estimate that the global temperature will keep on rising unless we act now.	[1283] evaluate

1182	중등 토익	1. 접다, 개다 2. 주름 3. -배의 (ex. twofold)	folder (폴더)
fold			
[fohld]		I know how to fold an envelope from a piece of paper.	

1183	초등	1. 혼자, 홀로, 단독으로 2. 외로운	[2843] lonely
alone			
[uh-LOHN]		I love being alone.	

1184	중등	~에도 불구하고	
despite			
[dih-SPAHYT]		Despite all the difficulties, he eventually succeeded.	

1185	공무원	1. 경로, 유통 체계 2. 채널, 주파수대 3. 수단, 방법 4. 물길, 수로	[5704] conduit
channel			
[CHAN-l]		Goods can be transported through various channels.	

1186	초등	1. 죽은 2. 작동을 안 하는 3. 활기가 없는 4. 무감각한 5. 완전한, 정확한	deadly (치명적인) [363] death
dead			
[ded]		I feel dead inside during work.	

1187	중등	1. 이기다 2. 때리다 3. 능가하다, 더 낫다 4. 맥박, 울림 5. 리듬, 박자, 비트	beating (매질) [1226] strike
beat			
[beet]		Nobody can beat his record.	

1188	중등	1. 수송(하다) 2. 이동시키다 3. 운송(업)	transportation (교통) [553] carry
transport			
[trans-PAWRT]		A ship that transports oil is called an oil tanker.	

1189	초등	1. 형, 오빠, 남동생, 형제 2. 수도사, 수사	[4212] monk
brother			
[BRUHTH-er]		He has three brothers.	

1190		1. 드레스, 원피스 2. 옷을 입다 3. 장식하다, 꾸미다	[1392] clothes
dress			
[dres]		She looks good in a red dress.	

1191	중등 토익	컨설턴트, 자문 위원, 상담가	consult (컨설팅하다) [1035] adviser
consultant			
[kuhn-SUHL-tnt]		Great consultants are good listeners.	

1192	중등	1. 예산 2. 예산을 세우다, 책정하다	
budget			
[BUHJ-it]		A government budget deficit can affect the overall economy.	

1193	중등	1. 드러내다, 폭로하다 2. 노출시키다	[1080] reveal
expose			
[ik-SPOHZ]		Her identity as a secret agent was exposed in a newspaper column.	

1194	중등 토익	1. 임차하다, 임대하다 2. 집세, 임차료	rental (임대) [2125] lease
rent			
[rent]		We will rent a car when we get there.	

1195	중등	역량, 능력	capable (역량이 있는) incapable (역량이 없는) [111] ability
capability			
[key-puh-BIL-i-tee]		Students need to build digital capabilities.	

1196		1. 샘플 2. 표본 3. 시식하다, 시음하다 4. 표본 조사를 하다	[3687] specimen
sample			
[SAM-puhl]		She sent the blood samples off to a laboratory.	

1197	중등 토익	1. 조리법, 레시피 2. 비결, 방안	[1559] formula
recipe			
[RES-uh-pee]		I need a recipe for cookies without eggs.	

1198	중등	1. 두려움, 공포 2. 두려워하다, 무서워하다 3. 우려하다, 염려하다	fearful (두려워하는) [3561] dread
fear			
[feer]		She is consumed by fear too often.	

1199	초등	1. 부유한, 부자인 2. 다채로운, 풍요로운 3. 사치스러운, 호화로운	enrich (풍요롭게 하다) riches (부) [1855] wealthy
rich			
[rich]		Everyone wants to be rich.	

1200	중등 토익	확정하다, 확인하다, 확실히 하다	confirmation (확인) [1778] verify
confirm			
[kuhn-FURM]		Your reservation has been confirmed.	

1201	중등 토익	1. 반복하다, 따라하다 2. 반복, 되풀이 3. 재방송	repeatedly (반복적으로) repetition (반복) repetitive (반복적인) [3337] reiterate
repeat			
[ri-PEET]		I don't like people who repeat the same things over and over.	

1202	수능 토익	이용하다, 활용하다, 적용하다	utility (실용성) [303] employ
utilize			
[YOOT-l-ahyz]		What are some companies that utilize AI?	

1203	중등 토익	1. 영향을 미치다 2. 영향(력)	influential (영향력 있는) [4408] sway
influence			
[IN-floo-uhns]		Parents influence their children in many ways.	

1204	초등	1. 휴가 2. 휴일, 공휴일	[1989] vacation
holiday			
[HOL-i-dey]		We are going on holiday next month.	

1205	중등	1. 위협 2. 협박	threaten (위협하다) threatened (위협당하는) [1223] danger
threat			
[thret]		Air pollution is a serious health threat.	

1206	수능 토익	제외하다, 배제하다	exclusive (독점적인) [1626] eliminate
exclude			
[ik-SKLOOD]		Injured players are excluded from the match.	

1207	중등	대단한, 최고의	
super			
[SOO-per]		What a super idea he has.	

1208	중등	1. 거리, 간격 2. 먼 곳 3. 거리를 두다	distant (멀리 떨어져 있는) [358] away
distance			
[DIS-tuhns]		The distance between us is growing too wide.	

1209	중등	엄청난, 놀라운, 믿기 힘든, 굉장한	credible (신뢰할 수 있는) [309] unbelievable
incredible			
[in-KRED-uh-buhl]		It's incredible how the world has changed so much in recent years.	

1210	중등	길, 방향	pathway (경로,통로) [1288] route
path			
[path]		We need to choose the right path in life.	

1211	초등	1. 산 2. 거대한, 산더미	[1272] mount
mountain			
[MOUN-tn]		He climbed up to the highest mountain in the world.	

1212	중등	생존하다, 살아남다	survival (생존)
survive			survivor (생존자)
[ser-VAHYV]		The company won't survive unless it pursues innovation.	[189] live

1213	중등	1. 임무 2. 사절단, 파견단 3. 사명, 철칙 4. 선교	missionary (선교사)
mission			[1039] task
[MISH-uhn]		Her mission in life was to help others.	

1214	초등	1. 전투, 투쟁 싸움 2. 싸우다	battlefield (전쟁터)
battle			battleship (전투함)
[BAT-l]		We won the battle.	[697] fight

1215	초등	1. 유리 2. 안경 3. 컵	
glass			
[glas]		Don't walk on that broken glass.	

1216	초등	추측(하다), 짐작(하다)	[6401] conjecture
guess			
[ges]		Can you guess my age?	

1217	초등	1. 간호사 2. 간호하다, 치료하다 3. 보살피다, 젖을 먹이다	nursery (탁아소)
nurse			[3744] nurture
[nurs]		She is a nurse.	

1218	중등 토익	1. 바람, 풍력 2. 숨, 호흡 3. (실을) 감다	windy (바람이 많이 부는)
wind			winding (감겨 있는)
[wind]		There's no wind today.	[3447] breeze

1219	중등	1. 이론 2. 학설 3. 의견, 생각	theoretical (이론적으로)
theory			[3152] hypothesis
[THEE-uh-ree]		In theory, her plan sounds reasonable.	

1220		1. 기술적인 2. 전문적인	technically (기술적으로)
technical			technicality (세부 디테일)
[TEK-ni-kuhl]		There were some technical problems.	[352] technological

1221	중등	1. 필터, 여과 장치 2. 여과하다, 거르다 3. 새어 들어오다	unfiltered (필터되지 않은)
filter			[6535] sieve
[FIL-ter]		I need to buy coffee filters.	

1222	수능	1. 패널, 토론 참석자 2. (금속)판, 판자	[515] board
panel			
[PAN-l]		We have two professors on our panel tonight.	

1223	초등	위험한	danger (위험)
dangerous			endangered (멸종 위기의)
[DEYN-jer-uhs]		Fake news is dangerous.	[2553] hazardous

1224	초등	1. 불에 타다, 태우다 2. 데다, 화상을 입다 3. 화상, 덴 상처	
burn			
[burn]		You should never burn papers at home.	

1225	중등 토익	1. 예약하다 2. 보류하다, 유보하다 3. (권한 등을)갖다 4. 비축물 5. 보호구역	reservation (예약) reserved (내성적인)
reserve [ri-ZURV]		I would like to reserve a table for five.	
1226	중등	1. 파업(하다) 2. 치다, 부딪치다 3. 때리다, 공격(하다) 4. (야구)스트라이크	strikingly (눈에 띄게)
strike [strahyk]		A record number of workers went on strike last year.	
1227	중등	1. 묶다, 매다 2. 비기다, 동점, 무승부 3. 넥타이 4. 유대 관계	
tie [tahy]		I tie back my hair when I'm studying.	
1228	중등	1. 반응하다 2. 대응하다, 대처하다	reaction (반응) overreact (과민반응하다)
react [ree-AKT]		We are not sure how she will react to the news.	
1229	중등	1. 근거, 이유 2. 기반, 기초	
basis [BEY-sis]		Her claim had no basis.	
1230	초등	1. 싼, 저렴한 2. 천박한 3. 인색한	[1130] inexpensive
cheap [cheep]		He bought a cheap car.	
1231	중등	1. 그렇지 않으면 2. 그 외에는 3. 다른, 달리	[117] differently
otherwise [UHTH-er-wahyz]		Shut the window; otherwise, it will get too cold.	
1232	중등	1. 구성 방식, 형식 2. 포맷, 서식	[220] form
format [FAWR-mat]		The exam format has been changed.	
1233	중등	1. 똑바로, 일직선으로 2. 곧장, 곧바로 3. 솔직하게 4. 내리, 잇달아	straighten (바로잡다) [112] right
straight [streyt]		He looked straight into my eyes.	
1234	중등	의견, 견해, 생각	opinionated (자기고집이 강한) [116] view
opinion [uh-PIN-yuhn]		It is important to have your own opinion.	
1235	중등	금속	metallic (금속의) [1733] iron
metal [MET-l]		Gold is a precious metal.	
1236	중등	1. 교통(량) 2. 통신 3. 밀거래	trafficking (불법 거래) [667] trade
traffic [TRAF-ik]		She is stuck in traffic.	
1237	중등	1. 승인하다, 허락하다 2. 인정하다 3. 보조금	
grant [grant]		The country refused to grant him political asylum.	
1238	초등 토익	사과	[1364] fruit
apple [AP-uhl]		An apple a day is good for your health.	

1239		1. 자전거 2. 오토바이	[1049] cycle
bike			
[bahyk]		My bike is broken.	

1240	중등	종교	religious (종교적인)
religion			[1380] faith
[ri-LIJ-uh n]		Some countries have official state religions.	

1241	중등 토익	1. 원, 원형, 동그라미 2. ~계, 사회 3. 빙빙 돌다 4. 동그라미를 그리다	circulation (순환)
circle			encircle (둘러싸다)
[SUR-kuhl]		I'm good at drawing circles.	[1271] ring

1242	중등	1. 첨부하다, 붙이다 2. 부여하다, 연관짓다	[4058] fasten
attach			
[uh-TACH]		Please check the attached file for your reference.	

1243	초등	1. 스트레스, 압박, 긴장 2. 중점, 강조(하다) 3. 강세(를 붙이다)	stressful
stress			(스트레스가 많은)
[stres]		She doesn't know how to handle stress.	[1789] emphasize

1244	중등	1. 군사의, 무력의 2. 군대	[1512] army
military			
[MIL-i-ter-ee]		What are the world military superpowers?	

1245	초등	1. 부드러운, 푹신한 2. 연한, 무른 3. 은은한	soften (부드럽게 하다)
soft			[2065] gentle
[sawft]		I prefer a soft mattress.	

1246	중등	1. 이웃, 동네 2. 지역, 지방 3. 근처, 인근	neighbor (이웃)
neighborhood			[177] area
[NEY-ber-hood]		I live in a rich neighborhood.	

1247	초등	1. 현금, 돈 2. 현금화하다	[368] money
cash			
[kash]		I'll pay in cash.	

1248	중등	1. 핵심(적인), 중심부 2. 가장 중요한	[619] heart
core			
[kawr]		We need to identify the core problem first.	

1249	초등 토익	얼음, 빙하	icy (얼음의)
ice			[2763] chill
[ahys]		Can I get some ice?	

1250	중등 토익	얻다, 구하다, 획득하다	unobtainable
obtain			(얻을 수 없는)
[uhb-TEYN]		Where did you obtain the information?	[1321] acquire

1251	중등 토익	1. 높게 평가하다, 인정하다 2. 고마워하다, 환영하다 3. 감상하다 4. 가치가 오르다	[378] enjoy
appreciate			
[uh-PREE-shee-eyt]		I came to appreciate the beauty of nature.	

1252	수능 토익	1. 소매 2. 유통	retailer (소매업자)
retail			[208] market
[REE-teyl]		What is the retail price of this car?	

1253 status [STEY-tuhs]	중등	1. 상황, 현상 2. 지위, 신분	status quo (현 상황) [1274] rank
		What is the current status of gene therapy research?	
1254 volunteer [vol-uhn-TEER]	중등	1. 봉사하다 2. 자원 봉사자 3. 자원하다 4. 자원자, 지원자	involuntary (의도하지 않은)
		He volunteered at a hospital.	
1255 destroy [dih-STROI]	중등	1. 파괴하다, 훼손하다 2. 죽이다	destruction (파괴) [2431] ruin
		That exam destroyed my life.	
1256 ultimate [UHL-tuh-mit]	중등	1. 궁극적인, 최종적인 2. 최고의 3. 근본적인	ultimately (궁극적으로) [360] final
		What is your ultimate goal in life?	
1257 therapy [THER-uh-pee]	수능	치료, 요법	therapist (치료사) [366] treatment
		She needs speech therapy.	
1258 background [BAK-ground]	초등	1. 배경 2. 출신 3. 경력	[341] history
		How do you take a picture with a bright background?	
1259 assign [uh-SAHYN]	중등 토익	1. 맡기다, 배정하다 2. 파견하다, 선임하다 3. 부여하다 4. 양도하다	assignment (과제) [2487] allocate
		His teacher never assigns homework.	
1260 enhance [en-HANS]	중등	높이다, 향상시키다	[401] improve
		The player is working to enhance his performance.	
1261 mechanism [MEK-uh-niz-uhm]	중등 토익	1. 기계 장치 2. 방법, 메커니즘 3. 구조, 기제	mechanical (기계적인) [562] device
		The mechanism of the machine is very complicated.	
1262 hide [hahyd]	중등	1. 숨기다, 감추다 2. 은신처 3. 가죽	hidden (숨겨진) [3580] conceal
		He is good at hiding his emotions at work.	
1263 flight [flahyt]	중등	1. 항공편 2. 비행, 여행 3. 탈출, 도피	
		My flight has been canceled.	
1264 constant [KON-stuhnt]	중등	1. 지속적인, 끊임없는 2. 일정한, 변함없는 3. 상수(常數)	
		She is in constant pain.	
1265 rare [rair]	중등	1. 드문, 희귀한 2. 살짝 익힌	rarity (희귀한)
		He has a rare disease.	
1266 volume [VOL-yoom]	중등	1. 양, 부피 2. 용량 3. 음량 4. (책)권	
		How do you measure the volume of a gas?	

1267 satisfy [SAT-is-fahy]	중등 토익	만족시키다, 충족시키다, 채우다	satisfaction (만족) satisfactory (만족스러운)
		It is hard to satisfy everyone.	
1268 emotional [ih-MOH-shuh-nl]	중등	정서적인, 감정적인	emotion (감정)
		She got very emotional watching the documentary.	
1269 organic [awr-GAN-ik]	중등	1. 유기농의 2. 유기적인	
		Many people favor organic food.	
1270 born [bawrn]	토익	1. 태어나다, 탄생하다 2. 태생의, 출신의 3. 타고난, 천부적인	newborn (갓 난) [1619] birth
		He was born in Korea.	
1271 ring [ring]	초등	1. 반지 2. 울리다, 울려퍼지다 3. 전화하다	[129] call
		She doesn't like wearing rings.	
1272 mount [mount]	중등	1. 서서히 증가하다 2. 올라가다 3. 탑재하다 4. 산	dismount (내리다) [1211] mountain
		The country's debt continues to mount.	
1273 chart [chahrt]	공무원	1. 도표, 차트 2. (과정을)기록하다 3. 지도를 만들다	uncharted (지도에 없는, 미지의) [2970] diagram
		He will present the information using a chart.	
1274 rank [rangk]	중등	1. 차지하다, 오르다 2. 지위 3. 계급 4. 등급	[971] grade
		She is ranked in the top five tennis players in the world.	
1275 camp [kamp]		1. 캠프 2. 야영지 3. 수용소 4. 진영	
		Summer camps can be really fun and great.	
1276 jump [juhmp]		1. 뛰다, 점프하다 2. 급증(하다) 3. 건너뛰다 4. 달려들다, 공격하다	[3114] leap
		He can jump really high.	
1277 fantasy [FAN-tuh-see]	초등	공상, 상상	fantastic (환상적인) [1073] dream
		She lives in a fantasy world.	
1278 square [skwair]	중등	1. 광장 2. 정사각형(모양의) 3. 제곱(의) 4. 직각의 5. 공정한, 정직한	
		There are many people in the square.	
1279 theme [theem]	중등	주제, 테마	[1126] topic
		What is the theme of this novel?	
1280 ahead [uh-HED]	초등	1. 앞서 2. 미리 3. 앞으로, 앞에	[713] forward
		He arrived ahead of time.	

1281	중등	1. 청중, 관중 2. 시청자, 독자	[333] public
audience			
[AW-dee-uhns]		There was loud applause from the audience.	

1282	중등 토익	1. 계산하다, 산출하다 2. 추정하다, 추산하다	calculation (계산)
calculate			calculator (계산기)
[KAL-kyuh-leyt]		Can you calculate the area of a circle?	calculated (계산된) [4149] reckon

1283	중등	평가하다, 감정하다	evaluation (평가)
evaluate			[1026] assess
[ih-VAL-yoo-eyt]		We need to evaluate how well the plan is working.	

1284	중등	1. 시민의 2. 민간의 3. 정중한, 예의 바른	civilian (민간인)
civil			civilized (문명화된)
[SIV-uhl]		The criminals were deprived of their civil rights.	uncivilized (미개한) [3824] polite

1285	중등	1. 사실인, 진실인 2. 진짜의	truly (진정으로)
true			truth (진실)
[troo]		What she said to me was true.	

1286	초등	1. 뇌, 두뇌 2. 지능, 똑똑한 사람	no-brainer (당연한 것)
brain			[494] mind
[breyn]		Our brains need oxygen.	

1287	중등	1. 달콤한, 단 2. 상냥한, 다정한 3. 좋아요! 4. 디저트	[2366] cute
sweet			
[sweet]		Honey is sweet.	

1288	중등	1. 경로, 노선 2. (경로에 따라) 보내다	[1210] path
route			
[root]		I know a shorter route.	

1289		겨울, 동계	
winter			
[WIN-ter]		There are so many reasons to love winter.	

1290		1. 식단, 식습관 2. 다이어트(하다)	dietary (식이 요법의)
diet			[332] food
[DAHY-it]		Try excluding sugar from your diet.	

1291	중등	1. 주된 2. 최고위자(인) 3. 추장, 족장	[301] head
chief			
[cheef]		The chief crop of our country is rice.	

1292	중등	1. 연료(를 공급하다), 기름을 넣다 2. 부채질하다	refuel
fuel			(연료를 다시 채우다)
[FYOO-uhl]		We ran out of fuel.	

1293	중등	1. 설문 조사(하다) 2. 점검(하다), 살피다	
survey			
[ser-VEY]		Our team conducted a survey recently.	

1294	초등	1. 날씨, 기상, 일기 예보 2. 견디다 3. (햇빛에)변하다	
weather			
[WETH-er]		How's the weather?	

1295	수능	1. 프로필 2.약력 3. 옆모습 4. 인지도, 관심	[2119] outline
profile [PROH-fahyl]		You need to edit your SNS profile.	

1296	초등	딸, 여식, 여성	[744] girl
daughter [DAW-ter]		He has two daughters.	

1297	중등 토익	1. 측면 2. 양상 3. 관점	[266] feature
aspect [AS-pekt]		It is important to consider every aspect of a problem.	

1298	중등	1. 저항하다, 반대하다 2. 참다	resistance (저항) irresistible (저항할 수 없는) [4022] withstand
resist [ri-ZIST]		We all need to resist tyranny.	

1299	중등	1. 풍부한, 충분한 2. 많이, 대단히	plentitude (충만함) [2566] abundance
plenty [PLEN-tee]		Drinking plenty of water can help you lose weight.	

1300	중등	1. 약속(하다) 2. 가능성, 장래성 3. 장담하다	promising (유망한) [3242] pledge
promise [PROM-is]		Don't make promises you can't keep.	

1301	초등	호수, 연못	[3196] pond
lake [leyk]		I saw kids skating over the frozen lake.	

1302	중등	1. 조사하다, 검토하다 2. 진찰하다 3. 확인하다, 관찰하다	examination (시험) [116] review
examine [ig-ZAM-in]		We need to examine the evidence first.	

1303	중등	1. 교환(하다) 2. 환전 3. 거래소	[667] trade
exchange [iks-CHEYNJ]		They exchanged gifts.	

1304	중등	1. 결론, 결말 2. 체결	conclude (결론짓다) inconclusive (결론이 나지 않은) [207] completion
conclusion [kuhn-KLOO-zhuhn]		The conclusion of the movie was very disappointing.	

1305	중등	1. 안정적인, 안정된 2. 마구간	stability (안정성) instability (불안정성) [1036] firm
stable [STEY-buhl]		He wants a stable relationship.	

1306	초등	1. 다리 2. 구간	[3728] limb
leg [leg]		She has long legs.	

1307	중등	1. 단단한, 고체의 2. 탄탄한, 확실한 3. 고체, 고형물	solidify (굳히다) [498] strong
solid [SOL-id]		Water becomes solid when it freezes.	

1308	중등 토익	감당할 만한 가격의, 알맞은 가격의	afford (~할 여유가 있다) [1230] cheap
affordable [uh-FAWR-duh-buhl]		It is hard to find affordable housing in major cities.	

1309	중등 토익	1. 유연한 2. 신축성 있는, 탄력적인	flexibility (유연성)
flexible [FLEK-suh-buhl]		You need to be flexible to learn ballet.	
1310	중등	1. 통나무 2. 일지, 기록 3. 기록하다 4. 항해하다, 운항하다	[342] record
log [lawg]		Can you put another log on the fire?	
1311	중등	시각의, 시각적인	visualize (시각화하다) [1532] visible
visual [VIZH-oo-uhl]		I have a very good visual memory.	
1312	중등	1. 생각하다, 추측하다 2. 가정하다 3. ~인 것 같다	supposedly (추측하기로)
suppose [suh-POHZ]		I suppose he hates me.	
1313	중등	해결하다, 타결하다, 풀다	[1172] resolve
solve [solv]		We need to solve this issue right now.	
1314	수능 토익	1. 관련있는, 적절한 2. 유의미한	irrelevant (관계가 없는) [979] appropriate
relevant [REL-uh-vuhnt]		Why don't you ask relevant questions?	
1315	중등	1. 부정적인, 나쁜 2. 비관적인 3. 음성의 4. 이하의, 마이너스의	negate (무효화하다) negativity (부정적인) [2835] adverse
negative [NEG-uh-tiv]		She is so negative all the time.	
1316	초등	1. 춤(추다) 2. 무도회, 댄스파티	
dance [dans]		I want to dance all night.	
1317	중등	1. 바퀴 2. 승용차, 차 3. 핸들 4. 선회하다, 빙 돌다	[981] roll
wheel [hweel]		Her bike has two wheels.	
1318		1. 미터 2. 계량기	[614] measure
meter [MEE-ter]		We are only 10 meters away from the beach.	
1319	중등	1. 목표(하다), 목적 2. 겨냥(하다), 조준(하다)	aimlessly (목적 없이) [768] purpose
aim [eym]		His aim is to become a doctor.	
1320	중등	1. 구멍 2. 허점 3. 공백 4. 구멍을 내다	[186] opening
hole [hohl]		There's a hole in your sock.	
1321	수능	1. 습득하다, 얻다 2. 획득하다, 취득하다	acquisition (취득, 인수) [1250] obtain
acquire [uh-KWAHYUHR]		She acquired Spanish quickly.	
1322	중등	결국, 마침내	[1256] ultimately
eventually [ih-VEN-choo-uh-lee]		We eventually finished the project.	

1323 **vision** [VIZH-uhn]	편입	1. 시력, 시야 2. 예지력, 선경지명 3. 영상, 화상	envision (상상하다) visionary (공상가) [1073] dream
		I want to improve my night vision.	
1324 **corner** [KAWR-ner]	초등	1. 모서리, 모퉁이 2. 구석, 외딴 곳 3. 곤경, 궁지(에 몰아넣다) 4. 다가가다	
		You should make a right turn at the corner.	
1325 **upgrade** [UHP-greyd]	토익	1. 개선하다 2. 승진, 승급시키다	[401] improve
		The company needs to update its website.	
1326 **occasion** [uh-KEY-zhuhn]	중등	1. 때, 경우 2. 행사 3. 이유, 원인	occasionally (때때로) [302] event
		There are occasions in life when you can't control what's happening.	
1327 **coast** [kohst]	중등	1. 해안, 연안 2. 부드럽게 움직이다 3. 수월하게 하다	coastal (해안의) coastline (해안선) [2866] shore
		We drove along the coast.	
1328 **fat** [fat]	초등	1. 비만인, 뚱뚱한 2. 지방, 기름 3. 두툼한, 많은	[7063] chubby
		He is fat.	
1329 **muscle** [MUHS-uhl]	중등	1. 근육 2. 힘, 근력 3. 힘으로 밀고 들어가다	muscular (근육적인)
		She pulled a muscle in her back.	
1330 **gun** [guhn]	중등	1. 총, 대포 2. 저격범 3. 고속으로 돌아가다 4. (총으로) 쏘다	gunshot (발포, 포격) [1467] weapon
		He was carrying a gun.	
1331 **hang** [hang]	초등	1. 걸다, 매달다 2. 내려오다, 처지다, 늘어지다	
		Will you hang the calendar on the wall?	
1332 **labor** [LEY-ber]	중등	1. 노동(의), 근로 2. 일, 업무 3. 분만, 진통(을 겪다)	laborious (열심히 일하는)
		More and more robots are displacing manual labor jobs.	
1333 **struggle** [STRUHG-uhl]	중등	1. 투쟁(하다), 분투(하다), 싸우다 2. 힘겹게 나아가다	[697] fight
		He struggled with the robber.	
1334 **secret** [SEE-krit]	중등	1. 비밀(의)진, 기밀 2. 은밀한, 숨겨진 3. 비결, 비법	secretly (비밀리에) secretive (비밀스러운) [1262] hidden
		She has many secrets.	
1335 **configuration** [kuhn-fig-yuh-REY-shuhn]	공무원 편입	1. 구성 2. 배열, 배치 3. 환경 설정	[854] structure
		The specifics for the configuration of the phone differ depending on the phone's manufacturer.	
1336 **wedding** [WED-ing]	초등	결혼(식)	wed (결혼하다) [1018] marriage
		He was invited to his friend's wedding.	

1337 consistent [kuhn-SIS-tuhnt]	중등 토익	1. 일관된, 한결같은 2. 거듭되는 3. ~와 일치하는	inconsistency (일관되지 못함) [2557] persistent
		Our findings are consistent with the theory.	

1338 aid [eyd]	중등	1. 원조, 지원, 도움 2. 보조 기구 3. 돕다	
		Financial aid from the government is of big help to students.	

1339 label [LEY-buhl]	중등	1. 상표, 라벨 2. 딱지, 꼬리표 3. 음반사, 레이블 4. 라벨을 붙이다, 정보를 적다	labeled (~로 분류된) [837] mark
		He thoroughly read the label on the bottle.	

1340 pop [pop]	중등	1. 튀어나오다, 떠오르다 2. 터트리다 3. 팝(음악 장르) 4. 아빠	pop-up (튀어오른) [980] dad
		A good idea popped into my mind.	

1341 default [dih-FAWLT]		1. 채무불이행, 부도 2. 기본값	[621] failure
		Puerto Rico defaulted on $1 billion worth of debt.	

1342 settle [SET-l]	중등	1. 합의하다, 마무리 짓다 2. 결정하다 3. 정착하다	settlement (정착) [1172] resolve
		It is time to settle on a resolution.	

1343 decade [DEK-eyd]	중등	10년	
		Many things can change in a decade.	

1344 capture [KAP-cher]	중등	1. 포착하다 2. 관심을 사로잡다 3. 억류하다	[965] catch
		A brilliant idea always captures people's attention.	

1345 valid [VAL-id]	수능 토익	1. 유효한, 법적 효력이 있는 2. 타당한	validate (입증하다) invalid (효력이 없는) [444] sound
		You need to provide valid information.	

1346 surround [suh-ROUND]	중등	1. 둘러싸다 2. 포위하다	surrounding (둘러싸는) surroundings (주위환경) [1241] encircle
		Korea is surrounded by waters.	

1347 husband [HUHZ-buhnd]	초등	남편	[2742] spouse
		My husband is at work right now.	

1348 dedicate [DED-i-keyt]	수능 토익	1. 헌신하다, 전념하다 2. 바치다, 헌정하다	[2427] devote
		Good parents dedicate their time to their kids.	

1349 pool [pool]	중등	1. 수영장 2. 웅덩이, 못 3. 이용가능한 인력/물자 (ex. 인력풀)	[3196] pond
		Let's play by the pool.	

1350 internal [in-TUR-nl]	중등	1. 내부의, 내재된 2. 내면의	internally (내부에) [1864] interior
		Internal bleeding is often hard to detect.	

1351 quarter [KWAWR-ter]	중등 토익	1. 사분의 일 2. 25센트 3. 사분기 4. 구역	quarterly (분기의) [1155] district
		The first quarter of the year went by smoothly.	
1352 root [root]	중등	1. 근원, 뿌리 2. 핵심 3. 기원	grass-roots (민중의) [534] source
		What is the root cause of the problem?	
1353 candidate [KAN-di-deyt]	중등 토익	1. 후보(자), 지원자 2. ~가 될 가능성이 있는 사람	[140] applicant
		There are many candidates for this job.	
1354 wave [weyv]	중등 토익	1. 파도, 물결 2. 파동, 파장 3. 흔들다	waver (흔들리다, 약해지다) wavelength (파장) [3170] surge
		We are seeing a wave of changes.	
1355 mental [MEN-tl]	중등	1. 정신(의) 2. 마음의	[1684] psychological
		Mental health is as important as physical health.	
1356 motor [MOH-ter]		1. 자동차의 엔진, 모터 2. 운동(신경)의	motorist (운전자) motorial (운동의)
		He owns a famous motor vehicle company.	
1357 wash [wosh]	초등	1. 씻다 2. 세척(하다), 세탁(하다) 3. 휩쓸다	washer (세탁기) washable (물빨래가 가능한)
		Washing hands can prevent many infections.	
1358 invite [in-VAHYT]	초등	1. 초대/초청하다 2. 청하다, 권하다 3. 자초하다	invitation (초대)
		I was invited to the party.	
1359 meal [meel]	중등	식사, 끼니, 한끼	[1113] dinner
		Two meals a day is enough.	
1360 reward [ri-WAWRD]	중등 토익	1. 보상 2. 보상금, 사례금 3. 보상하다, 보답하다	rewarding (가치가 있는) [1787] prize
		He was rewarded for the hard work.	
1361 cat [kat]	초등	고양이	[5767] feline
		Cats are a popular choice for pets.	
1362 athlete [ATH-leet]	중등 토익	운동선수	athletic (운동 신경의)
		He was an athlete when he was in college.	
1363 cloud [kloud]	초등 토익	1. 구름 2. 먹구름, 그림자	cloudy (흐린) [3751] obscure
		Clouds cover the sky right before the rain.	
1364 fruit [froot]	초등	1. 과일 2. 열매 3. 성과, 결실	fruitful (결실이 있는) [130] product
		I chose fruit for dessert.	

1365 appeal [uh-PEEL]	중등	1. 감동시키다, 매력적으로 다가오다 2. 항소 3. 호소 The movie appealed to the audiences' emotions.	[129] call
1366 hire [hahyuhr]	중등	1. 고용하다 2. 빌리다 The company hired a new engineer.	[1194] rent
1367 asset [AS-et]	중등	자산, 재산, 가치 있는 것 The semiconductor industry is our country's biggest asset.	[991] advantage
1368 arrange [uh-REYNJ]	중등 토익	1. 주선하다 2. (시간을)조율하다 3. 정리하다 4. 편곡하다 He arranged a meeting with the client.	arrangement (배열) [350] organize
1369 appointment [uh-POINT-muhnt]	중등	1. 약속 2. 예약 3. 임명 4. 직책 She has an appointment with a doctor.	appoint (임명하다) appointee (피임명자) [276] meeting
1370 waste [weyst]	중등	1. 쓰레기, 폐기물 2. 낭비, 허비하다 3. 쇠약해지다 Human waste is the biggest issue in many cities.	[435] lose
1371 detect [dih-TEKT]	중등	1. 발견하다 2. 탐지하다 3. 감지하다 Terrorists are often hard to detect.	detection (탐지) detective (형사) [857] discover
1372 talent [TAL-uhnt]	중등	1. 인재 2. 재주, 재능 Good schools foster talents.	
1373 spread [spred]	중등	1. 확산(하다), 분산(하다) 2. 펼치다 3. 나누다 4. 빵에 발라먹는 것 Words spread very quickly.	[1062] distribute
1374 infection [in-FEK-shuhn]	수능	감염 A bug bite caused an infection.	[960] disease
1375 magic [MAJ-ik]		1. 마법, 마술 2. 매력 There is no magic formula for success in life.	magical (마법의) magician (마법사) [5964] sorcery
1376 duty [DOO-tee]	중등	1. 의무, 임무 2. 업무 3. 세금, 관세 The government's duty is to protect the people.	[651] responsibility
1377 repair [ri-PAIR]	중등	1. 수리, 수선 2. 바로잡다 Your shoes need to be repaired.	reparation (보상, 수리) [1947] mend
1378 initiate [ih-NISH-ee-eyt]	중등	1. 시작하다 2. 착수하다 We recently initiated a project.	initiative (시작하는 새 계획, 주도권)

1379 **trend** [trend]	중등	1. 추세, 동향, 유행 2. 경향을 따다 We need to keep up with the latest trends.	trendy (유행의) [1417] fashion
1380 **faith** [feyth]	중등	1. 신뢰, 믿음 2. 신앙심 I have good faith in people.	faithful (신뢰하는) [882] trust
1381 **willing** [WIL-ing]	공무원	1. 할 의지가 있는 2. 자발적인 I am willing to make the sacrifice.	unwilling (꺼리는) willpower (의지력) [752] ready
1382 **highlight** [HAHY-lahyt]	편입	1. 강조하다 2. 주목하다 He highlighted the importance of this project.	[1789] emphasize
1383 **study** [STUHD-ee]		1. 공부(하다) 2. 연구(하다), 조사(하다) Study hard for your exam.	[1302] examine
1384 **peace** [pees]	초등	1. 평화, 강화 2. 화평, 화목 We need to bring peace on the Korean Peninsula.	peaceful (평화로운) [1739] quiet
1385 **creature** [KREE-cher]		생물, 생명체 Aliens are creatures from outer space.	[907] animal
1386 **quote** [kwoht]	수능	1. 인용(하다) 2. 옮기다 3. 시세를 매기다 4. 견적 가격 I love to quote famous people.	quotation (인용 글귀) [2142] cite
1387 **intend** [in-TEND]	중등	1. 의도하다 2. 뜻하다 I didn't intend to hurt you.	[184] plan [1527] intention
1388 **modify** [MOD-uh-fahy]	수능 토익	1. 수정, 변경하다 2. 수식하다 Plans have been modified.	modification (수정) [123] change
1389 **port** [pawrt]	중등	항구(도시), 항만 The ship is leaving the port.	[2595] harbor
1390 **billion** [BIL-yuhn]	중등	10억 The company's sales reached 3 billion dollars this year.	billionaire (억만장자) [464] million
1391 **kit** [kit]	중등 토익	장비 세트, 키트 We can easily build furniture with DIY kit products.	[2526] outfit
1392 **clothes** [klohz]		옷, 의류 We can always shop for clothes online.	clothing (의류) clothe (입히다)

1393 **god** [god]	초등	1. 신 2. 하느님, 하나님 He prayed to God at church.	goddess (여신) godly (신 같은) [5229] almighty
1394 **kitchen** [KICH-uhn]	초등	부엌, 주방 The fridge is in the kitchen.	[3531] cuisine
1395 **electronic** [ih-lek-TRON-ik]	중등 토익	전자의 Children these days use electronic devices frequently.	electron (전자 원소) [873] digital
1396 **warning** [WAWR-ning]	중등	경고(문), 주의 The teacher gave his students a warning.	warn (경고하다) [2038] alert
1397 **bright** [brahyt]	초등	1. 환한, 밝은 2. 머리가 좋은, 영리한 3. 유망한 The lights are very bright.	[2178] brilliant
1398 **flat** [flat]	중등	1. 납작한, 평편한 2. 아파트 This area used to be a hill but now it is flat.	flatten (납작하게 하다) [1759] apartment
1399 **tire** [tahyuhr]	중등	1. 피로하게 하다 2. 피곤해지다 3. 타이어 Playing with children tires me.	tired (피곤한) [5248] weary
1400 **symptom** [SIMP-tuhm]	중등	1. 증상, 증후 2. 조짐 The symptoms of a cold include coughing.	[221] sign
1401 **shift** [shift]	중등	1. 옮기다 2. 변화(하다), 전환(하다) 3. 교대(근무) His constantly shifting the chair disrupted the class.	[175] move
1402 **medicine** [MED-uh-sin]	중등	1. 약 2. 의술, 의학 You should take medicine if you are ill.	[1810] medication
1403 **union** [YOON-yuhn]	중등 토익	1. 노동조합 2. 연합, 합동 The union decided to protest against the abuse of workers.	reunion (재회) [500] association
1404 **honest** [ON-ist]	초등 토익	솔직한, 정직한 An honest person cannot lie.	honestly (솔직하게) [3338] sincere
1405 **hall** [hawl]	중등 토익	1. 복도 2. 현관 3. 넓은 방, 공간 My room is on the right side of the hall.	hallway (복도)
1406 **gear** [geer]	중등	1. 도구, 장비 2. 준비하다 3. 기어 I brought the gear to cut the tree.	[889] equipment

128

1407 **awesome** [AW-suh m]	중등	멋있는, 어마어마한	awe (경외감, 놀라움) [887] amazing
		Children think spaceships are awesome.	
1408 **tank** [tangk]		1. (물) 탱크 2. 저장하다 3. (군사) 탱크 4. 급락하다	[503] container
		The tank was almost empty.	
1409 **united** [yoo-NAHY-tid]	중등	통합한, 결합한	unite (연합하다) unity (통합) [642] joined
		East Germany and West Germany are now united.	
1410 **smooth** [smooth]	중등 토익	부드러운, 매끄러운	[1245] soft
		The table had a smooth surface.	
1411 **conversation** [kon-ver-SEY-shuhn]	중등	대화, 담화, 회화	converse (대화하다, 반대) [392] talk
		I had an interesting conversation with my friend.	
1412 **entertain** [en-ter-TEYN]	중등	1. 즐겁게 하다, 접대하다 2. 고려하다, 마음에 품다	entertainment (연예 오락, 즐거움) [3634] amuse
		The clowns were entertaining the children.	
1413 **browse** [brouz]	토익	훑어보다, 검색하다	[4843] graze
		I am browsing through the books at the library.	
1414 **boat** [boht]	초등	배, 보트	sailboat (돛단배) [659] ship
		The boat was sailing on the sea.	
1415 **adapt** [uh-DAPT]	중등 토익	적응하다, 조정하다	adaptation (각색) [985] adjust
		She adapted to the new school.	
1416 **signal** [SIG-nl]	편입	1. 신호, 통신 2. 신호를 보내다	[221] sign
		Wait for my signal before starting the race.	
1417 **fashion** [FASH-uhn]	편입	1. 패션, 유행 2. 하는 방식	fashionable (패션 감각이 있는) old-fashioned (구식의) [529] style
		You should study in Paris if you are interested in fashion.	
1418 **flower** [FLOU-er]	초등	꽃(을 피우다)	florist (플로리스트) [4292] blossom
		Thank you for the beautiful flowers.	
1419 **lord** [lawrd]		1. 왕 2. 하느님 3. 귀족, 경	[914] king
		In the past, lords ruled over civilians.	
1420 **math** [math]	초등	수학, 수리	mathematics (수학) mathematician (수학자) mathematical (수학적인)
		Her favorite subject is math.	

1421	중등	1. 연기 2. 담배를 피우다, 흡연하다	smoky (연기가 나는)
smoke			
[smohk]		Smoke was coming out from the chimney.	

1422		(책의) 장, 편	[522] section
chapter			
[CHAP-ter]		She read 8 chapters of the book.	

1423	초등	1. 수업, 교육 2. 교훈	[2385] lecture
lesson			
[LES-uhn]		I have English lessons from 10 am today.	

1424	초등	박물관, 미술관	[2023] gallery
museum			
[myoo-ZEE-uhm]		There are many paintings in the museum.	

1425	중등 토익	대체로, 대략	approximate (대략의)
approximately			
[uh-PROK-suh-mit-lee]		My dog is approximately three years old.	

1426	중등 토익	연구실, 실험실	laboratory (연구실)
lab			
[lab]		Please wear safety glasses when entering the lab.	

1427	중등	1. 출연진 2. 투표하다 3. 던지다, 쏟다, 투영하다	[1030] throw
cast			
[kast]		The director recruited the cast for the new movie.	

1428	수능	재산, 사유지	[502] property
estate			
[ih-STEYT]		The wealthy family owned a large estate.	

1429	중등	수술	surgical (수술의)
surgery			[351] operation
[SUR-juh-ree]		This surgery is very risky.	

1430	중등 토익	편리한, 간편한	convenience (편의)
convenient			[2530] handy
[kuhn-VEEN-yuhnt]		Public transporation in Korea is convenient.	

1431	중등	1. 입양하다 2. 채택하다	
adopt			
[uh-DOPT]		I would like to adopt a child in the future.	

1432	수능 토익	1. 물질 2. 실체, 본질	[902] essence
substance			
[SUHB-stuhns]		DNA is the substance composing our genes.	

1433	토익 편입	1. 안내책자 2. 손으로 하는, 수동의	manually (수동으로)
manual			[4217] handbook
[MAN-yoo-uhl]		You should follow the instructions from the manual.	

1434	초등	1. 돌 2. 돌을 던져 죽이다	[1010] rock
stone			
[stohn]		In the past, stones were carved and used as weapons.	

1435	중등	1. ~로 구성되어 있다. 2. ~에 존재하다 3 ~와 일치하다	[503] contain
consist [kuhn-SIST]		The gift basket consists of fruit and candles.	
1436	중등	1. 케이블 2. 전선, 굵은 철제 밧줄	[1028] wire
cable [KEY-buhl]		The TV isn't working, the cable lines must be disconnected.	
1437	중등	생산, 출력	[2032] exit
output [OUT-poot]		The new machine produced more output than 50 workers.	
1438	중등	여성의, 여자의	[744] girl
female [FEE-meyl]		There aren't many female police officers.	
1439	토익 공무원 편입	진단하다	diagnosis (진단) [2412] distinguish
diagnose [DAHY-uhg-nohs]		The doctor diagnosed her disease as cancer.	
1440	중등	은퇴, 퇴직	retire (은퇴하다) [2511] pension
retirement [ri-TAHYUHR-muhnt]		The average retirement age is 54.	
1441	중등 토익	협력, 공동	collaborate (협력하다) collaborative (협력적인) [2147] cooperation
collaboration [kuh-lab-uh-REY-shuhn]		The students worked in collaboration to finish the research.	
1442	중등	1. 외국의 2. 이질적인	foreigner (외국인) [2502] alien
foreign [FAWR-in]		She had a foreign accent.	
1443		센트 (1달러의 100분의 1)	
cent [sent]		One hundred cents is equivalent to a dollar.	
1444	수능	1. 실 2. 실로 꿰다	
thread [thred]		She used some thread and a needle to alter her clothes.	
1445	중등	약한, 힘없는	weakness (약점) [3609] feeble
weak [week]		The newborn puppy was weak.	
1446	중등	1. 문제, 어려움 2. 난처하게 하다, 괴롭히다	troublesome (문제의) troublemaker (문제를 일으키는 사람) [215] problem
trouble [TRUHB-uhl]		Children cause a lot of trouble.	
1447	중등	보장(하다), 보증(하다)	[607] ensure
guarantee [gar-uhn-TEE]		Can you guarantee that this investment is safe?	
1448	초등	노래하다	singer (가수)
sing [sing]		The choir is singing on stage.	

1449 seed [seed]	중등	씨, 씨앗, 종자	[2206] grain
		Farmers purchase seeds every year and plant them.	
1450 magazine [mag-uh-ZEEN]	중등	잡지	[322] store
		The magazine is about fashion.	
1451 bottle [BOT-l]	초등	1. 병 2. 병에 담다	[5613] flask
		The bottle is leaking.	
1452 predict [pri-DIKT]	중등 토익	예언하다, 예측하다	prediction (예측) predictable (예측가능한) [2429] forecast
		No one can predict the future.	
1453 transform [trans-FAWRM]	중등	변형시키다, 바꾸다	transformation (변신) [123] change
		He transformed the house and made it look like a palace.	
1454 sustain [suh-STEYN]	수능	버티다, 지지하다	sustainable (지속 가능한) unsustainable (지속할 수 없는) [172] support
		The pillars were sustaining the weight of the house.	
1455 episode [EP-uh-sohd]	중등	1. 사건 2. ~회	[1567] incident
		Episode 8 is my favorite episode of this show.	
1456 football [FOOT-bawl]	초등	축구	[2755] soccer
		She has football lessons after school.	
1457 capacity [kuh-PAS-i-tee]	공무원 편입	1. 용량, 수용력 2. 능력, 역량	incapacitate (능력을 없애다)
		The bag has a large storage capacity.	
1458 minor [MAHY-ner]	중등	1. 작은, 가벼운 2. 미성년자	minority (소수) [219] small
		Don't worry, this is a minor problem.	
1459 string [string]	중등	1. 끈, 줄 2. 일련(으로 묶다)	[227] line
		The string of my guitar broke.	
1460 shoe [shoo]	초등	신발(한 짝)	
		I lost one shoe and couldn't walk properly.	
1461 experiment [ik-SPER-uh-muhnt]	중등	1. 실험, 시도 2. 실험하다	[275] test
		Mice are often used in science experimentations.	
1462 universe [YOO-nuh-vurs]	중등	우주, 세계	universal (전 세계적인, 보편적인) [136] world
		There are numerous planets in the universe.	

1463	수능 토익	변화(하다), 전환(하다)	transit (운송, 통과)
transition			[1401] shift
[tran-ZISH-uhn]		The city is encouraging people to transition from cars that run on oil to cars that run on electricity.	

1464	중등 토익	1. (맞다고) 의심하다, 의혹을 갖다 2. 피의자 3. 의심스러운	suspicious (의심하는)
suspect			suspicion (의혹)
[suh-SPEKT]		I suspect him of stealing my car.	

1465	중등	1. 그물, 네트 2. 순, 최종의	
net			
[net]		The sailors used a net to catch fish	

1466	토익 공무원	영양	malnutrition (영양실조)
nutrition			[332] food
[noo-TRISH-uhn]		Please consider nutrition before ordering pizza.	

1467	중등	무기	weaponry (무기류)
weapon			[1001] arms
[WEP-uhn]		The criminals tried to hide the weapons from the police.	

1468	중등 토익	1. 애완동물 2. 쓰다듬다	
pet			
[pet]		I have a pet goldfish.	

1469	토익 공무원 편입	준수, 응낙	comply (준수하다)
compliance			[1175] observance
[kuhm-PLAHY-uhns]		The students showed compliance with the teacher's requests.	

1470	중등	하천, 개울	mainstream (주류,대세)
stream			[1178] flow
[streem]		In the summer, let's go to the stream.	

1471	중등 토익	1. 맛, 향미 2. 조미료	flavored (향미를 첨가한)
flavor			[1065] taste
[FLEY-ver]		Kimchi has a spicy flavor.	

1472	수능	제한하다, 한정하다	restriction (제한)
restrict			[402] limit
[ri-STRIKT]		The parents restricted the activity of the child.	

1473	수능 토익	거래, 매매	transactional (거래의)
transaction			[351] operation
[tran-SAK-shuhn]		Financial transactions are made at the bank.	

1474	중등	1. 단단한, 꽉 끼는 2. 빠듯한, 빈틈없는	tighten (꽉 조이다)
tight			[247] close
[tahyt]		The pants were too tight for him.	

1475	중등 GRE	열정, 격정	passionate (열정적인)
passion			[3570] affection
[PASH-uhn]		I am looking for a candidate with passion.	

1476	중등	의심(하다), 의문(을 가지다)	undoubtedly (의심할 여지없이)
doubt			[263] question
[dout]		I doubt he is telling the truth.	

1477	중등	추구하다, 추진하다	pursuit (추구)
pursue			[155] follow
[per-SOO]		You should pursue your dreams.	

1478	중등	접시, 그릇	[1758] dish
plate			
[pleyt]		He put spaghetti onto the plate.	

1479	중등	진화하다, 발달하다	evolution (진화)
evolve			[149] develop
[ih-VOLV]		The company evolved and became bigger.	

1480	중등 토익	1. 꼬리표(를 달다) 2. 붙어 다니다	[1339] label
tag			
[tag]		You didn't take off the price tag from your shirt.	

1481	초등 토익	화장실	[2658] toilet
bathroom			
[BATH-room]		She ran into the bathroom.	

1482	토익	가방, 배낭	[484] pack
backpack			
[BAK-pak]		I bought a new backpack.	

1483	토익	오토바이	
motorcycle			
[MOH-ter-sahy-kuhl]		Never ride a motorcycle without a helmet.	

1484	중등	여행, 여정	[945] trip
journey			
[JUR-nee]		She went on a six-month journey to Australia.	

1485	중등 토익	장학금	[1237] grant
scholarship			
[SKOL-er-ship]		The school gives scholarships to students from rural areas.	

1486	초등	1. 똑똑한 2. 맵시 좋은	[3031] clever
smart			
[smahrt]		If you want to become smart, you should read a lot of books.	

1487	수능 토익	구독하다, 가입하다, 응모하다	subscription (구독)
subscribe			[172] support
[suhb-SKRAHYB]		Please subscribe to my youtube channel.	

1488	중등	1. 공동의, 합동의 2. 관절	[485] common
joint			
[joint]		The research was a joint project conducted by 14 students.	

1489	중등	아무도 없는, 아무도 ~ 않는	
none			
[nuhn]		None of them listened to orders.	

1490	초등	1. 모험, 도전 2. 모험하다, 도전하다	adventurous (모험심이 강한)
adventure			[2317] venture
[ad-VEN-cher]		Traveling alone is an adventure.	

1491	수능	1. 사실상의 2. 가상의, 인터넷의	virtually (사실상)
virtual			[492] practical
[VUR-choo-uhl]		Virtual reality is taking over the world.	

1492	편입	음성의, 녹음의	auditory (청각의)
audio			[444] sound
[AW-dee-oh]		She had an audio recording of her phone call with her children.	

1493	중등	1. 들어 올리다 2. 높아지다, 들리다 3. 차 태워주기	[841] raise
lift			
[lift]		Can you help me lift the chair?	

1494	중등	폭력, 범죄	violent (폭력적)
violence			[395] force
[VAHY-uh-luhns]		Violence is not acceptable in our school.	

1495		저녁, 해질녘	[388] night
evening			
[EEV-ning]		What are you doing this evening?	

1496	중등	시민, 국민	citizenship (시민권)
citizen			[686] resident
[SIT-uh-zuhn]		All citizens have the right to vote.	

1497	공무원 편입	1. 매출, 수입 2. 세입	[1063] income
revenue			
[REV-uhn-yoo]		How much was our revenue today?	

1498	초등	달걀, 알	
egg			
[eg]		Which came first, the chicken or the egg?	

1499		1. 환불(하다) 2. 환불 금액	[160] repay
refund			
[ri-FUHND]		They refused to give me a refund.	

1500	중등	1. 대량의 2. 대중의 3. (형체가 없는) 덩어리 4. (가톨릭) 미사	[4139] heap
mass			
[mas]		A mass of ice was blocking the path for the boat.	

1501	중등	원칙, 법칙	principled (원칙에 의거한)
principle			[516] rule
[PRIN-suh-puhl]		What are your principles in life?	

1502	중등	모으다, 수집하다	gathering (모임)
gather			[420] collect
[GATH-er]		He gathers post stamps.	

1503	중등 토익	재료, 성분	[775] component
ingredient			
[in-GREE-dee-uhnt]		What are the ingredients for cake?	

1504	초등	설탕, 당분	[2603] honey
sugar			
[SHOOG-er]		Sugar is sweet.	

1505	중등	정의, 공평성	[886] fairness
justice [JUHS-tis]		Courts should protect justice.	

1506	수능	1. 헌법 2. 구성, 구조	constitute (구성하다) constituency (선거구, 유권자)
constitution [kon-sti-TOO-shuhn]		The constitution guarantees freedom of speech.	

1507	중등 토익	1. 구속하다, 속박하다 2. 묶다	binding (구속력이 있는) [4058] fasten
bind [bahynd]		A contract binds an employee to the company.	

1508	중등	기도, 기원	pray (기도하다)
prayer [prair]		God hears all our prayers.	

1509		드라마, 연극	dramatic (극적인)
drama [DRAH-muh]		She watches a drama every Sunday/.	

1510	중등	극장, 영화관	
theater [THEE-uh-ter]		I like getting popcorn at the theater.	

1511	중등	지역, 구역	
zone [zohn]		This zone is owned by the government.	

1512	중등	군대, 육군	
army [AHR-mee]		America has a big army.	

1513	중등	1. 실수, 잘못 2. 오인하다, 오해하다	[1092] error
mistake [mi-STEYK]		I'm sorry but it was a mistake.	

1514	중등	빚, 부채	debtor (채무자) indebted (빚이 있는) [1852] liability
debt [det]		University tuitions gave her a lot of debt.	

1515	초등	언덕, 작은 산	[1211] mountain
hill [hil]		A hill is lower than a mountain.	

1516	토익 공무원 편입	(선출될) 자격이 있는, 적임의	eligibility (적격성) [1076] qualified
eligible [EL-i-juh-buhl]		He is an eligible candidate for the president.	

1517		축제, 행사, 페스티벌	fest (=festival) [1134] celebration
festival [FES-tuh-vuhl]		Halloween is a festival for the dead.	

1518	중등	희생자, 피해자	[3868] prey
victim [VIK-tim]		He was a victim of bullying.	

1519	중등	종, 종류	[281] type
species [SPEE-sheez]		There are many species of animals in the world.	

1520	중등	입력, 투입	[365] entry
input [IN-poot]		The output was not worth the input.	

1521	중등 토익	상기시키다, 생각나게 하다	reminder (상기시키는 것) [622] remember
remind [ri-MAHYND]		Please remind me to do my assignment.	

1522	중등	~도 또한 아니다, ~도 ~않다	[1913] neither
nor [nawr]		He was neither smart nor kind.	

1523	중등	강렬한, 강한	intensity (강도) [498] strong
intense [in-TENS]		She experienced intense pain.	

1524	중등	유전자	genetic (유전적인)
gene [jeen]		Genes are inherited from our parents.	

1525	초등	1. 다리 2. ~사이에 다리를 놓다	
bridge [brij]		The bridge connects the islands.	

1526	중등	1. 전시하다 2. 전시회	exhibition (전시) [699] display
exhibit [ig-ZIB-it]		They were exhibiting paintings of French artists.	

1527	중등 토익	의지, 의도, 고의	intent (의도) intentionally (의도적으로) [768] purpose
intention [in-TEN-shuhn]		I had no intention of hurting you.	

1528	중등 토익	휴식을 취하다, 쉬다	relaxation (휴식)
relax [ri-LAKS]		Please relax when you are ill.	

1529	초등	1. 사슬, 쇠줄 2. 체인점 3. 연속, 연쇄	[1459] string
chain [cheyn]		She secured her bike to the fence with a chain.	

1530	중등	1. 부문, 분야 2. 업종	[177] area
sector [SEK-ter]		Workers from the public sector include police officers and firefighters.	

1531	중등 토익	포럼, 회의, 토론회	[2435] assembly
forum [FAWR-uhm]		The UN held a forum about environmental protection.	

1532	중등	가시의, 보이는	visibility (눈에 보이는) invisible (보이지 않는) [372] clear
visible [VIZ-uh-buhl]		The rise in sea levels was visible.	

1533	초등	1. (나뭇)잎 2. 넘기다	
leaf			
[leef]		There was an ant on the leaf.	

| 1534 | 중등 | ~대, 상대하다 | vs (=versus)
[344] against |
|---|---|---|---|
| versus | | | |
| [VUR-suhs] | | The football game was Korea versus Japan. | |

| 1535 | 중등 | 다양한, 여러가지의 | diversity (다양성)
diversify (다각화)
[762] various |
|---|---|---|---|
| diverse | | | |
| [dih-VURS] | | People have diverse personalities. | |

| 1536 | 중등 | 1. 공예 2. 만들다 3. 선박, 항공기 4. 기술 | handcraft (수공예)
[659] ship |
|---|---|---|---|
| craft | | | |
| [kraft] | | She was skilled at the craft of making jewelry. | |

1537	중등	비용, 지출	[297] cost
expense			
[ik-SPENS]		She kept records of her expenses to save money.	

| 1538 | 중등 | 두꺼운, 굵은 | thickness (두께)
[2258] dense |
|---|---|---|---|
| thick | | | |
| [thik] | | The tree had thick branches. | |

| 1539 | 중등 | 왕실의, 왕족의 | royalty (왕족의)
[6074] regal |
|---|---|---|---|
| royal | | | |
| [ROI-uhl] | | She was from the royal family. | |

1540	중등	단백질	
protein			
[PROH-teen]		Consuming protein is necessary to build muscles.	

1541	중등 토익	1. 악기 2. 도구, 기구	[505] tool
instrument			
[IN-struh-muhnt]		The violin is my favorite instrument.	

1542	수능 토익	1. 끝의, 종점의, 말기의 2. (공항) 터미널	[360] final
terminal			
[TUR-muh-nl]		She had terminal cancer.	

1543	중등	1. 힘든, 어려운 2. 강한	[308] hard
tough			
[tuhf]		Running a marathon is tough.	

| 1544 | 초등 | 1. 의자 2. 의장 | armchair (안락의자)
[584] president |
|---|---|---|---|
| chair | | | |
| [chair] | | Please sit down on this chair. | |

1545	중등 토익	남성의, 수컷의	[4718] masculine
male			
[meyl]		He had a deep male voice.	

| 1546 | 중등 토익 GRE | 1. 종합적인, 포괄적인 2. 이해가 빠른 | comprehend (이해하다)
[608] extensive |
|---|---|---|---|
| comprehensive | | | |
| [kom-pri-HEN-siv] | | The newspaper was comprehensive and covered many subjects. | |

1547 **wild** [wahyld]	중등	1. 야생의 2. 거친, 야만적인 Cats used to be wild animals.	[1776] crazy
1548 **enemy** [EN-uh-mee]	중등	적, 원수 A soldier must be prepared to kill his enemies.	[1169] opponent
1549 **pure** [pyoor]	중등 토익	1. 순수한 2. 완전한 The water was very pure.	purely (순수하게) purity (순수함)
1550 **abuse** [uh-BYOOZ]	중등 토플	1. 학대(하다) 2. 남용(하다) You shouldn't abuse animals.	
1551 **professor** [pruh-FES-er]	중등	1. 교수, 선생 2. 박사 My professor is very smart.	
1552 **module** [MOJ-ool]		모듈, (구성) 단위 This factory creates tires, handles, and other modules for bikes.	[633] unit
1553 **sheet** [sheet]	중등 토플	1. 판, 시트, 얇은 층 2. 침구 등의 커버 She changed the sheets on her bed.	[700] layer
1554 **icon** [AHY-kon]		1. (컴퓨터의) 아이콘, 상징 2. 존경받는 인물 Press this icon to use the internet.	[397] image
1555 **kick** [kik]	초등	(발로) 차다 He gave the ball a powerful kick.	[2594] punch
1556 **donate** [DOH-neyt]	중등 토익	기부하다, 기증하다 Please donate your unworn clothes.	donation (기부)
1557 **bowl** [bohl]	초등	1. 사발, 접시 2. 볼링 There were three apples in the bowl.	
1558 **minister** [MIN-uh-ster]	중등 토익 토플	1. 장관, 각료 2. 성직자, 목사 The minister of defense is on the news.	ministry (정부부처)
1559 **formula** [FAWR-myuh-luh]	수능 토익 토플	공식, 법식, 형식 If you follow the math formula, you will get the question correct.	
1560 **familiar** [fuh-MIL-yer]	중등 토익	익숙한, 친숙한 You look very familiar.	familiarize (익숙하게 하다) [426] usual

1561	중등 토플	1. 교도소, 감옥 2. 투옥하다	prisoner (죄수)
prison			imprisonment (투옥)
[PRIZ-uhn]		There are 100 prisoners in this prison.	[2619] jail

1562	초등	1. 부츠, 장화 2. 부팅하다	
boot			
[boot]		I wear boots when it rains.	

1563	중등 토익 토플	복원하다, 회복하다	[231] recover
restore			
[ri-STAWR]		Please restore the data on my phone.	

1564	중등	만(灣)	[4668] cove
bay			
[bey]		The waves rushed into the bay.	

1565	중등 토익	1. 산 2. 신맛(이 있는)	acidic (산성의)
acid			[3130] bitter
[AS-id]		Acid rain can melt stone.	

1566	중등	북돋우다, 증가하다	[280] increase
boost			
[boost]		She boosted my confidence.	

1567	중등 토익	사건, 사고	incidentally (우연히)
incident			[302] event
[IN-si-duhnt]		The police investigated the incident.	

1568	중등 토플	1. 불다 2. 타격	overblown (도가 지나친)
blow			[2431] ruin
[bloh]		The wind was blowing.	

1569	중등	1. 시력 2. 광경	
sight			
[sahyt]		She lost her sight when she was seven and cannot see.	

1570	중등	1. 줄 2. (노를 써서) 배를 젓다	
row			
[roh]		I will sit at the front row and watch you perform.	

1571	중등 토익 토플	1. 부탁 2. 호의, 친절 3. 이익, 유리함	favorable
favor			(유리한, 호의적인)
[FEY-ver]		Can you do me a favor and pick up that pen?	

1572	중등	1. 각도 2. 모서리	[5730] slant
angle			
[ANG-guhl]		The tree is leaning at an angle.	

1573	중등 토익 토플	점령하다, 차지하다, 거주하다	occupant (점유자)
occupy			[895] engage
[OK-yuh-pahy]		The army occupied the conquered territory.	

1574	중등	1. 미끄러지다 2. 하락하다 3. 미끄럼틀	landslide
slide			(산사태, 압도적 승리)
[slahyd]		His car slid down the slope.	[2086] slip

1575 수능 토익 토플	1. 조정하다, 조직화하다 2. 좌표	coordinated (합동된)
coordinate		
[koh-AWR-dn-it]	The leader should coordinate the works of the team.	

1576 중등	1. 화학물질 2. 화학의	
chemical		
[KEM-i-kuh l]	Do not pour chemicals into the river.	

1577 중등	강철, 스틸	
steel		
[steel]	Steel is used to make weapons such as swords.	

1578 수능 토익 토플 GRE	1. 관습, 관례 2. 협약, 약속 사항 3. 총회, 대표회의	conventional (관습적인) [276] meeting
convention		
[kuhn-VEN-shuhn]	It is a social convention to give presents on birthdays.	

1579 중등	냉동하다, 얼리다	frozen (냉동된) freezer (냉동고)
freeze		
[freez]	If you freeze water it turns into ice.	

1580 중등 토플	1. 동료, 동지 2. 녀석, 친구	[3510] buddy
fellow		
[FEL-oh]	The fellow worker promised to help me finish the task.	

1581 중등	1. 혼동하다 2. 혼란 시키다	[6326] confound
confuse		
[kuhn-FYOOZ]	The twins confused their parents.	

1582 중등 토익	1. 듣자 하니, 겉보기에는 2. 분명히, 명백히	apparent (분명한)
apparently		
[uh-PAR-uhnt-lee]	Apparently, she lied to her children.	

1583 중등 토익	1. 정말로, 확실히 2. 그뿐 아니라	[296] actually
indeed		
[in-DEED]	It is very cold indeed.	

1584 토익 공무원 편입	불쾌한, 무례한, 공격적인	offense (공격, 범죄) [3788] foul
offensive		
[uh-FEN-siv]	The teacher criticized his offensive actions.	

1585	세대	[2137] era
generation		
[jen-uh-REY-shuh n]	The younger generation loves Gucci.	

1586	1. 매개체 2. 중앙값	[1047] middle
medium		
[MEE-dee-uhm]	The radio was a very big medium.	

1587	1. 코트, 외투 2. 칠하다	[231] cover
coat		
[koht]	Please wear a coat, it is cold outside.	

1588 중등	1. 지능, 지성 2. 정보	intelligent (지능이 있는) intelligible (이해하기 쉬운)
intelligence		
[in-TEL-i-juhns]	Intelligence is a valued trait.	

1589	초등 토익	(음식을) 굽다	bakery (제과점)
bake			[1058] cook
[beyk]		He is backing a pie.	

1590	중등 토익 토플	1. 어조, 말투 2. 소리, 음성 3. 색조 4. 분위기	tonality (음조)
tone			[444] sound
[tohn]		Her scary tone made the children cry.	

1591	중등 토익	동기를 주다, 자극하다	motivation (동기부여)
motivate			motive (동기)
[MOH-tuh-veyt]		Please motivate the students to work hard.	[929] encourage

1592	초등	1. 모자 2. 뚜껑 3. 모자를 씌우다	[244] top
cap			
[kap]		It is hot outside, please wear a cap.	

1593	중등 토익	번역하다, 해석하다	translation (번역)
translate			[1651] interpret
[trans-LEYT]		Can you translate Korean to English?	

1594	초등	1. 희극의, 우스꽝스러운 2. 코메디언, 희극인	comedy (코미디)
comic			
[KOM-ik]		Everyone thought it was comic when he slipped and fell on the floor.	

1595	중등 토익 토플	1. 묘기, 속임수 2. 속이다	[3383] deceive
trick			
[trik]		The magician showed the audience a magic trick.	

1596	중등 토플	민주적인, 민주주의의	democracy (민주주의)
democratic			[735] popular
[dem-uh-KRAT-ik]		In democratic nations, the citizens vote for their leaders.	

1597	초등	사고, 재난	accidentally (우연히)
accident			[1788] crash
[AK-si-duhnt]		A car accident killed them both.	

1598	초등	새, 조류	
bird			
[burd]		My favorite bird is the parrot.	

1599	초등	몹시 싫어하다, 미워하다	hatred (증오)
hate			
[heyt]		I hate onions.	

1600	초등	1. 사냥하다 2. 추적하다	[2251] chase
hunt			
[huhnt]		They went hunting for geese.	

1601	중등	1. 외진, 외딴 2. 원격의	[1208] distant
remote			
[ri-MOHT]		Their destination was the remote valley.	

1602	중등	1. 출생의, 토착의 2. 원주민의	[3278] indigenous
native			
[NEY-tiv]		Native wildlife should be protected.	

1603 **pitch** [pich]	수능 토플	1. 투구하다, 던지다 2. 음색 3. (천막을) 치다	pitcher (투수) [2890] toss
		The baseball player pitched the ball at the stadium.	
1604 **column** [KOL-uhm]	중등 토플	1. 기둥 2. 열, 세로줄 3. 신문기고	columnist (기고가(칼럼니스트)) [3838] pillar
		The columns were supporting the roof.	
1605 **stretch** [strech]	중등 토플	1. 기지개를 켜다, 스트레칭하다 2. 잡아당기다, 늘리다	[608] extend
		Don't forget to stretch every day.	
1606 **graphic** [GRAF-ik]	중등 토익	1. 사실적인, 생생한 2. 도표의 3. 시각예술, 그래픽	[3937] vivid
		Scenes showing graphic violence have been censored.	
1607 **self** [self]	중등	자기 자신, 본인	selfish (이기적인) selfless (이타적인)
		While Molly was her usual quiet self, it was obvious she was excited.	
1608 **retain** [ri-TEYN]	수능 토익 토플	유지하다, 간직하다	retention (잔여, 보유) [147] keep
		I cannot retain so much information.	
1609 **seal** [seel]	중등 토플	1. 봉인(하다) 2. 물개	[247] close
		She sealed the letter with wax.	
1610 **possession** [puh-ZESH-uhn]	중등 토익 토플	재산, 소유물	possess (보유하다) possessor (소유자)
		Happiness is more important than having a large possession.	
1611 **upper** [UHP-er]	중등	위의, 상부의	
		Do you want to use the upper bunk or the lower bunk?	
1612 **phase** [feyz]	수능 토익 토플	1. 단계 2. 단계적으로 시행하다	[852] stage
		The next phase of growth for a caterpillar is to become a butterfly.	
1613 **twice** [twahys]		두 번	[1086] double
		He looked at me twice.	
1614 **bin** [bin]	중등	상자	
		Throw your trash into that bin.	
1615 **civilize** [SIV-uh-lahyz]		문명화 하다	[354] educate
		A civilized person will most likely not survive in the wilderness.	
1616 **republican** [ri-PUHB-li-kuhn]	중등 토익	1. 공화당원 2. 공화당의	republic (공화국)
		He was a devoted member of the Republican party, but not a politician in the strict sense.	

1617 **concentration** [kon-suhn-TREY-shuhn]	중등 토익	1. 집중 2. 수용소	concentrate (집중하다) [447] focus
		Don't lose your concentration, focus on the test.	
1618 **accommodate** [uh-KOM-uh-deyt]	중등 토익 토플	1. (손님 등을) 수용하다 2. (남의 의견 등을) 수용하다	accommodation (숙박) [1415] adapt
		This hotel can accommodate 250 guests.	
1619 **birth** [burth]	초등 토익 토플	탄생, 출생	birthday (생일)
		They celebrated the birth of their first child.	
1620 **blend** [blend]	중등	1. 섞다, 융화하다 2. 혼합물	[613] combine
		Blend the strawberries and bananas to make a smoothie.	
1621 **sponsor** [SPON-ser]	토익 토플	1. 후원자 2. 후원하다	sponsorship (후원) [172] support
		Our company will sponsor the Olympics this year.	
1622 **sister** [SIS-ter]	초등	1. 여동생 2. 언니 3. 누나 4. 자매	
		Do you have any sisters?	
1623 **wrap** [rap]	중등 토플	1. 포장하다, 싸다 2. 포장지	[3168] envelop
		She wrapped the presents and put them under the tree.	
1624 **discount** [DIS-kount]	중등	할인(하다)	[4503] rebate
		They are having a discount on clothes.	
1625 **transmit** [trans-MIT]	수능 토익 토플	1. 전송하다, 발송하다 2. 전염시키다	transmission (전송) [396] send
		The message has been transmitted.	
1626 **eliminate** [ih-LIM-uh-neyt]	중등 토익	제거하다, 삭제하다, 탈락시키다	elimination (탈락) [470] remove
		Eliminate the wrong answers and choose the correct one.	
1627 **forest** [FAWR-ist]	초등 토플	삼림, 숲	deforestation (삼림 파괴) rainforest (열대우림)
		The forest is becoming smaller each year.	
1628 **salt** [sawlt]	초등	소금	salty (짠)
		Can you add more salt to the soup?	
1629 **recruit** [ri-KROOT]	수능 토익 토플	1. 모집하다, 채용하다 2. 신입생, 신병	[259] enlist
		The company is recruiting new members.	
1630 **broad** [brawd]	중등 토익 토플	넓은, 광대한	broaden (넓히다) [579] wide
		The newspaper covers a broad range of issues.	

1631	중등	1. (병, 상처를)낫게 하다 2. 치유되다	[2239] cure
heal [heel]		The wound is healing slowly.	

1632	중등 토플	심각한, 엄숙한	severity (심각성) [2939] harsh
severe [suh-VEER]		She was in severe pain.	

1633		1. 원반 모양 2. 원반 레코드	
disk [disk]		Insert the compact disk(CD) into the computer to play the video.	

1634	중등 토익	동적인, 힘찬	[547] energetic
dynamic [dahy-NAM-ik]		The dynamic speaker inspired the crowd.	

1635	초등 토익	1. 군중, 관객 2. 붐비다	crowded (붐비는) [6969] throng
crowd [kroud]		The crowd began to cheer.	

1636	중등	1. 자랑스러운 2. 거만한	[4589] arrogant
proud [proud]		The parents were proud of their children.	

1637	수능 토플	1.법안 2. 입법	legislative (입법의) legislature (입법부) [732] legal
legislation [lej-is-LEY-shuhn]		The country's tax legislation is flawed.	

1638	중등	임신	pregnant (임신한)
pregnancy [PREG-nuhn-see]		She purchased a pregnancy test kit at the store.	

1639	초등 토익	끌다, 견인하다	[3442] haul
tow [toh]		The truck towed the broken car to the repair shop.	

1640		닭	chick (병아리) [5414] coward
chicken [CHIK-uhn]		Chickens were being raised at the farm.	

1641	중등 토익 토플	1. 가장 중요한 2. 전성기	primal (최초의, 근본의) primacy (최고) [968] primary
prime [prahym]		The prime concern these days is global warming.	

1642	초등 토익 토플	1. 벌레, 곤충 2. 오류, 버그 3. 괴롭히다	[2465] annoy
bug [buhg]		He is scared of bugs such as bees.	

1643	중등	영혼, 정신	[923] spirit
soul [sohl]		She has a kind and pure soul.	

1644	초등	1. 우유 2. 젖을 짜다	[3124] dairy
milk [milk]		Pour the milk into the cup.	

1645	공무원	1. 난타하다, 두드리다 2. 영국의 화폐 단위 3. 무게단위(lb)	pounding (강하게 치는, 두근두근하는)
pound			[1187] beat
[pound]		Someone was pounding at his door.	

1646	초등 토플	뼈	
bone			
[bohn]		She broke a bone playing football.	

1647	편입	1. 대본, 각본 2. 대본을 쓰다	scripted (각본이 있는)
script			[168] writing
[skript]		Actors should memorize their script.	

1648	수능 토익 토플	임시의	temporarily (임시로)
temporary			[5116] transient
[TEM-puh-rer-ee]		She found temporary employment.	

1649	중등 토익 토플	1. 성공하다 2. ~의 뒤를 잇다	successive (연속적인) successor (후계자)
succeed			succession (연속, 상속물)
[suhk-SEED]		Everyone wants to succeed in life.	

1650	중등 토익	통찰력, 간파력	[317] understanding
insight			
[IN-sahyt]		The book gives readers insight into World War II.	

1651	중등 토익 토플	1. 해석, 이해 2. 통역	interpret (해석하다) interpreter (통역사)
interpretation			misinterpret (오해석하다)
[in-tur-pri-TEY-shuhn]		A poem can have many interpretations.	[630] explanation

1652	중등 토플	관, 튜브	[1919] pipe
tube			
[toob]		The tube was clogged.	

1653	토익 토플	1. 인터페이스 2. 접속기, 접점 3. 접속하다, 접하다	
interface			
[IN-ter-feys]		The user interface should be simple and accessible.	

1654	중등 토익	1. 방식 2. 예의	mannerism (매너리즘, 버릇)
manner			[1417] fashion
[MAN-er]		People found his rapid manner of talking to be incomprehensible.	

1655	중등	부정/부인하다, 거절하다	undeniable (부정할 수 없는)
deny			[1690] refuse
[dih-NAHY]		The criminal denied his crime.	

1656		정말, 매우	[296] actually
really			
[REE-uh-lee]		It is really hot in here.	

1657		사업, 기업	businessman (사업가, 직장인)
business			
[BIZ-nis]		I started my own business.	

1658		조직, 기관	[854] structure
organization			
[awr-guh-nuh-ZEY-shuhn]		The UN is an international organization.	

1659	중등	이상한, 익숙지 못한	stranger (낯선 사람) [2265] weird
strange			
[streynj]		They saw many strange faces in the crowd.	

1660	중등 토익	1. 외부의 2. 외관의, 피상적인	
external			
[ik-STUR-nl]		External appearance is not as important as internal characteristics.	

1661	토플	1. 경계하다, 보호하다 2. 경비원, 보초	[476] watch
guard			
[gahrd]		Please stand guard and protect this painting.	

1662	초등	여성, 귀부인	[307] woman
lady			
[LEY-dee]		A nice lady at the library helped me find a book.	

1663		1. 마당, 운동장 2. 야드 (약 91cm)	[2981] backyard
yard			
[yahrd]		The children were playing in the yard.	

1664	수능 토플	1. 뒤, 배후 2. 양육하다	
rear			
[reer]		The chair's rear legs were broken.	

1665	토익	1. 막다 2. 마개 3. 플러그 4. 꽂다	unplug (플러그를 뽑다) [439] stopper
plug			
[pluhg]		She plugged the wine bottle with a cork.	

1666	중등	대답(하다), 답장(하다)	[540] answer
reply			
[ri-PLAHY]		Why aren't you replying to me?	

1667	중등 토익	꾸미다, 장식하다	decoration (장식) [4509] adorn
decorate			
[DEK-uh-reyt]		Would you like to decorate the Christmas tree with me?	

1668	중등	(마시는) 차	
tea			
[tee]		She preferred tea over coffee.	

1669	중등 토익	정밀 검사, 점검	inspect (검사하다) [1302] examination
inspection			
[in-SPEK-shuhn]		We had to wait for the inspection before we could use the elevator.	

1670	중등	빛나다, 번득임, 섬광	flashy (화려한) [5981] gleam
flash			
[flash]		As the lightning hit, there was a big flash.	

1671	중등	1. 짧은, 단시간의 2. 보고하다	briefing (간단한 보고) [443] short
brief			
[breef]		There was a brief pause.	

1672	수능	부분, 몫	
portion			
[PAWR-shuhn]		What will be my portion of the revenue?	

1673 noise [noiz]	중등 토익	소음 What was all the noise last night?	noisy (시끄러운) [444] sound
1674 alcohol [AL-kuh-hawl]		술, 알코올 Children cannot drink alcohol.	alcoholic (알코올 중독자) [4319] liquor
1675 rain [reyn]	초등 토익 토플	비(가 오다) The farmers were happy to see the rain.	rainy (비가 오는) rainfall (강우량)
1676 premium [PREE-mee-uhm]	수능 토익	1. 고품질, 고급 2. 상금, 상여금 (bonus) 3. 보험료, 할증금, 수업료 (fee) You can sign up for the premium service and remove ads from your application.	[1884] bonus
1677 grand [grand]	중등 토플 GRE	1. 웅장한, 장엄한 2. 1000$ Their house had a grand ballroom.	grandeur (장엄한) grandiose (거창한) [3408] magnificent
1678 perspective [per-SPEK-tiv]	수능 토익	관점, 시각 He has an interesting perspective.	
1679 objective [uhb-JEK-tiv]	중등 토익	1. 객관적인 2. 목표(의) Math has objective answers whereas literature does not.	[560] goal
1680 tune [toon]	중등 토익	1. 곡, 노래 2. 조율하다 He was humming a tune I didn't recognize.	[989] song
1681 climb [klahym]	초등 토플	오르다, 등반하다 I would like to climb that mountain.	[836] rise
1682 sorry [SOR-ee]	초등	유감스러운, 미안한 I'm sorry to hear that you are ill.	[3497] miserable
1683 context [KON-tekst]	중등 토익	1. (어떤 일의) 정황 2. 문맥 Please consider the historical context behind this event.	[1258] background
1684 psychology [sahy-KOL-uh-jee]	중등 토익 토플	심리학 He is studying psychology at university.	psychological (심리학의) [1060] behaviorism
1685 edition [ih-DISH-uhn]	공무원	판, 부수 The newspaper releases a new edition every week.	[517] version
1686 branch [branch]	초등 토플	1. 나뭇가지 2. 지점 3. 가지를 내다 The children broke the branch while climbing the tree.	[635] department

1687 scan [skan]	중등	1. 자세히 조사하다, 훑어보다 2. 스캔하다	scanner (스캐너) [1302] examine
		I scanned through the book to find relevant information.	
1688 motion [MOH-shuhn]	중등	1. 움직임, 동작 2. 몸짓으로 신호하다	[175] movement
		She shook her head rapidly and this motion made her dizzy.	
1689 horse [hawrs]	초등	말	horseback (말을 타서) [4683] pony
		There are horses on the farm.	
1690 refuse [ri-FYOOZ]	중등 토익 토플	거절하다, 사절하다	refusal (거절) [2030] reject
		She refused the offer to go hiking.	
1691 village [VIL-ij]	중등	마을, 촌락	
		The village is far away from the city.	
1692 sad [sad]	초등	슬픈, 슬퍼하는	sadly (슬프게도) sadness (슬픔) [594] unhappy
		She was sad that her dog died.	
1693 grandmother [GRAN-muhth-er]	초등	할머니	grandfather (할아버지) grandchild (손자) grandparent (조부모) granny (할머니)
		My grandmother bakes me cookies.	
1694 domain [doh-MEYN]	중등 토익	1. 범위, 분야 2. 영토, 영역	[2109] territory
		The paper had a big impact on the domain of biology.	
1695 planet [PLAN-it]	중등	행성, 유성	[136] world
		There are many planets in the universe.	
1696 illustrate [IL-uh-streyt]	중등 토익 토플	1. 삽화를 넣다 2. 설명하다	illustration (삽화)
		She illustrates a book with drawings	
1697 delay [dih-LEY]	중등	지연(시키다), 연기(하다)	[4705] postpone
		The train has been delayed.	
1698 supplement [SUHP-luh-muhnt]	수능 토익	보충(하다), 보완(하다)	[2660] complement
		You should supplement your diet by taking vitamin pills.	
1699 terror [TER-er]	공무원	1. 공포, 두려움 2. 테러	terrorist (테러범) terrorism (테러) terrifying (공포스러운) [1198] fear
		The ghost stories made the children feel terror.	
1700 symbol [SIM-buhl]	중등 토익	상징, 기호	symbolic (상징적인) symbolize (상징하다) [221] sign
		The eagle is a symbol of the United States	

1701	토익 공무원 토플	1. 뚜렷한, 독특한 2. 별개의	distinction (구별) distinctive (독특한)
distinct [dih-STINGKT]		Cinnamon has a distinct spice.	[372] clear

1702	수능 토익	1회분, 복용량	dosage (복용량) overdose (과다 복용)
dose [dohs]		Only consume one dose of medicine.	

1703	중등 토익	1. 수입하다 2. 수입품	
import [im-PAWRT]		Korea imports beef from Australia.	

1704	초등	영웅, 주인공	heroic (영웅의) heroine (여성 영웅/주인공)
hero [HEER-oh]		Thank you for saving me, you are my hero.	[1082] champion

1705	중등 토익	1. 빠른, 급속한 2. 급류	[421] quick
rapid [RAP-id]		Korea went through rapid development.	

1706	중등 토익 토플	기후, 날씨	[2004] atmosphere
climate [KLAHY-mit]		The climate is growing warmer and warmer.	

1707	중등 토익	1. 결속, 유대 2. 끈 3. 묶다 4. 채권	bonding (유대감) bondage (속박)
bond [bond]		The bond between a mother and a child is strong.	[493] link

1708	중등 토익 토플	1. 손해를 주다, 해치다 2. 피해	harmful (해로운) harmless (무해한)
harm [hahrm]		Do not harm other people.	[1745] hurt

1709	중등 토익	현명한, 영리한	wisdom (지혜) [383] sensible
wise [wahyz]		He was a wise old man.	

1710	중등 토플	떨어진, 분리된	[892] separate
apart [uh-PAHRT]		He lives apart from his parents.	

1711	중등 토익 토플	1. 직물, 천 2. 구조, 짜임새	[511] material
fabric [FAB-rik]		She used soft fabric to make clothes.	

1712	수능 토익 토플	통계학	[252] data
statistics [stuh-TIS-tiks]		The most recent statistics show the disease to be spreading.	

1713	중등 토익 토플	취소하다	
cancel [KAN-suhl]		She canceled plans for tomorrow because she was sick.	

1714	중등 토익 토플	선언하다, 공언하다	declaration (선언)
declare [dih-KLAIR]		He declared that he was innocent	

1715	초등	헤엄치다, 수영	swimming (수영)
swim			swimmer (수영선수)
[swim]		Swimming on a hot summer day is refreshing.	

1716		대규모의, 육중한, 거대한	[939] huge
massive			
[MAS-iv]		A massive crowd turned up at the protest.	

1717	중등 토익	갈등, 충돌	conflicting (상충되는)
conflict			[2329] dispute
[kuhn-FLIKT]		There was a conflict between the two children.	

1718	수능 토익	다수의, 수많은	
numerous			
[NOO-mer-uhs]		Numerous evidence proves global warming.	

1719	중등	1. 거친, 사나운 2. 함부로, 대충	[1543] tough
rough			
[ruhf]		She was rough and inconsiderate.	

1720	수능 토익 토플	1. 초안(을 쓰다) 2. 선발(하다), 징병(하다)	[162] design
draft			
[draft]		The artist drew a few rough sketches	

1721	중등 토익 토플	안심	relieve (해소시키다)
relief			
[ri-LEEF]		The news brought her relief.	

1722	수능 토익	1. 색인 2. 지표	[259] list
index			
[IN-deks]		The index of the book was well organized.	

1723	중등 토익	가정교사, 강사	tutorial (사용 지침서)
tutor			[961] coach
[TOO-ter]		They hired a personal tutor for the child.	

1724	중등 토익 토플	계획, 방법	[184] plan
scheme			
[skeem]		The robbers created a scheme to steal from the bank.	

1725	초등	1. 손가락 2. 손가락을 대다	forefinger (검지손가락)
finger			fingerprint (지문)
[FING-ger]		Her fingers were long and thin.	fingertip (손끝)
			[966] touch

1726	중등 토익 토플	결과	[235] result
outcome			
[OUT-kuhm]		I am satisfied with the outcome.	

1727	중등 토익	상담, 카운슬링	counselor (상담사)
counseling			
[KOUN-suh-ling]		If you are fighting with your wife, I suggest marriage counseling.	

1728	초등	1. 충격 2. 충격을 주다	shocking (충격적인)
shock			[959] surprise
[shok]		The news shocked him.	

1729 **origin** [AWR-i-jin]	중등 토익	기원, 태생 Where is the origin of this rumor?	originate (유래하다) [534] source
1730 **sudden** [SUHD-n]	중등	돌연한, 갑작스러운 He made a sudden decision to move to New York.	suddenly (돌연) [4793] abrupt
1731 **vegetable** [VEJ-tuh-buh l]	초등	야채, 채소 He grows vegetables in his garden.	[640] plant
1732 **attorney** [uh-TUR-nee]	수능 토익	대리인, 변호사 If you cannot afford an attorney, the state will assign one to you.	[338] lawyer
1733 **iron** [AHY-ern]	중등	철, 쇠 The machine was made of iron.	[1577] steel
1734 **sentence** [SEN-tns]	중등	1. 문장 2. 결정, 판결(을 내리다) Please write in full sentences.	[2344] punishment
1735 **circumstance** [SUR-kuhm-stans]	중등 토플	상황, 처지, 환경 He always tried to be happy, even in unfortunate circumstances.	circumstantial (상황에 의한, 추정의) [718] situation
1736 **steal** [steel]	중등 토플	훔치다, 도둑질하다 Someone stole my wallet on the train.	stolen (도난당한)
1737 **holy** [HOH-lee]	중등	신성한, 거룩한 The church is a holy place.	[2519] divine
1738 **excess** [ik-SES]	중등 토익 토플	과도, 과다, 과잉 I am trying to lose excess weight.	excessive (과도한) [4176] surplus
1739 **quiet** [KWAHY-it]	초등	1. 조용한 2. 달래다 Please be quiet in the library.	quietly (조용히) [2260] calm
1740 **delete** [dih-LEET]	중등 토익	삭제하다, 지우다 Please delete my name from the list of participants.	indelible (잊을,지울 수 없는) [470] remove
1741 **murder** [MUR-der]	중등	살인(하다) The murder happened last week.	murderer (살인자) [682] kill
1742 **sufficient** [suh-FISH-uhnt]	중등 토익	충분한 We have sufficient food for the winter.	insufficient (불충분한) suffice (충분하다) [2096] adequate

1743	중등 토익	1. 갑판 2. 층 3. 꾸미다, 단장하다 4. 카드 한 세트	[4509] adorn
deck			
[dek]		It was windy and cold on the deck.	

1744	중등	성서, 성경책	[2878] scripture
bible			
[BAHY-buhl]		All members of the church should read the bible.	

1745	중등	상처(를 입히다), 부상(을 입히다)	[1708] harm
hurt			
[hurt]		He hurt my feelings.	

1746	토익 공무원 토플 편입	결과, 결말	consequently (결과적으로)
consequence			consequential (당연한, 중대한)
[KON-si-kwens]		The consequence of not recycling is pollution.	

1747	중등 토익 토플	1. 정식의, 격식 있는 2. 의례적인, 형식적인	informal (비공식) formality (형식적 절차)
formal			[879] proper
[FAWR-muhl]		This is a formal event, please dress up accordingly.	

1748	중등	1. 휴양지 2. (최종 대안으로) 선택하고 의지하다	[2448] refuge
resort			
[ri-ZAWRT]		We are going to a resort in Hawaii for vacation.	

1749	중등 토익 토플	무작위의, 임의의	[7036] haphazard
random			
[RAN-duhm]		She chose a random student and asked the question.	

1750	수능 토익 토플	합병하다, 통합하다, 포함하다	
incorporate			
[in-KAWR-puh-reyt]		The book incorporated the arguments of both sides.	

1751	중등 토익 토플	영구적인, 영속하는	[143] lasting
permanent			
[PUR-muh-nuhnt]		He regretted getting a permanent tattoo.	

1752	중등 토익 토플	즉시, 즉각적인	instantaneous (즉각적인)
instant			[856] moment
[IN-stuhnt]		Fast food can be cooked instantly.	

1753	중등	1. (옷이나 머리를 고정하는 용도의) 핀 2. 꼭 누르다, 못 박다	[769] fix
pin			
[pin]		She used pins to style her hair.	

1754		마른	[1768] thin
skinny			
[SKIN-ee]		Skinny people should eat more.	

1755	초등	(식용의) 고기	[2683] beef
meat			
[meet]		I prefer fish to meat.	

1756	중등 토익	감소(하다), 저하(하다)	[509] reduce
decrease			
[dih-KREES]		The amount of homework decreased.	

1757	중등	잡다, 쥐다	
grab			
[grab]		She grabbed the child's hand and ran out of the room.	

1758	초등 토익	1. 접시 2. 요리	dishwasher (식기세척기)
dish			[1478] plate
[dish]		We gave them a set of dishes for their wedding present.	

1759		아파트	
apartment			
[uh-PAHRT-muhnt]		They have been living in an apartment for 13 years.	

1760	중등 토익 토플	완수하다, 성취하다	accomplishment (업적)
accomplish			[748] achieve
[uh-KOM-plish]		The spy accomplished her mission.	

1761	토익	암호, 비밀번호	
password			
[PAS-wurd]		He forgot the password again.	

1762	토익 공무원 토플 편입	조정하다, 길을 찾다, 항해하다	navigation (항해)
navigate			circumnavigate (세계 일주하다)
[NAV-i-geyt]		It is difficult to navigate on a rainy day.	[609] guide

1763	수능 토플	1. 방아쇠 2. 촉발하다, 유발하다	
trigger			
[TRIG-er]		She pulled the trigger and shot the gun.	

1764	중등 토익	요약	summarize (요약하다)
summary			[2119] outline
[SUHM-uh-ree]		I didn't have time to read the book so I read a summary.	

1765	중등	맥주	[2234] brew
beer			
[BEER]		Beer is made of wheat.	

1766	중등	1. 눈물 2. 찢다	[2136] rush
tear			
[teer]		His story brought tears to her eyes.	

1767	중등 토익 토플	정확한, 세심한	precision (정확성)
precise			[741] exact
[pri-SAHYS]		Being precise when treating patients is extremely important.	

1768	중등	얇은, 가는	[3259] slim
thin			
[thin]		The thin coat wasn't enough to keep him warm.	

1769	중등 토익 토플	목적지	[845] target
destination			
[des-tuh-NEY-shuhn]		Wake up, we have reached the destination.	

1770	중등 토익 토플	1. 동맹국 2. 동맹하다	alliance (동맹)
ally			[500] associate
[uh-LAHY]		France and England were allies.	

1771 **wing** [wing]	중등	1. 날개 2. (정치) 진영 The bird spread its wings and flew away.	[1686] branch
1772 **legend** [LEJ-uhnd]	중등 토익	전설 Zeus and Hera are from Greek legends.	legendary (전설적인) [2724] myth
1773 **mouth** [mouth]	초등	1. 입 2. 말하다 He stuffed his mouth with candy.	mouthful (한가득) [392] talk
1774 **butter** [BUHT-er]	토익	1. 버터(를 바르다) 2. 아첨하다 Can I have some butter with my toast?	[외래어] cream
1775 **auto** [AW-toh]	중등 토익	1. 자동차 2. 자동의 (automatic의 약자) The auto industry is producing electric cars these days.	
1776 **crazy** [KREY-zee]	초등	미친, 흥분해 있는 When the celebrity appeared, the crowd went crazy.	[2693] insane
1777 **sand** [sand]	초등	모래 Sand got in her shoes.	
1778 **verify** [VER-uh-fahy]	토익 공무원 편입	검증하다, 확인하다 Please verify if this story is true.	verification (인증) [304] check
1779 **yellow** [YEL-oh]	초등	황색의, 노란 Bananas are yellow.	
1780 **depression** [dih-PRESH-uhn]	중등 토익	우울증 She is suffering from depression.	depressed (우울한) [3497] misery
1781 **sharp** [shahrp]	중등 토익	날카로운, 뾰족한 The knife had a sharp blade.	sharpener (연필깎이) [2938] keen
1782 **complaint** [kuhm-PLEYNT]	중등	불만, 투덜거림 He always has so many complaints.	complain (불평하다) [5206] grievance
1783 **attribute** [uh-TRIB-yoot]	중등 토익 토플	1. 속성, 특질 2. ~에 돌리다, ~탓으로 돌리다 The key attributes of our students are passion and enthusiasm.	[374] quality
1784 **valley** [VAL-ee]	중등	골짜기, 계곡 During the summer, many people go to the valley.	

1785	고등	1. 사면(하다), 용서(하다) 2. (실수를 했을 때)실례지만, 죄송합니다	
pardon [PAHR-dn]		He asked for my pardon.	

1786	중등 토익 토플	전망, 가능성	prospectus (설립취지서)
prospect [PROS-pekt]		His prospects as a writer are excellent.	

1787	초등	1. 상, 경품 2. 소중히하다, 귀하게 여기다	prized (소중한)
prize [prahyz]		The prize for winning the tournament was a free trip to Europe	

1788	중등 토익	1. 충돌하다, 붕괴하다 2. 충돌 (사고)	
crash [krash]		Two cars crashed on a rainy day.	

1789	중등 토익 토플	강조, 강세	
emphasis [EM-fuh-sis]		She used a highlighter to put an emphasis on important words.	

1790	초등	왕자, 군주	princess (공주)
prince [prins]		The prince wore a crown.	

1791	중등 토익	보존하다, 유지하다	preservation (보존) [147] keep
preserve [pri-ZURV]		Cultural artifacts should be preserved.	

1792	중등 토익 토플	1. 쇠퇴(하다), 감소(하다) 2. 거절하다	[1756] decrease
decline [dih-KLAHYN]		The economy was in decline.	

1793	중등	무시하다	[654] disregard
ignore [ig-NAWR]		She ignored his phone calls.	

1794	수능 토익 토플	등록하다	enrollment (등록) [675] register
enroll [en-ROHL]		She enrolled her son in school	

1795	중등 토플	승리	victorious (승리한) [3500] triumph
victory [VIK-tuh-ree]		It was a narrow victory.	

1796	중등 토익 토플	1. 단지, 항아리 2. 대마초	pottery (도자기) potable (마실 수 있는) [2995] weed
pot [pot]		She stored honey and sugar in the pot.	

1797	중등 토플	1. 철자를 말하다, 쓰다, 스펠링 2. 주문, 마법	misspelling (틀린 철자) [2312] charm
spell [spel]		Do you know how to spell this word?	

1798		1. 비행기 2. 단면, 평면	[212] level
plane [pleyn]		There is a plane in the sky.	

1799	초등	1. 붓 , 솔 2. 빗다	[3537] scrub
brush			
[bruhsh]		She several brushes to pain.	

1800	수능 토익 토플	1. 분할하다, 분열시키다 2. 갈린, 찢어진	[920] divide
split			
[split]		You should split the pie evenly.	

1801	중등	1. 달아나다, 탈출하다, 도피하다 2. 탈출	
escape			
[ih-SKEYP]		The criminals wanted to escape from prison.	

1802	초등	시험	[275] test
exam			
[ig-ZAM]		He is studying for the exam.	

1803	중등	고대의, 옛날의	[243] older
ancient			
[EYN-shuhnt]		I am interested in ancient history.	

1804	중등 토익 토플	혁명, 격변	revolutionary (혁명적인) revolt (반란)
revolution			
[rev-uh-LOO-shuhn]		The industrial revolution brought permanent changes to society.	

1805	초등	이, 치아	
tooth			
[TOOth]		Her tooth was wobbly.	

1806	중등 토익	1. 신문, 학술지 2. 일기	[810] diary
journal			
[JUR-nl]		Her paper was published in a famous journal.	

1807	중등 토익	사업, 기업	
enterprise			
[EN-ter-prahyz]		This enterprise has the potential to grow.	

1808	중등 토익 토플	1. 확신을 주다, 안심을 주다 2. 보장하다	assurance (확언) [607] ensure
assure			
[uh-SHOOR]		I assured him that traveling to Cambodia was safe.	

1809	중등 토익 토플	삽입하다, 끼워 넣다	[761] introduce
insert			
[in-SURT]		Insert your ticket here.	

1810	토익 공무원	약물	medicate (약물치료하다) [1402] medicine
medication			
[med-i-KEY-shuhn]		He was taking medication for his cold.	

1811	중등 토익	1. 크루즈 2. 유람선 3. 순항(하다)	[2088] sail
cruise			
[krooz]		We signed up for a cruise in the Caribbean sea.	

1812	초등	1. 깨우다 2. 일어나다	[2819] awaken
wake			
[weyk]		I need to wake up at 7 am.	

1813	중등	1. 연설 2. 말, 언어	speechless (말할 수 없는, 말문이 막힌)
speech			[392] talk
[speech]		He enjoyed giving speeches in front of an audience.	

1814	중등	1. 일상적인, 규칙적으로 하는 일 2. 일과	[426] usual
routine			
[roo-TEEN]		Everyone should make routine visits to the doctor.	

1815	초등	1. 테이프 2. 녹화된 영상 3. 녹화하다	[342] record
tape			
[teyp]		I used tape to stick the poster to the wall.	

1816	중등 GRE	1. 체포하다, 붙들다 2. 막다, 저지하다 3. 정지, 저지	[439] stop
arrest			
[uh-REST]		The police arrested the criminals.	

1817	중등 토익 토플	복잡한, 뒤얽힌	[1088] complex
complicated			
[KOM-pli-key-tid]		It was a complicated problem.	

1818	중등 토플	1. 목격자 2. 목격하다 3. 증언	[2291] testify
witness			
[WIT-nis]		Were there any witnesses of the crime?	

1819	초등	하늘	
sky			
[skahy]		The sky was clear and blue.	

1820	중등	1. 경관, 풍경 2. 풍경화	[2417] geography
landscape			
[LAND-skeyp]		The landscape of the countryside was beautiful.	

1821	중등 토플	1. 민속의 2. 일반적인 사람들, 민족	folks (사람들)
folk			
[fohk]		Folk music is very different from modern music.	

1822	중등 토익 토플	1. 훈련(하다) 2. 훈계하다 3. 학문 분야	disciplinary (징계하는)
discipline			[2344] punish
[DIS-uh-plin]		You should discipline your children.	

1823	중등	1. 국경 2. 가장자리, 경계 3. (경계에 붙어) 접하다, 이웃하다	[1070] edge
border			
[BAWR-der]		Canada and the US have adjoining borders.	

1824	초등	주머니	pickpocket (소매치기)
pocket			[4180] pouch
[POK-it]		I keep my wallet and cellphone in my pocket.	

1825	중등 토익	건축학, 설계	[842] construction
architecture			
[AHR-ki-tek-cher]		He studies architecture in school because he is interested in designing buildings.	

1826	중등	어깨	
shoulder			
[SHOHL-der]		She hurt her shoulder while playing basketball.	

1827 **deposit** [dih-POZ-it]	수능 토플	1. 보증금 2. (돈을) 맡기다, 예금하다, 넣다 His deposit was refunded when he returned the car.	
1828 **giant** [JAHY-uhnt]	초등	1. 거인 2. 거대한 The villain of the movie was an evil giant.	[939] huge
1829 **ocean** [OH-shuhn]	초등	바다, 대양 The ocean is home to many creatures.	[1950] marine
1830 **soil** [soil]	중등	1. 흙, 땅 2. 더럽히다 You can grow many crops in fertile soil.	[766] ground
1831 **template** [TEM-plit]	토익	1. 템플릿, 샘플, 본 뜨는 공구 2. 디자인 서식 The teacher taught his students how to write an essay by providing them a template.	[431] model
1832 **sin** [sin]	중등 토익	1. 죄 2. 죄를 짓다 Stealing is a sin.	[5742] trespass
1833 **nerve** [nurv]	중등 토플	1. 신경, 긴장 2. 신경, 뉴런 3. 용기, 강심장 She drank tea to calm her nerves.	nervous (초조해하는) [929] courage
1834 **carbon** [KAHR-buhn]		탄소 Releasing carbon into the air causes pollution.	
1835 **violation** [vahy-uh-LEY-shuhn]	토익 공무원	위배, 침해 Discriminating someone because of their religion is a violation of their human rights.	violate (위반하다) [2628] breach
1836 **smell** [smel]	초등	1. 냄새(를 맡다) 2. 후각 3. 냄새가 나다 She loved the smell of roses	smelly (냄새나는) [2944] scent
1837 **philosophy** [fi-LOS-uh-fee]	중등 토익	철학, 원리 Many ancient Greek scholars studied philosophy.	[3022] doctrine
1838 **tap** [tap]	중등	(가볍게) 치다, 두드리다 He tapped me on the shoulder.	[2320] knock
1839 **liquid** [LIK-wid]	중등 토플	액체, 수분 He sipped the hot liquid and burned his tongue.	liquidity (유동성) [2106] fluid
1840 **charity** [CHAR-i-tee]	중등 토익	자선 단체, 자선 행위 Donating money to charity helps the less fortunate.	charitable (자선의, 베푸는) [2160] goodwill

1841 ease [eez]	중등	1. 쉬움, 편의성 2. 완화하다, 안심시키다	uneasy (불안한) [4170] alleviate
		She got a perfect score on the exam with ease.	

1842 hell [hel]	중등	지옥	
		If you do evil things, you will go to hell.	

1843 odd [od]	중등 토플	1. 기이한, 특이한 2. 홀수의	odds (가능성, 승산) [1659] strange
		Everyone thought he was an odd person.	

1844 supervisor [SOO-per-vahy-zer]	수능 토익 토플	감독관, 관리자	supervision (관리 감독) supervise (감독하다) [167] manager
		A supervisor monitored the children during exams.	

1845 reverse [ri-VURS]	수능 토익 토플	1. 뒤바꾸다, 역행하다 2. 반대, 배후	reversal (반전하다) irreversible (돌이킬 수 없는) [2026] opposite
		The decision was reversed in court.	

1846 suspension [suh-SPEN-shuhn]	수능	1. 정직, 정학 2. 정지	suspend (중단하다) [2824] interruption
		Suspension is used to discipline misbehaving students.	

1847 faculty [FAK-uhl-tee]	수능 토익	1. 교수단, 교직원 2. 능력, 재능	
		The faculty is very intelligent.	

1848 strip [strip]	수능 토플	1. 옷을 벗다 2. 박탈하다	[1190] undress
		He stripped his clothes to go swimming.	

1849 debate [dih-BEYT]	중등 토익 토플	토론(하다), 논쟁(하다)	[647] discuss
		We had a heated debate on the issue of environment protection.	

1850 ear [eer]	초등	귀	[379] hearing
		He whispered in my ear.	

1851 afternoon [af-ter-NOON]	초등	오후	[808] noon
		He spent a quiet afternoon in the park.	

1852 liability [lahy-uh-BIL-i-tee]	토익 공무원 편입	책임, 의무	liable (책임이 있는, 하기 쉬운) [651] responsibility
		Parents have liability over their children.	

1853 chip [chip]	중등	1. 깨진 흔적 2. 조각	[3352] fragment
		There was a chip in the glass.	

1854 luxury [LUHK-shuh-ree]	중등	1. 사치스러운, 고급의 2. 사치품	luxurious (호화로운) [5574] extravagance
		Luxury bags are very expensive.	

1855	중등 토익	재력, 부	wealthy (부유한)
wealth			[368] money
[welth]		Some people like to show off their wealth.	

1856	토익 편입	태양의	
solar			
[SOH-ler]		Solar energy is environmentally friendly.	

1857	중등	빌려주다	lender (빌려준 사람)
lend			[1166] loan
[lend]		I will lend you my car	

1858	초등 토플	갈색	[5813] hazel
brown			
[broun]		The branches of trees are brown.	

1859	중등 토익	논리	logical (논리적인)
logic			illogical (비논리적인)
[LOJ-ik]		His argument does not have any logic.	[1837] philosophy

1860	중등 토플	1. 불길 2. 정열	[655] fire
flame			
[fleym]		The match lit up a flame.	

1861	수능 토익 토플	순서, 차례	sequential (순차적)
sequence			[290] order
[SEE-kwuhns]		The names are in alphabetical sequence.	

1862	토익	최적화하다	optimization (최적화)
optimize			optimum (최적의)
[OP-tuh-mahyz]		The computer program was optimized for the users.	[1046] maximize

1863	중등	1. 웃음 2. 웃다	laughter (웃음)
laugh			[2293] joke
[laf]		His joke made everyone laugh.	

1864		실내, 내부	[692] inside
interior			
[in-TEER-ee-er]		She is decorating the interior of the home.	

1865	중등	닫다, 잠그다	shutter (셔터)
shut			[247] close
[shuht]		Can you please shut the door?	

1866	초등 토익	1. 자르다, 다듬다 2. 동영상, 클립 3. 핀	[3656] clamp
clip			
[klip]		The gardener clipped the branches of the tree.	

1867	중등 토익	처방전	prescribe (처방하다)
prescription			[1402] medicine
[pri-SKRIP-shuhn]		The doctor gave the patient a prescription.	

1868	중등 토플	1. 절정, 정점 2. (산) 꼭대기 3. 정점을 찍다	[2801] summit
peak			
[peek]		Becoming CEO was the peak of his career.	

1869	중등	아주 작은, 미세한	[219] small
tiny			
[TAHY-nee]		Ants are tiny.	

1870	중등	의회	congressman (국회의원) [2435] assembly
congress			
[KONG-gris]		Politicians in congress vote on important policies.	

1871	중등	갈라진 틈, 간격	[6087] hiatus
gap			
[gap]		Drivers should always maintain a gap with the preceding car.	

1872	중등 토익	1. 수출하다 2. 수출품	
export			
[ik-SPAWRT]		Korea exports cars and smartphones.	

1873	중등 토익 GRE	1. 새로운, 신기한 2. 소설	novelist (소설가) [1103] fresh
novel			
[NOV-uhl]		He came up with a novel idea.	

1874	중등 토플	승무원, 선원	[174] team
crew			
[kroo]		The competent crew kept the passengers safe through the rough voyage.	

1875	수능 토익 토플	1. 제휴하다, 관계시키다 2. 합병하다 3. 관련 회사, 회원	affiliation (관계) [500] associate
affiliate			
[uh-FIL-ee-eyt]		The company is affiliated with a university.	

1876	초등 토플	1.옆에, 곁에 2. 비교하여	[389] near
beside			
[bih-SAHYD]		The boy who sat beside him was his son.	

1877	초등	점심	[1113] dinner
lunch			
[luhnch]		I had pizza for lunch.	

1878	중등	폭풍우, 큰비	[3161] rage
storm			
[stawrm]		The storm continued most of the night.	

1879	중등 토플	폭로, 노출	disclose (밝히다) [1080] revelation
disclosure			
[dih-SKLOH-zher]		Celebrities risk disclosure of personal information.	

1880	초등 토익	1. 경쟁, 경기 2. 싸우다, 겨루다	contestant (경기 참가자) [583] competition
contest			
[KON-test]		The school had a math contest.	

1881	중등 토익 토플	1.~의 의무가 있는 2. 묶인, 얽매인 3. ~로 가는 길인, 반드시 하게 될 4. 뛰다, 튀다	boundary (경계선) inbound (안으로 향하는) outbound (밖으로 향하는) rebound (리바운드)
bound			
[bound]		Because she left in such a hurry, she was bound to have left something.	

1882	중등 토익	패드(를 덧대다)	
pad			
[pad]		The chair had a pad on the seat which made it comfortable.	

1883 **proof** [proof]	중등	증명, 증거	proove (증명하다) [956] evidence
		The lawyer provided proof of her client's innocence.	
1884 **bonus** [BOH-nuhs]	토익	보너스, 상여금	[1360] reward
		She received a bonus for the high quality work.	
1885 **perceive** [per-SEEV]	중등 토익 토플	인식하다, 지각하다	perception (인식)
		He finally perceived the truth.	
1886 **glad** [glad]	초등	1. 기쁜 2. 반가운 3. 기꺼이 ~를 하려는	
		I am glad we agree on that matter.	
1887 **literally** [LIT-er-uh-lee]	수능 토플	(말)그대로, 정말로, 실제로	literal (글자 그대로의)
		She literally failed her graduation exam.	
1888 **consciousness** [KON-shuh s-nis]	중등 토익 토플	1. 의식 2. 인식, 생각	conscious (의식하는) unconscious (무의식의)
		He was hit hard and lost consciousness.	
1889 **empty** [EMP-tee]	중등	1. 비어 있는 2. 공허한 3. ~이 없는 4. 비우다	
		We need an empty box.	
1890 **prompt** [prompt]	수능 토익 토플	1. 즉각적인 2. 신속한 3. 촉구하다	promptly (신속히) [421] quick
		Prompt action is necessary.	
1891 **loose** [loos]	중등 토플	1. 느슨해진, 풀린, 헐렁한 2. ~을 마구 늘어놓다	loosen (느슨하게 하다) [216] free
		This screw is loose.	
1892 **passenger** [PAS-uh n-jer]	중등	승객, 탑승객	[757] rider
		No passengers are allowed to smoke in the vehicle.	
1893 **crack** [krak]	중등	1.금, 균열, 틈 2. 갈라지다, 깨지다 3. 해결하다	crackdown (단속) [445] break
		There's a crack in the wall.	
1894 **province** [PROV-ins]	중등 토익 토플 GRE	1. 지방, 주(州) 2. 분야	[2109] territory
		Canada is divided into ten provinces.	
1895 **official** [uh-FISH-uh l]	중등	1. 공식적인 2. 관계자 3. 심판	[179] officer
		Official documents need to be kept safe.	
1896 **stain** [steyn]	중등	1. 얼룩, 때 2. 오점 3. 더러워지다, 더럽히다	stainless (녹슬지않는) [5156] smear
		You have an ink stain on your face.	

1897 **mighty** [MAHY-tee]	막강한, 거대한	[498] strong
	The mighty army planned an attack.	

1898 **snow** [snoh] 초등 토익	눈(이 내리다)	snowflake (눈꽃)
	It snowed a lot last night.	

1899 **enlist** [en-LIST]	입대(하다)	[1629] recruit
	He had to enlist in the army.	

1900 **shade** [sheyd] 중등	1. 그림자, 그늘 2. 색조 3. 빛 가리개	shady (그늘진, 은밀한) [1963] shadow
	Let's go sit in the shade.	

1901 **ideal** [ahy-DEE-uhl]	이상적인	[414] perfect
	She was the ideal person for the job.	

1902 **sole** [sohl] 수능 토익	1. 유일한, 단독의 2. 바닥, 밑창	[548] single
	His sole purpose in life is to be happy.	

1903 **physician** [fi-ZISH-uhn] 토익 공무원	(내과)의사	[877] doctor
	Her father is a physician.	

1904 **rose** [rohz]	1. 장미(색) 2. 올랐다	[외래어] pink
	Roses are red and violets are blue.	

1905 **organ** [AWR-guhn]	1. 몸 속의 장기 2. (악기) 오르간	[1541] instrument
	The patient had to go through an organ transplant.	

1906 **sick** [sik] 초등	1. 아픈 2. 멀미가 나는, 신물나는, 역겨운	sickness (질병) sickening (역겨운) [2113] ill
	She still came to school even though she was sick.	

1907 **ratio** [REY-shoh] 토익	비율	[2241] proportion
	What is your school's ratio of students to teachers?	

1908 **circuit** [SUR-kit] 토익 편입 GRE	1. (전기)회로 2. 순환, 순회	[1241] circle
	Electricity flows through an electric circuit.	

1909 **juice** [joos] 토익	1. 주스, 즙(을 내다) 2. 육즙 3. (위)액	juicy (즙이 많은) [1839] liquid
	Can I have some apple juice?	

1910 **infrastructure** [IN-fruh-struhk-cher] 토익 공무원 토플	인프라, 공공 기반 시설	[250] base
	Creating good infrastructure can contribute to economic growth.	

1911	초등	공장	
factory			
[FAK-tuh-ree]		This factory produces semiconductors.	
1912	수능 토플	1.육성하다, 사육하다 2. 새끼를 낳다 3. 품종, 유형	[410] kind
breed			
[breed]		She owns a ranch where she breeds cattle.	
1913	중등	1. 어느 것도 아니다 2. ~도 아니고 ~도 아니다	
neither			
[NEE-ther]		Neither of us can be there tonight.	
1914	초등	1. 먼지 2. 흙 3. 추문	dirty (더러운)
dirt			[1830] soil
[durt]		My car is covered with dirt.	
1915	수능	1. 베테랑, 전문가 2. 퇴역 군인, 재향 군인, 참전 용사	vet (참전용사, 수의사, 조사하다)
veteran			[171] experienced
[VET-er-uhn]		She went to seek help from a veteran worker.	
1916	초등	1. 깃발, 국기 2. 표시를 하다 3. 지치다, 약해지다	[외래어] banner
flag			
[flag]		Do you know how to draw the national flag?	
1917	중등 토플	1. 날것의, 안 익힌 2. 원자재의, 다듬어지지 않은 3. 노골적인	[1103] fresh
raw			
[raw]		I am allergic to raw oysters.	
1918	중등	1. 축복하다 2. 기도하다 3. 세상에, 맙소사	[2986] sanctify
bless			
[bles]		Bless you, for your kindness.	
1919		1. 관, 배관 2. 파이프 3. 관으로 수송하다	[1652] tube
pipe			
[pahyp]		There's a leak in that pipe.	
1920		토너먼트, 경기, 시합	[1880] contest
tournament			
[TOOR-nuh-muhnt]		He has a soccer tournament next month.	
1921	고등	눈썹	[4892] brow
eyebrow			
[AHY-brou]		He has thin eyebrows.	
1922	중등 토플	1. ~의 것이다 2. 속하다, 알맞은 위치에 있다 3. 소속감을 느끼다	
belong			
[bih-LAWNG]		This book belongs to her.	
1923	중등 토익	1. 대조(하다), 차이(를 보이다) 2. 명암	
contrast			
[kuhn-TRAST]		It is interesting to contrast the styles of the two poets who were best friends.	
1924	토익 편입	1. 도보 여행, 하이킹(을 가다) 2. 급등 3. 대폭 인상하다	[533] walk
hike			
[hahyk]		We are going on a hike.	

1925	수능 토플	1. 장관의, 극적인 2. 화려한 공연	spectacle (장관) [5199] splendid
spectacular [spek-TAK-yuh-ler]		The view from my room is just spectacular.	

1926	편입	1. 수수께끼, 미스터리 2. 신비, 불가사의 3. 추리 소설	mysterious (비밀의) [5599] enigma
mystery [MIS-tuh-ree]		Nature is full of mysteries.	

1927	수능 토익 토플	1. 필수적인, 중요한 2. 생명의 3. 활력이 넘치는	revitalize (다시 활력을 주다) [902] essential
vital [VAHYT-l]		Endurance is vital to success.	

1928	토익	1. 고리, 순환, 회로 2. 순환하며 움직이다	[1271] ring
loop [loop]		Her mind kept turning in an endless loop.	

1929	중등 토플	협상, 협의, 교섭	negotiate (협상하다) negotiable (협상이 가능한)
negotiation [ni-goh-shee-EY-shuhn]		The issue is under negotiation.	

1930	중등	1. 사악한, 악마의, 악랄한 2. 악, 폐해	[3791] wicked
evil [EE-vuhl]		Some people are very evil.	

1931	초등	웃다, 미소(짓다)	[4850] grin
smile [smahyl]		What makes you smile?	

1932	중등 토익 토플	1. 문학 2. 문헌	[168] writing
literature [LIT-er-uh-cher]		She majored in American literature.	

1933	중등	1. 엉망 2. 지저분한 사람, 문제가 있는 사람 3. 엉망으로 만들다	messy (지저분한) [290] disorder
mess [mes]		Your house is a mess.	

1934	중등 토익 GRE	1. 지지자, 옹호자 2. 지지하다, 옹호하다 3. 변호사, 대변자	[172] support
advocate [AD-vuh-keyt]		He is an advocate of free trade.	

1935	중등 토익 토플	1. 촉구하다, 요구하다 2. 재촉하다 3. 강한 욕구, 충동	urgent (급박한)
urge [urj]		We urged him to leave immediately.	

1936	고등	한숨짓다, 탄식하다	
sigh [sahy]		My mom sighed after seeing my report card.	

1937	초등 토익	맛있는, 먹음직스러운	
delicious [dih-LISH-uhs]		That apple looks so delicious.	

1938	수능 토익 토플	1. 의무 2. 채무	oblige (의무로 하게 하다) obligtae (의무화하다) obligatory (의무적인) [1376] duty
obligation [ob-li-GEY-shuhn]		Companies have an obligation to treat all workers equally.	

1939	토익 공무원	1. 거의 ~하지 않는 2. 아주 가끔	[1265] rarely
seldom [SEL-duhm]		He seldom smokes.	

1940	중등	1. 제쳐두고, 제외하고 2. 한쪽으로 3. 따로 4. 여담	[358] away
aside [uh-SAHYD]		We need to set aside our personal opinions for a moment.	

1941	중등 토익	실망한, 실의에 잠긴, 낙담한	[594] unhappy
disappointed [dis-uh-POIN-tid]		She was disappointed with her exam results.	

1942	수능	1. 나사, 못 2. 돌려서 고정시키다, 조이다	[2991] bang
screw [skroo]		You have to tighten those screws.	

1943	공무원	1. 주택 담보 대출, 융자 2. 저당 잡히다	[1166] loan
mortgage [MAWR-gij]		He bought that condo without a mortgage.	

1944	중등	놀라운, 주목할 만한, 대단한	remark (발언) [2704] extraordinary
remarkable [ri-MAHR-kuh-buhl]		She has made remarkable progress.	

1945	토익 공무원 토플	1. 회전하다 2. 교대로 하다	rotation (회전) rotary (순환교차로) [278] turn
rotate [ROH-teyt]		You are supposed to rotate the wheel when making turns.	

1946	공무원	1. 입찰(하다) 2. 가격을 제시하다 3. 유치하다	[164] offer
bid [bid]		I bid $200 for that painting.	

1947	공무원 토플 편입	1. 개정, 수정 2. 미국 헌법 수정 조항, 개정안	amend (개정하다) mend (고치다, 수정하다)
amendment [uh-MEND-muhnt]		Many amendments have been proposed but they were defeated at the polls.	

1948	초등	여왕, 왕비, 왕후	[1393] goddess
queen [kween]		The queen is only a figurehead.	

1949	수능 토익 토플	1. 아카이브, 기록 보관소 2. 파일을 보관하다	[342] record
archive [AHR-kahyv]		Most historians are heavily dependent on archives.	

1950	중등	1. 해양의, 해상의 2. 해병대	submarine (잠수함) [4315] maritime
marine [muh-REEN]		Whales and seals are marine animals.	

1951	초등	어제(의), 과거	[513] past
yesterday [YES-ter-dey]		I visited her yesterday.	

1952		1. 감촉, 질감 2. 직물	
texture [TEKS-cher]		I love the smooth texture of silk.	

1953	수능 토익 토플	각각, 각기	respective (각각의)
respectively			
[ri-SPEK-tiv-lee]		The coffee and cakes cost $5 and $8 respectively.	

1954	중등	1. 곡선, 커브 2. 커브볼 3. 곡선으로 나아가다	[2140] bend
curve			
[kurv]		You need to slow down when approaching a sharp curve.	

1955	수능 토플	평판, 명성, 신용	reputable (평판이 좋은)
reputation			
[rep-yuh-TEY-shuhn]		She has a good reputation.	

1956		1. 계산서, 비용 2. 색인표 3. 일컫다, 묘사하다 4. 탭 키	[1480] tag
tab			
[tab]		He didn't pay the tab.	

1957	초등	아침 식사, 조식	[외래어] brunch
breakfast			
[BREK-fuhst]		I always skip breakfast.	

1958	공무원 토플 편입	1. 큰 감동을 받다 2. 놀라게 하다 3. 기절시키다	stunning (놀랍게 아름다운)
stun			
[stuhn]		I was stunned by her beauty.	

1959	공무원 토플	1. 압축 2. 요약	compress (압축하다)
compression			
[kuhm-PRESH-uhn]		The effectiveness of file compression depends on the format of the file.	

1960	중등 토플	1. 회전(하다), 돌다 2. 돌리다	[278] turn
spin			
[spin]		My head is spinning.	

1961	중등 토플	무서운, 공포스러운	scare (겁을 주다) scared (겁먹은) [5238] spooky
scary			
[SKAIR-ee]		She hates scary movies.	

1962	중등	1. 반짝이다, 환하다 2. 비추다 3. 윤기, 광택	shiny (반짝이는) [5981] gleam
shine			
[shahyn]		I will shine your shoes.	

1963	중등 토플	1. 그림자 2. 어둠, 그늘 3. 일말의 4. 배우기 위해 함께하다	overshadow (가리다) foreshadow (전조가 되다) [1900] shade
shadow			
[SHAD-oh]		Ghosts don't have shadows.	

1964	수능 토익 토플	1. 호환이 되는 2. 양립 가능한 3. 화합할 수 있는	[1337] consistent
compatible			
[kuhm-PAT-uh-buhl]		The new system will be compatible with existing devices.	

1965	중등	항공기	[1798] plane
aircraft			
[AIR-kraft]		There were 20 crew members on the aircraft.	

1966		치즈	
cheese			
[cheez]		I like cheese pizza.	

1967	초등	1. 지붕, 천장 2. 지붕을 덮다	[2567] ceiling
roof [roof]		Fix the roof while the sun is shining.	
1968	수능 토익 토플	1. 추출하다, 뽑다 2. 발췌하다 3. 초록, 발췌 4. 추출물	[470] remove
extract [ik-STRAKT]		Various methods are used to extract olive oil.	
1969	중등 토익	1. 흔들다 2. 털다 3. 악수를 하다 4. 떨다, 떨림	shaky (흔들리는) [5700] tremble
shake [sheyk]		He shook her by the shoulder.	
1970	중등 토익	1. 생물학의, 생물학적 2. 생물체의	biology (생물학) biodiversity (생물의 다양성) [1269] organic
biological [bahy-uh-LOJ-i-kuhl]		He is her biological father.	
1971	중등 토익	가이드라인, 지침	[609] guide
guideline [GAHYD-lahyn]		There are guidelines on how the work should be carried out.	
1972	초등 토익	1. 달력 2. 일정표, 행사표	[913] schedule
calendar [KAL-uhn-der]		Do you have next year's calendar?	
1973	토익 공무원 편입	자동의, 자동화(된)	automation (자동화) [1158] automatic
automated [AW-tuh-mey-tid]		The company's manufacturing process has been completely automated.	
1974	중등	설득하다, 납득시키다	convincing (설득력있는) [3205] persuade
convince [kuhn-VINS]		I can't convince him.	
1975	중등	1. 속도 2. 걸음, 보폭 3. 속도를 유지하다, 보조를 맞추다	
pace [peys]		The world is changing at a rapid pace.	
1976		1. 비행사, 조종사 2. 시범 사용하다, 시험하다	
pilot [PAHY-luht]		He wants to be a pilot in the future.	
1977	중등 토익 토플	1. 좌절감, 욕구 불만 2. 혼란	frustrating (불만스러운)
frustration [fruh-STREY-shuhn]		She felt like crying with frustration.	
1978	초등	목(부분)	
neck [nek]		His neck is broken.	
1979	초등 토익	버릇, 습관	habitual (습관적인)
habit [HAB-it]		Smoking is a bad habit.	
1980	중등 토익 토플	1. 도덕적인, 도의상인 2. 교훈	morality (도덕) immoral (비도덕적)
moral [MAWR-uhl]		He aims to live a moral life.	

1981	수능 토플	1. 부분 2. 조각 3. 부분을 덧대다	[1947] mend
patch [pach]		She has a bald patch.	

1982		소통하다, 상호작용하다	interation (소통, 상호작용)
interact [in-ter-AKT]		We interact with people everyday.	[2147] cooperate

1983	중등 토익 토플	넘다, 초과하다	[3970] surpass
exceed [ik-SEED]		Don't exceed the speed limit.	

1984	중등	1. 일, 문제, 사건 2. 불륜 관계	
affair [uh-FAIR]		He has nothing to do with the affair.	

1985	중등 토익	1. 양, 수량 2. 다수의, 다량의	quantitative (양적) [455] amount
quantity [KWON-ti-tee]		Consumers tend to prefer quantity to quality.	

1986	수능 토익 토플	진품인, 진짜인	[1285] true
authentic [aw-THEN-tik]		She doesn't know if the painting she bought is authentic.	

1987	초등	1. 화난, 성난 2. 곪은	anger (화) [3576] furious
angry [ANG-gree]		The teacher was angry at the students.	

1988	토익 공무원	1. 정제, 약제 2. 태블릿	[2924] pill
tablet [TAB-lit]		Take only one tablet a day.	

1989	중등 토익	1. 방학, 휴가 2. 휴가를 보내다	vacate (비우다) [1204] holiday
vacation [vey-KEY-shuhn]		Enjoy your vacation.	

1990	토익 편입	1. 행상인, 노점상 2. 판매 회사	vending (판매하는) [375] seller
vendor [VEN-der]		She works as a street vendor, selling fruits.	

1991	수능 토익 토플	보상, 보상금, 배상	compensate (보상하다)
compensation [kom-puhn-SEY-shuhn]		He received some compensation for lost items from the insurance company.	

1992	중등	얼마간, 다소, 어느 정도	
somewhat [SUHM-hwuht]		She somewhat resembles her mother.	

1993	중등 토익 토플	1. 섬유(질), 섬유 조직 2. 기질, 성질, 근성 3. 강도	[1444] thread
fiber [FAHY-ber]		His diet contains lots of fiber.	

1994	초등	1. 천국, 낙원 2. 하늘	haven (피난처) [3519] paradise
heaven [HEV-uhn]		With you, this is heaven to me.	

1995	수능 토익 토플	그저, 한낱(의)	mere (겨우,단순한)
merely			[229] simply
[MEER-lee]		It was merely a matter of luck.	

1996	중등 토익 토플	1. 일치하다, 상응하다 2. ~와 서신을 주고받다	correspondence (일치)
correspond			correspondent (특파원)
[kawr-uh-SPOND]		Her actions do not correspond with her words.	[688] match

1997	토익	1. 분사하다, 뿌리다 2. 스프레이, 분무기	
spray			
[sprey]		He is spraying his back garden.	

1998	중등 토익	1. 흡수하다, 받아들이다 2. 차지하다, 잡아먹다	absorption (흡수)
absorb			[2622] engross
[ab-SAWRB]		Plants absorb carbon dioxide.	

1999	토익	1. 포트폴리오 2. 서류 가방 3. 장관 직 4. 상품 목록	[294] file
portfolio			
[pawrt-FOH-lee-oh]		She needs to update her portfolio to be submitted.	

2000	중등 토익	경우, 예, 사례	[218] case
instance			
[IN-stuhns]		Many instances already show that this plan is not feasible.	

#2001~ #3000

대다수의 한국인의 어휘력이다.

텍스트의 몇 가지 주요한 아이디어와 정보는 이해하지만, 문장의 뉘앙스나 연결 관계를 파악할 수 없어서 해석이 불완전하다. 특히 시험에서 지문의 패러프레이징이 어려워 정확한 독해가 안 된다. 만약 레벨3에서 익숙하지만 명확한 뜻을 설명할 수 없는 어휘가 종종 있다면, 여기서부터 차근차근 학습해나가자. 문장 해석 훈련도 병행하길 권장한다.

LEVEL 03

2001	중등 토익 토플	1. (양)극 2. 막대기, 기둥	polar (극의) bipolar (양극의, 조울증)
pole		It is extremely cold at the South Pole.	polarizing (양극화, 분열시키는)
[pohl]			

2002	토익	1. 집합체, 무리 2. 배열하다, 진열하다	[290] order
array		Her garden offers an impressive array of flowers.	
[uh-REY]			

2003	수능	1. 고리 2. ~에 걸다, 걸고 가다 3. 낚다	[965] catch
hook		Hang your coat on the hook.	
[hook]			

2004	중등 토플	1. (지구)대기 2. 공기 3. 분위기, 기운	[532] environment
atmosphere		The atmosphere is composed of many gases including oxygen.	
[AT-muhs-feer]			

2005	중등 토익	1. 학장, 교장 2. 주요한, 주된 3. (투자한)원금 4. 본인(법문서 작성 시)	[1291] chief
principal		Our principal is very old.	
[PRIN-suh-puhl]			

2006	수능 토익 토플	1. 도덕, 윤리 2. 윤리학	ethical (윤리적인)
ethics		She studied environmental ethics.	
[ETH-iks]			

2007	수능 토익	1. 차원, 관점 2. 규모, 범위 3. 크기, 치수	dimensional (차원의)
dimension		It was a dimension of poverty I hadn't seen before.	
[dih-MEN-shuhn]			

2008	중등 토플	1. 껍데기 2. 조개 3. 포탄 4. 뼈대 5. 겉모습	
shell		I like collecting shells.	
[shel]			

2009	중등 토익 토플	1. 국내의 2. 가정용, 집안의 3. 사육되는, 애완용의	domesticate (길들이다)
domestic		Thankfully, domestic demand has been increasing.	
[duh-MES-tik]			

2010		1. (칼)날 2. 날개 3. 풀잎	[2080] knife
blade		This blade is very sharp.	
[bleyd]			

2011	공무원 편입	1. 부분, 부문 2. 나누다, 분할하다	segmentation (분할)
segment		A large segment of the population supports the new government.	
[SEG-muhnt]			

2012	중등	~할 자격이 있다, ~을 받을 만하다	[3093] merit
deserve		He deserves to win.	
[dih-ZURV]			

2013	토익 공무원 토플 편입	1. 동등한 2. 등가(물), ~에 상당 하는 것	[861] equal
equivalent		These two words are equivalent in meaning.	
[ih-KWIV-uh-luhnt]			

2014	중등 토플	1. 패배시키다, 물리치다 2. 무산시키다, 좌절시키다 3. 패배	undefeated (불패의) [1187] beat
defeat		We defeated the enemy.	
[dih-FEET]			

2015	중등	군인, 전사, 병사	
soldier			
[SOHL-jer]		Many soldiers died from starvation during the Civil War.	

2016	중등	1. 은 2. 은색, 은빛 3. 은화	[368] money
silver			
[SIL-ver]		Gold is heavier than silver.	

2017	중등 토익 토플	1. 새다, 유출되다, 누설되다 2. 누출, 누설 3. 틈, 구멍	leakage (누수)
leak			
[leek]		The roof leaks.	

2018	중등	1. 숨을 쉬다, 호흡하다 2. 속삭이듯 말하다	breath (숨)
breathe			
[breeth]		He can barely breathe.	

2019	중등	방대한, 막대한, 광대한	[3448] immense
vast			
[vast]		She has a vast amount of knowledge.	

2020	토익 공무원 토플 편입	1. 회계 감사(를 하다) 2. (품질)검사 3. 수업 청강하다	[304] check
audit			
[AW-dit]		The company has an audit at the end of each year.	

2021	초등	1. 달 2. 위성	[2731] satellite
moon			
[moon]		The moon is shining.	

2022	초등	1. 높은, 키가 큰 2. 키	
tall			
[tawl]		He is very tall.	

2023		1. 갤러리, 미술관, 화랑 2. 좁고 긴 건물/공간	[1405] hall
gallery			
[GAL-uh-ree]		Her family owns a gallery.	

2024	중등	1. 샤워(하기) 2. 샤워실 3. 소나기 4. 쏟아지다	
shower			
[SHOU-er]		I take a shower every morning.	

2025	중등 토익	1. 인정하다 2. 감사를 표하다 3. (받았음을)확인하다	
acknowledge			
[ak-NOL-ij]		He acknowledged his faults.	

2026	공무원 편입	1. 맞은편의, 건너편의 2. 반대의 3. 상대(역)	
opposite			
[OP-uh-zit]		Their house is just opposite the bus stop.	

2027	토익 공무원	계속 진행 중인, 진행중의	
ongoing			
[ON-goh-ing]		Air pollution is an ongoing issue.	

2028	수능 토익 토플	1. 배수하다 2. 비우다 3. 소비하다, 소모하다 4. 배수관	draining (배수, 힘든)
drain			
[dreyn]		The pool gets drained once a month.	

| 2029
wet
[wet] | 초등 | 1. 젖은, 축축한 2. 비가 오는 3. 적시다

The ground is still wet from the rain last night. | wetland (습지대)
wetness (축축함) |

| 2030
reject
[ri-JEKT] | 중등 토익 | 1. 거절하다, 거부하다 2. 불량품, 불합격품

I couldn't reject her offer. | rejection (거절)
[1690] refuse |

| 2031
animation
[an-uh-MEY-shuhn] | 편입 | 1. 활기, 생기 2. 만화 영화

We were full of animation as we talked about our good old days. | animated (생기있는)
[3873] liveliness |

| 2032
exit
[EG-zit] | 초등 토익 | 1. 출구 2. 퇴장(하다) 3. 종료하다

Where is the emergency exit? | [241] leave |

| 2033
accessory
[ak-SES-uh-ree] | 토익 토플 편입 | 1. 부수적인, 보조적인 2. 장신구, 액세서리 3. 종범, 방조자 4. 부대용품

Accessory organs basically have no function. | [6915] accomplice |

| 2034
designate
[DEZ-ig-neyt] | 수능 토익 | 1. 지정하다, 지명하다 2. 표시하다

He was designated as the new director. | [1369] appoint |

| 2035
arise
[uh-RAHYZ] | 중등 토익 토플 | 1. 발생하다, 일어나다 2. 유발되다

Accidents arise from carelessness. | [836] rise |

| 2036
occupation
[ok-yuh-PEY-shuhn] | | 1. 직업 2. 점유

Please state your name, nationality, and occupation. | preoccupation
(집착, 몰입)
[321] profession |

| 2037
partial
[PAHR-shuhl] | 공무원 편입 | 1. 부분적인 2. 편파적인

The president ordered a partial withdrawal of troops from Afghanistan. | impartial (공정한)
[207] incomplete |

| 2038
alert
[uh-LURT] | 중등 토익 토플 | 1. 경계하는 2. 경보를 발행하다, 위험을 알리다 3. 기민한

We have to stay alert to the possible dangers. | [476] watchful |

| 2039
align
[uh-LAHYN] | 토익 토플 | 1. 일렬의, 나란히 2. ~에 맞춰 조정, 조절하다

The desks are all aligned properly thanks to the teacher. | |

| 2040
treasure
[TREZH-er] | 중등 토플 | 1. 보물, 귀중품 2. 귀하게 여기다

They were looking for buried treasure. | treasury (재무부)
[1787] prize |

| 2041
powder
[POU-der] | 중등 토익 토플 | 1. 가루, 분말 2. 화장품 파우더(를 바르다)

I don't like powdered sugar. | [2102] dust |

| 2042
fundamental
[fuhn-duh-MEN-tl] | 중등 토익 | 1. 근본적인, 본질적인 2. 핵심적인, 필수적인 3. 원리, 근본, 핵심

The company has to make fundamental changes in order to survive. | [648] basic |

2043	중등 토플	1. 좁은 2. 아슬아슬한 3. 한정된, 제한된 4. 좁히다, 줄이다	[402] limited
narrow [NAR-oh]		The road is too narrow for cars.	
2044	중등 토익	1. 고요, 정적 2. 침묵, 묵념 3. 무소식 4. 정숙시키다	silent (침묵의) [1739] quiet
silence [SAHY-luhns]		He and I walked together in silence.	
2045	중등	1. 이야기를 나누다 2. (인터넷)채팅하다 3. 담소, 수다	chatter (수다) [392] talk
chat [chat]		Let's have a chat.	
2046	중등 토익	1. 처벌, 형벌 2. 불이익 3. 벌금, 위약금 4. 페널티 킥	penalize (처벌하다) penal (처벌의) [2344] punishment
penalty [PEN-l-tee]		There will be a penalty for being late.	
2047	초등	1. 장난감 2. 갖고 놀다	
toy [toi]		I bought her a toy.	
2048	초등 토익	1. 선장, 기장 2. 대위, 대령 3. (팀의)주장	[1012] commander
captain [KAP-tuhn]		He is the captain of this ship.	
2049	중등	1. (세포)조직 2. 화장지 3. 얇은 종이	
tissue [TISH-oo]		His lung tissue has been damaged from years of smoking.	
2050	토익 공무원 토플 편입	1. ~로 만들다, ~가 되게 하다 2. 제시하다, 제출하다 3. 표현하다, 연주하다	
render [REN-der]		Her words rendered me speechless.	
2051	중등 토플	1. 평범한, 소박한 2. 숨김없는, 솔직한 3. 평원, 평지 4. 무늬가 없는	[372] clear
plain [pleyn]		I love plain bagels.	
2052		전압	
voltage [VOHL-tij]		What is the standard voltage in the United States?	
2053	토익 공무원 토플 편입	1. 증가 2. 승진, 승격 3. 해발 높이, 고도	elevate (높이다) elevator (엘리베이터)
elevation [el-uh-VEY-shuhn]		Elevation of blood pressure can cause migraines.	
2054	토익	1. 구멍을 뚫다 2. 드릴 3. 반복 연습, 훈련(하다)	[311] train
drill [dril]		We need to drill holes in the wall.	
2055	중등 토익 토플	1. 태도, 사고방식 2. (몸의)자세	[487] position
attitude [AT-i-tood]		I don't appreciate his rude attitude.	
2056	중등 토익 토플	이루다, 성취하다	fulfillment (성취)
fulfill [fool-FIL]		We can all fulfill our dreams.	

2057	중등 토익 토플	1. 발명하다, 개발하다 2. 지어내다, 날조하다	invention (발명품)
invent [in-VENT]		Thomas Edison invented the light bulb.	
2058	중등 토플	1. 터지다, 폭발하다 2. 급격히 증가하다	explosion (폭발) explosive (폭발적인)
explode [ik-SPLOHD]		The bomb exploded with a loud noise.	
2059	초등	1. 폭탄 2. 대실패 3. 큰 돈 4. 폭격하다	bombshell (폭탄선언, 예쁜여성)
bomb [bom]		An unknown terrorist group detonated a nuclear bomb.	
2060	중등 토플	1. 동반하다, 동행하다 2. 동반되다, 딸려오다	accompaniment (동행, 반주) [4138] escort
accompany [uh-KUHM-puh-nee]		He accompanied me on a walk.	
2061	초등	1. 물다 2. 한 입, 소량의 식사 3. 악영향이 나타나다	[6429] nibble
bite [bahyt]		I accidentally bit my tongue.	
2062	중등 토플	1. 금지하다 2. 금지법, 규제	[851] bar
ban [ban]		The treaty bans the use of chemical weapons.	
2063	중등 토플	위기, 고비	[1005] emergency
crisis [KRAHY-sis]		There could be another economic crisis in the near future.	
2064	중등	수분, 습기, 촉촉한 느낌	moist (촉촉한) [3136] dampness
moisture [MOIS-cher]		These plants need rich soil that can retain moisture.	
2065	중등	1. 온화한, 친절한 2. 가벼운, 완만한	gently (부드럽게) [1245] soft
gentle [JEN-tl]		He is a very gentle person.	
2066	중등 토플	1. 12개 묶음, 한 다스 2. 다수, 여러 개의	[기타] twelve
dozen [DUHZ-uhn]		She boiled a half-dozen eggs.	
2067	중등 토플	1. 덫, 올가미, 함정 2. 가두다	trapped (갇힌) [965] catch
trap [trap]		He was lured into a trap.	
2068	초등	1. 울다 2. 외치다 3. 비명, 고함 4. 간절한 요청, 요구	[5459] howl
cry [krahy]		She began crying.	
2069	중등 GRE	1. 기쁨을 주다, 즐겁게 하다 2. 기쁨, 즐거움	delighted (기쁜) [270] pleasure
delight [dih-LAHYT]		His success delighted his parents.	
2070	중등	1. 다발, 묶음 2. 많음 3. 사람들 무리 4. 단단해지다	[223] group
bunch [buhnch]		I want a small bunch of grapes.	

2071	중등 토익 토플	1. 변경하다, 고치다 2. 변하다, 달라지다	
alter			
[AWL-ter]		He needs to alter his sleeping patterns.	

2072	초등	1. 문, 출입문 2. 게이트, 탑승구 3. 관중 수	[506] door
gate			
[geyt]		Lock the gate before you leave.	

2073	수능	1. 제대로 된 2. 예의 바른, 품위 있는 3. 적절한, 온당한	[1059] respectable
decent			
[DEE-suhnt]		I want her to have a decent life.	

2074	중등 토플	1. 끌다, 끌어내다 2. 힘들게 움직이다 3. 장애물, 방해물	[912] pull
drag			
[drag]		She dragged him out of bed.	

2075	중등 토익	1. 철도, 기차 2. 난간	railroad (철도) railway (철로)
rail			
[reyl]		Rail passengers are tired of delays.	

2076	중등 토익	1. 뛰어들다, 다이빙하다 2. 잠수(하다) 3. 급락하다	[4018] plunge
dive			
[dahyv]		He learned to dive when he was six.	

2077	중등	1. 유방, 가슴 2. 가슴살 3. (꼭대기에)오르다	[2173] chest
breast			
[brest]		I like roasted chicken breasts.	

2078	토익 공무원 토플 편입	다음의, 차후의, 뒤따르는	[199] later
subsequent			
[SUHB-si-kwuhnt]		Subsequent studies confirmed the results.	

2079	중등 토플	1. (이야기의)구성, 줄거리 2. 음모(하다), 계획(하다) 3. 작은 땅	[1724] scheme
plot			
[plot]		She didn't like the plot of the movie.	

2080	초등	1. 칼, 나이프 2. 칼로 찌르다	[2010] blade
knife			
[nahyf]		I need a knife to cut the cake.	

2081	중등	1. 가죽 2. 피부	[749] skin
leather			
[LETH-er]		She bought a leather jacket.	

2082	수능 토익	1. 탈퇴하다 2. 철수하다, 철회하다 3. 인출하다	withdrawal (철수) [2994] retreat
withdraw			
[with-DRAW]		The country withdrew from the agreement.	

2083	초등	1. 거울 2. 반영하다, 잘 보여주다 3. 비추다 4. 따라하다	[1108] reflect
mirror			
[MIR-er]		He looked at himself in the mirror.	

2084	중등	1. 괴물 2. 잔인한 인간 3. 거대한	monstrous (엄청난)
monster			
[MON-ster]		He'd have to be a monster to hit a baby like that.	

2085	초등	상사, 보스	bossy (갑질하는)
boss			
[baws]		She tried hard to impress her boss.	

2086	중등	1. 미끄러지다 2. 살짝 빠지다 3. 풀려나다 4. 조각, 쪽지	slippery (미끄러운)
slip			slippage (미끄러짐)
[slip]		I slipped and fell.	

2087	중등	1. ~를 싸우다 2. 전투, 싸움	
combat			
[kuhm-BAT]		All governments need to take urgent action to combat climate change.	

2088	중등	1. 항해하다, 출항하다 2. 나아가다 3. 돛	sailor (선원)
sail			
[seyl]		I'd like to sail around the world.	

2089	토익 공무원 토플 편입	방사선, 복사	irradiate (방사능을 쬐다, 비추다)
radiation			radiator (라디에이터)
[rEY-dee-ey-shuhn]		Even a brief exposure to radiation is very dangerous.	

2090	수능 토익 토플	평가 기준	[450] standards
criteria			
[krahy-TEER-ee-uh]		No candidate fulfills all the criteria for this position.	

2091	수능 토익	교육 과정, 교과 과정	extracurricular (정식 교과 이외의)
curriculum			
[kuh-RIK-yuh-luhm]		Languages are almost always included in the school curriculum.	

2092	중등 토익 토플	1. 무덤, 묘 2. 심각한, 중대한	[896] serious
grave			
[greyv]		We put flowers on his grave.	

2093	중등 토익	1. 청소년의 2. 2학년의 3. 어린 아들 4. 하급의	[399] younger
junior			
[JOON-yer]		The team won the junior championship.	

2094		1. 벨트, 허리띠 2. 지대 3. 강타하다	[1067] band
belt			
[belt]		Fasten your seat belt.	

2095	중등	1. 비서 2. 총무, 서기 3. 정부 부처의 장관	[3472] clerk
secretary			
[SEK-ri-ter-ee]		He hired a new secretary.	

2096	중등 토익	충분한, 적당한, 적합한	inadequate (부적합한)
adequate			[1742] sufficient
[AD-i-kwit]		We didn't have an adequate amount of food.	

2097	중등	1. 은총, 은혜 2. 유예 기간 3. 우아함, 품위	gracious (은혜로운)
grace			disgrace (불명예)
[greys]		She has natural grace and elegance.	[2947] mercy

2098	초등	1. 쥐 2. 마우스	
mouse			
[mous]		Cats catch mice.	

2099	중등 토익 토플	1. 우수한, 우월한 2. 상급의 3. 선배, 상급자 4. 거만한	superiority (우월성)
superior			[724] excellent
[suh-PEER-ee-er]		This dictionary is superior to that one in quality.	

2100	중등 토익	도시의	suburban (교외 지역의)
urban			urbane (도시풍의)
[UR-buhn]		More and more people are moving to urban areas.	[261] city

2101	토익 공무원	1. 기업, 단체 2. 독립체 3. 존재, 실체	[925] object
entity			
[EN-ti-tee]		The two companies will combine to form a new entity.	

2102	중등	1. 흙, 먼지 2. 가루 3. 먼지를 털다 4. 뿌리다	[2041] powder
dust			
[duhst]		I'm allergic to dust.	

2103	중등 토익 토플	처분, 폐기	dispose (폐기하다)
disposal			
[dih-SPOH-zuhl]		Waste disposal is a huge problem.	

2104	초등 토익	1. 배트, 방망이 2. 공을 치다 3. 박쥐	batter (타자)
bat			[765] club
[bat]		He hit a ball with the bat.	

2105	수능	1. 범죄, 악행, 악 2. 부(직책) (ex.부통령)	vicious (악랄한)
vice			[1980] immorality
[VAHYs]		We all try to abstain from vice.	

2106	수능 토익 토플	1. 유체 2. 유동성의, 부드러운	[1839] liquid
fluid			
[FLOO-id]		Fluid includes both gasses and liquids.	

2107	중등	1. 앞으로 2. 밖으로, ~에서 멀리	forthright (솔직한)
forth			[713] forward
[fawrth]		My dog springs forth whenever I come home.	

2108	토익 공무원 편입	튼튼한, 오래가는, 내구성이 있는	durability (내구성)
durable			[498] strong
[DOOR-uh-buhl]		These leather shoes are very durable.	

2109	중등 토익 토플	1. 영토, 영역 2. 구역	[177] area
territory			
[TER-i-tawr-ee]		ISIS lost all of its territories.	

2110	중등 토익	1. 유래하다, 생기다 2. 줄기 3. 막다, 저지하다	[439] stop
stem			
[stem]		His problems stem from his unhappy childhood.	

2111	수능 토익	1. 현대의, 당대의 2. 동시대의 3. 동년배	[258] current
contemporary			
[kuhn-TEM-puh-rer-ee]		The museum exhibits 2,000 contemporary and modern artworks.	

2112	중등 토익	길, 도로, 차선	[611] road
lane			
[leyn]		We drove down the small lane to the main road.	

2113	중등	1. 아픈, 병 든 2. 나쁜, 유해한 3. 문제, 병, 해악	[1906] sick
ill [il]		I went home early because I felt ill.	
2114	초등 토플	1. 왕관 2. 왕위, 왕권 3. 왕관을 씌우다	[1868] peak
crown [kroun]		The king likes to wear a fancy crown.	
2115	초등 토플	1. 호기심이 많은, 궁금한 2. 별난, 특이한	curiosity (호기심) [4511] peculiar
curious [KYOOR-ee-uhs]		They were curious about the noise last night.	
2116	수능 토익	1. 수확량, 총수익 2. 생산하다 3. 양도하다, 양보하다 4. 항복하다	unyielding (굽히지 않는) [3682] surrender
yield [yeeld]		In the last two years, the average yield of rice went up.	
2117	중등 토플	1. 간신히, 겨우 2. 거의 ~않다	bare (맨 살의, 추가된게 없는) [308] hardly
barely [BAIR-lee]		I can barely eat.	
2118	중등	1. 죄책감이 드는 2. 유죄의, 책임이 있는	guilt (죄, 죄책감) [651] responsible
guilty [GIL-tee]		She feels guilty about the team's defeat.	
2119	중등 토익	1. 개요(를 서술하다, 설명하다) 2. 윤곽(을 나타내다)	[3085] sketch
outline [OUT-lahyn]		He briefly went over the outline of the project.	
2120	중등 토플	1. 혐의를 제기하다 2. 고발하다, 기소하다 3. 비난하다	accusation (혐의) [415] charge
accuse [uh-KYOOZ]		They accused him of lying.	
2121	중등 토익	1. 노예 2. 고되게 일하다	slavery (노예제도) enslave (노예로 만들다) [269] servant
slave [sleyv]		She treated him like a slave.	
2122	초등 토플	1. 동전 2. (새로운 단어를)만들다 3. 주조하다	[368] money
coin [koin]		We need coins for parking meters.	
2123	중등 토익	급여, 월급	[2245] wage
salary [SAL-uh-ree]		She overspent her salary last month.	
2124	중등 토익	1. 정도, 규모 2. 범위, 크기	
extent [ik-STENT]		I was surprised at the extent of her knowledge.	
2125	수능 토익	1. 임대하다, 대여하다 2. 리스, 임대차 계약	
lease [lees]		He signed the lease today.	
2126	중등	1. 홍수 2. 폭주, 쇄도 3. 범람하다, 쇄도하다	
flood [fluhd]		Their house was damaged by the flood.	

2127	중등	1. 무릎 2. 무릎으로 치다	
knee			
[nee]		I'm down on bended knee.	

2128	초등 토익	1. 브레이크, 제동 2. 속도를 줄이다	
brake			
[breyk]		The brake pedal needs replacement.	

2129	중등	중독	addictive (중독성의)
addiction			
[uh-DIK-shuhn]		I'm trying hard to fight my addiction to alcohol.	

2130	수능 토익	1. 쌓다, 포개다 2. 무더기, 더미 3. 다량의	[2696] pile
stack			
[stak]		Dishes are stacked up by the sink.	

2131	중등 토익 토플 GRE	1. 열렬한 지지자 2. 광팬 3. 열정적인 사람	enthusiasm (열정)
enthusiast			[2427] devotee
[en-THOO-zee-ast]		She is a real sports enthusiast.	

2132	중등	1. 방송(하다) 2. 광고하다, 널리 알리다	
broadcast			
[BRAWD-kast]		Their performance was broadcast live on TV.	

2133	중등	1. 영광, 영예 2. 찬양 3. 장관, 아름다움	glorious (영광스러운)
glory			glorified (미화된)
[GLAWR-ee]		What a glory it is to be a student of yours.	[2458] praise

2134	초등	1. 빵 2. 생계 수단	[2958] dough
bread			
[bred]		Can I eat this bread?	

2135	중등	1. (농)작물 2. 잘라 내다	[2515] harvest
crop			
[krop]		Our family grows a variety of crops.	

2136	중등 토플	1. 서두르다, 재촉하다 2. 난입(하다), 돌진(하다) 3. 혼잡, 분주함	[807] hurry
rush			
[ruhsh]		Don't rush yourself.	

2137	중등	시대, 시기	[545] period
era			
[EER-uh]		We live in a new era of transformation.	

2138	중등 토익	1. 잘못, 실수 2. 고장, 결함 3. 나무라다, 탓하다	[2643] flaw
fault			
[fawlt]		It wasn't his fault that she left.	

2139	중등 토익	1. 빈틈없는, 철저한 2. 완전한	[207] complete
thorough			
[THUR-oh]		He needs a thorough understanding of the problem.	

2140	중등	1. 굽히다, 구부리다, 휘다 2. 굽은 곳	bent (구부러진)
bend			[1954] curve
[bend]		I can't bend my elbow.	

2141	중등 토익	1. 공격적인 2. 배짱이 있는, 적극적인	[3603] hostile
aggressive [uh-GRES-iv]		She hates talking to aggressive people.	

2142	중등 토익 토플	1. 인용하다 2. 소환하다 3. 표창하다 4. 예로 들다	citation (인용) [1386] quote
cite [sahyt]		He enjoys citing famous authors.	

2143	중등 토플	1. 뜨다, 띄우다, 부유하다 2. 제시하다, 내놓다	afloat (물에 떠있는) [3393] drift
float [floht]		She saw fallen leaves floating in the pool.	

2144	토익	1. 마스크 2. 가면 3. 팩 4. 가리다, 감추다	[3948] disguise
mask [mask]		Put your mask on.	

2145	중등 토플	1. 파다, 캐내다 2. 뒤지다, 헤집다 3. (회화) 아주 좋아하다	[3392] poke
dig [dig]		My dog likes to dig in the ground.	

2146	초등	1. 내일 2. 미래, 향후의	[488] future
tomorrow [tuh-MAWR-oh]		Meet me tomorrow.	

2147	중등 토익 토플	1. 협력 2. 공조 3. 조합	cooperative (협력적인) cooperate (협력하다)
cooperation [koh-op-uh-REY-shuh n]		The government needs cooperation from the private sector.	

2148	토익	(특별 행사가 열리는) 장소	
venue [VEN-yoo]		We need to book a venue for this conference.	

2149	중등 토익	1. 주의, 경고 2. 조심, 신중함 3. 주의를 주다, 경고를 하다	precaution (사전 주의) cautious (신중한) [1396] warn
caution [KAW-shuhn]		Proceed with caution.	

2150	초등	모자	[1592] cap
hat [hat]		He wore a hat.	

2151	중등 토플	1. 해군 2. 군청색	naval (해군의) [2554] fleet
navy [NEY-vee]		She will join the navy.	

2152	초등	1. 책상 2. 프런트, 접수처, 안내소	[2811] bureau
desk [desk]		I have two desks.	

2153	수능 토익	1. 범위 2. 기회, 여지 3. 자세히 살피다	[411] range
scope [skohp]		The issue is beyond the scope of my understanding.	

2154	초등	1. 회색 2. 흐린, 우중충한 3. 백발의	
gray [GREY]		The sky is gray.	

2155 **mature** [muh-TOOR]	중등 토익	1. 성숙한, 성인인 2. 숙성된 3. 만기가 된 He is very mature for his age.	maturity (성숙) immature (미성숙한)
2156 **boil** [boil]	중등	1. 끓다, 끓이다 2. 삶다, 데치다 Water boils at 100℃ at sea level.	boiler (보일러)
2157 **intervene** [in-ter-VEEN]	수능 토익 토플	1. 개입하다, 중재하다 2. 가로막다, 끼어들다 3. 사이에 있다 The teacher intervened in the fight between two students.	intervention (개입)
2158 **keynote** [KEE-noht]		기조, 가장 중요한 부분 Steve Jobs gave a keynote speech.	
2159 **headquarters** [HED-kwawr-terz]	수능 토익	본부, 사령부 Many companies have headquarters in New York.	
2160 **goodwill** [GOOD-wil]		선의 The leader was known for his goodwill.	[6008] benevolence
2161 **setback** [SET-bak]	공무원 편입	시련, 좌절 He faced many setbacks.	[1845] reversal
2162 **backbone** [BAK-bohn]	공무원	척추 I went to the doctor because my backbone hurt.	[2615] spine
2163 **treadmill** [TRED-mil]	공무원	런닝머신 He ran 1 kilometer on the treadmill.	
2164 **entitle** [en-TAHYT-l]		권한을 주다 A membership at Costco entitles you to shop there.	[2719] empower
2165 **anesthesia** [an-uhs-THEE-zhuh]		마취 Anesthesia is a loss of sensation in a body part.	
2166 **turnout** [TURN-out]		(특히 선거의) 참여자 수 Heavy rain on election day caused the poor turnout.	[453] attendance
2167 **backlash** [BAK-lash]	공무원	반발 The politician faced fierce backlash.	lash (비난하다, 공격하다) [2517] recoil
2168 **frankly** [FRANGK-lee]	중등 GRE	1. 솔직히 2. 사실대로 말하면 I have to answer frankly to his questions.	frank (솔직한) [1404] honestly

2169		몰락	[2431] ruin
downfall			
[DOUN-fawl]		The scandal led to the downfall of the celebrity.	

2170		소용돌이	[6058] vortex
whirlpool			
[HWURL-pool]		There was a whirlpool in the ocean.	

2171	토플	마천루, 높은 빌딩	
skyscraper			
[SKAHY-skrey-per]		Dubai has many skyscrapers.	

2172	초등	항공사	[3234] aviation
airline			
[AIR-lahyn]		I always use the same airline.	

2173	중등	1. 가슴, 흉부 2. 상자, 궤, 서랍장	[2077] breast
chest			
[chest]		I have a sharp pain in my chest.	

2174	토익	1. 해킹하다 2. 자르다, 난도질하다	
hack			
[hak]		He hacked into the company's system.	

2175	중등	가구	
furniture			
[FUR-ni-cher]		She ordered new furniture.	

2176	중등 토익	농업	
agriculture			
[AG-ri-kuhl-cher]		Many countries depend on agriculture.	

2177	중등 토익 토플 GRE	1. ~에서 비롯되다, ~로부터 파생하다 2. 유도하다	derivative (파생된)
derive			
[dih-RAHYV]		A lot of English words are derived from Latin.	

2178	중등	1. 훌륭한 2. 성공적인 3. 뛰어난, 우수한 4. 밝은, 선명한, 눈부신	
brilliant			
[BRIL-yuhnt]		What he told me was a brilliant idea.	

2179	초등	신문(지)	
newspaper			
[NOOZ-pey-per]		I try to read a newspaper every morning.	

2180	중등 토익	팬, 냄비	
pan			
[pan]		She needs to buy a pan.	

2181	중등 토익 토플 GRE	1. 자유 2. 제멋대로 구는	liberalism (자유주의) liberate (해방하다) liberal (진보적인) [216] freedom
liberty			
[LIB-er-tee]		They fought for their liberty.	

2182	중등 토익	1. 면역성의, 면역이 된 2. 면제된	immunity (면역, 면제) immunization (예방 접종)
immune			
[ih-MYOON]		She is immune to smallpox.	

2183 중등 토익 토플 GRE **margin** [MAHR-jin]	1. 여백 2. 차이 3. 수익, 마진 4. 가장자리 He left a note in the margin of the paper.	marginal (미미한) marginalize (과소평가하다, 밖으로 쫓아내다) [1070] edge
2184 중등 토익 토플 **clarity** [KLAR-i-tee]	1. 명확성, 명료함 2. 선명도, 투명도 We should learn to write with clarity.	clarify (명백히하다) clarification (설명) [372] clearness
2185 토익 공무원 토플 **pharmacy** [FAHR-muh-see]	1. 약국 2. 약학, 약제학 Is there a pharmacy nearby?	pharmaceutical (약학의) [2630] chemist
2186 중등 **swing** [swing]	1. 전후, 좌우로 흔들다, 휘두르다 2. 선회하다, 바꾸다 3. 그네 Let your arms swing as you walk.	[4408] sway
2187 중등 토익 토플 **framework** [FREYM-wurk]	1. 체제, 체계 2. 뼈대, 골조, 틀 We need to create a legal framework for environmental protection.	[1120] frame
2188 수능 **rid** [rid]	1. 없애다, 제거하다 2. 면하다, 벗어나다 I got rid of old textbooks.	[372] clear
2189 중등 토익 토플 **accelerate** [ak-SEL-uh-reyt]	1. 가속화하다, 속도를 높이다 2. 촉진시키다 The company needs to accelerate its effort to innovate its system.	decelerate (감속하다) [5296] expedite
2190 공무원 편입 **ceremony** [SER-uh-moh-nee]	1. ~식, 의식 2. 양식, 형식 They attended her graduation ceremony.	ceremonial (의식의) [2814] rite
2191 중등 토플 **blind** [blahynd]	1. 시각장애인, 맹인인 2. 눈멀게 하다 3. 맹목적인 4. 비논리적인 He is blind in one eye.	[683] screen
2192 토익 공무원 토플 편입 **vulnerable** [VUHL-ner-uh-buhl]	취약한, 연약한, 상처 입기 쉬운 Children are particularly vulnerable to the effects of air pollution.	vulnerability (취약성) [1193] exposed
2193 중등 토익 **absence** [AB-suhns]	1. 부재, 결석 2. 없음, 결핍 We didn't notice her absence.	absent (결석한) [1091] lack
2194 중등 **pose** [pohz]	1. 제기하다 2. 자세를 취하다 3. 으스대다 4. 포즈 Smoking poses a risk to your health.	[3865] posture
2195 중등 **romantic** [roh-MAN-tik]	1. 로맨틱한, 낭만적인 2. 몽상적인 사람, 낭만파 This place is so romantic.	romance (로맨스) [3346] sentimental
2196 수능 토익 토플 **moderate** [MOD-er-it]	1. 적당한, 적정한 2. 중도의, 온건한 3. 보통의, 중간의 4. 조정하다, 관리하다 Moderate exercise is good for you.	moderator (토론 사회자) [1245] soften

2197	중등 토익 토플	냉장고	refrigerator (=fridge)
fridge			
[frij]		Will you put this in the fridge?	

2198	고등 토익 토플 GRE	1. 배기(관) 2. 지치다, 기진맥진하게 만들다 3. 고갈시키다	exhaustion (지침)
exhaust			exhausting (지치는)
[ig-ZAWST]		Exhaust fumes are bad for our health.	[2028] drain

2199	수능	1. 최고의, 제1의 2. 총리 3. 주지사	[1641] prime
premier			
[pri-MEER]		She is one of the nation's premier physicians.	

2200	고등	1. 꽉 잡다, 움켜쥐다 2. 사로잡다 3. 악력 4. 이해, 파악	[3371] grasp
grip			
[grip]		He gripped her arms.	

2201	고등 토익	고속도로, 하이웨이	beltway (순환도로)
highway			[611] road
[HAHY-wey]		There was a terrible accident on the highway.	

2202	고등	1. 비틀다, 돌리다 2. 삐다, 접질리다 3. 왜곡하다, 꼬다	[278] turn
twist			
[twist]		She twisted his arm.	

2203	수능	당뇨병	
diabetes			
[dahy-uh-BEE-tis]		He was diagnosed with diabetes.	

2204	고등 토익	1. 손톱, 발톱 2. 못 3. ~을 이루어 내다	[965] catch
nail			
[neyl]		She was biting her nails out of frustration.	

2205	고등 토익 토플	1. 주사 2. 주입, 투입	inject (주입하다)
injection			[473] shot
[in-JEK-shuhn]		The injection relieved her pain.	

2206	고등	1. 곡물, 알갱이 2. 티끌, 아주 조금 3. 촉감, 결	[외래어] cereal
grain			
[greyn]		Rice is one of my favorite grains.	

2207	고등 토익 토플	1. 예상하다, 예측하다 2. 기대하다, 고대하다	[357] expect
anticipate			
[an-TIS-uh-peyt]		What he did was something we didn't anticipate.	

2208	고등	1. 견과 2. 너트, 나사 3. 괴짜, 미친 사람	[3350] freak
nut			
[nuht]		He is allergic to nuts.	

2209	초등 토익	대화	[647] discussion
dialogue			
[DAHY-uh-lawg]		She refused to participate in the dialogue.	

2210	초등	빌리다, 꾸다, 차용하다	
borrow			
[BOR-oh]		Can I borrow $20?	

2211	고등	1. 증기, 물방울 2. 찌다	[3339] vapor
steam			
[steem]		Steam engines brought about the First Industrial Revolution.	

2212	고등	1. 내기(하다) 2. ~이 틀림없다고 확신하다 3. 짐작, 추측	[3370] gamble
bet			
[bet]		She won the bet.	

2213	토익 공무원 토플	기자, 저널리스트	journalism (저널리즘)
journalist			[226] reporter
[JUR-nl-ist]		Journalists should never walk away from the hard truth.	

2214	토익 공무원	1. 영향력 2. 지렛대 효과(를 이용하다) 3. (금융) 레버리지	lever (지레)
leverage			
[LEV-er-ij]		His wealth gave him some leverage in social circles.	

2215	고등 토익	1. 끔찍한, 극심한 2. 기분, 몸이 안 좋은 3. 형편없는	
terrible			
[TER-uh-buhl]		That movie was terrible.	

2216	토플	1. 허브, 약초 2. 초식의	herbal (약초의)
herb			
[urb]		This herb has a variety of uses.	

2217	초등 토익	1. 연주회, 음악회, 콘서트 2. 일치, 단합	concerted (합심한)
concert			
[KON-surt]		I went to a concert last night.	

2218	고등 토익 토플	동료	
colleague			
[KOL-eeg]		I am loyal to my colleagues.	

2219	수능 토플	1. 빨다 2. 엉망이다, 형편없다	
suck			
[suhk]		The baby is sucking her thumb.	

2220	초등	1. 겁내는, 무서워하는 2. 걱정하는, 염려하는	[1961] scared
afraid			
[uh-FREYD]		He is afraid of cats.	

2221	초등	천사, 천사 같은 사람	[2986] saint
angel			
[EYN-juhl]		She must be an angel.	

2222	고등	1. 구하다, 구제하다 2. 구출, 구조	[390] save
rescue			
[RES-kyoo]		They rescued a boy from drowning.	

2223	토익	1. 밸브 2. (심장, 혈관의)판막	[5299] faucet
valve			
[valv]		I wasn't able to open the valve without a tool.	

2224	수능 토익	1. 편찬하다, 엮다 2. 모으다	compilation (모음집)
compile			[420] collect
[kuhm-PAHYL]		It took us 10 years to compile this book.	

2225	고등 토익 토플	1. 자석 2. ~을 매료하는 사람/것	[1069] attraction
magnet [MAG-nit]		A magnet attracts iron.	
2226	고등 토익 토플	1. 자취, 흔적 2. 추적하여 찾아내다 3. 따라가다, 베끼다 4. 소량	retrace (흔적을 따라 추적하다) [561] track
trace [treys]		She disappeared without a trace.	
2227	토익 공무원 토플	1. 재고(품) 2. (물품)목록	[868] stock
inventory [IN-vuhn-tawr-ee]		The store's inventory is very limited.	
2228	고등	1. 가라앉다, 침몰하다, 주저앉다 2. 싱크대, 개수대 3. 망치다	[4018] plunge
sink [singk]		He saw the boat sinking yesterday.	
2229	토익	보석, 쥬얼리, 장신구	jewel (보석)
jewelry [JOO-uhl-ree]		I don't like wearing jewelry.	
2230	고등 토플	1. 따르다, 붓다 2. 쏟아지다, 퍼붓다	[1470] stream
pour [pawr]		He poured me some tea.	
2231	고등	1. 살아 있는 2. 생기, 활기 넘치는 3. 의식하는, 알고 있는	[189] live
alive [uh-LAHYV]		She is happy to be alive.	
2232	토익 공무원	다가오는, 다음 번의	[4621] forthcoming
upcoming [UHP-kuhm-ing]		He is excited about the upcoming match.	
2233	토익	1. 공평, 공정 2. 자기 자본, 가치 3. 주식	[886] fairness
equity [EK-wi-tee]		Social justice and equity go hand in hand.	
2234	수능	1. 끓이다, 우리다 2. 양조하다 3. 태동하다 4. 혼합, 조합	brewery (양조장) [862] drink
brew [broo]		He asked her to brew some coffee.	
2235	수능 토익 GRE	1. 촉진하다, 활성화하다 2. 용이하게 하다	facilitator (촉진자) [636] assist
facilitate [fuh-SIL-i-teyt]		The government is taking new measures to facilitate economic growth.	
2236	고등 토익	1. 출발 2. 일탈, 벗어남	depart (떠나다) [241] leaving
departure [dih-PAHR-cher]		We postponed our departure.	
2237	수능 토익 토플	1. 지명하다, 임명하다 2. 정하다	nomination (임명) nominee (임명된 후보) [1369] appoint
nominate [NOM-uh-neyt]		I would like to nominate him as the new director.	
2238	초등	1. 시계 2. 기록하다, 측정하다	
clock [klok]		This clock is broken.	

2239	고등 토익 토플	1. 치료하다, 치유하다 2. 해결책	incurable (치유 불가능한)
cure [kyoor]		This pill will help you cure your cold.	[1631] heal

2240	고등	1. 씨름하다, 해결하다 2. 따지다 3. 태클	[544] address
tackle [TAK-uhl]		He did his best to tackle the problem.	

2241	수능 토익 GRE	1. 비율 2. 크기, 규모 3. 균형	proportional (비례의) disproportionate (불균형의)
proportion [pruh-PAWR-shuhn]		A large proportion of old people live alone.	[271] share

2242	고등	1. 아무도, 그 누구도 2. 보잘 것 없는 사람	
nobody [NOH-bod-ee]		Nobody wants to be sad.	

2243	고등 토익	1. 고립시키다 2. 분리하다, 따로 떼어내다	isolation (격리)
isolate [AHY-suh-leyt]		The village was isolated by the storm.	[892] separate

2244	고등 토익 토플	1. 식민지 2. 집단, 거주지 3. 작은 마을 4. 군집	colonist (식민지) colonize (식민지로 가다)
colony [KOL-uh-nee]		Brazil was a Portuguese colony.	[1342] settlement

2245	고등	1. 임금, 급여 2. (전쟁을)벌이다	[2123] salary
wage [weyj]		What's the minimum wage in Korea?	

2246		운동	[1044] exercise
workout [WURK-out]		She got ready for her morning workout.	

2247	고등	1. 긁다, 할퀴다 2. 흠집, 자국 3. 취소하다	[3658] scrape
scratch [skrach]		A cat scratched me.	

2248	토익	전술, 전략	tactical (전술적인)
tactic [TAK-tik]		We changed our tactics in line with the current situation.	[184] plan

2249	고등 토익 토플	1. 합, 합계, 총합 2. 계산, 산수 3. 액수	[508] total
sum [suhm]		The whole is greater than the sum of the parts.	

2250	토익 공무원 토플 편입	사업가, 기업인	entrepreneurship (기업가정신)
entrepreneur [ahn-truh-pruh-NUR]		It requires a great deal of courage to be a successful entrepreneur.	

2251	고등 토플	1. 뒤쫓다, 추구하다 2. 서둘러 가다 3. 추격	[1600] hunt
chase [cheys]		We should all chase our dreams.	

2252	수능 토익 토플 GRE	1. 혼합물 2. 합성의, 복합의 3. 증가하다 4. 복리 5. 구내, 지역 내	compounding (쌓이는)
compound [KOM-pound]		Salt is a compound of sodium and chlorine.	[3574] composite

2253	고등 토플	~와 함께, 나란히, 동시에	[1876] beside
alongside			
[uh-LAWNG-sahyd]		The students lined up alongside the teacher.	

2254	토플	소스	[1190] dressing
sauce			
[saws]		Try this sauce.	

2255	수능	수의사	vet (수의사,조사)
veterinarian			vetting (심사하는)
[vet-er-uh-NAIR-ee-uhn]		She took her vomiting dog to a veterinarian.	

2256	고등 토익	1. 정당화시키다, 해명하다 2. 타당함을 보여주다	justification (정당화)
justify			[2592] excuse
[JUHS-tuh-fahy]		I am sick of her justifying herself all the time.	

2257	고등 토플	1. 재난, 재해 2. 재앙, 불행 3. 실패작, 실패자	disastrous (재앙의)
disaster			[4119] catastrophe
[dih-ZAS-ter]		Floods are one of the most devastating natural disasters.	

2258	고등 토익 토플	1. 밀집한, 밀도가 높은 2. 짙은 3. 난해한	density (밀도)
dense			[1538] thick
[dens]		She couldn't drive because of the dense fog.	

2259	수능 토익 토플	1. 배출, 방출 2. 배기가스	emit (방출하다)
emission			[415] discharge
[ih-MISH-uhn]		We need to reduce carbon dioxide emissions at home.	

2260	초등	1. 침착한, 차분한 2. 잔잔한, 바람이 없는 3. 진정시키다	[1739] quiet
calm			
[kahm]		She always seems so calm.	

2261	초등 토익 토플	시끄러운, 큰 소리의	aloud (소리내어)
loud			[1673] noisy
[loud]		He has a loud voice.	

2262		최고의, 최대의, 최상의	supremacy (우위, 패권)
supreme			[2099] superior
[suh-PREEM]		The Pope is the supreme leader of the Roman Catholic Church.	

2263	수능 토플	1. 다듬다, 손질하다, 잘라내다 2. 장식(하다)	
trim			
[trim]		I had my hair trimmed recently.	

2264	고등	1. 핵의 2. 원자력의	nuke (=nuclear)
nuclear			[2583] atomic
[NOO-klee-er]		Nuclear weapons are a threat to all humanity.	

2265	고등	1. 기이한, 이상한 2. 섬뜩한, 기괴한, 수상한	[1659] strange
weird			
[weerd]		He is so weird that nobody wants to talk to him.	

2266	고등 토익	1. 정정, 수정사항 2. 검토	revise (수정하다)
revision			
[ri-VIZH-uhn]		This plan needs some revisions.	

2267	고등 토익	충성심, 의리	loyal (충성스러운)
loyalty			disloyal (충성이 없는)
[LOI-uhl-tee]		Can I count on your loyalty?	[1380] faithfulness

2268	초등 토익	농구(공)	
basketball			
[BAS-kit-bawl]		We played basketball yesterday.	

2269		1. 마주치다, 대면하다 2. 직면하다 3. 마주침, 직면	[276] meet
encounter			
[en-KOUN-ter]		Have you ever encountered a homeless person?	

2270		회복	recover (회복하다)
recovery			[1563] restoration
[ri-KUHV-uh-ree]		She was very helpful during my recovery.	

2271		전자레인지	
microwave			
[MAHY-kroh-weyv]		I sold my old microwave.	

2272		조심하는, 신중한	[4610] prudent
discreet			
[dih-SKREET]		I admire his discreet personality.	

2273		강하지 않은, 평소보다 얌전한	[1739] quiet
subdued			
[suh b-DOOD]		He seemed subdued today.	

2274		떠오르다, 나타나다	emerging (떠오르는)
emerge			[367] appear
[ih-MURJ]		Many questions emerged during the talk.	

2275		동화, 우화	[2450] tale
fable			
[FEY-buh l]		I love Aesop's fables.	

2276		점진적인	gradually (점진적으로)
gradual			[1040] progressive
[GRAJ-oo-uhl]		There was a gradual decline in revenue.	

2277		1. 중력 2. 심각성	gravitate (서서히 끌려 움직이다)
gravity			[896] seriousness
[GRAV-i-tee]		Gravity caused the apple to fall.	

2278		집중시키다	engrossed (몰두한)
engross			[1998] absorb
[en-GROHS]		Molly was engrossed in the movie.	

2279		중요한 역할을 하는	
instrumental			
[in-struh-MEN-tl]		Her contribution was instrumental in our success.	

2280		중재하다	[3672] arbitrate
mediate			
[MEE-dee-eyt]		The woman agreed to mediate the argument.	

2281		동양의	[911] eastern
oriental [awr-ee-EN-tl]		Westerners have much interest in oriental art.	

2282		실용적인	
practical [PRAK-ti-kuhl]		My mentor gave me practical advice.	

2283		심판	[993] judge
referee [ref-uh-REE]		The athlete screamed at the referee.	

2284		1. 볼트 2. 빗장 3. 번개 4. 달아나다	[3003] dash
bolt [bohlt]		He will help you tighten these bolts.	

2285	고등	1. 부러지다, 꺾다 2. 사진을 찍다 3. 성급한, 불시의	[1893] crack
snap [snap]		A twig snapped under my feet.	

2286	수능 토플	1. 압박, 부담 2. 종류, 유형 3. 무리하게 사용하다	strenuous (힘을 많이 쏟는) [1243] stress
strain [streyn]		You should try not to put too much strain on your muscles.	

2287	고등 토익 토플	1. 엄격한 2. 엄밀한, 철저한	[3400] rigorous
strict [strikt]		He is very strict about manners.	

2288	고등 토익	1. 불안감 2. 걱정거리, 염려 3. 열망	anxious (불안한,열망하는) [1198] fear
anxiety [ang-ZAHY-i-tee]		Her anxiety about the work was apparent to everyone.	

2289	고등	1. 거리, 길, ~가 2. 방안	[611] road
avenue [AV-uh-nyoo]		We walked down a broad avenue.	

2290	고등 토플 GRE	1. 확신 2. 신념 3. 유죄 선고	convict (유죄 선고하다) convicted (유죄 선고받은) [1110] confidence
conviction [kuhn-VIK-shuhn]		I have a strong conviction that our judgment was right.	

2291	수능	증거, 증언	testify (증언하다) [956] evidence
testimony [TES-tuh-moh-nee]		He is scheduled to give a testimony in the courtroom tomorrow.	

2292	고등 토익	체육관, (실내)경기장	gym (=gymnasium)
gymnasium [jim-NEY-zee-uhm]		Our school has a huge gymnasium.	

2293	고등	농담(하다), 장난(하다)	jokingly (농담으로) [5593] prank
joke [johk]		She told him a joke.	

2294	고등 토익 토플	1. 침략하다, 침입하다 2. 침범하다, 침해하다	invasion (침략)
invade [in-VEYD]		The press can unknowingly invade people's privacy.	

| 2295 | 고등 | 1. 묘사, 이야기 2. 서술, 서사 | narrator (내레이터) narration (서술) |
| narrative [NAR-uh-tiv] | | The author has great narrative skills. | [377] story |

| 2296 | | 용 | |
| dragon [DRAG-uhn] | | Dragons are imaginary animals. | |

| 2297 | 수능 토익 | 1. 자극하다, 활성화시키다 2. 흥분시키다, 고무하다 | stimulus (자극제) stimulation (자극) stimulant (각성제) |
| stimulate [STIM-yuh-leyt] | | The country's priority is to stimulate its economy. | [929] encourage |

| 2298 | 고등 | 1. 시위(하다) 2. 이의를 제기하다 3. 항의(하다), 항변(하다) | [925] object |
| protest [PROH-test] | | We protested against the reduction in wages. | |

| 2299 | 고등 | 선반, 책꽂이 | bookshelf (책꽂이) |
| shelf [shelf] | | I am too short to reach the top shelf. | [2514] rack |

| 2300 | 공무원 편입 | 1. 보수적인 2. 보수주의자 3. 적게 잡은 | |
| conservative [kuhn-SUR-vuh-tiv] | | She comes from a conservative family. | |

| 2301 | 토익 공무원 편입 | 1. 행동 의례, 의전 2. 프로토콜 | [외래어] etiquette |
| protocol [PROH-tuh-kawl] | | The delegates have to be seated according to protocol. | |

| 2302 | 수능 토익 토플 | 수직의, 세로의 | [3975] upright |
| vertical [VUR-ti-kuhl] | | She is good at drawing vertical lines. | |

| 2303 | 고등 | 1. 진실한, 진심으로, 진정으로 2. 진짜의, 진품의 | [1285] true |
| genuine [JEN-yoo-in] | | I would like to express my genuine appreciation to you. | |

| 2304 | 고등 | 1. ~에 의지하다, 기대다 2. 기울다, 기울이다 3. 군살이 없는 | [3341] incline |
| lean [leen] | | You can always lean on me. | |

| 2305 | 고등 토익 | 1. 긴장, 갈등 2. 긴장감, 불안감 3. 팽팽함, 장력 | tense (긴장된, 시제) [1243] stress |
| tension [TEN-shuhn] | | Tensions between the two countries are increasing. | |

| 2306 | 수능 토익 토플 | 전례 없는, 유례없는, 기록적인 | precede (앞서다) [2334] unparalleled |
| unprecedented [uhn-PRES-i-den-tid] | | We are witnessing unprecedented changes in our daily lives. | |

| 2307 | 수능 토익 토플 | 1. 광을 내다, 닦다 2. 다듬다, 손질하다 3. 윤, 광택 4. 폴란드의 | [3816] gloss |
| polish [POL-ish] | | I polished my shoes. | |

| 2308 | 토익 | 1. 문의 사항, 의문(을 제기하다) 2. 묻다, 질문하다 | [263] question |
| query [KWEER-ee] | | What was their response to your query? | |

2309 **nose** [nohz]	초등	1. 코 2. 후각 3. ~을 알아보는 능력	nosy (참견을 좋아하는) [1836] smell
		He blew his nose.	
2310 **wound** [woond]		1. 상처, 부상 2. 상처를 입히다, 감정을 상하게 하다	wounded (상처를 입은) [1745] hurt
		Her wound has not healed yet.	
2311 **garage** [guh-RAHZH]	고등 토익	1. 차고, 주차장 2. 차량 정비소 3. 차고에 넣다	
		I left the car in the garage.	
2312 **charm** [chahrm]	고등	1. 매력 2. 부적 3. 매료하다, 사로잡다	charming (매력적인) [3366] captivate
		I was mesmerized by her charm.	
2313 **console** [kuhn-SOHL]	공무원 편입	1. 위로하다, 달래다 2. 콘솔	[694] comfort
		Nothing could console him.	
2314 **orientation** [awr-ee-uhn-TEY-shuhn]	고등 토익	1. 방향, 지향 2. 성향 3. 오리엔테이션	[1094] direction
		The orientation of the planet's orbit is changing all the time.	
2315 **fiction** [FIK-shuhn]	공무원 편입	1. 소설, 픽션 2. 허구, 거짓	nonfiction (논픽션) fictitious (지어낸) [377] stories
		She prefers poetry to fiction.	
2316 **blame** [bleym]	고등 토플	1. ~을 탓하다, 비난하다 2. 책임, 탓	[2138] fault
		I don't blame you for what has happened.	
2317 **venture** [VEN-cher]	고등	1. 벤처(사업) 2. 모험(하다), 위험을 무릅쓰고 하다	[531] risk
		Venture capital investments are usually considered as high-risk investments.	
2318 **slice** [slahys]	고등	1. 조각 2. 몫, 부분 3. 얇게 썰다, 자르다 4. 베다 5. 삭감하다	[599] piece
		I'd like to have a slice of cake.	
2319 **intellectual** [in-tl-EK-choo-uhl]	고등 토익 토플	1. 지성의, 지능의 2. 지적인, 이지적인 3. 지식인	intellect (지성인) [3360] genius
		He enjoys intellectual conversations.	
2320 **knock** [nok]	고등	1. 노크하다, 두드리다 2. 때리다, 타격하다 3. 찧다, 부딪치다	[1187] beat
		Please knock on my door before you come in.	
2321 **poetry** [POH-i-tree]	고등	시	poet (시인) poetic (시적인) [2468] verse
		I love poetry and music.	
2322 **baseball** [BEYS-bawl]	초등 토익	야구(공)	[1054] ball
		What's your favorite baseball team?	

| 2323
quest
[kwest] | 편입 | 1. 탐구(하다), 추구(하다) 2. 도전 | [571] search |
| | | Nothing will stop him in his quest for truth. | |

| 2324
till
[til] | 고등 | ~까지, ~때까지 | [331] until |
| | | I can't wait till winter. | |

| 2325
meanwhile
[MEEN-hwahyl] | 수능 토플 | 1. 한편 2. 그 사이, 그 동안에 | |
| | | They went out for dinner; meanwhile, I stayed home. | |

| 2326
vessel
[VES-uhl] | 수능 토익 토플 | 1. 선박 2. 그릇, 용기 3. 혈관 | [659] ship |
| | | The vessel will be arriving at the port tomorrow. | |

| 2327
chairman
[CHAIR-muhn] | 고등 토익 | 1. 의장 2. 회장 3. 사무장 | [1544] chair |
| | | The chairman spoke for an hour at the meeting. | |

| 2328
dear
[deer] | | 1. 소중한, 사랑하는 2. (편지 첫 부분에)친애하는 ~께 3. 어머나, 맙소사 | [5175] darling |
| | | My professor is very dear to me. | |

| 2329
dispute
[dih-SPYOOT] | 수능 | 1. 분쟁 2. 논쟁 3. 반박하다, 이의 제기하다 | [4678] quarrel |
| | | The dispute was finally settled. | |

| 2330
refresh
[ri-FRESH] | 토익 공무원 | 1. 상쾌하게 하다 2. 기억을 되살리다 3. 다시 채우다 | refreshing (상쾌하게 하는)
[3215] revive |
| | | A cold bath will refresh you. | |

| 2331
gender
[JEN-der] | 고등 | 성, 성별, 양성 | |
| | | She still believes in traditional gender roles. | |

| 2332
bump
[buhmp] | 고등 토플 | 1. ~에 부딪치다, 찧다 2. 혹 3. 이동시키다 4. 마주치다 | bumpy (울퉁불퉁한)
[2320] knock |
| | | The truck bumped into her car. | |

| 2333
bass
[beys] | | 1. 베이스, (최)저음, 베이스 기타 2. (어류) 배스 | [595] deep |
| | | He always plays his stereo with the bass turned up. | |

| 2334
parallel
[PAR-uh-lel] | 수능 토익 토플 GRE | 1. 평행인 2. 유사한 3. 병행, 병렬의 | unparalleled (견줄데 없는) |
| | | The road runs parallel to the river. | |

| 2335
assault
[uh-SAWLT] | 수능 토플 | 1. 폭행(하다) 2. 공격, 맹비난 3. 괴롭히다 | |
| | | He was charged with sexual assault. | |

| 2336
overwhelming
[oh-ver-HWEL-ming] | 수능 | 1. 압도적인, 엄청난, 너무 강력한 2. 가슴 벅찬 | |
| | | She felt an overwhelming desire to hit him. | |

2337	공무원	1. 기소하다 2. 고발하다, 고소하다 3. 공소를 제기하다	prosecutor (검사)
prosecute			prosecution (기소, 고소)
[PROS-i-kyoot]		The police decided not to prosecute for the lack of sufficient evidence.	

2338	고등 토익	1. 신나게, 황홀하게 만들다, 열광시키다 2. 설렘, 흥분 3. 전율	thriller (긴장감 높은 영화)
thrill			
[thril]		She was thrilled to see her favorite artist.	

2339	수능 토플 GRE	1. 포용하다, 수용하다, 받아들이다 2. 안다, 포옹하다 3. 포괄하다 아우르다	
embrace			
[em-BREYS]		We must embrace all the changes brought about by technological development.	

2340	수능	1. 뇌졸중 2. 쓰다듬다, 어루만지다 3. (노)젓기 4. 획	
stroke			
[strohk]		Air pollution can certainly cause strokes.	

2341	고등 토익	1. 거르다, 건너뛰다 2. 깡충깡충 뛰며 가다 3. 이것저것 바꾸다	[1276] jump
skip			
[skip]		I skipped dinner last night.	

2342		1. 곰팡이 2. 주형, 틀 3. 유형 4. (틀을 활용해) 만들다	[949] shape
mold			
[mohld]		This bread tastes of mold.	

2343	수능 토익	금지하다	prohibition (금지)
prohibit			prohibited (금지된)
[proh-HIB-it]		Smoking is prohibited on the train.	[3590] forbid

2344	고등 토익 토플	1. 처벌, 형벌 2. 징계	punish (처벌하다)
punishment			
[PUHN-ish-muhnt]		He deserved the punishment he received.	

2345	수능	1. 방패, 보호자, 보호막 2. 보호하다, 가리다 3. 경찰관 배지	
shield			
[sheeld]		The immune system is our body's shield against infection.	

2346	수능 토익	1. 세입자, 소작농인, 임차인 2. 세 들어 살다, 소작하다	
tenant			
[TEN-uhnt]		The sofa was left by the previous tenant.	

2347	토익 공무원 편입	1. 예언자, 선지자 2. 선도자	prophecy (예언)
prophet			
[PROF-it]		I'm afraid I'm no weather prophet.	

2348	고등 토플	후자의, 후반의, 마지막의	
latter			
[LAT-er]		Of the two choices, I prefer the latter.	

2349	수능 토플	1. 방, 특수목적실, 공간 2. (심)실, 기계실	[382] room
chamber			
[CHEYM-ber]		Meetings will be held in the chamber.	

2350	고등 토익	장벽, 한계, 장애물	[3084] obstacle
barrier			
[BAR-ee-er]		They fell in love in spite of the language barrier.	

2351	초등	풀, 잔디		[2995] weed
grass [gras]		Let's sit on the grass.		

2352	고등 토익 토플	1. ~을 대신하여, 대표하여 2. ~을 위해		
behalf [bih-HAF]		I welcome you on behalf of the company.		

2353		1. 향신료, 양념 2. 묘미, 흥취		spicy (매운)
spice [spahys]		This store has a variety of spices.		

2354	고등 토익	10대의		teenager (=teen)
teen [teen]		He is still in his late teens.		

2355	고등	1. 여론 조사(를 하다) 2. 투표, 개표 3. 득표하다	
poll [pohl]		The poll showed that 60% of the population supported the new administration.	

2356	수능 토익 토플	1. 유산 2. 혈통, 민족	
heritage [HER-i-tij]		This building is part of our national heritage.	

2357	고등	1. 희생(하다) 2. 희생물 3. 제물(을 바치다)	
sacrifice [SAK-ruh-fahys]		He sacrificed everything for you.	

2358	고등 토플	1. 친구, 또래, 동료 2. 유심히 보다, 눈여겨보다	
peer [peer]		Don't give in to peer pressure.	

2359	고등 토익 GRE	중대한, 중요한, 결정적인	
crucial [KROO-shuhl]		Right evidence is crucial when drawing up policies.	

2360	고등 토익 토플	꿰매다, 바느질하다		sewing (바느질) [2618] stitch
sew [soh]		She knows how to sew by hand.		

2361	토익	1.자리, 시간대 2. 구멍 3. 넣다, 끼우다		[186] opening
slot [slot]		Visitors can book a time slot a week in advance.		

2362	고등	1. 녹다, 녹이다 2. 용해되다		meltdown (무너짐) [5522] thaw
melt [melt]		The sun melted the snow.		

2363		1. 은하(수) 2. 기라성 같은 사람들		galactic (은하계의) [4661] cosmos
galaxy [GAL-uh k-see]		There are many galaxies in the universe.		

2364	수능 토익	1. 떠맡다, 책임을 지다 2. 착수하다		[895] engage
undertake [uhn-der-TEYK]		The professor decided to undertake a new research project.		

2365	토익 공무원 토플 편입	1. 의무적인 2. 필수적인	mandate (지령)
mandatory [MAN-duh-tawr-ee]		Attendance is mandatory at all meetings.	[5093] compulsory

2366	초등	귀여운, 사랑스러운	
cute [kyoot]		Dogs are cute.	

2367	초등	1. 목욕 2. 욕조, 욕실	bathe (목욕하다)
bath [bath]		She takes a bath once a day.	sunbathe (일광욕하다) [1357] wash

2368	공무원 편입	1. 익명의, 숨은 2. 특색 없는	
anonymous [uh-NON-uh-muhs]		The donor prefers to remain anonymous.	

2369	초등 토익 토플	1. 콩 2. 열매	soybean (콩)
bean [been]		Chocolate is made from cocoa beans.	

2370	수능 토익	1. 동의(하다), 허락(하다) 2. 합의 3. 만장일치로	[1072] approval
consent [kuhn-SENT]		Silence often implies consent.	

2371	고등 토익	1. 크리스탈, 수정 2. 결정체 3. 유리	[4900] quartz
crystal [KRIS-tl]		These expensive glasses are made of crystal.	

2372	토익	1. 내각, 각료 2. 캐비닛, 수납장	[4961] cupboard
cabinet [KAB-uh-nit]		There will be a cabinet meeting this afternoon.	

2373	고등 토익	재활용하다, 재사용하다	
recycle [ree-SAHY-kuhl]		This shop uses recycled paper.	

2374	토익 편입	1. 들러붙다, 부착되다 2. 고수하다, 충실히 지키다	adhesive (접착제) adherence (충실하다)
adhere [ad-HEER]		Wet clothes adhere to the skin.	adherent (충신) [915] stick

2375	수능 토익	1. 합병하다, 합치다 2. 어우러지다, 융합되다	merger (합병)
merge [murj]		They decided to merge the two companies into one.	[613] combine

2376	고등	쌀, 밥, 벼	
rice [rahys]		Would you like another bowl of rice?	

2377	수능 토익	1. 시뮬레이션, 모의 실험 2. 가장함	simulate (가장하다)
simulation [sim-yuh-LEY-shuhn]		The pilot's skills are tested through simulation.	[431] model

2378	초등	1. 몹시 화난 2. 미친, 제정신이 아닌 3. 열광하는, 사족을 못 쓰는	madness (미친 것)
mad [mad]		He was mad at her for calling him stupid.	[2693] insane

2379	고등	1. 구절, 관용구 2. 표현하다	paraphrase (바꿔쓰다)
phrase			[380] word
[freyz]		She taught him some useful phrases in French.	

2380	공무원	1.인원, 인력, 직원 2. 인사과	[634] staff
personnel			
[pur-suh-NEL]		All personnel had to carry security badges.	

2381	수능 토익	1. 재개하다, 다시 시작하다 2. 자기 자리로 다시 돌아가다 3. 이력서, 레쥬메	
resume			
[ri-ZOOM]		She resumed reading after dinner.	

2382	고등 토익	1. 미네랄, 광물, 무기물 2. 광천수	[3514] fossil
mineral			
[MIN-er-uhl]		She likes drinking mineral water.	

2383	수능 토익 토플	(과학) 분자	molecular (분자의)
molecule			[2701] particle
[MOL-uh-kyool]		A water molecule is composed of two hydrogens and an oxygen.	

2384	토익	1. 배럴 2. 통	
barrel			
[BAR-uhl]		How many barrels of oil are produced daily?	

2385	고등 토익	1. 강의, 강연 2. 잔소리, 설교	[392] talk
lecture			
[LEK-cher]		I slept in and missed the morning lecture.	

2386	수능 토익	1. 대신하다, 대체하다, 교체되다 2. 대리자, 대용물 3. 교체선수	substitution (대체)
substitute			[673] replacement
[SUHB-sti-toot]		You can substitute oil for butter in this recipe.	

2387	수능 토익 토플	이주, 이동	migrate (이동)
migration			[2423] immigration
[mahy-GREY-shuhn]		Scientists have been studying the migration patterns of salmon.	

2388	고등 토익 토플	유능한	competency (능력)
competent			incompetent (무능한)
[KOM-pi-tuhnt]		He is a very competent employee.	[1195] capable

2389	고등 토익	허리, 엉덩이	
hip			
[hip]		The lady slipped and broke her hip.	

2390	수능 토익 토플	문의	inquire (문의하다)
inquiry			[1004] investigation
[in-KWAHYUHR-ee]		For inquiries, please contact us via email.	

2391	고등 토익	1. 땀 (흘리다) 2. 열심히 일하다	sweaty (땀에 젖은)
sweat			[7020] perspire
[swet]		His t-shirt was soaked in sweat.	

2392	토익 토플 편입	엘리트, 지식인	elitism (엘리트주의)
elite			
[ih-LEET]		Elite level players compete in the Olympics.	

2393	고등 토플	파묻다, 매장하다	[1262] hide
bury [BER-ee]		The man buried cash in his backyard.	

2394	고등 토플	병력	[1512] army
troops [troops]		Many US troops are based in Korea.	

2395	고등 토익	경매(에 부치다)	
auction [AWK-shuhn]		The painting was put up for auction.	

2396	수능 토익	두 개의, 이중의	[1086] double
dual [DOO-uhl]		He received a dual degree in Math and Economics.	

2397	고등	솔로, 혼자서	[1183] alone
solo [SOH-loh]		I travelled across the world solo.	

2398	초등	감자	
potato [puh-TEY-toh]		I had a baked potato this morning.	

2399	고등 토익 토플	버리다	[241] leave
abandon [uh-BAN-duhn]		We had to abandon the ship.	

2400	고등 토익	문단, 단락	[522] section
paragraph [PAR-uh-graf]		The first paragraph is the hardest to write in an essay.	

2401	고등	극복하다	[3501] conquer
overcome [oh-ver-KUHM]		Learn how to overcome your fears.	

2402		솔기(를 내다)	seamless (끊김없이) [3268] vein
seam [seem]		The seam of the pants tore apart during exercise.	

2403		지퍼(로 잠그다)	zipper (지퍼) unzip (지퍼를 열다) [3003] dash
zip [zip]		Can you zip up my bag?	

2404	수능 토익	1. 그러므로 2. 이제부터	[1746] consequently
hence [hens]		He lied to me, hence I dislike him.	

2405	수능 토익 토플	도입하다, 부과하다	imposing (강한 인상을 주는, 위압하는) [395] enforce
impose [im-POHZ]		The government imposes taxes on citizens.	

2406	토익	스타디움, 경기장	[3186] arena
stadium [STEY-dee-uhm]		There are many athletes in the stadium.	

2407	토익	기와, 타일	
tile			
[tahyl]		The tiles of the bathroom are white.	

2408	공무원 토플	1. 경보기, 자명종 2. 놀라게 하다	alarming (걱정스러운) [2038] alert
alarm			
[uh-LAHRM]		Please turn off the alarm.	

2409	고등 토플	1. 콘크리트(로 만들어진) 2. 확실한, 확고한	[1307] solid
concrete			
[KON-kreet]		Concrete walls are more sturdy than wooden walls.	

2410	토익 공무원	1. 마디, 옹이 2. 교점 3. (전자) 노드	[3344] knot
node			
[nohd]		The old tree had many nodes.	

2411	고등	1. 쌍둥이(의) 2. (닮은) 한 쌍	[1086] double
twin			
[twin]		It is hard to distinguish twins.	

2412	토익 공무원 토플 편입	구별하다, 분류하다	
distinguish			
[dih-STING-gwish]		She couldn't distinguish the gender of the puppy.	

2413	토익 공무원	1. 투명한 2. 솔직한, 속보이는	transparency (투명성) [372] clear
transparent			
[trans-PAIR-uhnt]		Glass is transparent.	

2414		통풍, 환기	vent (통풍구)
ventilation			
[ven-tl-EY-shuhn]		The ventilation is bad in the office.	

2415	초등	오늘밤	[388] night
tonight			
[tuh-NAHYT]		What are you doing tonight?	

2416		1. 미혼남 2. 학사	[548] single
bachelor			
[BACH-uh-ler]		He has been a bachelor for 10 years.	

2417	고등	1. 지리학 2. 지리, 지형	geographic (지리적인)
geography			
[jee-OG-ruh-fee]		I study geography at university.	

2418	고등	기분, 감정	[4080] temper
mood			
[MOOD]		He has been in a grumpy mood since he woke up.	

2419	토익 공무원 토플	1. 번식하다 2. 복사하다, 복제하다	reproduction (번식) [931] copy
reproduce			
[ree-pruh-DOOS]		Rabbits reproduce quickly.	

2420	고등	1. (제복, 교복 등의) 유니폼 2. 일정한, 한결같은	uniformity (균일성) [1337] consistent
uniform			
[YOO-nuh-fawrm]		Students wear uniforms to school.	

2421	토익 토플	1. 소형의, 휴대용의 2. 밀집한, 빽빽하게 찬	[219] small
compact [kuhm-PAKT]		She packed a compact hairdryer for the trip.	
2422	고등 GRE	1. 지방의 2. 시골의, 전원의	[4466] rustic
rural [ROOR-uhl]		Rural areas are less polluted.	
2423	수능 토익	이민자, 이주민	immigration (이주)
immigrant [IM-i-gruh nt]		It is difficult for immigrants to learn the native language.	
2424	토익	마감일자	
deadline [DED-lahyn]		You must finish everything by the deadline.	
2425	고등 토익	우아한, 품위있는	elegance (우아함)
elegant [EL-i-guhnt]		He is a very elegant dancer.	
2426	고등 토익	1. 고무 2. (영국) 지우개	
rubber [RUHB-er]		Rubber is used to make erasers.	
2427	고등 토플	~에 몰두하다, 헌신하다	devotion (헌신)
devote [dih-VOHT]		She devoted her time to her career.	
2428	고등 토플	1. 치료법, 교정법 2. 치료하다, 구제하나	
remedy [REM-i-dee]		What is the remedy for a cold?	
2429	고등	예상(하다), 예보(하다)	[1452] predict
forecast [FAWR-kast]		According to the national weather forecast, it will rain today.	
2430	초등 토플	입술	
lip [lip]		He bit his lip while chewing food.	
2431	고등	1. 망치다 2. 잔해, 옛터	[1255] destroy
ruin [ROO-in]		The rain ruined their plans to have a picnic.	
2432	수능	뒤집다, 젖히다, 넘기다	
flip [flip]		Flip the pancake now.	
2433	토플	1. 소화제 2. 소화의	digest (소화하다) indigestion (소화불량)
digestive [dih-JES-tiv]		If you feel queasy you should take a digestive.	
2434	수능 토플	1. 절충안 2. 타협하다, 절충하다 3. 위험에 노출되다	[1342] settlement
compromise [KOM-pruh-mahyz]		The compromise made everyone satisfied.	

2435	고등 토익	1. 모으다, 집합하다 2. 조립하다	disassemble (해체하다)
assemble			assembly (국회, 조립)
[uh-SEM-buhl]		Please assemble all students to the classroom.	[1502] gather

2436	고등 토플	1. 자부심, 자존심 2. 자부하다, 자랑하다	[3675] vanity
pride			
[prahyd]		He takes pride in his son's success.	

2437	초등	1. 접착제, 풀 2. 붙이다	[2655] paste
glue			
[gloo]		You can use glue or tape to stick the paper to the book.	

2438	토익 공무원	1. (유통) 기한이 지나다 2. 만기가 되다, 만료되다	expiration (만료)
expire			[4782] perish
[ik-SPAHYUHR]		This cheese expired last month.	

2439	공무원 편입	1. 사기 2. 사기꾼	fraudster (사기꾼)
fraud			defraud (속이다)
			fraudulent (사기성의)
[frawd]		He lost a lot of money due to fraud.	[2774] cheat

2440		귀걸이	[1271] ring
earring			
[EER-ring]		She spent the whole day looking for here lost earring.	

2441		고향	
hometown			
[HOHM-toun]		The athlete was happy to be back in his hometown.	

2442	토익 토플	야생	[1547] wild
wildlife			
[WAHYLD-lahyf]		We have to protect the wildlife.	

2443	고등 토플	널리 퍼진	[329] general
widespread			
[WAHYD-spred]		The tornado caused widespread damage along the east coast.	

2444	토익	시내	[261] city
downtown			
[DOUN-toun]		My office is located downtown.	

2445	토익	노트북	[575] computer
laptop			
[LAP-top]		I bought a new laptop.	

2446	토익	여행 가방	[218] case
suitcase			
[SOOT-keys]		I carry my laptop in my suitcase.	

2447		점수판	
scoreboard			
[SKAWR-bawrd]		The player looked up at the scoreboard.	

2448	공무원 토플 편입 GRE	피난민	refuge (피난)
refugee			[6280] fugitive
[ref-yoo-JEE]		Refugees cannot return to their country because of persecution.	

2449	수능 토익 토플 GRE	특허(권)	[1079] obvious
patent [PAT-nt]		If you have a good idea, you should apply for a patent.	
2450	고등	이야기, 소문	folktale (민화) fairytale (동화) [377] story
tale [teyl]		Cinderella is a tale about being kind.	
2451	고등	1. 괴롭히다, 귀찮게 하다 2. 신경 쓰다	[1446] trouble
bother [BOTH-er]		Don't bother your brother, he is trying to study.	
2452	고등 토익	1. 후추 2. 고추	[2353] spice
pepper [PEP-er]		Add more pepper to the soup.	
2453	고등 토플	1. 부족, 집단 2. 패거리	[3776] clan
tribe [trahyb]		This tribe lives in the Amazon.	
2454	초등	성	[2879] palace
castle [KAS-uhl]		The prince lives in the castle.	
2455	수능 토플	1. 지배하다, 군림하다 2. 우세하다	dominant (지배적인) dominance (지배력) indomitable (불굴의) [273] control
dominate [DOM-uh-neyt]		The dictator dominated the country.	
2456	고등	1. 사막, 불모지 2. 버리다	deserted (버려진) [2399] abandon
desert [DEZ-ert]		No animals live in the desert.	
2457	초등	1. (동물 등의) 꼬리 2. 미행하다 3. 동전 뒷면	[1664] rear
tail [teyl]		Horses have long tails.	
2458	고등 토플	칭찬(하다), 찬양(하다)	[2646] compliment
praise [preyz]		The parents praised their children for their grades.	
2459	공무원	멍청한, 어리석은	stupidity (멍청함) [3659] dumb
stupid [STOO-pid]		Don't do anything stupid.	
2460		지루한, 재미없는	boredom (지루함) bore (지루하게 하다) [3731] dull
boring [BAWR-ing]		The movie was boring.	
2461	고등	제국, 왕국	[914] kingdom
empire [EM-pahyuhr]		The British created a great empire.	
2462	고등 토익	1. 대륙 2. 육지, 본토	
continent [KON-tn-uhnt]		There are seven continents in the world.	

2463	수능 토익 토플	만성의, 고질적인	[2557] persistent
chronic [KRON-ik]		He is a chronic smoker.	

2464	수능	1. 대피소, 은신처 2. 보호하다	[2448] refuge
shelter [SHEL-ter]		After the earthquake, the government provided shelter for homeless people.	

2465	고등 토익 GRE	짜증나는, 귀찮은	annoy (귀찮게하다) [2895] irritating
annoying [uh-NOI-ing]		Her brother kept annoying her.	

2466	고등 토플	닦아내다	wiper (와이퍼) [559] clean
wipe [wahyp]		Can you please wipe the table?	

2467	토익 공무원	알레르기	allergen (알레르기 덩어리) allergic (알레르기의)
allergy [AL-er-jee]		Many people have an allergy to peanuts.	

2468	수능 토플	1. (시의) 절 2. 운문	[2321] poetry
verse [vurs]		What is your favorite verse of the poem?	

2469	고등	흥미로운, 매혹적인	fascinate (흥미를 사로잡다) [2312] charming
fascinating [FAS-uh-ney-ting]		He is a fascinating man.	

2470	초등 토익	배고픈, 공복의	hunger (배고픔) [3977] starving
hungry [HUHNG-gree]		Are you hungry?	

2471	공무원 편입	유산	[2356] heritage
legacy [LEG-uh-see]		He left a large legacy for his children.	

2472	고등 토플	성직자, 목사, 사제	[1558] minister
priest [preest]		Priests take care of their clergy.	

2473	고등 토플	1. 유독성의 2. 중독적인	detoxify (해독하다) toxin (독소) [2686] poisonous
toxic [TOK-sik]		Toxic oil spills killed many sea creatures.	

2474	고등 토플	구두의, 구술의	[440] spoken
oral [AWR-uhl]		The oral exam will last for 10 minutes.	

2475	초등 토익	1. 수수께끼, 난문 2. 혼란스럽게 만들다	[5291] riddle
puzzle [PUHZ-uhl]		She loved solving puzzles.	

2476	공무원	중심부, 중추	[447] focus
hub [huhb]		Cities are hubs of economic activity.	

2477 strap [strap]		1. (가죽) 끈 2. 끈으로 묶다	[2094] belt
		The strap of the bag tore apart.	
2478 dot [dot]	고등	점(을 찍다)	
		Ladybugs have dots on their shells.	
2479 comprise [kuhm-PRAHYZ]	수능 토플	~으로 구성되다, ~로 이뤄지다	
		Each hotel room is comprised of two bathrooms and three beds.	
2480 anniversary [an-uh-VUR-suh-ree]	고등 토익 토플	기념일	[1134] celebration
		They went to a fancy restaurant to celebrate their 10th anniversary.	
2481 shed [shed]	공무원	1. (허물이나 옷을) 벗다, 없애다 2. (눈물을) 떨어트리다 3. 헛간	[5457] shack
		Mark shed his clothes on the floor.	
2482 tolerate [TOL-uh-reyt]	공무원 토플	참다, 견디다, 묵인하다	tolerance (참음) intolerable (참을 수 없는) [2516] endure
		The teacher couldn't tolerate her students being rude.	
2483 steady [STED-ee]	고등 토익 토플	1. 꾸준한, 지속적인 2. 견고한, 안정적인	[1305] stable
		Birth rates are in a steady decline.	
2484 rod [rod]	수능 토플	1. 막대기 2. 낚싯대 3. 매	
		The hikers used a rod to climb the mountain.	
2485 rival [RAHY-vuhl]	고등	경쟁자, 적수	
		Rivals can inspire you to work hard.	
2486 whereas [hwair-AZ]	수능 토플	1. ~와 대조되게 2. ~임에도 불구하고, 그러나, 그런데	
		I don't like milk whereas my brother loves it.	
2487 allocate [AL-uh-keyt]	수능 토익	배분하다, 할당하다	allocation (배분) reallocate (재분배하다)
		During the war, the government allocated food to citizens.	
2488 cheer [cheer]	고등 토익	격려(하다), 응원(하다)	cheerful (쾌활한)
		The crowd cheered the athletes.	
2489 privilege [PRIV-uh-lij]	수능 토플	특권, 특혜	privileged (특권을 가진)
		Voting is a right, not a privilege.	
2490 bulk [buhlk]	수능 토익 토플	부피, 크기	
		The package was difficult to carry because of its large bulk.	

2491	수능	1. 젓다, 섞다 2. 동요시키다	stir-fry (볶다)
stir			
[stur]		The chefs stirred the soup.	

2492	고등	시장, 구청장	
mayor			
[MEY-er]		The mayor was elected by the citizens.	

2493		중년의, 노인층	elder (손위의, 노인)
elderly			eldest (가장 나이가 많은)
[EL-der-lee]		The elderly should be respected.	[432] aged

2494	수능	암시하다, 의미하다	implied (암시된)
imply			[591] suggest
[im-PLAHY]		Her criticism implied she was better than him.	

2495	고등 토플	중립적인	neutralize (중립으로 만들다)
neutral			[2753] unbiased
[NOO-truhl]		Spain is a very neutral country.	

2496	고등 토플	감사한, 고마운	[289] thankful
grateful			
[GREYT-fuhl]		I am so grateful for your help.	

2497	수능	통합하다, 접목하다	[1750] incorporate
integrate			
[IN-ti-greyt]		Integrate exercise into your daily routine.	

2498		관심, 주의력	[447] focus
attention			
[uh-TEN-shuhn]		The child requires much attention.	

2499		위원회	[1051] council
committee			
[kuh-MIT-ee]		The committee gathered to discuss a severe issue.	

2500		축 쳐진	[1891] loose
baggy			
[BAG-ee]		Baggy pants symbolize hiphop.	

2501		꾸벅 졸다	
snooze			
[snooz]		My friend snoozed in front of the teacher.	

2502	고등 토플 GRE	1. 외국의, 외국인의 2. 외계인 3. 생소한	alienate (멀리하다)
alien			[1442] foreign
[EYL-yuhn]		She had a hard time getting used to alien customs in Spain.	

2503	고등 토플	보통의, 평범한	[485] common
ordinary			
[AWR-dn-er-ee]		It was just an ordinary day.	

2504	고등 GRE	1. 남는, 여분의 2. 아끼다, 절약하다 3. 용서해주다, 면제하다	sparingly (절약하여, 조금씩)
spare			[216] free
[spair]		Do you have a spare tire?	

2505	토익	1. 간식, 가벼운 식사 2. 과자	[2061] bite
snack [snak]		We are having dinner soon, do not eat any snacks.	

2506	고등	무한한, 끝없는	infinity (무한대) finite (유한의)
infinite [IN-fuh-nit]		There is an infinite number of stars in the universe.	

2507	고등 토익 토플	관대한, 마음이 넓은	generosity (관대함) [1840] charitable
generous [JEN-er-uhs]		Generous people donate money to charity.	

2508	토익	1. 굽다 2. 엄하게 심문하다	[외래어] barbecue
grill [gril]		Sausages should be grilled for five minutes.	

2509	공무원 토플	검, 칼	[2010] blade
sword [sawrd]		Be careful, the sword is very sharp.	

2510	수능 토익 토플	정련하다, 정제하다	refinement (정제) [401] improve
refine [ri-FAHYN]		You can refine sugar by boiling it.	

2511	공무원	1. 연금 2. 펜션	[1440] retirement
pension [PEN-shuhn]		People over the age of 65 can get pensions.	

2512	수능 토플	1. 생식력, 다산의 2. 비옥함, 풍요로움	fertilizer (비료) fertile (비옥한) infertility (불임성)
fertility [fer-TIL-i-tee]		Obesity used to be seen as a sign of fertility.	

2513	고등	아주 아름다운, 아주 멋진	
gorgeous [GAWR-juhs]		That dress is gorgeous.	

2514	토익	거치대, 받침대, 선반	
rack [rak]		Please fold the towels and put them on the rack.	

2515	고등 토플	수확(하다), 추수(하다)	[420] collect
harvest [HAHR-vist]		Farmers harvest crops during fall.	

2516	고등	1. 견디다, 인내하다 2. 지속하다	endurance (지구력) [1109] bear
endure [en-DOOR]		The child couldn't endure the pain.	

2517		1. 코일, (철사 등의) 뭉치 2. 똘똘 감다, 고리를 이루다	recoil (움찔하다) [2202] twist
coil [koil]		There is a coil of rope in the cabinet.	

2518	공무원	1. 상원 2. 입법부 3. 의회	senator (상원의원) [1870] congress
senate [SEN-it]		There are 100 politicians in the Senate.	

2519	수능	신의, 신성한	divinity (신)
divine			[1994] heavenly
[dih-VAHYN]		Churches and temples are divine places.	

2520	토플	에이커 (약 4,800 평방미터의 땅)	[외래어] hectare
acre			
[EY-ker]		The farmer owns 10 acres of land.	

2521	토플 편입 GRE	1. 완충제 2. 완충액	buffering (버퍼링)
buffer			[3238] cushion
[BUHF-er]		The DMZ is a buffer between South and North Korea.	

2522	고등 토플	1. 불꽃, 스파크 2. 촉발하다	[3441] sparkle
spark			
[spahrk]		When he cut the wire, there was a small spark.	

2523	초등	사자	
lion			
[LAHY-uh n]		There are lions in the zoo.	

2524	편입	1. 암시, 힌트 2. 넌지시 비추다, 암시하다	
hint			
[hint]		This question is too difficult. Can I have a hint?	

2525	고등	위, 복부, 배	stomachache (복통)
stomach			
[STUHM-uhk]		Her stomach hurts when she drinks too much milk.	

2526	토익 공무원	옷, (특별한 날의) 복장	
outfit			
[OUT-fit]		What's your outfit for the party?	

2527	토플	시각의	
optical			
[OP-ti-kuh l]		Optical illusions can confuse people.	

2528	고등 토익	비누	
soap			
[sohp]		He smells like soap.	

2529	토익 공무원	1. 인턴 2. (정치범이나 포로를) 억류하다, 구금하다	
intern			
[in-TURN]		Some interns work without getting paid.	

2530	토익 공무원	1. 유용한 2. 손재주가 있는	
handy			
[HAN-dee]		You should always take an umbrella. It is very handy.	

2531	공무원	섭취량, 수용량	
intake			
[IN-teyk]		Her caffeine intake is too high.	

2532	고등	1. 용서하다 2. (빚을) 탕감하다	
forgive			
[fer-GIV]		I forgive you for your mistake.	

2533	공무원 편입 GRE	1. 다재다능한, 다방면에 능한 2. 변덕스러운	versatility (다재다능함)
versatile [VUR-suh-tl]		He is a versatile employee with many skills.	

2534	고등	1. 화살표 2. 화살	
arrow [AR-oh]		The arrow is pointing to the left.	

2535	초등	1. 거품, 기포 2. 끓다	
bubble [BUHB-uhl]		There are many bubbles in champagne.	

2536	수능	1. 의회 2. 국회	
parliament [PAHR-luh-muh nt]		Politicians vote on laws in parliament.	

2537	고등 토플	주장하다, 끝까지 우기다	insistence (고집, 주장)
insist [in-SIST]		He insisted he was correct.	

2538	고등 토플 GRE	찬반 논란, 논쟁	controversial (논란의)
controversy [KON-truh-vur-see]		There is a controversy about which political candidate is most suitable.	

2539	토익	출구, 배출구	
outlet [OUT-let]		The Pacific ocean is the outlet for many rivers.	

2540		격자무늬, 그리드	[3167] mesh
grid [grid]		The shirt had a grid pattern.	

2541	고등 토익	1. 영수증 2. 수령, 받기	[230] receiving
receipt [ri-SEET]		A receipt shows how much money you spent.	

2542	고등 토익	1. 저작권, 판권 2. 저작권으로 (작품을) 보호하다	
copyright [KOP-ee-rahyt]		The movie is protected with copyright.	

2543	고등	부정부패, 비리, 타락	corrupt (부패한) [1980] immorality
corruption [kuh-RUHP-shuhn]		The government was criticized for corruption.	

2544	편입	1. 신임장을 주다 2. 공인하다	accredited (공인된)
accredit [uh-KRED-it]		After passing the exam, she was accredited as a teacher.	

2545	토익	1. 치아의 2. 치과의	
dental [DEN-tl]		He has many dental problems.	

2546	초등	유령, 귀신, 망령	
ghost [gohst]		I think I saw a ghost in the kitchen.	

2547	공무원 토플	굉장한, 기막힌	
fabulous			
[FAB-yuh-luhs]		This vacation was fabulous.	

2548		님, 선생님, 남자에 대한 경칭	
sir			
[sur]		Sir, may I ask you a question?	

2549	고등	1. 짝, 친구 2. 짝짓기	
mate			
[meyt]		Peacocks have colorful feathers to attract mates.	

2550	고등 토익	그만두다, 사퇴하다	[439] stop
quit			
[kwit]		She quit her job as a teacher.	

2551	토익 공무원 편입	1. 공제, 차감 2. (연역적) 추론, 추정	[4210] inference
deduction			
[dih-DUHK-shuhn]		Police officers made deductions about the identity of the criminal.	

2552	공무원 편입	1. 가짜의, 위조의 2. 속이다	[5303] counterfeit
fake			
[feyk]		Fake diamonds are very popular these days.	

2553	고등 토익	1. 위험(한 일) 2. 모험	hazardous (위험한)
hazard			[531] risk
[HAZ-erd]		Drinking alcohol is a health hazard.	

2554	토익 토플 GRE	1. 함대, 선대 2. 빠르게 움직이고 사라지다	fleeting (빨리 지나가는, 덧없는)
fleet			[3860] swift
[fleet]		A fleet of ships entered the port.	

2555	공무원 편입	1. 혼종, 잡종 2. 혼합된, 혼성의	[656] mixed
hybrid			
[HAHY-brid]		Hybrid crops can withstand harsh temperatures.	

2556	고등 토익	1. 제트기 2. (빠르게) 분출되다	[6323] gush
jet			
[jet]		Jets are faster than planes.	

2557	수능 토플	1. 끈기 있는, 고집하는 2. 지속적인	persist (지속하다)
persistent			[1036] firm
[per-SIS-tuhnt]		Persistent students have good grades.	

2558		종업원, 웨이터	waitress (여종업원)
waiter			[외래어] bartender
[WEY-ter]		The waiter's services were excellent.	

2559	편입	1. 거품(을 일게 하다) 2. 스펀지, 발포 고무	[6742] froth
foam			
[fohm]		The beer had a thick layer of foam.	

2560	토플	1. 갈다, 분쇄하다 2. 지루한 반복 업무	[2692] crush
grind			
[grahynd]		Grind coffee beans to make coffee powder.	

2561		통일시키다	unified (통일된)
unify			reunification (재통일)
[YOO-nuh-fahy]		Music unifies the whole world.	[1409] unite

2562		1. 임원 2. 행정부 3. 경영의, 행정의	
executive			
[ig-ZEK-yuh-tiv]		Two executives of the firm were fired.	

2563		1. 에세이, 수필, 평론 2. 시도(하다)	[982] attempt
essay			
[ES-ey]		The assignment is to write a 3000-word essay.	

2564	토플	1. 소총, 라이플총 2. (공 등을) 날리다, 차다	
rifle			
[RAHY-fuhl]		He got a rifle for Christmas.	

2565	공무원	(신체의) 간	
liver			
[LIV-er]		Drinking harms the liver.	

2566	고등 토플 GRE	풍부, 다량	abundant (풍부한)
abundance			abound (풍부하다)
[uh-BUHN-duhns]		The country has an abundance of natural resources.	[1299] plenty

2567	고등 토익 토플	1. 천장 2. (가격, 요금 등의) 최고 한도	[1967] roof
ceiling			
[SEE-ling]		The ceiling began to crumble.	

2568	고등	1. 숭배(하다) 2. 예배(하다)	
worship			
[WUR-ship]		Many people worship God.	

2569	수능 GRE	1. 미묘한, 미세한 2. 포착하기 어려운	[3126] delicate
subtle			
[SUHT-l]		There is a subtle change in his expression.	

2570	수능	1. 청소하다, 쓸다 2. 확 지나가다 3. 싹쓸이	
sweep			
[sweep]		Please sweep the floor with a broom.	

2571	고등 토익	1. 캐주얼의, 평상시의 2. 무심한, 태평한	[1747] informal
casual			
[KAZH-oo-uhl]		Her outfit was very casual.	

2572	수능 토플	1. 폭발(하다) 2. 발사하다 3. 신나는 경험	[2828] burst
blast			
[blast]		The terrorists blasted the building.	

2573	수능 토익 토플 GRE	1. 방해하다 2. 분열하다	[2665] disturb
disrupt			
[dis-RUHPT]		The event was disrupted by gunfire.	

2574	고등	1. 희미한, 가냘픈 2. 실신(하다)	faintly (희미하게)
faint			[1445] weak
[feynt]		I could see a faint outline of the criminal.	

2575 **charter** [CHAHR-ter]		1. 리스, 전세 2. 공립의 3. 공식문서, 선언문	[2125] lease
		The prince chartered a plane for his trip to Hawaii.	
2576 **conversely** [kuhn-VURS-lee]		정반대로	
		I liked the movie. My friend, conversely, did not like it at all.	
2577 **lodge** [loj]	공무원	1. 숙박하다, 임시로 거주하다 2. 오두막집	[2642] cabin
		Could I lodge at your home?	
2578 **steer** [steer]	토익 토플	1. (차 등을) 조종하다, 몰다 2. 이끌다	steering wheel (자동차 핸들) [609] guide
		Steer your car to the right.	
2579 **inflation** [in-FLEY-shuhn]	수능 토익 토플	물가 상승, 인플레이션	inflate (부풀리다) [280] increase
		During inflation, everything gets more valuable except money.	
2580 **raid** [reyd]	토플	1. 급습(하다), 기습(하다) 2. 불시 단속	[709] attack
		The thieves raided the museum.	
2581 **creek** [kreek]	수능 토플	1. 시내, 개천 2. (바다나 강 등의) 작은 만	[1470] stream
		Small fish are living in the creek.	
2582 **fuse** [fyooz]	수능 토플	1. (녹여서) 융합하다 2. 퓨즈, 도화선	fusion (융합) [2375] merge
		Metal can be fused to other substances at high temperatures.	
2583 **atom** [AT-uhm]	고등	1. 원자 2. 원자력 3. 미진, 미량	[6669] speck
		Everything is made of atoms.	
2584 **fence** [fens]	토플 편입	1. 울타리 2. 펜싱, 검술	fend off (받아넘기다)
		Fences protect houses from stray animals.	
2585 **horror** [HAWR-er]	고등 토플	공포, 무서움	[1699] terror
		Photographs revealed the horror of war.	
2586 **intermediate** [in-ter-MEE-dee-it]	고등 토플	1. 중간 단계의, 중급의 2. 중개자, 중재자	[1047] middle
		She is an intermediate level swimmer.	
2587 **span** [span]	수능	1. (지속) 기간 2. 폭 3. (일정 시공간에) 걸치다, 걸리다	wingspan (날개폭) [2124] extent
		The job was finished in the span of an hour.	
2588 **duration** [doo-REY-shuhn]	토익 토플	지속 기간, ~동안	[545] period
		The duration of the exam is one hour.	

2589	토익	학기	[343] term
semester [si-MES-ter]		There are two semesters in one year.	

2590	고등	자살(하다)	suicidal (자살의)
suicide [SOO-uh-sahyd]		Many people are committing suicide these days.	

2591	고등	1. 대담한, 용감한 2. 두꺼운	[2865] brave
bold [bohld]		Don't be so timid, be bold.	

2592	고등	1. 변명, 구실 2. 용서하다, 면제하다	inexcusable (용서할 수 없는) [1785] pardon
excuse [ik-SKYOOZ]		Students create excuses for not doing their homework.	

2593	수능 GRE	조종하다, 다루다	manipulation (조작) [273] control
manipulate [muh-NIP-yuh-leyt]		The politicians were manipulating the public.	

2594	고등	1. 때리다, 주먹질하다 2. 타격, 힘 3. (구멍을) 뚫다	
punch [puhnch]		She punched a friend who mocked her.	

2595	고등 토플	1. 항구, 항만 2. 피난처를 제공하다, 숨기다, 품다	
harbor [HAHR-ber]		There are many boats at the harbor.	

2596	고등 토플	1. (살짝) 담그다, 적시다 2. 떨어지다, 내려가다	
dip [dip]		Dip the meat in egg and batter.	

2597		1. 들이받다, 격돌하다 2. 숫양 3. 컴퓨터 주기억장치(RAM)	
ram [ram]		A car rammed into a building.	

2598	고등	1. 무리, 집단 2. (포도, 꽃 등의) 송이	[223] group
cluster [KLUHS-ter]		There is a large cluster of students in front of the school.	

2599	고등 토익	1. 온화한, 유순한 2. (병이) 가벼운	[2065] gentle
mild [mahyld]		The weather is sunny and mild in spring.	

2600	공무원 토플 편입	1. 착취하다 2. 이용하다	exploitation (착취) [1202] utilize
exploit [EK-sploit]		Some companies exploit child labor.	

2601	수능 토익 토플	1. 저명한, 유명한 2. 두드러진, 돌출한	[5148] eminent
prominent [PROM-uh-nuhnt]		A prominent scientist wrote this book.	

2602	수능	1. 설득력 있는, 시선을 끄는 2. 강제적인, 억지의	compel (강제하다) compulsory (의무적인) compulsive (강박적인) [201] powerful
compelling [kuhm-PEL-ing]		The police discovered new and compelling evidence.	

2603	초등	1. 꿀 2. 자기, 여보	
honey [HUHN-ee]		Bees make honey.	

2604	고등 토플	1. 붕괴(하다), 무너지다 2. 폭락(하다)	[454] fall
collapse [kuh-LAPS]		The building collapsed due to an earthquake.	

2605	고등 토익	끈, 밧줄	[1459] string
cord [kawrd]		The cord of the phone was disconnected.	

2606	수능 토플	1. 스펙트럼, 분광 2. 범위, 범주	spectral (스펙트럼의) [411] range
spectrum [SPEK-truhm]		Our eyes are only capable of seeing a narrow spectrum of color.	

2607	토플	갑옷, 방호복	[2345] shield
armor [AHR-mer]		The knight is wearing armor.	

2608		1. (같은 일을 하는) 단체, 단 2. 군단, 부대	[335] body
corps [kawr]		Medical corps are rescuing the survivors of the earthquake.	

2609	고등	1. 우표 2. 도장(을 찍다) 3. (거세게) 밟다	[837] mark
stamp [stamp]		You need a stamp to send a letter.	

2610		카탈로그, (책, 물품 등의) 목록	[259] list
catalog [KAT-l-awg]		You can search the library catalog by title or author.	

2611		1. 새가 지저귀다 2. 짹짹	[5363] twitter
tweet [tweet]		Birds are tweeting in the forest.	

2612	고등	1. 단지, 병, 항아리 2. 삐걱거리다, 거슬리다 3. 충격을 주다	jarring (거슬리는, 충격적인)
jar [jahr]		I keep honey in a jar.	

2613		산소	
oxygen [OK-si-juhn]		Oxygen is crucial for survival.	

2614	초등	강아지	
puppy [PUHP-ee]		Puppies are playful and friendly.	

2615		등뼈, 척추	[2162] backbone
spine [spahyn]		He hurt his spine in a car accident.	

2616	수능	온스 (28.35 그램과 동일한 무게의 단위)	
ounce [ouns]		The puppy weighs 10 ounces.	

2617	수능	보호자, 수호자	[429] protector
guardian			
[GAHR-dee-uhn]		My parents are my guardians.	

2618	수능 토플	1. 꿰매다, 바느질하다, 봉합하다 2. 바늘땀	[2360] sew
stitch			
[stich]		The doctors stitched his wound.	

2619	고등	1. 교도소, 감옥 2. 투옥하다	[1561] prison
jail			
[jeyl]		Their daughter is in jail for stealing.	

2620	수능 토익	1. 강화하다, 장려하다 2. 지원하다	reinforcement (보강) [1007] strengthen
reinforce			
[ree-in-FAWRS]		Let's reinforce good behavior.	

2621	고등	부끄러움, 수치, 불명예	shameless (창피를 모르는) shameful (창피한) [2097] disgrace
shame			
[sheym]		One mistake brought shame to all his family.	

2622	수능 토플	1. 총합의 2. 징그러운, 더러운	[4011] disgusting
gross			
[grohs]		The gross revenue of the company was 24 million dollars.	

2623		빈티지, 오래된 멋이 있는 물건	[3286] antique
vintage			
[VIN-tij]		She bought a vintage dress.	

2624	고등	해외에, 외국에	[1085] overseas
abroad			
[uh-BRAWD]		He lives abroad.	

2625	수능 토플	1. 차별 2. 구별, 식별	discriminate (차별하다) [4060] discernment
discrimination			
[dih-skrim-uh-NEY-shuhn]		Racial discrimination is a serious problem.	

2626	고등	1. 자르다, 썰다 2. (고기의) 갈비	
chop			
[chop]		Chop the onions into thin slices.	

2627	수능 토플	1. 세련된, 고상한 2. 복잡한, 정교한	sophistication (세련미, 복잡도) [1088] complex
sophisticated			
[suh-FIS-ti-key-tid]		She is a sophisticated woman.	

2628	공무원	위반(하다), 파기(하다)	[1835] violation
breach			
[breech]		He breached the contract.	

2629	토익 공무원 편입	휴대용의, 이동식의	
portable			
[PAWR-tuh-buhl]		Portable cellphones were invented in the 20th century.	

2630	고등 토익	1. 화학 2. (좋은) 궁합	chemist (화학자)
chemistry			
[KEM-uh-stree]		Chemistry is my favorite subject.	

2631 hop [hop]		(깡충깡충) 뛰다 Rabbits hop quickly.	[3114] leap
2632 squad [skwod]	공무원 토플	1. 팀, 반 2. 분대 The assassination squad successfully accomplished its mission.	
2633 cotton [KOT-n]	초등	목화, 면화 Cotton is used to make blankets.	
2634 palm [pahm]	고등	1. 손바닥 2. 야자수 Her palms get sweaty during summer.	
2635 owe [oh]	고등	빚지고 있다, 은혜를 입고 있다 You owe me money.	
2636 tragedy [TRAJ-i-dee]	고등 토플	비극, 참사 His death was a tragedy.	tragic (비극적인)
2637 apologize [uh-POL-uh-jahyz]	고등 토익	사죄하다, 사과하다 You need to apologize to your mom.	apology (사과)
2638 grocery [GROH-suh-ree]	고등 토익	1. 식료품점, 슈퍼마켓 2. 식료품류 We went to the grocery store to buy milk.	
2639 interfere [in-ter-FEER]	고등 토익 토플	1. 방해하다, 훼방하다 2. 간섭하다 Your talking interferes with my work.	interference (방해)
2640 divorce [dih-VAWRS]	고등	이혼 They wanted to get a divorce.	[892] separate
2641 medal [MED-l]		메달, 훈장, 상패 The athlete won a medal.	medallion (메달)
2642 cabin [KAB-in]	고등 토익	1. 오두막집 2. 객실 There are cabins near the forest.	[5457] shack
2643 flaw [flaw]	고등 토익	흠, 결점, 결함 He had his flaws, but he was great nonetheless.	[2138] fault
2644 fool [fool]	초등	1. 바보 2. 우롱하다, 속이다 He was a fool to believe her again.	foolish (어리석은) [3666] idiot

2645	고등 토플	1. 쓰레기 더미 2. 버리다	[676] drop
dump [duhmp]		Throw away the trash at the dump.	

2646	토익 공무원 편입 GRE	1. 찬사, 경의 2. 칭찬하다	complimentary (축하의, 무료의)
compliment [KOM-pluh-muhnt]		The teacher complimented his neat handwriting.	[2458] praise

2647		1. 속임수(를 치다), 사기(를 치다) 2. 범죄자, 전과자 3. 반대측, 반대편	[1595] trick
con [kon]		He conned his friends into buying unnecessary insurances.	

2648	초등 토익	1. (기름에) 튀기다 2. 감자튀김	[2156] boil
fry [frahy]		I am going to fry chicken for dinner tonight.	

2649		교환하다, 바꾸다	[1303] exchange
swap [swop]		The children swapped toys.	

2650		자랑하다, 과시하다	[5008] brag
boast [bohst]		She boasted about her good grades.	

2651	토플	법령, 규칙	[1637] legislation
statute [STACH-oot]		There is a statute banning excessive pollution from companies.	

2652		구리	
copper [KOP-er]		Copper is used in making coins.	

2653	고등 토익 GRE	1. 절실한, 간절한 2. 절망적인, 자포자기의	desperation (절망)
desperate [DES-per-it]		He was desperate to make money.	[384] hopeless

2654	토익	중개인, 중개업자	brokerage (중개소)
broker [BROH-ker]		The broker connected customers to producers.	[558] agent

2655		1. 붙이다 2. 풀 3. 반죽	[2437] glue
paste [peyst]		The child pasted a picture on her diary.	

2656	공무원 토플	지름, 직경	[579] width
diameter [dahy-AM-i-ter]		The diameter of the circle is 5 meters.	

2657	토익 공무원 토플 편입	1. 결함, 결점 2. 도망치다	defector (탈북자)
defect [DEE-fekt]		The diamond had several defects.	[2643] flaw

2658	고등 토익	화장실, 변소	toiletry (세면도구)
toilet [TOI-lit]		I need to use the toilet.	[1481] bathroom

| 2659 | 공무원 토플 편입 | 1. 구술된 내용을 글로 기록한 것, 대본 2. 성적 증명서 | transcribe (글로 기록하다) |
| transcript [TRAN-skript] | | He read a transcript of the interrogation. | [931] copy |

| 2660 | 고등 토플 | 보완하다, 보충하다, 완전케하다 | complementary (보완적인) |
| complement [KOM-pluh-muhnt] | | Wine complements cheese. | [1698] supplement |

| 2661 | 고등 토플 | 범죄자, 가해자 | offend (성나게 하다) [4703] perpetrator |
| offender [uh-FEN-der] | | He is an offender of a heinous crime. | |

| 2662 | | 한 묶음, 한 집단, 1회 분 | [223] group |
| batch [bach] | | He baked a batch of cookies. | |

| 2663 | 고등 토플 | 방앗간, 제분소 | [1911] factory |
| mill [mil] | | If you want to make flour, go to the mill. | |

| 2664 | 수능 | 1. 붙잡다 2. 압류하다, 몰수하다 | seizure (압수, 경련) [1757] grab |
| seize [seez] | | The police seized the criminal. | |

| 2665 | 고등 토플 | 1. 방해하다 2. 어지럽히다 | disturbance (방해) [2705] upset |
| disturb [dih-STURB] | | I'm sorry, didn't mean to disturb you. | |

| 2666 | 초등 토익 | (숨이 겨워) 헐떡이다 | pants (바지) panties (팬티) [5372] gasp |
| pant [pant] | | The runners reached the finish line, panting heavily. | |

| 2667 | 고등 | 1. 화려한, 멋있는 2. 원하다, 좋아하다 3. 생각하다 | [1100] desire |
| fancy [FAN-see] | | This is a fancy necklace. | |

| 2668 | 공무원 GRE | 복제하다, 모사하다 | replica (모조품) [3016] duplicate |
| replicate [REP-li-kit] | | She could replicate her teacher's voice. | |

| 2669 | 고등 | 1. 발뒤꿈치 2. (구두 등의) 굽 | |
| heel [heel] | | A snake bit his heel. | |

| 2670 | | 탄수화물 | |
| carbohydrate [kahr-boh-HAHY-dreyt] | | Rice and flour have carbohydrates. | |

| 2671 | 수능 토익 | 구두의, 말의 | nonverbal (말로하지 않는) verb (동사) [2474] oral |
| verbal [VUR-buhl] | | She verbally abused her children. | |

| 2672 | 고등 토익 | 주의를 돌리다, 관심을 딴 데로 돌리다 | distraction (방해) [3904] divert |
| distract [dih-STRAKT] | | Be quiet, don't distract me. | |

2673	수능 토플	1. (수술을) 받다 2. (안 좋은 일을) 겪다, 당하다	
undergo			
[uhn-der-GOH]		She has to undergo a long surgery.	
2674	고등	유아, 소아	infantile (어린아이 같은) [970] baby
infant			
[IN-fuhnt]		Infants should be vaccinated.	
2675	공무원 토플 편입 GRE	1. 고결함, 도덕성, 진실성 2. 완전한 상태, 본래 모습	[1404] honesty
integrity			
[in-TEG-ri-tee]		Employers value integrity.	
2676	고등 토플	1. 성단, 신전 2. 절 3. 관자놀이	[4445] shrine
temple			
[TEM-puhl]		People worship God at temples.	
2677	고등	총알	[473] shot
bullet			
[BOOL-it]		A bullet pierced his skull.	
2678	공무원	(의사나 변호사 등의) 개업자	[1903] physician
practitioner			
[prak-TISH-uh-ner]		At our hospital, skilled practitioners treat patients.	
2679	고등	1. 닻 2. 뉴스 앵커	
anchor			
[ANG-ker]		If you want to stop the boat, let down the anchor.	
2680	수능 토익 GRE	1. 양육하다, 돌보다 2. 발전시키다, 촉진하다	[774] promote
foster			
[FAW-ster]		The orphanage is fostering 20 children.	
2681	고등	공백의, 백지의	[1889] empty
blank			
[blangk]		She didn't do her homework so the page was blank.	
2682	공무원 편입	노력하다, 분투하다	[1333] struggle
strive			
[strahyv]		Everyone strives for success.	
2683	초등	1. 쇠고기 2. 불평	[6393] gripe
beef			
[beef]		My favorite meat is beef.	
2684		허파, 폐	
lung			
[luhng]		She had lung cancer.	
2685	고등	1. (고기를) 굽다, 가열하다 2. (남에게) 열불내다	[2508] grill
roast			
[rohst]		It takes 20 minutes to roast chicken.	
2686	고등 토플	1. 독 2. 독을 넣다, 독살하다	poisoning (독) poisonous (독성의) [2473] toxin
poison			
[POI-zuhn]		He put poison in the king's food.	

2687	수능 토익 토플	1. (수색을 허용하는) 영장 2. 보장하다	unwarranted (보증되지 않는)
warrant			warranty (보증)
[WAWR-uh nt]		The courts issued a warrant to search his home.	

2688	고등 토익	상인, 무역상인	[413] dealer
merchant			
[MUR-chuh nt]		The merchant sells jewels.	

2689	고등	1. 뛰어오르다, 튀다 2. 뛰어오름, 튀어오름	[1276] jump
bounce			
[bouns]		The rubber ball bounced.	

2690	수능 토플 GRE	반역자, 반란자	rebellion (반란)
rebel			rebellious (반항하는)
[REB-uhl]		The rebels organized protests.	

2691	토플	유수한, 순종적인	disobedient (순종적이지 않은)
obedient			[969] submissive
[oh-BEE-dee-uhnt]		My dog is very loyal and obedient.	

2692	고등	1. 눌러부수다, 뭉개다 2. 좋아하는 사람, 짝사랑의 대상	[4025] squash
crush			
[kruhsh]		Crush some garlic and add it to the stew.	

2693		미친, 제정신이 아닌	insanity (미친 상태)
insane			sane (제정신인)
[in-SEYN]		The patient was declared insane.	[1776] crazy

2694	초등 토익	사탕	[1287] sweet
candy			
[KAN-dee]		Children love candy.	

2695	수능 토플	1. 합법의 2. 정당한, 타당한	legitimacy (타당성)
legitimate			[732] legal
[li-JIT-uh-mit]		Abusing a child is not a legitimate action.	

2696	고등	1. 더미 2. 쌓다, 포개다	[4139] heap
pile			
[pahyl]		There is a pile of dirty laundry in his room.	

2697	고등 토플	1. 광선, 빛의 줄기 2. 대들보	beaming (빛나는)
beam			[1962] shine
[beem]		There was a beam of light coming from the flashlight.	

2698	수능 토플 GRE	1. 만연하다 2. 이기다, 우세하다	prevalent (만연한)
prevail			[2455] dominate
[pri-VEYL]		Though it was a hard fight, the champion prevailed.	

2699	고등	1. 옥수수 2. 곡식	
corn			
[kawrn]		Corn is used to feed chickens.	

2700	토익 공무원 토플 편입	면제	exempt (면제된)
exemption			[216] freedom
[ig-ZEMP-shuhn]		Bad eyesight can lead to exemption from military service.	

2701	수능 토플	입자, (작은) 조각	[6669] speck
particle			
[PAHR-ti-kuhl]		The cup shattered into small glass particles.	

2702	고등 토플	1. 활 2. (허리를 굽혀) 인사하다, 절하다 3. 리본	[2140] bend
bow			
[bou]		In the past, hunters used a bow and arrow to catch animals.	

2703	고등 GRE	1. 무시하다, 기각하다 2. 해고하다	[2030] reject
dismiss			
[dis-MIS]		She dismissed his ideas as foolish.	

2704	수능 토플	비범한, 뛰어난	[1944] remarkable
extraordinary			
[ik-STRAWR-dn-er-ee]		The child had extraordinary intelligence.	

2705	고등 토플	1. 화난 2. 속상하게 하다 3. (배)탈	[2665] disturb
upset			
[uhp-SET]		When you lie it makes me upset.	

2706		대마(초)	[2995] weed
marijuana			
[MAR-uh-wah-nuh]		Smoking marijuana is illegal.	

2707		피를 흘리다, 출혈하다	
bleed			
[bleed]		Her finger is bleeding.	

2708	수능 토플	우스꽝스러운, 말도 안 되는	ridicule (조롱하다) [4103] absurd
ridiculous			
[ri-DIK-yuh-luhs]		What a ridiculous thought.	

2709		독수리	[4195] hawk
eagle			
[EE-guh l]		The eagle is a symbol of America.	

2710	수능 토익	조각품	sculpt (조각하다) [3101] statue
sculpture			
[SKUHLP-cher]		There are many sculptures in the museum.	

2711	고등 토익	야망, 대망	ambitious (야망있는) [2868] aspiration
ambition			
[am-BISH-uhn]		Her ambition is to become the president.	

2712	고등 토플	유인책, 장려금, 보상물	incentivize (장려하다) [2297] stimulus
incentive			
[in-SEN-tiv]		The government is giving an incentive to young couples to have more children.	

2713	고등	1. 동료, 동반자 2. 친구, 벗	[3510] buddy
companion			
[kuhm-PAN-yuhn]		My dog Delano is my companion.	

2714		상당한 양의	[221] significant
substantial			
[suhb-STAN-shuhl]		A substantial amount of heroin was smuggled into Korea.	

2715 **abort** [uh-BAWRT]		중단하다	abortion (낙태)
		The team had to abort their mission after severe criticism.	
2716 **thrive** [thrahyv]	공무원 편입	번영하다, 성공하다	[3945] flourish
		Her business is thriving.	
2717 **cart** [kahrt]	초등 토익	수레, 마차	[4288] wagon
		Two horses drove the cart.	
2718 **gut** [guht]	토플	1. 배짱 2. 내장, 배 3. 직감 4. 내부를 파내다	[1864] interior
		Nobody had the guts to jump out the window.	
2719 **empower** [em-POU-er]	공무원	권한을 주다	empowerment (권한 부여)
		Parents should be empowered to make decisions for their children.	
2720 **pit** [pit]	공무원 토플 편입	구덩이, 구멍	[5962] abyss
		They dug a pit to bury the body.	
2721 **mortality** [mawr-TAL-i-tee]	수능 토플	필사, 죽을 운명	mortal (죽을 운명인) immortal (죽지 않는) [363] death
		The idea of mortality is scary for young children.	
2722 **celebrity** [suh-LEB-ri-tee]	고등 토익	1. 연예인, 유명 인사 2. 유명도, 명성	[669] star [1159] fame
		I would like to meet a celebrity.	
2723 **harmony** [HAHR-muh-nee]	공무원 토플 편입	1. 조화, 화합 2. 화음	[479] accord
		Man and nature should live in harmony.	
2724 **myth** [mith]	고등	신화, 꾸민 이야기	[1772] legend
		According to myths, a bear and tiger are the ancestors of the Korean people.	
2725 **dividend** [DIV-i-dend]	토익	배당금, (배당) 이익	[3831] perks
		The investors received large dividends.	
2726 **bulb** [buhlb]	토익 토플	전구	
		The light bulb turned on.	
2727 **nest** [nest]	고등	둥지, 소굴	
		Birds live in a nest.	
2728 **admire** [ad-MAHYUHR]	고등 GRE	감탄하다, 찬미하다	admiration (존경) [1059] respect
		Many people admired her beauty.	

2729	고등 토익	의상, 복장	[2526] outfit
costume			
[KOS-toom]		What costume are you wearing for Halloween?	

2730	수능 GRE	서로 간의, 공통의	mutually (공통으로) [271] shared
mutual			
[MYOO-choo-uhl]		They had mutual respect.	

2731	고등 토익	인공위성	
satellite			
[SAT-l-ahyt]		Images from satellites show water on Mars.	

2732	수능 토익 토플	모으다, 누적하다	[420] collect
accumulate			
[uh-KYOO-myuh-leyt]		The dust keeps accumulating.	

2733	고등 토플	적시다, (물에) 담그다	[3523] immerse
soak			
[sohk]		Soak the laundry in soapy water.	

2734	토플	정육면체	[849] block
cube			
[kyoob]		Cut the cheese into small cubes.	

2735	수능 토익	유혹하다, 꾀다, 부추기다	temptation (유혹) tempting (유혹하는) [4495] entice
tempt			
[tempt]		The snake tempted Eve to eat the apple.	

2736	고등 토익	실마리, 단서	clueless (단서가 없는) [2524] hint
clue			
[kloo]		The criminal left clues about his identity.	

2737		오줌, 소변	urinate (소변을 보다)
urine			
[YOOR-in]		The dark street smelled like urine.	

2738	토익	수프	[4657] broth
soup			
[soop]		If you're sick, I'll cook soup for you.	

2739	토익	밀가루, 가루	[2041] powder
flour			
[FLOUuhr]		Flour is used to make bread.	

2740	수능	부풀어오르다, 붓다	swollen (부은) [280] increase
swell			
[swel]		Her wound swelled up.	

2741	고등	채굴, 광업	mine (광산) [1968] extraction
mining			
[MAHY-ning]		There are many diamond mining businesses in Congo.	

2742	수능 토익	배우자, 부부	[598] partner
spouse			
[spous]		Do you have a spouse?	

2743		1. 동성애자(인) 2. 쾌활한	[4040] homosexual
gay			
[gey]		She is gay.	

2744		복음(서), (종교의) 교리	[1285] truth
gospel			
[GOS-puhl]		The gospel says 'love your neighbors as you love yourself'.	

2745	고등	보라색	[5529] violet
purple			
[PUR-puhl]		Plums are purple.	

2746	초등 토익	1. 장갑 2. (야구, 권투용) 글러브	[5974] mitten
glove			
[gluhv]		I wear gloves when my hands get cold.	

2747	공무원 토플 편입 GRE	1. 결정권, 재량 2. 신중한 선택	[4610] prudence
discretion			
[dih-SKRESH-uhn]		You have the discretion to decide which university to attend.	

2748	수능	1. 보존하다, 유지하다 2. 아끼다	conservation (보존) [1791] preserve
conserve			
[kuhn-SURV]		We must conserve energy.	

2749	고등 토플	더욱 더, 게다가	[2862] moreover
furthermore			
[FUR-ther-mawr]		He is kind. Furthermore, he is smart.	

2750		중간의, 가운데의	
mid			
[mid]		The actor stopped mid-speech because she forgot the script.	

2751	고등	발가락	tiptoe (까치발로 살금살금 걷기) [657] foot
toe			
[toh]		Her toe was bruised.	

2752	공무원 토플 편입	1. 암시하는 것, 의미하는 것 2. 연루	implicate (암시하다) [221] significance
implication			
[im-pli-KEY-shuhn]		The implication of the evidence is that she is the criminal.	

2753	고등 GRE	편견, 차별적 생각	biased (편향된) [494] mindset
bias			
[BAHY-uhs]		Don't be biased against people because of their race.	

2754	고등 토플	1. 간격 2. 막간, 휴식 시간	[545] period
interval			
[IN-ter-vuhl]		There is a 15-minute interval before the next show starts.	

2755	초등 토익	축구	[1456] football
soccer			
[SOK-er]		Soccer is a very popular sport.	

2756	토익	1. 재단하다, 재봉하다 2. 재단사	tailored (맞춤화된) [1415] adapt
tailor			
[TEY-ler]		I tailored my pants and made them shorter.	

2757	고등	1. 다발, 꾸러미 2. 다발로 묶다	[2070] bunch
bundle [BUHN-dl]		He received a bundle of flowers.	

2758	수능 토익 토플	1. 대단한, 굉장한 2. 무시무시한	[2777] enormous
tremendous [trih-MEN-duhs]		Thank you for your tremendous help.	

2759		1. 대리, 부대표 2. 보안관	[636] assistant
deputy [DEP-yuh-tee]		The shop owner employed a deputy.	

2760	고등 토플	1. 부담, 짐 2. 짐을 지우다	[844] load
burden [BUR-dn]		The excessive expectation from her parents was a burden.	

2761	공무원 편입	1. 극단적인, 급진적인 2. 근본적인	[1804] revolutionary
radical [RAD-i-kuhl]		She has radical political opinions.	

2762	토익	1. (밀려오는) 파도 2. 파도를 타다, 서핑 3. 인터넷 서핑하다	surfer (서핑하는 사람) surfing (서핑) [1413] browse
surf [surf]		The surf hit the shore.	

2763	고등 토익 토플	1. 냉기, 한기 2. 오싹함, 으스스함	chilly (쌀쌀한) [1163] cold
chill [chil]		There was a chill in the breeze now.	

2764	수능 토플	동시에	
simultaneously [sahy-muhl-TEY-nee-uhs-lee]		They spoke simultaneously.	

2765	공무원 토플 편입	시의, 지방 자치의	
municipal [myoo-NIS-uh-puhl]		The municipal government decided to build a new public school.	

2766	토익 공무원	1. 기기, (가전) 제품 2. 적용	
appliance [uh-PLAHY-uhns]		The house didn't have any electric appliances yet.	

2767	토플 편입	아치 형태의, 활 모양의	overarching (무엇보다 중요한) [2140] bend
arch [ahrch]		Most bridges are built in the shape of an arch.	

2768	고등	문지르다, 비비다	[3537] scrub
rub [ruhb]		Puppies like having their stomachs rubbed.	

2769	고등 토플	1. 추상적인 2. (특히 논문의) 요약문 3. 추출물, 추출하다	abstraction (관념) [1219] theoretical
abstract [ab-STRAKT]		Modern art is difficult to understand because it is abstract.	

2770	토익	1. 전망, 예측 2. 관점	[1678] perspective
outlook [OUT-look]		Her outlook on life was very pessimistic.	

2771	편입	1. 관할권 (지역) 2. 사법권	[771] authority
jurisdiction			
[joor-is-DIK-shuhn]		This area is not the jurisdiction of your department.	

2772		암호화, 부호화	
encryption			
[en-KRIP-shuh n]		Use encryption to hide personal information.	

2773	고등 토익 토플	건축가, 설계가	
architect			
[AHR-ki-tekt]		My friend is the architect who designed this building.	

2774	공무원	속이다, 부정 행위를 하다	cheater (사기꾼) [2439] fraud
cheat			
[cheet]		Do not cheat in exams.	

2775	공무원 토플 편입	영원한, 영구의	eternity (영원)
eternal			
[ih-TUR-nl]		Love is not eternal.	

2776		1. 실험 단계의, 미완성의 2. 그러스어 알파벳 둘째 자	
beta			
[BEY-tuh]		This program is a beta version.	

2777	고등	거대한, 막대한	[939] huge
enormous			
[ih-NAWR-muhs]		The pumpkin is enormous.	

2778	고등 토플	벽돌	[849] block
brick			
[brik]		The house was built with bricks.	

2779	고등 토익	1. 청소기(를 돌리다) 2. 진공	[3280] void
vacuum			
[VAK-yoom]		Using a vacuum makes cleaning faster.	

2780		1. 두루마리, 스크롤 2. 지나치다, 넘기다	[981] roll
scroll			
[skrohl]		The ancient document was written on a scroll.	

2781		1. 엄청난, 장대한 2. 영웅담, 서사시	[1772] legend
epic			
[EP-ik]		The Spanish Flu was an epic tragedy.	

2782		1. 집다, 들다 2. (차에) 태워주다	
pickup			
[PIK-uhp]		The garbage truck picks up trash every Tuesday.	

2783	고등 토플 GRE	친밀한, 친숙한	intimacy (친밀함) [610] private
intimate			
[IN-tuh-mit]		He is my best friend who knows my intimate secrets.	

2784	고등	1. 소리지르다 2. 비명	[3718] yell
scream			
[skreem]		Don't scream at night, you will wake people up.	

2785	고등	1. 개척자, 선구자 2. 개척하다	[870] explorer
pioneer [pahy-uh-NEER]		American astronauts were the pioneers of space research.	

2786	토익 공무원	등록금, 수업료	[354] education
tuition [too-ISH-uhn]		University tuition is very expensive.	

2787	수능 GRE	1. 주장하다 2. 다투다, 싸우다	contender (도전자) contention (싸움) [962] argue
contend [kuhn-TEND]		Many football fans contend that the referee was wrong.	

2788	공무원 토플	가난, 결핍	[7039] destitution
poverty [POV-er-tee]		Many people suffer from poverty.	

2789	공무원 토플 편입 GRE	전제	[1041] assumption
premise [PREM-is]		The premise of marriage is love.	

2790		픽셀, 화소	
pixel [PIK-suhl]		Images online are made up of many pixels.	

2791	토익	타월, 수건	[2833] cloth
towel [TOU-uhl]		May I have a towel to dry my hair?	

2792	수능	1. 집회, 시위 2. (불러) 모으다 3. (테니스) 랠리 4. (주식이) 반등하다	[5727] muster
rally [RAL-ee]		They organized a rally against government corruption.	

2793		1. 문, 입구 2. (인터넷) 포털	[2072] gate
portal [PAWR-tl]		The portals of the cathedral are very majestic.	

2794	공무원	(신체의) 종양	[1074] cancer
tumor [TOO-mer]		She had a tumor in a brain.	

2795	수능 토플 GRE	아마, 예측하건대	presume (추정하다) presumption (추정) [458] probably
presumably [pri-ZOO-muh-blee]		He left late so presumably, he missed the train.	

2796	토익	소매	
sleeve [sleev]		Roll up your sleeves if it's too hot.	

2797	고등	악마	[3047] demon
devil [DEV-uhl]		The devil seduces people to make bad decisions.	

2798	수능 GRE	불가피한, 부득이한	[848] unavoidable
inevitable [in-EV-i-tuh-buhl]		Death is inevitable.	

2799	고등	1. 짐승, 가축 2. 야수, 괴물	[3041] brute
beast [beest]		A wild beast ruined the farmer's crops.	

2800	고등	인사하다, 반기다, 맞이하다	greeting (인사) [1111] welcome
greet [greet]		He greeted his friend.	

2801	고등	1. 정상 회담 2. 꼭대기, 정상, 절정	[1868] peak
summit [SUHM-it]		The presidents met at the summit.	

2802	고등	1. 희미해지다, 바래다 2. 자취를 감추다, 사라지다	[367] disappear
fade [feyd]		Her hair faded and became gray.	

2803	공무원 편입	(단열이나 방음 등의) 절연 처리하다	
insulate [IN-suh-leyt]		No sound left the room because the room was insulated.	

2804	고등 토플	의제, 안건	[913] schedule
agenda [uh-JEN-duh]		The agenda of the meeting was climate change.	

2805	공무원 편입	1. 명상하다 2. 숙고하다, 꾀하다	meditation (명상) [4788] ponder
meditate [MED-i-teyt]		If you are feeling anxious, try meditating.	

2806	고등	기적, 불가사의한 일	miraculous (기적적인) [605] wonder
miracle [MIR-uh-kuhl]		Her recovery was a miracle.	

2807	수능 토플	묘사하다, 그리다	depiction (묘사) [3139] portray
depict [dih-PIKT]		The artist depicted the happy moment on canvas.	

2808	고등	초상화, 인물 사진	[564] picture
portrait [PAWR-trit]		I requested the photographer to take a portrait of me.	

2809	고등 토플	(바느질용 혹은 주사) 바늘	[2895] irritate
needle [NEED-l]		Many children are scared of injection needles.	

2810	고등	떡갈나무	[5894] chestnut
oak [ohk]		Oak trees can live up to more than 100 years.	

2811	공무원	1. (기관의) ~국, 특정 부서 2. 책상	
bureau [BYOOR-oh]		The bureau of education decided to increase history lessons.	

2812	공무원	가로의, 수평선의	horizon (수평선, 지평선)
horizontal [hawr-uh-ZON-tl]		The child drew a horizontal line to represent the sea.	

2813	초등 토익	1. 바구니 2. (농구의) 네트	
basket			
[BAS-kit]		What's in your basket?	

2814	공무원 토플 편입	의식, 제사	rite (의식)
ritual			
[RICH-oo-uhl]		Some tribes used to have religious rituals involving human sacrifice.	

2815	고등 토익 토플	공해, 오염	pollutant (오염물질) pollute (오염시키다)
pollution			
[puh-LOO-shuhn]		Air pollution is a grave issue.	

2816	공무원 편입	구원, 구제	salvage (구조)
salvation			
[sal-VEY-shuhn]		Religious people ask God for salvation.	

2817	편입	기증자, 기부자	
donor			
[DOH-ner]		I am a blood donor.	

2818	토플	원기둥, 원통	
cylinder			
[SIL-in-der]		This water bottle is shaped like a cylinder.	

2819	고등	깨어있는, 일어난	awaken (깨다) awakening (깨닫게 되는 계기)
awake			
[uh-WEYK]		I was awake half the night.	

2820	고등	동일한, 같은	
identical			
[ahy-DEN-ti-kuhl]		The twins look identical.	

2821	공무원	1. (손)해, 나쁜 짓 2. (주로 짓궂은) 장난	mischievous (장난기가 많은)
mischief			
[MIS-chif]		You should try to stay out of mischief.	

2822	공무원 토플 편입 GRE	추측하다	speculation (추측, 투기) [6401] conjecture
speculate			
[SPEK-yuh-leyt]		Scientists speculate that many dinosaurs could fly.	

2823	고등	1. 곱슬곱슬하게 하다, 말다 2. 곱슬, 컬	[2202] twist
curl			
[kurl]		She curled her hair.	

2824	고등 토익	방해하다	interruption (방해) [439] stop
interrupt			
[in-tuh-RUHPT]		Please don't interrupt me when I am studying.	

2825		1. 측정하다 2. 측정기	[614] measure
gauge			
[geyj]		We can use instruments to gauge the depth of the ocean.	

2826		1. 3월 2 .행군하다	[533] walk
march			
[mahrch]		March is spring in Korea.	

2827	고등	1. 폭력단, 범죄 조직 2. 집단을 이루다	[1067] band
gang			
[gang]		The gang committed many crimes.	

2828	고등 토플	터지다, 폭발하다, 파열하다	[2058] explode
burst			
[burst]		The balloon burst and made a loud noise.	

2829	고등 토플	1. 내리다 2. 내려가다 3. 타락하다, 질이 떨어지다	[454] fall
descend			
[dih-SEND]		Snow descended from the sky.	

2830	편입	무서운, 끔찍한	[3052] awful
horrible			
[HAWR-uh-buhl]		There was a horrible terrorist attack.	

2831	수능	비숍, 주교	[2472] priest
bishop			
[BISH-uhp]		The bishop comforted the clergy.	

2832	고등 토플	1. 감탄하다 2. 경이로운 것, 놀라운 것	marvelous (놀라운) [605] wonder
marvel			
[MAHR-vuhl]		I marvel at the beauty of nature.	

2833	초등 토익	옷감, 천	[1711] fabric
cloth			
[klawth]		This cloth is very scratchy.	

2834	토익 공무원 편입	탄원(하다), 청원(하다)	
petition			
[puh-TISH-uhn]		She started a petition for stricter environmental regulations.	

2835	수능	1. 불리한 2. 역의, 반대의	adversity (역경) adversary (적)
adverse			
[ad-VURS]		He worked hard despite adverse circumstances.	

2836	공무원 토플	증후군, 일정한 행동 양식	
syndrome			
[SIN-drohm]		Fever and coughs are syndromes of a cold.	

2837		1. 통계 2. 곧, 급히	statistics (통계학)
stat			
[stat]		Stats prove that pollution is a serious problem.	

2838		1. 스카우트, 소년/소녀 단원 2. 정찰(하다) 3. 신인 발굴자	
scout			
[skout]		Scouts learn how to survive in the wild.	

2839	고등	1. 장례식 2. 장례의	
funeral			
[FYOO-ner-uhl]		You should wear black clothes to a funeral.	

2840	고등	1. 인공의, 인조의 2. 부자연스러운	[2552] fake
artificial			
[ahr-tuh-FISH-uhl]		This is an artificial island.	

2841	토플 GRE	상쇄하다, 벌충하다	[897] counterbalance
offset [AWF-set]		The revenue offsets spendings.	

2842	고등 토플 GRE	단언하다, 주장하다	assertion (주장) [3157] affirm
assert [uh-SURT]		Some people assert that the earth is flat.	

2843	수능 토플	1. 외로운, 쓸쓸한 2. 혼자의, 고립된	loneliness (외로움) [1183] alone
lonely [LOHN-lee]		Everyone gets lonely sometimes.	

2844	수능 토익	1. (사업으로) 음식물을 조달하다 2. 비위를 맞추다	
cater [KEY-ter]		The bakery caters to birthday parties.	

2845		신장, 콩팥	[410] kind
kidney [KID-nee]		You can survive with one kidney.	

2846	토익 공무원 편입	교차점, 교선	intersect (교차하다) [3741] junction
intersection [in-ter-SEK-shuhn]		There are many car accidents at intersections of roads.	

2847	고등 토익	1. 소포 2. 통, 갑, 곽	[484] package
packet [PAK-it]		I received a packet from Japan.	

2848	초등 토익	1. 영화관 2. 영화	[924] movie
cinema [SIN-uh-muh]		I am going to the cinema with my friends today.	

2849		용접(하다), 결합(하다)	[2582] fuse
weld [weld]		She welded metal to make an ornament.	

2850	고등 토익	전기, 자서전	autobiography (자서전) [341] history
biography [bahy-OG-ruh-fee]		Have you ever read the president's biography?	

2851	고등 토익	램프, 등불	[257] light
lamp [lamp]		I am scared of the dark so I always keep the lamp turned on.	

2852	고등 토익	소문, 풍설	[5009] gossip
rumor [ROO-mer]		There is a rumor that he is a cheater.	

2853	초등	(꿀)벌	
bee [bee]		Bees can sting people.	

2854		양파	
onion [UHN-yuhn]		Chopping onions can make you cry.	

2855	초등	호랑이	
tiger			
[TAHY-ger]		Tigers are endangered animals.	

2856	고등 토익	1. 라운지, 대합실 2. 여유 부리다, 빈둥거리다	
lounge			
[lounj]		I'll meet you at the lounge in ten minutes.	

2857	토익 토플	열대의, 열대적인	
tropical			
[TROP-i-kuhl]		Tropical forests have many rare plants and animals.	

2858	고등	1. 호황, 인기 2. (북,천둥 등이) 쾅,쿵 하는 소리	
boom			
[boom]		This boom may be temporary.	

2859		1. 씨름 (경기) 2. 씨름하는	wrestler (레슬링 선수)
wrestling			
[RES-ling]		Wrestling is a violent sport.	

2860		강간(하다)	rapist (강간범)
rape			[1835] violate
[reyp]		The woman was raped.	

2861	고등	엄지	[1725] finger
thumb			
[thuhm]		Raise your thumb if you are happy.	

2862	고등	게다가, 더욱	[2749] furthermore
moreover			
[mawr-OH-ver]		She is intelligent. Moreover, she is kind.	

2863	고등 토플	1. 혀 2. 언어	[880] language
tongue			
[tuhng]		I burned my tongue while eating stew.	

2864	공무원 토플 편입 GRE	지지하다, 보증하다, 후원하다	endorsement (지지)
endorse			
[en-DAWRS]		I endorse this presidential candidate.	

2865	초등 토플	용감한	[929] courageous
brave			
[breyv]		Be brave and go on many adventures.	

2866	고등	1. 해안가, 호숫가 2. 언덕, 기슭	ashore (해변에, 물가에)
shore			[1327] coast
[shawr]		There are many seashells on the shore.	

2867	고등	1. 망치 2. (망치로) 두드리다	[1645] pound
hammer			
[HAM-er]		The hammer is in the toolbox.	

2868	고등 토플 GRE	갈망, 야망	aspire (열망하다)
aspiration			[1100] desire
[as-puh-REY-shuhn]		My aspiration is to stop global warming.	

2869	고등 토플	직면하다, 맞서다	confrontation (직면)
confront			[404] face
[kuh n-FRUHNT]		Don't run away from your fears, confront them.	

2870	토익 공무원 편입	되찾다, 회수하다	[231] recover
retrieve			
[ri-TREEV]		She retrieved her lost necklace.	

2871	고등	(문학작품 중의) 시	[2468] verse
poem			
[POH-uh m]		I love poems about nature.	

2872	초등	돼지	[4756] hog
pig			
[pig]		The farmer raises pigs on the farm.	

2873	고등	현상, 경이	phenomenal (경이적인)
phenomenon			
[fi-NOM-uh-non]		Auroras are a beautiful natural phenomenon.	

2874	토익	1. 전화를 걸다, 숫자판을 누르다 2. 숫자판	
dial			
[DAHY-uh l]		Please dial this telephone number.	

2875		1. 돈, 달러 2. 수사슴 3. (껑충) 뛰다	
buck			
[buhk]		Save several bucks by cooking at home.	

2876	수능	집착하는, 빠져있는	obsession (집착)
obsessed			[1573] preoccupled
[uh b-SEST]		He is obsessed with celebrities.	

2877		1. 왁스(를 바르다), 밀랍(을 입히다) 2. 커지다, 증가하다	[280] increase
wax			
[waks]		You can use wax to style your hair.	

2878		경전, 성서	[1744] bible
scripture			
[SKRIP-cher]		Religious people read scriptures.	

2879	초등 토플	궁전	[2454] castle
palace			
[PAL-is]		The royal family lives in the palace.	

2880	초등 토익 GRE	1.억양, 악센트, 말씨 2. 강세	accentuate (강조하다)
accent			[1243] stress
[AK-sent]		He has a British accent.	

2881		1. 계층 2. 괄호 부호 3. 받침	[223] group
bracket			
[BRAK-it]		Students from lower income brackets can receive scholarships.	

2882	고등 토플	후생, 복지	
welfare			
[WEL-fair]		We should increase welfare for soldiers.	

2883	편입	최적의, 최상의	
optimal [OP-tuh-muhl]		Summer is the optimal weather for growing watermelons.	

2884	고등 토플	1. 밧줄, 로프 2. 묶다	
rope [rohp]		Hold the rope in both hands.	

2885	공무원 토플 편입	1. 경사로 2. 날뛰다, 질주하다	rampant (사나운) rampage (난폭한 행동) ramp up (늘리다)
ramp [ramp]		All buildings should have ramps for people using wheelchairs.	

2886	고등 토플	1. 동굴, 굴 2. 함몰하다, 움푹 꺼지다	
cave [keyv]		Bats live in caves.	

2887	고등 토익 토플	비슷한, 유사한	
alike [uh-LAHYK]		Mothers and daughters often look alike.	

2888		1. 로켓, 우주선 2. 상승하다	
rocket [ROK-it]		There are ten astronauts on the rocket.	

2889	공무원	1. (내기, 경기 등에 건) 돈, 상품 2. 말뚝	sweepstake (상금이 걸린 내기)
stake [steyk]		100 dollars is at stake.	

2890	고등 토플	1. (가볍게) 던지다 2. 뒤척이다	[1030] throw
toss [taws]		We can toss a coin to make the decision.	

2891	토익 공무원 편입	예의, 정중	courteous (예의바른) courtly (공손한) [3824] politeness
courtesy [KUR-tuh-see]		Please treat your friends with courtesy.	

2892	수능 토플 GRE	1. 나타내다 2. 명시하다 3. 당연하다	manifesto (선언서) manifestation (명시) [1079] obvious
manifest [MAN-uh-fest]		The ghost manifests each year on the same day.	

2893		1. 축, 축선 2. 중심축	[3906] axle
axis [AK-sis]		The earth revolves on its axis once every 24 hours.	

2894	수능	1. 살금살금 가다 2. 몰래 하다, 가져가다	sneaky (교활한) [2086] slip
sneak [sneek]		The stranger sneaked up from behind and shoved her.	

2895	고등 토익	1. 염증 2. 짜증, 화 3. 자극하는 것	irritate (화나게 하다) irritant (자극제) irritable (성미가 급한) [2465] annoyance
irritation [ir-i-TEY-shuhn]		Skin irritation occurs due to rough scrubbing.	

2896	고등 토플	1. (아이, 자식을)버릇없게 키우다 2. 망치다 3. 상하다	spoiled (버릇없게 자란) [2431] ruin
spoil [spoil]		Too much love can spoil a child.	

2897 **rip** [rip]	1.찢다 2. 떼어내다, 뜯어내다	R.I.P. ((묘비에 쓰이는) Rest in Peace=평화롭게 잠들다) [1766] tear
	I ripped my pants.	

2898 　　　　고등 토플 **innocent** [IN-uh-suhnt]	1. 무죄인, 결백한, 무고한 2. 순수한, 순진한 3. 악의 없는, 선량한	innocence (결백) [5081] naive
	He was declared innocent of all charges.	

2899 　　　　공무원 **throne** [throhn]	1. 왕좌, 왕위 2. 즉위, 보위	dethrone (퇴위시키다) enthrone (왕좌에 앉히다) [4118] stool
	The prince will succeed to the throne.	

2900 　　수능 토익 토플 **delegate** [DEL-i-git]	1. 대표(단), 사절(단) 2. 위임하다	delegation (대표단) [528] representative
	The Korean government sent a delegate to the US.	

2901 　토익 공무원 토플 **landlord** [LAND-lawrd]	1. 주인 2. 임대주, 건물주 3. 회사	[3194] proprietor
	Many landlords raise the rent when renewing tenancy agreements.	

2902 　　　고등 토익 **convey** [kuhn-VEY]	1. 전달하다, 전하다 2. 실어 나르다, 운반하다, 수송하다	[1625] transmit
	I would like to convey my sincere gratitude.	

2903 **wolf** [woolf]	늑대, 이리	[2799] beast
	Wolves travel in packs.	

2904 　　수능 토플 GRE **rational** [RASH-uh-nl]	1. 이성적인 2. 합리적인, 논리적인	irrational (비이성적인) rationalize (합리화하다) [306] reasonable
	Logical and rational thinking is important.	

2905 　　공무원 편입 **hydrate** [HAHY-dreyt]	수분을 공급하다	dehydration (탈수) hydrant (소화전) [2064] moisturize
	You should keep your body hydrated.	

2906 　　　　공무원 **echo** [EK-oh]	1. 울리다, 메아리(치다) 2. 공감하다 3. 따라말하다	[3337] reiterate
	My own voice echoes in my ears.	

2907 　공무원 토플 편입 **inherit** [in-HER-it]	1. 상속받다 2. 일을 물려받다 3. 유전되다	inheritance (상속) [230] receive
	I have inherited a house from my father.	

2908 　　　수능 토익 **warehouse** [WAIR-hous]	창고, 창고형 매장	[322] store
	I got a temporary job at a warehouse.	

2909 　　토익 공무원 **invoice** [IN-vois]	송장(을 보내다), 청구서	[1057] bill
	I just sent an invoice by e-mail.	

2910 　　　　　고등 **precious** [PRESH-uhs]	1. 소중한, 귀중한 2. 값비싼	[2328] dear
	This necklace is very precious to me.	

2911	토플	가사, 노랫말	lyrical (감동적인) [380] words
lyrics [LIR-iks]		This song has beautiful lyrics.	

2912		1. 3배의 2. 3부분으로 된, 3개로 이뤄진	quadruple (4배의) quintuple (5배의) [6085] threefold
triple [TRIP-uhl]		The company is expecting to triple its profits next year.	

2913	공무원 편입	1. 튼튼한, 강한 2. 건강한, 팔팔한	[498] strong
robust [roh-BUHST]		This table is robust and durable.	

2914	수능	1. 째깍거리다 2. 체크 표시를 하다 3. 진드기	[304] check
tick [tik]		I can hear the clock ticking.	

2915	수능 토플	1. 증폭시키다 2. 부연하다	amplifier (앰프, 증폭기) [4239] magnify
amplify [AM-pluh-fahy]		Social media amplifies fake news.	

2916	공무원 GRE	정적인, 고정된, 정지 상태의	[4823] stationary
static [STAT-ik]		This is a very old and static city.	

2917	수능	개념, 이념, 생각	[262] idea
notion [NOH-shuhn]		A group of scientists publicly challenged the notion.	

2918	수능 토플	1. 짜서 만들다, 엮다 2. 누비다	woven (짜여진) [4137] braid
weave [weev]		Some spiders weave webs in circles.	

2919	고등 토플	1. 배심원단 2. 심사위원단	
jury [JOOR-ee]		Local juries tend to issue lighter sentences to defendants.	

2920	고등 토익	1. 깔끔한, 단정한, 정돈된 2. 멋진, 훌륭한	[4525] tidy
neat [neet]		Your handwriting is very neat.	

2921	공무원 토플	(신진)대사	metabolite (대사에 필요한 것)
metabolism [muh-TAB-uh-liz-uhm]		Eating plenty of protein can boost your metabolism.	

2922	토익	1. 상습적인, 연쇄적인 2. 순차적인 3. 연재물, 연속극	[3026] consecutive
serial [SEER-ee-uhl]		Serial killers should be sentenced to death.	

2923	공무원 편입 GRE	1. (인위적인) 합성 2. 종합, 통합	synthesize (합성하다) synthesizer (합성기) synthetic (합성의) [613] combination
synthesis [SIN-thuh-sis]		This chapter discusses the first artificial synthesis of a DNA molecule.	

2924	고등 토익	1. (알)약, 정제 2. 피임약	[1988] tablet
pill [pil]		Have you taken your pills?	

2925	고등	석탄	[1834] carbon
coal [kohl]		North Korea illegally exports coal to China.	

2926		통화, 화폐	[368] money
currency [KUR-uhn-see]		The dollar is the strongest currency.	

2927	토익 공무원	1. 혼잡, 교통 체증 2. 고장, 걸림 3. 잼 4. 밀어넣다, 집어넣다 5. 즉흥 연주	[5267] cram
jam [jam]		We are stuck in a traffic jam.	

2928	수능	1. 명쾌하게 2. 솔직하게	explicit (명쾌한) inexplicable (설명할 수 없는) explicate (설명하다)
explicitly [ik-SPLIS-it-lee]		He did not explicitly explain why he is leaving the company.	

2929	고등 토익	여권	[448] pass
passport [PAS-pawrt]		I lost my passport while traveling.	

2930	고등 토익	1. 교통 요금, 운임 2. 승객 3. 하다, do (ex. 잘하다, 못하다)	
fare [fair]		Egypt has the cheapest taxi fare in the world.	

2931	토익 공무원 토플 편입	음료	[862] drink
beverage [BEV-er-ij]		What is your favorite beverage?	

2932	토플	1. 활기찬, 활발한 2. 생생한, 선명한 3. 진동하는	[3873] lively
vibrant [VAHY-bruhnt]		Seoul is a vibrant city.	

2933	수능 토플 GRE	1. 심미적인, 미적인 2. 미학, 아름다움	[316] artistic
aesthetic [es-THET-ik]		My aesthetic standards are very different from yours.	

2934	수능 토플	1. 가파른, 경사의 2. 급격한, 극단적인	
steep [steep]		It is difficult to climb a steep hill.	

2935	공무원 토플	1. 직관적인 2. 이해하기 쉬운	intuition (통찰) [7382] visceral
intuitive [in-TOO-i-tiv]		People tend to believe that women are more intuitive than men.	

2936	수능 토플	1. 일부의, 부분 2. 파편 3. (수학)분수	[1672] portion
fraction [FRAK-shuhn]		Only a tiny fraction of people recycle garbage cans in the US.	

2937		1. 해적 2. 불법 복제, 저작권 침해(자) 3. 저작권을 침해하다	piracy (저작권 침해) [6819] corsair
pirate [PAHY-ruht]		Do you like pirate movies?	

2938	수능 GRE	1. 예리한, 예민한, 날카로운 2. 명민한 3. 간절한, 열망하는	keenly (날카롭게) [1781] sharp
keen [keen]		Dogs have a keen sense of smell.	

2939	고등 토플	1. 가혹한, (날씨, 생활 환경이) 혹독한 2. 귀에 거슬리는, 듣기 싫은	[1719] rough
harsh [hahrsh]		My father was rather harsh on me.	

2940		사랑스러운	adore (사모하다)
adorable [uh-DAWR-uh-buhl]		That little child is so adorable.	[2366] cute

2941	공무원 토플	1. 맥박 2. 진동, 파동 3. 활기 넘치다	[1187] beat
pulse [puhls]		I can hear the pulse in my neck.	

2942	고등	1. 황소 2. 주식 시세가 오르다	
bull [bool]		He was attacked by a bull.	

2943	편입	1. 증거 2. 구약성서, 신약성서	
testament [TES-tuh-muhnt]		Her success is a testament to her skills and hard work.	

2944		1. 향기, 냄새, 자취 2. 향수	[1836] smell
scent [sent]		I don't like the scent of the perfume.	

2945	고등	1. 빛나다 2. 상기되다 3. 타오르다	glow-in-the-dark (야광의)
glow [gloh]		Her eyes started to glow with happiness.	[1962] shine

2946	수능	1. 경사, 기울기 2. 슬로프	[3341] incline
slope [slohp]		They climbed the steep slope.	

2947	공무원 편입	1. 자비 2. 고마운 일	merciful (자비로운) merciless (무자비한)
mercy [MUR-see]		ISIS shows no mercy to hostages.	[3146] compassion

2948	공무원 편입 GRE	1. 실행 가능한 2. (독자)생존 가능한	viability (가능성)
viable [VAHY-uh-buhl]		Despite endless discussions, no viable plan came forward.	[3908] feasible

2949	토익 공무원	포기(각서)	waive (포기하다)
waiver [WEY-ver]		Click here to fill out a waiver form.	[438] release

2950	토익	1. 필요(성) 2. 필수품 3. 불가피한 사정	necessitate (필요로 하다)
necessity [nuh-SES-i-tee]		Students should understand the necessity of studying.	

2951	초등	1. 삼각형 2. 트라이앵글(악기)	
triangle [TRAHY-ang-guhl]		The sum of all the angles of a triangle is 180 degrees.	

2952	수능 GRE	1. 억제하다, 저해하다 2. 금하다, 제지하다	inhibitor (억제제)
inhibit [in-HIB-it]		Smoking could inhibit bone healing.	[740] prevent

2953	고등 토플	1. 바삭바삭한, 아삭아삭한 2. 상쾌한, 산뜻한	[1103] fresh
crisp [krisp]		I like to wear a crisp white shirt.	

2954		파이프라인, 수송관	[227] line
pipeline [PAHYP-lahyn]		The government initiated a project to supply water through a pipeline.	

2955	고등 토익	세탁(물), 빨래	laundromat (빨래방) [1357] wash
laundry [LAWN-dree]		I have to do laundry right now.	

2956	토익 공무원	1. 수리, 재건 2. 쇄신 3. 혁신	renovate (개조하다) [1563] restoration
renovation [REN-uh-vey-shuh n]		This hotel recently finished the renovation.	

2957	공무원 편입 GRE	1. 장애 2. 손상, 손실	impair (손상하다) [719] damage
impairment [im-PAIR-muhnt]		He has a visual impairment.	

2958		(밀가루)반죽	[368] money
dough [doh]		This pizza dough recipe is very simple and great for beginners.	

2959		1. 양동이, 통 2. 다량의	
bucket [BUHK-it]		I flushed the toilet with a bucket of water.	

2960	수능	서식지	habitable (서식 가능한) [532] cnvironment
habitat [HAB-i-tat]		Habitat destruction is a serious environmental issue.	

2961		마늘	
garlic [GAHR-lik]		Garlic is known to lower blood pressure.	

2962	고등 토플	혼돈, 혼란	chaotic (혼돈 상태의) [290] disorder
chaos [KEY-os]		The city was in chaos.	

2963	공무원	보석, 보물, 보배	[2229] jewel
gem [jem]		Diamonds are an expensive piece of gem.	

2964	고등 토익 토플	1. 닮다, 유사하다 2. 연상되다	resemblance (유사성) [688] match
resemble [ri-ZEM-buhl]		She resembles her mother.	

2965	토익	스케이트(를 타다)	
skate [skeyt]		People were skating on the lake.	

2966	고등	도둑질하다, 약탈하다	robbery (강도 사건) [1736] steal
rob [rob]		A group of thieves robbed a bank.	

2967	고등 토플	1. 짜다, 압착하다 2. 밀어넣다, 압박하다	[442] press
squeeze			
[skweez]		Many refugees are squeezed together in makeshift huts.	

2968	토플 GRE	1. 통합하다 2. 굳히다, 강화하다	[2375] merge
consolidate			
[kuhn-SOL-i-deyt]		Three kingdoms became consolidated into a larger kingdom.	

2969	초등 토익	취미	[6404] pastime
hobby			
[HOB-ee]		I like to play the violin as a hobby.	

2970	토익 토플	도표	[1273] chart
diagram			
[DAHY-uh-gram]		You can see the diagram on the left.	

2971	토익 토플	1. 로비(장소) 2. 로비 활동을 하다	lobbyist (로비 활동가)
lobby			[1405] hall
[LOB-ee]		Meet me at the lobby.	

2972	고등	1. 후회(하다), 유감스럽게 생각하다 2. 아쉬움, 애석함	[4508] sorrow
regret			
[ri-GRET]		I regret to inform you that I am resigning from my position.	

2973	공무원 GRE	목사	[1558] minister
pastor			
[PAS-ter]		Martin Luther King Jr. was a pastor.	

2974	초등 토플	1. 오리 2. 피하다, 모면하다	
duck			
[duhk]		I can see the ducks swimming by the river.	

2975		매트, 깔개	
mat			
[mat]		There is a mat to wipe your feet.	

2976	토익 공무원	(주로 월급) 수표	
paycheck			
[PEY-chek]		I receive a monthly paycheck.	

2977	초등 토익	비행기	
airplane			
[AIR-pleyn]		I first rode an airplane when I was 6.	

2978	토익 공무원	대변인	
spokesperson			
[SPOHKS-pur-suhn]		The spokesperson started reading the announcement.	

2979		등대	[4736] beacon
lighthouse			
[LAHYT-hous]		We survived thanks to the lighthouse.	

2980		정자	
sperm			
[spurm]		My mother conceived me using a sperm donor.	

2981		뒷마당	[1663] yard
backyard [BAK-yahrd]		My dog is running arround the backyard.	

2982		관점, 견해	[1678] perspective
viewpoint [VYOO-point]		I disagree with his viewpoint.	

2983	공무원	소송	
lawsuit [LAW-soot]		Mr. Kim will represent me in the lawsuit.	

2984		아이를 돌봐주다	
babysit [BEY-bee-sit]		Somebody has to babysit our son tonight.	

2985	토익 공무원	절도, 도둑질	thief (절도) [1736] stealing
theft [theft]		Identity theft is common in the United States.	

2986		1. 성자, 성인 2. 성자처럼 덕이 높은 사람	sanctify (신성하게 하다) saintly (성스러운)
saint [seynt]		St. Nicholas Day is celebrated on December 6th.	

2987	수능 공무원 편입	상호관계, 연관성, 상관관계	uncorrelated (상관관계 가 없는)
correlation [kawr-uh-LEY-shuhn]		There is a high correlation between smoking and lung cancer.	

2988	고등	1. 따르다, 지키다 2. 순종하다, 복종하다	disobey (복종하지 않다)
obey [oh-BEY]		You must obey the law.	

2989	수능	1. 설교하다 2. 전하다, 전도하다	preacher (설교자) [2385] lecture
preach [preech]		Missionaries were sent to preach the Gospel.	

2990	편입	1. 발표하다, 선보이다 2. 공개하다, 사실을 밝히다	veil (덮개, 가리다) [1080] reveal
unveil [uhn-VEYL]		Companies are gathered here to unveil their latest models.	

2991	고등 토플	1. 쾅 소리, 굉음 2. 부딪침 3. 치다, 때리다	bangs (일자 앞머리) [2320] knock
bang [bang]		He heard a loud bang and then saw black smoke.	

2992	토익	1. 부두, 선창 2. 정박하다 3. 도킹하다	[6040] wharf
dock [dok]		Parents took their children to the dock to see the ships.	

2993	공무원 편입	1. 포함하다, 아우르다 2. 둘러싸다	[1241] encircle
encompass [en-KUHM-puhs]		Biochemistry encompasses biology, chemistry, and physics.	

2994	수능 토익	1. 철수하다, 후퇴하다 2. 후퇴, 퇴각, 도피 3. 은신처, 수련회, 피서지 등	[2082] withdraw
retreat [ri-TREET]		The enemy was forced to retreat.	

2995	수능	1. 잡초 2. 담배, 마리화나 3. 잡초를 뽑다	[2351] grass
weed			
[weed]		The lake is full of weed.	

2996	토익	1. 포크 2. 갈래 3. 갈라지다, 나뉘다	[1686] branch
fork			
[fawrk]		She picked up her fork and knife.	

2997	고등 토플	1. 살, 고기 2. 육체 3. 과육	[1755] meat
flesh			
[flesh]		The dog bit deep into the flesh.	

2998	토플	1. 목소리의, 발성의 2. 소리 높여 표현하는	vocally (목소리로) vocalist (노래하는 자)
vocal			[2474] oral
[VOH-kuhl]		He loved singing as a child and started vocal training at 13.	

2999	고등 토익	잔디밭	[2351] grass
lawn			
[lawn]		We mow our lawn once a week.	

3000		1. 알파 (그리스 알파벳 첫 글자) 2. 우두머리 3. 처음의	[279] beginning
alpha			
[AL-fuh]		Alpha is the first letter of the Greek alphabet.	

Allvoca.com

수능	고3, 1~2등급
공무원	70
토익	800+
지텔프	65+
텝스	400+
토플	95+
아이엘츠	6.5
편입	기초 단어
SAT	기초 단어
GRE	기초 단어

#3001~ #4000

외국인으로서 중급 수준의 어휘력이다.
유학 생활이나 회사 업무에서 기본적인 의사소통이 가능하고, 논리 정연한 영문 텍스트의
핵심과 개요를 파악할 수 있다. 국내에서 가장 많이 요구되는 실력이기에, 대부분의 학습
자는 레벨3~4의 학습만으로도 비약적인 성장을 기대할 수 있다. 레벨4의 학습 보조수단
으로는 뉴베리상(Newbery Award) 수상도서들이나 자신의 관심사와 관련된 미디어 콘
텐츠(영문 기사, 영화, 다큐멘터리 등)를 추천한다.

LEVEL 04

3001	고등	1. 뱀 2. 꿈틀거리다	[5269] serpent
snake		A little boy screamed when he saw a snake.	
[sneyk]			

3002	공무원 토플 편입	특색, 특징, 성격의 한 부분	[374] quality
trait		Arrogance is a very unattractive personality trait.	
[treyt]			

3003	고등	1. 돌진(하다), 질주(하다) 2. 소량 3. 단거리 경주	[2136] rush
dash		She jumped off the bus and made a dash for the nearest restaurant.	
[dash]			

3004	수능	1. 처녀, 동정남 2. 성모 마리아 3. 자연 그대로의, 처녀의	virginity (순결) [1549] pure
virgin		I was a virgin until I was thirty years old.	
[VUR-jin]			

3005	수능 토플	1. 명령(하다), 지시(하다) 2. 좌우하다 3. 받아쓰다	dictator (독재자) [290] order
dictate		Don't try to dictate the rules to children.	
[DIK-teyt]			

3006	공무원 토플	1. 외부(의), 외관 2. 겉(모습)	
exterior		The exterior of the building was elegant and beautiful.	
[ik-STEER-ee-er]			

3007	고등 토플	1. 운명, 천명, 숙명 2. 죽음	[3851] destiny
fate		She wept over her sad fate.	
[feyt]			

3008		외과의사, 외과 전문의	[1903] physician
surgeon		He is a good surgeon.	
[SUR-juhn]			

3009	토익 공무원 편입	1. 생활 편의 시설 2. 오락시설	[1430] conveniences
amenities		This small town has all the amenities of a large city.	
[uh-MEN-i-teez]			

3010		1. 화음, 코드 2. 현 3. 감정	[1459] string
chord		Can you remember the chords to this song?	
[kawrd]			

3011		1. 상어 2. 사기꾼, 고리 대금업자	
shark		A shark can smell blood at a distance.	
[shahrk]			

3012	고등	신부	[1152] wife
bride		The bride looked truly radiant on her wedding day.	
[brahyd]			

3013	수능	1. 말하다 2. 완전, 매우	utterly (순전히) [1124] absolute
utter		She uttered John's name but he did not reply.	
[UHT-er]			

3014	고등	1. 껍질(을 벗기다, 깎다) 2. 벗겨지다	
peel		Would you peel me an apple?	
[peel]			

3015 **rig** [rig]	1. 부정한 방법으로 조작하다 2. 계략	
	There are widespread fears that any poll would be rigged.	
3016　　토익 공무원 토플 **duplicate** [DOO-pli-keyt]	1. 복사하다, 복제하다 2. 중복되다 3. 똑같은, 사본의	
	Can you duplicate the key for me?	
3017　　　공무원 편입 **regime** [ruh-ZHEEM]	1. 정권 2. 체제, 제도	
	The North Korean regime has been criticized for failing to uphold human rights.	
3018　　고등 토익 토플 **contrary** [KON-trer-ee]	1. 반대의, ~와는 다른 2. 모순된	
	Contrary to popular belief, many cats dislike milk.	
3019　　　　고등 **lid** [lid]	1. 뚜껑 2. 눈꺼풀	
	She put the lid on the jar.	
3020 **zoom** [zoom]	1. 급등하다 2. 아주 빨리 가다 3. 확대/축소하다	[728] speed
	Overnight trading caused share prices to zoom.	
3021　　공무원 GRE **arid** [AR-id]	1. 건조한, 불모의 2. 무미 건조한, 흥미로운 것이 없는	[5989] barren
	Nothing will grow in this arid ground.	
3022　　공무원 토플 편입 **doctrine** [DOK-trin]	1. 교리, 신조, 주의, 정책 2. 원칙	[1837] philosophy
	The doctrine had a far-reaching, devastating impact.	
3023　　　수능 GRE **deliberately** [dih-LIB-er-it-lee]	1. 의도적으로, 계산된 2. 신중히, 찬찬히	deliberate (의도적인, 신중한) [1527] intentionally
	He has been deliberately left off the guest list.	
3024　　　　토플 **vibration** [vahy-BREY-shuhn]	1. 진동, 떨림 2. 동요	vibrate (진동하다) [4634] oscillation
	Even at full speed, the ship's engines cause very little vibration.	
3025　　　고등 토플 **cease** [sees]	1. 중단하다, 그치다 2. 사라지다 3. 중지, 정지	cessation (중단) [439] stop
	She never ceases to amaze me.	
3026　　토익 공무원 편입 **consecutive** [kuhn-SEK-yuh-tiv]	연이은, 연속되는, 계속되는	[1861] sequential
	He was absent for five consecutive days.	
3027　　　　공무원 **underneath** [uhn-der-NEETH]	1. 아래에, 밑에, 안에 2. 저변의 3. 밑면	[474] below
	She sat underneath the tree in the shade.	
3028　　　　공무원 **cleanse** [klenz]	1. 세척하다 2. 깨끗이 되다 3. 죄책감을 씻어주다	[559] clean
	Cleanse your face thoroughly and take off any residue with toner.	

3029	토익 공무원 편입	유명한, 명성있는, 저명한	[1159] famous
renowned [ri-NOUND]		He was a renowned newspaper editor.	

3030	고등 토플	1. 아래에, 밑에 2. ~보다 못한 3. ~의 이면에	bequeath (물려주다) [474] below
beneath [bih-NEETH]		A dog was beneath the table.	

3031	초등	1. 똑똑한, 영리한 2. 솜씨 좋은 3. 기발한, 재치있는	[1486] smart
clever [KLEV-er]		He is a very clever young boy.	

3032	고등 토익 GRE	1. 간절히 염원하는, 열심인 2. 열렬한	eagerness (열망) [2131] enthusiastic
eager [EE-ger]		She was eager to get into politics.	

3033	고등	술집	
pub [puhb]		Let's go to the pub for a drink.	

3034	수능 토플	1. 뻣뻣한, 뻑뻑한, 경직된 2. 강한 3. 시체	stiffen (경직되다) [308] hard
stiff [stif]		I felt stiff after a long walk.	

3035		촬영 장면, 화면	[외래어] video
footage [FOOT-ij]		People can now see live footage of the war at home on their televisions.	

3036	고등	벌레, 곤충	[3762] pest
insect [IN-sekt]		The little girl caught the insect by inverting her cup over it.	

3037		1. 큰 덩어리 2. 상당히 많은 양 3. 부분	[3684] lump
chunk [chuhngk]		She bit off a large chunk of bread.	

3038	초등 토익	1. 양말 2. 강타, 세게 치다	[2594] punch
sock [sok]		A toe peeked through the hole in her sock.	

3039	수능	1. 돌아다니다, 거닐다 2. 길을 잘못 들다, 헤매다 3. 산만해지다	[3984] roam
wander [WON-der]		I will wander around the mall for an hour.	

3040	공무원 토플	1. 위함, 이유, 목적 2. 부디, 제발 3. (일본) 사케	[428] benefit
sake [seyk]		I stopped smoking for the sake of my health.	

3041	수능 토플	1. 잔혹한, 악랄한, 잔인한 2. 폭력적인 3. 야만적인	brute (짐승) brutality (잔인함) [3470] cruel
brutal [BROOT-l]		She was the victim of a very brutal murder.	

3042	고등 토익 토플	1. 달성하다, 이루다, 획득하다 2. 이르다, 달하다 3. 확보	[748] achieve
attain [uh-TEYN]		The important thing in life is to have a great aim and the determination to attain it.	

3043	수능 토플	1. 치명적인, 죽음을 초래하는 2. 불행한 3. 결정적인	fatality (사망)
fatal			[1186] deadly
[FEYT-l]		His children's death is a fatal blow on him.	

3044	고등 토익	교외, 외곽	suburban (교외의)
suburb			
[SUHB-urb]		They live in a wealthy suburb of Chicago.	

3045	수능	1. 경적 2. 뿔, 뿔제품	[4738] trumpet
horn			
[hawrn]		She continued to honk the horn.	

3046	고등	1. 절 2. 조항 3. 약관	[638] article
clause			
[klawz]		We should add this clause to the contract.	

3047	고등	1. 악령, 악마 2. 귀재 3. 마음을 괴롭히는 것	[2797] devil
demon			
[DEE-muhn]		Your son is a little demon.	

3048	고등	1. 그럼에도 불구하고 2. 어쨌거나	[3738] nonetheless
nevertheless			
[nev-er-thuh-LES]		She was very tired; nevertheless, she kept on working.	

3049		계기판	
dashboard			
[DASH-bawrd]		The car's interior is impressive—wonderful leather seats and a wooden dashboard.	

3050	공무원	1. 공작 2. 군주	[1419] lord
duke			
[dook]		The duke was the king's most trusted advisor.	

3051	수능 토플	시작하다, 개시하다	commencement (졸업식, 시작)
commence			
[kuh-MENS]		The meeting is scheduled to commence at noon.	

3052	고등	1. 끔찍한, 지독한 2. 엄청난 3. 무시무시한	[2215] terrible
awful			
[AW-fuhl]		I feel awful about forgetting my best friend's birthday.	

3053	고등	1. 자백하다, 고백하다 2. 인정하다	confession (자백)
confess			[1078] admit
[kuhn-FES]		We persuaded him to confess his crime.	

3054		마법사, 귀재	[1375] magician
wizard			
[WIZ-erd]		The wizard recited a spell.	

3055		1. 수직 통로 2. 손잡이 3. 축대 4. 날카로운 발언 5. 속이다	[2697] beam
shaft			
[shaft]		A fire broke out in the main lift shaft.	

3056	공무원 토플 편입	1. 관통하다 2. 침투하다 3. 간파하다	penetration (관통)
penetrate			impenetrable (관통할 수 없는)
[PEN-i-treyt]		Fine dust particles penetrate deep into the lungs.	[5056] permeate

3057	토플	1. 급증(하다) 2. 못, 뽀족한 것 3. 못을 박다, 찌르다 4. (배구) 스파이크	[915] stick
spike [spahyk]		In the last six months, there has been a spike in unemployment.	

3058		1. ~에, ~에게 2. ~까지	
unto [UHN-too]		The angel appeared unto her in a dream.	

3059	수능 GRE	1. 제약 2. 제한, 통제 3. 조건	constrain (강제하다) [3449] restraint
constraint [kuhn-STREYNT]		At last, we could relax and talk without constraint.	

3060	고등 토익	쟁반, 얕은 접시	[5320] platter
tray [trey]		She brought her breakfast in bed on a tray.	

3061	수능 토플	1. 민족, 종족의 2. 혈통의 3. 인종의	ethnicity (민족성) [693] cultural
ethnic [ETH-nik]		Different ethnic groups have different cultures.	

3062	고등	1. 면도(하다) 2. 깎다	shaver (면도기)
shave [sheyv]		My brother has to shave twice a day.	

3063	고등 토플	1. 밀물과 썰물, 조류 2. 흐름	tidal (파도의) [3170] surge
tide [tahyd]		We swam till the tide began to ebb.	

3064	고등	1. 무릎 2. 한 바퀴 3. 한 구간	
lap [lap]		Come and sit on my lap and I will read you a story.	

3065	고등	1. 점토, 찰흙 2. 진흙	[1064] earth
clay [kley]		My children like making houses with clay and sticks.	

3066	토플	1. 머리기사, 표제어 2. 주인공을 맡다	[301] heading
headline [HED-lahyn]		Every morning, I read all the daily headlines.	

3067		사다리꼴	
trapezoid [TRAP-uh-zoid]		A trapezoid has four sides, two of which are parallel.	

3068	토플	1. 자동차 경적을 울리다 2. 경적 소리	[5477] beep
honk [hongk]		An impatient driver honked from behind.	

3069	토익	길가의 보도	[3102] pavement
sidewalk [SAHYD-wawk]		Kids gathered on the sidewalk.	

3070		폐쇄(하다), 정지(하다)	[247] closure
shutdown [SHUHT-doun]		Government shutdowns should always be the last resort.	

3071		전시(하다)	[699] display
showcase			
[SHOH-keys]		There will be a time to showcase your skills.	

3072	토익	하락	[1792] decline
downturn			
[DOUN-turn]		The economic downturn affected thousands of workers.	

3073		1. 새로운, 획기적인 2. 기공(식)	[1165] innovative
groundbreaking			
[GROUND-brey-king]		Groundbreaking research proved the world to be flat.	

3074	공무원 토플 편입	발전, 돌파구	[857] discovery
breakthrough			
[BREYK-throo]		There was a major breakthrough in the treatment of cancer.	

3075	공무원	1. 매우 힘이 있는 집단 2. 발전소	
powerhouse			
[POU-er-hous]		That company is a marketing powerhouse.	

3076	토플	생리학	
physiology			
[fiz-ee-OL-uh-jee]		Physiology studies the mechanisms within a living being.	

3077	공무원	여유로운, 느긋한	
easygoing			
[EE-zee-goh-ing]		I like him for his easygoing personality.	

3078		모두가 의존하는 것, 매우 중요한 것, 초석	
cornerstone			
[KAWR-ner-stohn]		Vocabulary is the cornerstone of English proficiency.	

3079	편입	타고난	[5266] innate
inborn			
[IN-bawrn]		Most of his talents are inborn.	

3080	고등	1. 수평선, 지평선 2. 시야	
horizon			
[huh-RAHY-zuhn]		The sun went down below the horizon.	

3081	고등	1. 주거, 주택 2. 사는	dwell (머물다)
dwelling			
[DWEL-ing]		Tell me about your ideal dwelling place.	

3082	공무원 토플 GRE	1. 충돌, 부딪침 2. 상충, 대립	collide (충돌하다) [831] impact
collision			
[kuh-LIZH-uhn]		The two ships came into collision.	

3083	고등	1. 발음하다 2. 표명하다 3. 두드러지다	pronunciation (발음)
pronounce			
[pruh-NOUNS]		What is the most difficult English word to pronounce?	

3084	공무원 토플 편입 GRE	1. 장애, 방해 2. 장애물	[4133] hindrance
obstacle			
[OB-stuh-kuhl]		The greatest obstacle to progress is prejudice.	

3085	토익	1. 스케치(하다) 2. 밑그림 3. 개요	sketchy (대강의)
sketch			[2119] outline
[skech]		My mother made a sketch of my sister reading a book.	

3086	공무원 토플 GRE	1. 녹다, 용해되다 2. 끝내다 3. 사라지다, 흩어지다	[2362] melt
dissolve			
[dih-ZOLV]		Both salt and sugar dissolve easily in water.	

3087	토익	1. 쓰레기, 잡동사니 2. 부수다, 엉망으로 만들다 3. 맹비난하다	[4865] rubbish
trash			
[trash]		Don't throw trash here.	

3088	고등	1. 부끄러운, 난처한 2. 당혹스러운	embarrass (부끄럽게하다)
embarrassing			
[em-BAR-uh-sing]		It was so embarrassing having to sing in public.	

3089	고등	밴, 승합차	
van			
[van]		We hired a van for transport.	

3090	토익 공무원 편입 GRE	1. 파괴적인, 충격적인 2. 인상적인, 강력한	devastation (파괴)
devastating			[1255] destructive
[DEV-uh-stey-ting]		It is the most devastating storm in 25 years.	

3091		1. 기준 타수, 파 2. 동등, 평균 3. 액면 가격	parity (동등함, 동격)
par			[727] average
[pahr]		He went around the course in three under par.	

3092	고등	1. 캔버스 천 2. 화폭, 유화 3. 도화지	[2088] sail
canvas			
[KAN-vuhs]		The painter swept a brush over his canvas.	

3093	고등 토익	1. 가치, 뛰어남 2. 장점, 혜택 3. (칭찬, 상금 등을) 받을 만하다	demerit (약점)
merit			[724] excellence
[MER-it]		The film has no artistic merit whatsoever.	

3094		1. 세트 2. 결합체	[613] combination
combo			
[KOM-boh]		She played trumpet professionally in a jazz combo.	

3095		보안관	[5096] marshal
sheriff			
[SHER-if]		He was appointed Sheriff of New York.	

3096	수능 토플	1. 살금살금 움직이다 2. 슬며시 다가오다 3. 타고 오르다 4. 소름끼치게 싫은 사람	creepy (오싹하는)
creep			[3406] crawl
[kreep]		Someone could easily creep up behind us.	

3097	고등	1. 괴롭히는 사람, 불량배 2. 괴롭히다, 왕따시키다	[3630] intimidate
bully			
[BOOL-ee]		A bully is always a coward.	

3098	고등 토익	최고의, 최상의, 훌륭한	[724] excellent
superb			
[soo-PURB]		The house has a superb staircase made from marble.	

3099	고등 토플	신성한, 성스러운, 신성시되는	[1737] holy
sacred [SEY-krid]		A church is a sacred building.	

3100	편입	1. 총액, 합계, 전체 2. 모으다, 종합하다	[508] total
aggregate [AG-ri-git]		They purchased an aggregate of 5000 shares in the company.	

3101	고등 토익 토플	동상, 조각상	[2710] sculpture
statue [STACH-oo]		The statue of the dictator was toppled by the crowds.	

3102	수능 토플	1. 길을 열다 2. 기반을 마련하다 3. (도로를) 포장하다	
pave [peyv]		I hope the treaty will pave the way to peace in the Middle East.	

3103	고등	1. 어리석은, 바보같은 2. 어처구니없는, 유치한 3. 심각하지 않은	[2459] stupid
silly [SIL-ee]		Don't be silly, that insect can't hurt you.	

3104	GRE	1. 헌사, 찬사 2. ~의 효력을 입증하는 것 3. 조공	[1151] honor
tribute [TRIB-yoot]		The president paid tribute to the brave soldiers who had lost their lives.	

3105		1. 비틀기 2. 수정(하다) 3. 비틀다, 잡아당기다	[3709] pinch
tweak [tweek]		She gave the boy's ear a painful tweak.	

3106	토익	쇼핑센터	
mall [mawl]		I usually go to the mall to get new clothes.	

3107		1. 대응(하다), 반박(하다) 2. 계산대, 카운터 3. 반대로	counteract (반대로 대응하다) [2087] combat
counter [KOUN-ter]		She had a hard time countering John's arguments.	

3108		1. 상기하다 2. 리콜, 소환하다	[622] remember
recall [ri-KAWL]		I don't recall screaming for help.	

3109		1. 방송보도 2. 범위, 보급률	
coverage [KUHV-er-ij]		His controversial remarks received nationwide coverage.	

3110		그나저나, 어쨌든	
anyway [EN-ee-wey]		She did not read books, but bought one anyway.	

3111		1. 공학자, 기술자 2. 설계 및 제작하다	
engineer [en-juh-NEER]		My dad is a famous engineer.	

3112		학자	scholastic (학업의)
scholar [SKOL-er]		I aspire to be a scholar.	

3113	고등	1. 대처하다, 대응하다 2. 극복하다	
cope			
[kohp]		It must be difficult to cope with three small children and a job.	

3114	고등	1. 뛰다, 뛰어오르다 2. 도약(하다) 3. 급증(하다)	[1276] jump
leap			
[leep]		Small animals can easily leap from tree to tree.	

3115	수능	1. 붉어지다, 상기되다 2. 물을 내리다 3. 씻어내다 4. 홍조, 흥분	[3293] rinse
flush			
[fluhsh]		He began to flush with excitement.	

3116	고등	1. 아픈, 따가운 2. 화가 난, 기분이 상한 3. 상처, 염증	soreness (아픔) [863] painful
sore			
[sawr]		I had a sore throat and it hurt to swallow.	

3117		신입생	[3753] rookie
freshman			
[FRESH-muhn]		She is a freshman at Harvard.	

3118		1. 총애받는, 인기 많은 2. 가장 사랑하는 3. 애인	[2328] dear
beloved			
[bih-LUHV-id]		He lost his beloved wife two years ago.	

3119	고등	목, 목구멍	[1978] neck
throat			
[throht]		Antibiotics are effective in curing throat infection.	

3120		1. (약품)캡슐 2. 작은 플라스틱 용기 3. (우주선의)캡슐	encapsulate (짧게 요약 하다) [2924] pill
capsule			
[KAP-suhl]		The doctor advised me to take a capsule this afternoon.	

3121		매트리스	[1132] bedding
mattress			
[MA-tris]		He kept his money under the mattress.	

3122	토플	1. (사건이)동시 발생 2. 접속사 3. 연대, 협력 4. 결합	[3741] junction
conjunction			
[kuhn-JUHNGK-shuhn]		The conjunction of drought and heat wave caused wildfires.	

3123	공무원 토플	1. 영역, 범주 2. 왕국 3. 국토	[1694] domain
realm			
[relm]		A philosopher dwells in the realm of ideas.	

3124	고등	1. 유제품의 2. 낙농업(의) 3. 유제품 회사	[1644] milk
dairy			
[DAIR-ee]		I am allergic to dairy products.	

3125	토플	양초	
candle			
[KAN-dl]		A candle had set the curtains on fire.	

3126	고등 토익 토플	1. 연약한, 여린 2. 섬세한 3. 정교한	[383] sensitive
delicate			
[DEL-i-kit]		She has been in delicate health for a long time.	

3127	고등 토플	1. 쥐 2. 배신자, 비열한 인간	
rat			
[rat]		A rat squeaked and ran into the bushes.	

3128		1. 민트, 박하 2. 박하사탕 3. 조폐국 4. 많은 돈 5. 주조하다	[2122] coin
mint			
[mint]		I like using a mint-flavored toothpaste.	

3129	공무원 편입 GRE	1. 수동적인, 소극적인 2. 간접	
passive			
[PAS-iv]		She is very passive in the relationship.	

3130	고등 토플	1. 쓴 2. 씁쓸한 3. 격렬한, 신랄한	[7355] acrimonious
bitter			
[BIT-er]		The outside of orange is bitter, but the inside is sweet.	

3131	고등 토플	1. 진흙, 진창 2. 오명	muddy (진흙의)
mud			[6363] muck
[muhd]		There was a lot of mud on the ground.	

3132	고등	1. 공포, 공황 2. 패닉상태 3. 겁에 질려 어쩔 줄 모르다	[1198] fear
panic			
[PAN-ik]		She felt a spasm of panic sweeping over her.	

3133	수능 토플	1. 채찍(질하다) 2. 휘저어 거품을 내다	[1187] beat
whip			
[hwip]		The cruel man lashed the horse with his whip.	

3134	공무원	1. 항생제, 항생물질 2. 항균	[1402] medicine
antibiotic			
[an-ti-bahy-OT-ik]		Antibiotic ointment will prevent infection.	

3135	수능 토플	1. 욕을 하다 2. 맹세하다 3. 선서하다	[1300] promise
swear			
[swair]		He swears all the time.	

3136	고등 토플 GRE	1. 축축한, 눅눅한 2. 적시다 3. 낙담시키다	dampen (적시다)
damp			[2064] moist
[damp]		I don't like damp weather.	

3137		1. 전달하다 2. 중계(하다) 3. 계주 4. 교대용 팀	[2132] broadcast
relay			
[REE-ley]		They will relay your message.	

3138	공무원 토플 편입	글을 읽고 쓸 줄 아는 능력, 이해력	illiteracy (문맹)
literacy			[772] knowledge
[LIT-er-uh-see]		Some people have some problems with literacy and numeracy.	

3139	공무원 GRE	1. 그리다, 묘사하다 2. 표현하다 3. 연기하다	portrayal (묘사)
portray			[2807] depict
[pawr-TREY]		Many fairy tales portray women as victims.	

3140	고등	1. 조각하다, 깎아서 만들다 2. 새기다 3. 개척하다, 이뤄내다	[2318] slice
carve			
[kahrv]		He used a hammer to carve out a figure from the marble.	

3141	고등	1. 아무데도 2. 어디에도 없다	
nowhere [NOH-hwair]		I have no job and nowhere to live.	

3142	고등 토익	1. 담요 2. 장막 3. 뒤덮다	
blanket [BLANG-kit]		The baby was wrapped in a blanket.	

3143	토익 공무원 편입	1. 명성이 높은, 일류의 2. 명문 3. 권위	prestige (명성) [5148] eminent
prestigious [pre-STIJ-uhs]		He graduated from a prestigious university.	

3144	토익 공무원 토플 편입	1. 피로, 피곤 2. 피곤하게 하다	[2198] exhaust
fatigue [fuh-TEEG]		They were all suffering from fatigue at the end of their journey.	

3145	고등 토익	1. 줄무늬 2. 수장	striped (줄무늬가 있는) [3532] streak
stripe [strahyp]		The plates have a black stripe around the edge.	

3146	공무원 편입 GRE	연민, 동정심	compassionate (동정하는) [3321] sympathy
compassion [kuhm-PASH-uhn]		I was hoping he might show a little compassion.	

3147	공무원 편입	1. 지형 2. 지역	[2417] geography
terrain [tuh-REYN]		A jeep is ideal for driving over rough terrain.	

3148	수능 토플	도망치다, 달아나다	[1801] escape
flee [flee]		They were forced to flee their homeland during the war.	

3149	고등	1. 감히 ~하다 2. ~해 보라고 부추기다 3. 용기	daring (대담한) [602] challenge
dare [dair]		He didn't dare to look at her in the face.	

3150	고등 토플	담배	[1421] smoking
tobacco [tuh-BAK-oh]		This shop is licensed to sell tobacco.	

3151	편입	1. 통치(하다), 치세 2. 책임 맡는 기간 3. 재임하다	[516] rule
reign [reyn]		The dictator's ten-year reign of terror left thousands dead.	

3152	수능 토플	1. 가설 2. 추측	hypothetical (가설적인) [1219] theory
hypothesis [hahy-POTH-uh-sis]		We hope that further research will confirm our hypothesis.	

3153		1. 전속력으로 질주하다 2. 단거리 경기	sprinter (단거리 선수) [646] race
sprint [sprint]		They had to sprint to catch the bus.	

3154	토익	1. 탄약통 2. 카트리지, 프린터 잉크통 3. 약포	[1450] magazine
cartridge [KAHR-trij]		This rifle only holds one cartridge.	

3155 **incur** [in-KUR]	토익 공무원	1. 초래하다 2. 발생시키다	incursion (침입)
		He wondered what he had done to incur his displeasure this time.	
3156 **virtue** [VUR-choo]	수능 토플	1. 미덕, 덕행 2. 선, 선행 3. 장점	virtuous (미덕이 있는)
		Humility is the foundation of all virtue.	
3157 **affirm** [uh-FURM]	토익 공무원 편입	1. 단언하다 2. 확인하다	affirmative (단언하는, 찬 성하는) affirmation (단언)
		I can affirm that no one will lose their job.	
3158 **abortion** [uh-BAWR-shuhn]	수능 토플	낙태	
		Abortion is a highly controversial issue.	
3159 **distortion** [dih-STAWR-shuhn]	수능 GRE	1. 왜곡 2. 찌그러뜨림	
		That is a gross distortion of the truth.	
3160 **cultivate** [KUHL-tuh-veyt]	고등	1. 경작하다 2. 재배하다 3. 구축하다 4. 양성하다	[3744] nurture
		The land is too rocky to cultivate.	
3161 **rage** [reyj]	수능	1. 격노, 분노 2. 화를 내다 3. 급속히 번지다	enrage (격분하게 하다) [1987] anger
		Her face turned purple with rage.	
3162 **pretend** [pri-TEND]	고등 토플	1. ~인 척하다 2. 가장하다 3. 거짓의	pretender (~인 척하는 사 람) [2552] fake
		I am tired of having to pretend all the time.	
3163 **firearm** [FAHYUHR-ahrm]		1. 화기 2. 소화기	[1467] weapon
		He was found guilty of possessing an unlicensed firearm.	
3164 **niche** [nich]		틈새	[5342] nook
		The company has created a niche market for itself.	
3165 **pause** [pawz]	고등	1. 잠시 멈추다 2. 일시정지(시키다) 3. 휴식	[445] break
		They had to pause frequently for breath.	
3166 **rim** [rim]		1. 테두리 2. 가장자리 3. 둘러싸다	[1070] edge
		The rim of the cup was broken.	
3167 **mesh** [mesh]	공무원	1. 그물망, 철망 2. 들어맞게 하다 3. 맞물리다	[2540] grid
		The windows were covered in wire mesh to keep out flies.	
3168 **envelope** [EN-vuh-lohp]	고등	봉투	envelop (감싸다)
		An envelope was waiting for me when I got home.	

3169	토익	벽장, 옷장, 클로젯	[3670] wardrobe
closet [KLOZ-it]		Hang your coat in the closet.	

3170	공무원 토플 편입 GRE	1. 급상승 2. 밀려듦 3. 급증하다	[836] rise
surge [surj]		There has been a surge in house prices in recent months.	

3171	고등 토플 GRE	1. 급성의 2. 예리한	[1781] sharp
acute [uh-KYOOT]		She is suffering from an acute infection of the lower respiratory tract.	

3172	고등	1. 외치다, 소리지르다 2. 한턱내다 3. 환성	[3718] yell
shout [shout]		There is no need to shout, I can hear you perfectly.	

3173	토익 공무원 편입	통근(하다)	[1303] exchange
commute [kuh-MYOOT]		Many may eventually be able to work from home rather than commute to an office.	

3174	수능 토익 토플	1. 가구를 비치하다 2. 제공(하다) 3. 갖추다	unfurnished (가구가 없는)
furnish [FUR-nish]		We will furnish our house with expensive furniture.	

3175	고등 토플	계단	staircase (계단)
stair [stair]		She heard soft footsteps coming up the stair.	

3176	수능	1. 양육권 2. 구금, 구속 3. 유치, 구류	custodian (관리인, 보호자) [3390] detention
custody [KUHS-tuh-dee]		The court awarded custody to the child's mother.	

3177	고등 토플	1. 주민 2. 서식 동물	inhabit (거주하다) [686] resident
inhabitant [in-HAB-i-tuhnt]		The local inhabitants do not like noisy tourists in summer.	

3178	토익	지하(실)	[5053] cellar
basement [BEYS-muhnt]		The basement has been made into a workshop.	

3179	공무원 편입 GRE	1. 겸손한 2. 변변치 않은 3. 소박한 4. 겸허하게 하다	[3348] modest
humble [HUHM-buhl]		She is very humble about her success.	

3180		1. 기하학 2. 기하학적 구조	geometric (기하학적인)
geometry [jee-OM-i-tree]		I study spherical geometry.	

3181	토익 토플	1. 퍼레이드, 행진 2. 열병식 3. 정렬시키다	[699] display
parade [puh-REYD]		Marchers in the parade carried colorful banners.	

3182	토플	1. 뿌리다 2. 섞다 3. 물을 주다 4. 보슬비	[1997] spray
sprinkle [SPRING-kuhl]		I sprinkled chocolate on top of the cake.	

| 3183
matrix
[MEY-triks] | 1. 행렬 2. 모체 3. 망 | [1831] template |
| | A two by three matrix normally contains six elements. | |

| 3184　고등
stare
[stair] | 1. 쳐다보다, 응시하다 2. 노려보다 | [4197] gaze |
| | It is impolite to stare at a stranger. | |

| 3185　고등
upward
[UHP-werd] | 1. 위쪽을 향한 2. 증가하는 | |
| | The missile rose upward into the sky. | |

| 3186
arena
[uh-REE-nuh] | 1. 경기장, 공연장 2. 무대 3. 활동장소 | [482] field |
| | The circus elephants were led into the arena. | |

| 3187　공무원 토플 편입
agile
[AJ-uhl] | 1. 날렵한, 민첩한 2. 기민한, 명민한 | agility (민첩성)
[5943] nimble |
| | Monkeys are very agile climbers. | |

| 3188　고등 토플
neglect
[ni-GLEKT] | 1. 방치하다, 소홀히하다, 등한시하다 2. (의무, 일 등을) 게을리하다 | [1793] ignore |
| | Don't neglect your duties. | |

| 3189　토익 공무원 토플 편입
recurring
[ri-KUR-ing] | 1. 거듭 발생하는, 되풀이하여 발생하는 2. 순환하는 | recurrence (반복)
recursion (반복)
recursive (반복되는)
[1201] repeated |
| | Love is a recurring theme in the book. | |

| 3190　공무원 편입
forge
[fawrj] | 1. 구축하다, 만들다 2. 위조하다 3. 나아가다 | [949] shape |
| | He pledged to forge ahead with his plans for reform. | |

| 3191
enzyme
[EN-zahym] | 효소 | [4302] catalyst |
| | Enzymes help speed up chemical reactions in the body. | |

| 3192　편입
rehabilitation
[ree-huh-BIL-i-tey-shuh n] | 1. 사회 복귀 2. 복직, 복위 3. 재건 4. 재활 | rehabilitate (재활하다) |
| | The prison service has the goals of punishment and rehabilitation. | |

| 3193　공무원
roster
[ROS-ter] | 1. 근무자/직원 명단 2. 등록부 | [259] list |
| | You will see when you are working if you look on the duty roster. | |

| 3194
proprietary
[pruh-PRAHY-i-ter-ee] | 1. 소유주의 2. 상표권이나 저작권에 의해 보호받는 3. 소유자 | |
| | He has a proprietary right to the property. | |

| 3195　수능 토익
monument
[MON-yuh-muhnt] | 1. 기념물 2. 기념비적인 건축물 3. 표지 | monumental (기념비적
인)
[830] memorial |
| | There is a big monument in the square. | |

| 3196　고등
pond
[pond] | 1. 연못 2. 우물 | [1349] pool |
| | I own a small pond in my yard. | |

3197	토플	1. 인지의 2. 인식의	cognition (인지) [1355] mental
cognitive [KOG-ni-tiv]		Teachers are trained to stimulate students' cognitive processes.	
3198	공무원 편입	1. 나눠주다 2. 제외하다 3. 조제하다	dispenser (자판기) indispensable (없이는 안되는) [1062] distribute
dispense [dih-SPENS]		The government's aim is to dispense food and clothing to the people in need of help.	
3199		1. 산맥 2. 길쭉하게 솟은 부분	ridged (줄기 모양이 있는) [4451] crest
ridge [rij]		They finally reached the crest of the ridge.	
3200	고등	1. 소나무, 솔 2. 잣	
pine [pahyn]		There is an old pine tree in the garden.	
3201	토익	베개	[3238] cushion
pillow [PIL-oh]		She used to hide her diary under her pillow.	
3202		1. 테이블스푼(큰 숟가락) 2. 테이블스푼 하나 가득한 양	[795] spoonful
tablespoon [TEY-buh1-spoon]		Mix the flour with one tablespoon of water.	
3203	토익	1. 필수적인, 완전한 2. 포함되어 있는, 내장된 3. (수학) 적분	integrate (통합하다) disintegrate (분해하다)
integral [IN-ti-gruhl]		The internet has become an integral part of our lives.	
3204		1. 토스트 2. 건배(하다) 3. 불로 따뜻이 하다	toaster (토스터) [862] drink
toast [tohst]		I had a piece of toast for lunch.	
3205	고등 토플	설득하다, 납득시키다, 종용하다	persuasive (설득력 있는) persuasion (설득) [1974] convince
persuade [per-SWEYD]		I tried to persuade my mother but failed.	
3206	수능	1. 줄어들다 2. 감소하다 3. 위축되다	shrinkage (줄어듦) [738] contract
shrink [shringk]		This soap will shrink woolen clothes.	
3207	공무원 토플 편입	1. 문지방, 문턱 2. 한계점, 임계점	[402] limit
threshold [THRESH-ohld]		He caught his foot on the threshold and stumbled.	
3208	수능	교황	
pope [pohp]		The Pope is the supreme leader of the Roman Catholic Church.	
3209	수능 토익 토플	1. 사직하다, 내려오다 2. 사임, 사퇴, 퇴진	resignation (사직) [2550] quit
resign [ri-ZAHYN]		He was under pressure to resign.	
3210	공무원 편입 GRE	1. 진압하다 2. 억제하다 3. 감추다, 삭제하다 4. 참다	suppression (진압) [4779] repress
suppress [suh-PRES]		The autocratic government tried to suppress the people.	

3211	수능 토플	내재하는, 고유의, 타고난	[5266] innate
inherent [in-HEER-uhnt]		There are risks inherent in every sport.	

3212	공무원 토플	1. 이용하다 2. 벨트 3. 마구(를 채우다) 4. 지배하다	[2600] exploit
harness [HAHR-nis]		The company is trying to harness the power of frontier technologies.	

3213	편입	1. 탄력, 가속도 2. 힘 3. 운동량	[6456] impetus
momentum [moh-MEN-tuhm]		The team has lost momentum in recent months.	

3214	고등	1. 경찰관 2. 겪다	
cop [kop]		A cop pulled me over and gave me a speeding ticket.	

3215	고등	1. 활기를 되찾다 2. 소생시키다	revival (부활) [1927] revitalize
revive [ri-VAHYV]		The global economy is beginning to revive.	

3216	수능 토익 토플	1. 흐르다, 쏟다 2. 엎질러지다 3. 유출	[2481] shed
spill [spil]		The water is so full that it might spill over.	

3217	공무원	1. 등급 2. 단계 3. 표시 4. 달성하다	top-notch (최고등급)
notch [noch]		The quality of the food has dropped a notch recently.	

3218	공무원 편입 GRE	1. 연합, 동맹 2. 연립정부	coalesce (연합하다) [1770] alliance
coalition [koh-uh-LISH-uhn]		The two parties have united to form a coalition.	

3219	수능 토플	1. 궤도 2. 궤도를 돌다 3. 영향권	[1241] circle
orbit [AWR-bit]		The satellite is in a stable orbit now.	

3220	공무원 토플 편입	1. 오염 2. 혼합 3. 타락	contaminate (오염시키다) contaminant (오염 물질) [2815] pollution
contamination [kuhn-tam-uh-NEY-shuhn]		Environmental contamination is impacting wildlife.	

3221	공무원 편입 GRE	1. 전제조건, 사전에 필요한 2. 빠뜨릴 수 없는	requisite (필요한) [446] precondition
prerequisite [pri-REK-wuh-zit]		This course is a prerequisite to more advanced studies.	

3222	고등 토플	1. 고결한 2. 귀족의 3. 숭고한 4. 귀족	[1677] grand
noble [NOH-buhl]		She died for a noble cause.	

3223		1. 욕조 2. 통	
tub [tuhb]		We found him lying in the tub.	

3224	고등 토플	1. 동시에 일어나다 2. 일치하다	coincidence (우연의 일치) coincidentally (동시에 일치하는) [3847] concur
coincide [koh-in-SAHYD]		Their views on this issue closely coincide with yours.	

3225 vinyl [VAHYN-l]		1. 비닐 2. 레코드 음반	[342] record
		This type of vinyl is a good substitute for leather.	
3226 thermal [THUR-muhl]	편입	1. 열의 2. 뜨거운 3. 보온성이 좋은	
		The government will build another thermal power station.	
3227 hesitate [HEZ-i-teyt]	고등 토익	1. 망설이다, 주저하다 2. 거리끼다	hesitation (망설임) hesitant (망설이는) [3165] pause
		Please do not hesitate to contact me.	
3228 macro [MAK-roh]		1. 대형의, 대규모의 2. 거시적인 3. 매크로(컴퓨터 프로그램 일종)	
		Climate change is a macro issue.	
3229 canal [kuh-NAL]	공무원	1. 운하, 수로 2. 체내의 관	[1185] channel
		This canal has been closed to shipping.	
3230 wrist [rist]		손목, 팔목	[291] hand
		He seized me by the wrist.	
3231 lateral [LAT-er-uhl]	공무원 편입	1. 옆의 2. 측면으로의	unilateral (일방적인) bilateral (두 가지 면이 있는) [292] side
		This wall is weak and needs lateral support.	
3232 luggage [LUHG-ij]	토익 편입	짐, 수하물	[1052] baggage
		I left my luggage at the hotel.	
3233 clutch [kluhch]	공무원	1. 꽉 잡다 2. 클러치 3. 손아귀	[3371] grasp
		We had no time to gasp or clutch at each other.	
3234 aviation [EY-vee-ey-shuhn]	공무원	1. 항공 2. 비행	[1263] flight
		There were huge advances in aviation technology during World War Two.	
3235 brass [bras]		1. 놋쇠, 황동 2. 금관 악기 4. 돈, 엽전	
		Brass tarnishes quickly in wet weather.	
3236 intriguing [in-TREE-ging]	수능 토플 GRE	1. 아주 흥미로운 2. 음모를 꾸미는	intrigue (흥미를 유발하 다) [2469] fascinating
		He found the story rather intriguing.	
3237 toll [tohl]	토익 토플	1. 사상자 수 2. 통행료 3. 대가 4. 종소리	[415] charge
		The death toll has risen to 88.	
3238 cushion [KOOSH-uhn]	토익 토플	1. 쿠션, 방석 2. 완화하다 3. 대비책	[2521] buffer
		The cat was curled on a cushion on the sofa.	

3239	토익 공무원 토플 편입	1. 인접한 2. 가까운 3. 이웃의	[389] near
adjacent [uh-JEY-suhnt]		We work in adjacent buildings.	

3240	공무원	1. 물류, 화물, 군수 2. 실행 계획	
logistics [loh-JIS-tiks]		Blockchain could be used to facilitate logistics handling.	

3241	공무원 편입	1. 토큰 2. 상품권 3. 증거로서 주어진 (상징, 선물)	
token [TOH-kuhn]		Subways used to accept tokens.	

3242	공무원	1. 약속(하다), 맹세(하다) 2. 저당(을 잡히다) 3. 공약하다	[1300] promise
pledge [plej]		The government should fulfill its pledge.	

3243	수능 토플	편견, 차별적인 생각	[2753] bias
prejudice [PREJ-uh-dis]		There is a prejudice that men should not be nurses.	

3244		시제품, 원형, 견본 (을 만들다)	[4529] paradigm
prototype [PROH-tuh-tahyp]		The company is developing a prototype for an electric vehicle.	

3245		1. 식초 2. 찡그린 표정	[813] sour
vinegar [VIN-i-ger]		He flavored the fish with vinegar and sugar.	

3246	고등	1. 밀 2. 밀가루 반죽	[2206] grain
wheat [hweet]		The price of wheat had reached an all-time high.	

3247		1. 받치다 2. 지주 3. 버팀목 4. 소품 5. 명제	
prop [prop]		We had to prop up the tree with long poles under the branches.	

3248	고등	1. 모순적이게도 2. 비꼬아 3. 반어적으로	irony (모순) [4695] paradoxically
ironically [ahy-RON-i-kuhl-lee]		Ironically, the book he felt was his worst sold more copies than any of his others.	

3249	수능	1. 서리(가 내리다) 2. 성에 3. 결빙	defrost (해동하다) [1579] freeze
frost [frawst]		The plants all died in the last frost.	

3250		1. 모자 2. 덮개(를 씌우다)	[외래어] bonnet
hood [hood]		You can detach the hood from the coat.	

3251		1. 녹 2. 녹슬다, 부식하다 3. 못쓰게 되다	rusty (녹슨)
rust [ruhst]		Rust has corroded the steel rails.	

3252	고등	1. 꽃이 피다 2. 혈색이 돌다	blooming (꽃이 활짝 핀) [4292] blossom
bloom [bloom]		The roses are in full bloom.	

3253 **ammunition** [am-yuh-NISH-uhn]	토플	1. 탄약 2. 무기	[1467] weapon
		The soldiers need to be resupplied with ammunition.	
3254 **illuminate** [ih-LOO-muh-neyt]	공무원 편입	1. 비추다 2. 밝게 하다 3. 조명을 설치하다 4. 눈부시게 꾸미다	
		He used table lamps to illuminate dark corners.	
3255 **cannabis** [KAN-uh-bis]		대마초	
		The legalization of cannabis is a political minefield.	
3256 **grease** [grees]		1. 기름(을 바르다) 2. 지방 3. 뇌물	
		She puts grease on her hair to make it shiny.	
3257 **dye** [dahy]	공무원	1. 염색하다 2. 물들이다 3. 염료, 염색제	
		I want to dye my hair blonde.	
3258 **lightning** [LAHYT-ning]		1. 번개, 번갯불 2. 벼락	[1670] flash
		The big tree was struck by lightning.	
3259 **slim** [slim]	고등 토플	1. 날씬한, 호리호리한 2. 얇은 3. 희박한	[1768] thin
		She works out very hard to stay slim.	
3260 **vector** [VEK-ter]		1. 벡터 2. (질병의)매개체 3. 궤도 4. (비행기의)진로	[255] course
		Acceleration and velocity are vectors.	
3261 **thereby** [thair-BAHY]		그렇게 함으로써, 그 때문에	[1121] thus
		He became an American citizen, thereby gaining the right to vote.	
3262 **trophy** [TROH-fee]	고등	1. 트로피, 우승컵 2. 전리품	[1787] prize
		She lifted the trophy up and kissed it.	
3263 **debit** [DEB-it]	토익	1. 체크카드 2. 차변 3. 인출액	[1514] debt
		You can pay via debit or credit card.	
3264 **whale** [hweyl]	고등 토익 토플	고래	[1828] giant
		We may live to see the extinction of the whale.	
3265 **floral** [FLAWR-uhl]		꽃의	[1418] flowery
		They chose a delicate floral pattern for their bedroom curtains.	
3266 **treaty** [TREE-tee]	수능 토플	1. 조약 2. 협약 3. 협정	[427] agreement
		Both sides have agreed to sign the treaty.	

3267	1. 콘센트 2. 푹 들어간 구멍	[1665] plug
socket		
[SOK-it]	There is an electric socket on the wall.	

3268	1. 정맥 2. 잎맥 3. 맥락	
vein		
[veyn]	The nurse was having trouble finding a vein in his arm.	

3269	1. 작은 조각 2. 조금 3. 남은 음식 4. 폐지하다	
scrap		
[skrap]	He wrote down her phone number on a scrap of paper.	

3270 공무원 토플 편입	노력(하다), 시도(하다)	[982] attempt
endeavor		
[en-DEV-er]	They always endeavor to please their customers.	

3271 공무원 토플 편입	1. 잔류물 2. 잔여 유산 3. 찌꺼기 4. 남아있는	residual (잔여의) [537] remains
residue		
[REZ-i-doo]	Wipe the residue off with a tissue.	

3272	1. 델타, 그리스 알파벳의 넷째 글자 2. 삼각주	[1773] mouth
delta		
[DEL-tuh]	Delta is the fourth letter of the Greek alphabet.	

3273 편입	속도, 속력	[728] speed
velocity		
[vuh-LOS-i-tee]	The speedboat reached a velocity of 130 mph.	

3274 공무원 편입 GRE	1. 가판대, 노점, 칸 2. 지연(시키다)	forestall (앞질러 방해하다, 기선 제압하다) [1697] delay
stall		
[stawl]	He sells fruits at a market stall.	

3275 공무원 편입	괴롭힘, 희롱	harass (괴롭히다) [5104] torment
harassment		
[huh-RAS-muhnt]	Sexual harassment in the workplace is a grave issue.	

3276	호박	
pumpkin		
[PUHMP-kin]	I just made a pumpkin pie.	

3277 공무원 토플	1. 싹 2. 꽃봉오리 3. 싹을 틔우다 4. 친구	[1189] bro
bud		
[buhd]	The plants began to bud in April.	

3278 공무원 토플 편입 GRE	1. 원산의, 토착의 2. 고유의	[1602] native
indigenous		
[in-DIJ-uh-nuhs]	Pandas are indigenous to China.	

3279 토익 토플 편입	1. 습도 2. 습함 3. 습기	humid (습한) humidifier (가습기) [3136] dampness
humidity		
[hyoo-MID-i-tee]	I don't like the humidity of this climate.	

3280 토플 편입	1. 빈 공간 2. ~이 없는 3. 쓸모 없는, 무효의	[1345] invalid
void		
[void]	The void left by his father's death was never filled.	

3281 **deer** [DEER]		사슴	[2875] buck
November is a good month to hunt deer.			
3282 **activist** [AK-tuh-vist]		사회 운동가	
She is a environmental activist.			
3283 고등 **sheep** [sheep]		양	sheepishly (소심하게) [3892] lamb
Sheep are farmed for their meat and wool.			
3284 **ankle** [ANG-kuhl]		발목	
You should call your doctor right away if you sprain your ankle.			
3285 고등 토익 토플 **bargain** [BAHR-guhn]		1. 헐값 2. 흥정(하다)	[413] deal
The car was a bargain at that price.			
3286 토익 공무원 편입 **antique** [an-TEEK]		1. (귀중한)골동품 2. 옛날의	antiquated (구식의)
We have a lot of antique furniture.			
3287 수능 **judicial** [joo-DISH-uhl]		1. 사법의 2. 재판의	
After the trial, they had lost all faith in the judicial system.			
3288 수능 토플 **induce** [in-DOOS]		1. 설득하다, 유도하다, 유인하다 2. 초래하다	[323] cause
We could not induce our mother to travel by air.			
3289 공무원 토플 편입 **patriot** [PEY-tree-uht]		애국자	patriotism (애국심)
She regards herself as a patriot.			
3290 토익 **hurricane** [HUR-i-keyn]		허리케인, 태풍, 폭풍	[1878] storm
A hurricane hit the city last week.			
3291 공무원 편입 **ignorance** [IG-ner-uhns]		1. 무식, 무지, 모르는 2. 무시	ignorant (무시하는) [1560] unfamiliarity
People derided him for his ignorance.			
3292 수능 토플 **profound** [pruh-FOUND]		1. 엄청난, 지대한 2. 깊은, 심오한	[595] deep
The celebrity's death had a profound effect on her.			
3293 **rinse** [rins]		1. 씻다, 헹궈내다 2. 씻기, 헹구기	[1357] wash
Rinse thoroughly after you shampoo your hair.			
3294 고등 **silk** [silk]		실크, 비단	silky (비단의)
Her silk dress rustled as she moved.			

3295	토익 공무원 편입	상품, 물품, 제품	
merchandise			
[MUR-chuhn-dahyz]		We delivered the merchandise to her.	

3296	고등	담배	[1421] smoke
cigarette			
[sig-uh-RET]		The company monopolized the entire cigarette industry.	

3297		1. 구슬, 염주, 방울 2. 구슬선을 꿰다	[676] drop
bead			
[beed]		The woman is wearing a bead necklace.	

3298		1. 뜨개질을 하다 2. 뜨다, 짜다 3. 결합하다, 접합하다 4. (옷) 니트	[4995] entwine
knit			
[nit]		My grandmother taught me how to knit.	

3299	수능	1. 흩어지다 2. (흩)뿌리다	[4160] disperse
scatter			
[SKAT-er]		Police used tear gas to scatter the crowd.	

3300		1. 창백한, 힘없는 2. 병약한	[3563] pale
wan			
[won]		He gave me a wan smile.	

3301	공무원	자폐증	
autism			
[AW-tiz-uhm]		The cause of autism is unknown.	

3302		고기 덩어리, 햄버거 패티	
patty			
[PAT-ee]		I squeezed ketchup onto my patty.	

3303		반딧불	
firefly			
[FAHYUHR-flahy]		There were fireflies in my backyard.	

3304		매수하다	
buyout			
[BAHY-out]		Google negotiated a buyout of my company.	

3305	공무원	방관자	[4311] spectator
bystander			
[BAHY-stan-der]		The athlete started attacking innocent bystanders.	

3306		소문자	[7239] minuscule
lowercase			
[LOH-er-keys]		Lowercase means letters are not capitalized.	

3307		조개	
shellfish			
[SHEL-fish]		I have a shellfish allergy.	

3308	공무원	아가미	
gill			
[gil]		Fish breathe using their gills.	

3309 **bittersweet** [bit-er-SWEET]		달콤씁쓸한	
		I have many bittersweet memories of my high school life.	
3310 **jellyfish** [JEL-ee-fish]		해파리	
		There were so many jellyfish in the ocean.	
3311 **clone** [klohn]	공무원	1. 클론, 복제 생물 2. 복사품 3. 복제하다	[3016] duplicate
		He is an exact clone of his brother.	
3312 **mitigate** [MIT-i-geyt]	공무원 편입 GRE	1. 완화하다, 경감하다 2. 줄이다 3. 저감, 경감	mitigation (완화) unmitigated ((나쁨을 강 조할 때) 완전한) [509] reduce
		I know how to mitigate stress and fear.	
3313 **torque** [tawrk]		회전력, 토크	
		Bigger capacity engines produce more torque.	
3314 **bronze** [bronz]	공무원	1. 동 2. 청동 3. 구릿빛	
		He won a bronze medal in judo.	
3315 **glance** [glans]	고등	1. 흘긋 봄, 곁눈질 2. 흘긋 보다	
		She gave another impatient glance at her watch.	
3316 **pupil** [PYOO-puhl]	고등	1. 학생, 제자 2. 눈동자, 동공	
		The pupil echoed his teacher's words.	
3317 **sphere** [sfeer]	수능 토플	1. 구 2. 영역 3. 범위	
		The sculptor rounded the clay into a perfect sphere.	
3318 **beg** [beg]	고등 토플	1. 간청하다 2. 구걸하다 3. 부탁하다	beggar (거지)
		He begged her not to leave him.	
3319 **ambassador** [am-BAS-uh-der]	고등 토익	대사, 사절	
		He has been appointed British ambassador to the UN.	
3320 **commodity** [kuh-MOD-i-tee]	수능 토플	1. 상품, 물품 2. 원자재 3. 유용한 물건	
		Clean water is a precious commodity in many countries.	
3321 **sympathy** [SIM-puh-thee]	고등 토플	1. 동정, 연민, 공감, 애도 2. 동의, 찬성	sympathetic (공감하는) sympathize (공감하다) [3146] compassion
		We express our sincere sympathy to you and your family.	
3322 **collar** [KOL-er]	고등	1. 칼라, 깃 2. (장식용) 목걸이 3. 이음 고리 4. 붙잡다, 체포하다	[1816] arrest
		The collar of her shirt was dirty.	

| 3323 | 수능 | 1. 번영하다, 번창하다 2. 발전하다 | prosperity (번창)
prosperous (번창하는) |
| **prosper**
[PROS-per] | | He prospered as a businessman. | [3945] flourish |

| 3324 | 공무원 토플 | 1. 고통, 괴로움 2. 고난 3. 걱정 4. 조난 5. 괴롭히다, 피로하게 하다 | [1446] trouble |
| **distress**
[dih-STRES] | | Many people are in financial distress. | |

| 3325 | 토플 | 1. 배, 복부 2. 둥그런 부분 3. 부풀다 | [2525] stomach |
| **belly**
[BEL-ee] | | He was lying on his belly. | |

| 3326 | 수능 토익 | 1. 파산, 파탄 2. 부도 | [621] failure |
| **bankruptcy**
[BANGK-ruhpt-see] | | Many established companies were facing bankruptcy. | |

| 3327 | | 1. 땅콩 2. 하찮은 3. 아주 적은 액수 | |
| **peanut**
[PEE-nuht] | | Around 1.5 million Americans are allergic to peanuts. | |

| 3328 | 고등 | 1. 씹다 2. 물어뜯다 | [2061] bite |
| **chew**
[choo] | | This meat is difficult to chew. | |

| 3329 | | 1. 부수다, 고장내다 2. 급습하다, 불시단속하다 3. 상반신 4. 실패작 | [445] break |
| **bust**
[buhst] | | It was her drinking that bust up her marriage. | |

| 3330 | 고등 토익 토플 | 1. 마찬가지로 2. 똑같이, 비슷하게 3. 마찬가지야, 동감이야 | [2862] moreover |
| **likewise**
[LAHYK-wahyz] | | His third marriage was likewise unhappy. | |

| 3331 | | 1. 레이스 2. 끈(을 묶다) 3. 포함하다 | [4137] braid |
| **lace**
[leys] | | She wore a white gown with trimmed lace. | |

| 3332 | | 1. 행위, 행동 2. 증서 3. 공적 | [2600] exploit |
| **deed**
[deed] | | We felt that we had done our good deed for the day. | |

| 3333 | 공무원 | 1. 골절, 균열, 부러짐 2. 부서지다, 분열되다 | [445] break |
| **fracture**
[FRAK-cher] | | Fracture of any part of the body can be very serious in old people. | |

| 3334 | 고등 | 1. 악몽 2. 끔찍한 일 | [2761] radical |
| **nightmare**
[NAHYT-mair] | | I had a nightmare that felt real. | |

| 3335 | | 초-, 엄청난 | [2761] radical |
| **ultra**
[UHL-truh] | | Ultra fine dust particles can penetrate our lungs. | |

| 3336 | | 1. 주사위 2. 주사위 모양으로 자르다 | [2734] cube |
| **dice**
[dahys] | | You roll the dice and whoever gets the highest score goes first. | |

3337 공무원 편입 GRE	반복 , 되풀이	reiterate (되풀이하다) [1201] repetition
iteration [it-uh-REY-shuhn]	It was easy for me to learn the chorus because of its iteration in the song.	

3338 토익 공무원 편입	1. 진실된, 진심 어린 2. 진지한 3. 성실한	sincerely (진실된 마음으로)
sincere [sin-SEER]	I would like to say a sincere thank you to everyone who has supported me.	insincere (진실되지 못한) [1404] honest

3339 공무원 토플	1. 증기 2. 공상, 환상	vaporize (증발하다) [2211] steam
vapor [VEY-per]	Water vapor is water in the form of a gas.	

3340	1. (신용)사기 2. 사기치다	[2439] fraud
scam [skam]	They got involved in a credit card scam.	

3341 수능	1. ~하고 싶은, 마음이 내키는 2. ~하는 경향이 있는 3. 경사가 진	inclination (성향) [2103] disposed
inclined [in-KLAHYND]	She writes only when she feels inclined to.	

3342 토익 편입	1. 상품권, 할인권, 쿠폰 2. 보증인, 증명인	[외래어] coupon
voucher [VOU-cher]	The voucher can be used at most supermarkets.	

3343 고등 토익	여가	
leisure [LEE-zher]	Many people enjoy shorter working hours and more leisure time.	

3344 수능 토플	1. 매듭 2. 엉키다	
knot [not]	You should tie the knot as tight as you can.	

3345	상당한	significance (중요성)
significant [sig-NIF-i-kuhnt]	His most significant accomplishment was the invention of the dynamite.	

3346 수능 토플	1. 정서, 감정 2. 감상	
sentiment [SEN-tuh-muhnt]	The local sentiment is against any change to the law.	

3347 고등	1. 박살내다 2. 부서지다 3. 충돌하다	[2692] crush
smash [smash]	If I see him, I will smash his face in.	

3348 수능	1. 보통의 2. 겸손한 3. 얌전한, 정숙한	modesty (겸손) [3179] humble
modest [MOD-ist]	The global economy continues to grow at a modest pace.	

3349 고등 GRE	1. 제국의, 황제의 2. 제국주의의	[1539] royal
imperial [im-PEER-ee-uhl]	Past imperial glories are hardly relevant to the present day.	

3350 공무원	1. 열광자, 괴짜, 괴물 2. 아주 기이한	[1776] crazy
freak [freek]	People think he is a freak.	

276

3351	공무원 편입	1. 비만, 비대 2. 과체중	obese (비만)
obesity [oh-BEE-si-tee]		Further reducing childhood obesity will require broader changes.	

3352	공무원 토플 편입	1. 조각, 파편 2. 분열하다, 부서지다	[599] piece
fragment [FRAG-muhnt]		He heard only a fragment of their conversation.	

3353		활성화시키다	[1763] trigger
activate [AK-tuh-veyt]		Press the button to activate the system.	

3354	토익	1. 한 줄기, 광선, 빛살 2. 방사선, 복사선 3. 가오리	[2697] beam
ray [rey]		His visit brought a ray of sunshine into the old woman's life.	

3355	고등 토익 토플 GRE	1. 낙관적인, 낙관하는 2. 긍정적인	optimism (낙관주의) [384] hopeful
optimistic [op-tuh-MIS-tik]		Being optimistic has benefits for your health.	

3356	공무원 편입	생태계	
ecosystem [EK-oh-sis-tuhm]		Ecosystems are essential to our well-being and prosperity.	

3357	고등 토플	1. 작은집 2. 오두막	[2577] lodge
cottage [KOT-ij]		The old woman lived in a cottage.	

3358	수능	1. 저주하다, 욕하다 2. 욕설, 악담, 저주	[6622] bane
curse [kurs]		She cursed him silently.	

3359	공무원	1. 줄 2. 줄을 서다 3. 대기 행렬(을 만들다)	
queue [kyoo]		There was a long queue at the post office.	

3360	고등	1. 천재 2. 비범한 3. 특별한 재능	[1372] talent
genius [JEEN-yuhs]		She was a genius.	

3361	수능 토플 GRE	1. 결핍, 부족 2. 결점, 결함	deficient (부족한) [1091] lack
deficiency [dih-FISH-uhn-see]		Vitamin deficiency can lead to illness.	

3362	공무원 토플 편입	1. 인구(통계)학의 2. 인구통계적 집단	[1099] population
demographic [dem-uh-GRAF-ik]		Companies should evolve amid rapid demographic change.	

3363		1. 향기, 향 2. 향수	[4294] perfume
fragrance [FREY-gruhns]		The perfume has a light, fresh fragrance.	

3364	공무원 편입	1. 관련되다 2. 존재하다, 적용되다	
pertaining [per-TEY-ning]		She is interested in anything pertaining to folklore.	

3365	토익 공무원 편입	1. 환대, 후대 2. 접대, 대접	[288] friendliness
hospitality [hos-pi-TAL-i-tee]		We greatly appreciate your warm hospitality.	

3366	공무원 편입	1. 사로잡힌, 감금된 2. 어쩔 수 없는 3. 포로	captivating (마음을 사로 잡는) captivity (감금) [1561] prisoner
captive [KAP-tiv]		We were held captive by masked gunmen.	

3367	공무원 편입	1. 점화, 발화 2. 점화 장치 3. 연소	ignite (점화하다) [655] firing
ignition [ig-NISH-uhn]		The ignition of methane gas killed five men.	

3368	토익 편입	1. 입단식, 취임식 2. 끌어들임, 유도 3. 귀납법	induct ((취임,입대 등)가 입시키다) [1378] initiation
induction [in-DUHK-shuhn]		The team celebrated Mike's induction into the Hall of Fame.	

3369	토익	1. 셔틀 버스 2. 오가다, 왕복하다 3. 실어 나르다	[659] ship
shuttle [SHUHT-l]		There is a shuttle bus that goes to the airport.	

3370	고등 토플	도박, 노름, 갬블링	
gambling [GAM-bling]		He has been gambling all night long.	

3371	수능 토플	1. 이해(하다), 파악(하다) 2. 꽉 잡다, 움켜쥐다 3. 능력	[2200] grip
grasp [grasp]		I'm trying to grasp the current situation before I take any action.	

3372	공무원 토플 편입	1. 조사(하다), 수사(하다) 2. 살피다, 탐색하다	[1004] investigate
probe [prohb]		A team of astronauts was sent to Mars to probe its atmospheric condition.	

3373	토익	1. 부스, 칸막이 공간 2. 노점	[3274] stall
booth [booth]		There is a photo booth inside the train station.	

3374	토익 편입	수습생, 견습생, 도제	
apprentice [uh-PREN-tis]		She became an apprentice shoemaker.	

3375	토익	졸업장, 수료증, 학위	[885] certificate
diploma [dih-PLOH-muh]		He hasn't received his diploma yet.	

3376		가을	[454] fall
autumn [AW-tuhm]		Autumn in New York is beautiful.	

3377	수능 토플 GRE	1. 포식자, 포식 동물 2. 약탈자 3. 범죄자, 가해자	[1600] hunter
predator [PRED-uh-ter]		Tigers are one of the most well-known predators.	

3378	고등 토익	1. 모직, 울 2. 양털, 양모	[5341] fleece
wool [wool]		She is wearing a wool sweater.	

| 3379
spawn
[spawn] | 1. 산란하다, 알을 낳다 2. 결과를 낳다 3. 알 덩어리 | [6845] engender |
| | Fish normally spawn in rivers. | |

| 3380　　　　토익
gum
[guhm] | 1. 껌 2. 잇몸, 치은 3. 고무 | [2437] glue |
| | She is chewing gum. | |

| 3381　　공무원 토플
volcano
[vol-KEY-noh] | 화산 | [4109] eruption |
| | It is dangerous to live near a volcano. | |

| 3382　　　　고등
altogether
[awl-tuh-GETH-er] | 1. 완전히, 전적으로 2. 총, 합쳐서 3. 대체로 | [639] entirely |
| | These issues cannot be solved altogether. | |

| 3383　공무원 토플 편입 GRE
deceive
[dih-SEEV] | 속이다, 기만하다, 현혹하다 | deception (속임)
deceptive (속이는)
deceit (속임수)
[1595] trick |
| | Don't be deceived by appearances. | |

| 3384
straightforward
[streyt-FAWR-werd] | 1. 간단한, 복잡하지 않은 2. 직접적인 3. 솔직한 | |
| | I am asking you a straightforward question. | |

| 3385　　　공무원
implant
[im-PLANT] | 1. 심다 2. 이식하다 | [640] plant |
| | The teacher knew how to implant good habits in students. | |

| 3386
radar
[REY-dahr] | 1. 레이더, 전파 탐지기 2. 감시망 | [1371] detector |
| | The submarine is impossible to detect on radar. | |

| 3387　　　　고등
stove
[stohv] | 1. 스토브, 난로 2. 가스레인지 | |
| | Household stoves are known to emit air pollutants. | |

| 3388　　　공무원
crave
[kreyv] | 1. 갈망하다, 열망하다 2. ~을 청하다 | craving (갈망)
[1100] desire |
| | I am craving chocolate ice cream. | |

| 3389　　　　편입
landmark
[LAND-mahrk] | 1. 획기적인 사건 2. 주요 지형지물, 랜드마크 3. 역사적인 장소 | [1147] milestone |
| | The agreement reached was seen as a major landmark in the peace process. | |

| 3390　　공무원 편입
detention
[dih-TEN-shuhn] | 1. 구금, 구류 2. 방과 후 남게 하는 처벌 | detain (구금하다)
detainee (구금된 자)
[3176] custody |
| | She was held in detention for seven years. | |

| 3391　　공무원 편입
saturated
[SACH-uh-rey-tid] | 1. 포화된 2. 흠뻑 젖은 3. 강렬한 | saturation (포화)
[2733] soaked |
| | Consuming saturated fat may not be bad for health as people once believed. | |

| 3392
poke
[pohk] | 1. 찌르다 2. 삐져나오다 3. 힘 | [6536] prod |
| | He kept on poking her with a sharp stick. | |

3393	공무원 토플	1. 떠가다, 표류하다 2. (서서히) 이동(하다)	[2143] float
drift [drift]		Her swimsuit drifted down the river.	
3394	수능 토플	1. 규범 2. 기준, 표준, 일반적인 것	normative (규범의, 표준의)
norm [nawrm]		Non-smoking is now the norm in most workplaces.	[450] standard
3395	토플	1. 목장, 농장 2. 축산	[1050] farm
ranch [ranch]		My friend owns a huge ranch.	
3396		1. 정신 의학의 2. 정신 질환의 3. 정신과의	
psychiatric [si-KAHY-uh-trik]		She is trying to seek psychiatric help.	
3397	고등	1. 버섯 2. 우후죽순처럼 늘어나다	[280] increase
mushroom [MUHSH-room]		Would you like some mushroom soup?	
3398	고등 토익 GRE	1. 따르다, 순응하다 2. 일치하다	conformity (일치)
conform [kuhn-FAWRM]		Students need to conform to relevant school rules.	[688] match
3399	고등 토플	1. 트렁크(가방) 2. (나무의)줄기, 몸통 3. (코끼리)코	[2173] chest
trunk [truhngk]		I am bringing my own trunk to the trip.	
3400	토플 편입	1. 엄한, 엄격한 2. 철저한, 정확한 3. 혹독한	rigor (엄격함)
rigorous [RIG-er-uhs]		The semiconductor factory is subject to rigorous regulations.	[2287] strict
3401		1. 칸막이 벽 2. 분할, 구획	[1800] split
partition [pahr-TISH-uhn]		There's a partition separating the room into two.	
3402	고등	1. 나체의 2. 적나라한, 노골적인	[2117] bare
naked [NEY-kid]		She was lying on a bed naked.	
3403	공무원	1. 게으른, 태만한 2. 활용되지 않고 있는, 무용의 3. 실직 상태인	
idle [AHYD-l]		He seems idle all the time.	
3404		철저한 채식주의자	[3866] vegetarian
vegan [VEE-guhn]		I prefer a vegan diet.	
3405	수능	1. 순찰 돌다 2. 순회하다, 돌아다니다 3. 순찰, 경찰	[1661] guard
patrol [puh-TROHL]		Several policemen were patrolling the street.	
3406	고등 토플	1. 기어가다 2. 느릿느릿 걷다	[3096] creep
crawl [krawl]		I always crawl out of bed in the morning.	

3407 공무원 편입 GRE		
concession	1. 양보, 양여 2. 인정	concede (인정하다)
[kuhn-SESH-uhn]		[1237] grant
	Both parties were not willing to make a concession.	

3408 수능 토플		
magnificent	1. 장엄한, 웅대한 2. 훌륭한, 아름다운	[5199] splendid
[mag-NIF-uh-suhnt]		
	This condo has a magnificent view.	

3409		
apostle	1. 사도 2. 주창자, ~의 옹호자	[3657] disciple
[uh-POS-uhl]		
	Can you name all the apostles of Jesus?	

3410 토익 편입		
omit	1. 생략하다 2. 누락하다, 빠지다	omission (누락)
[oh-MIT]		
	You should omit all the redundant sentences.	

3411 고등 토익		
ferry	1. 페리, 여객선 2. 수송하다 3. 공수하다	[1414] boat
[FER-ee]		
	We took a ferry to get to the mainland.	

3412		
spider	거미	
[SPAHY-der]		
	Many people hate spiders.	

3413 공무원		
strand	1. 가닥 2. 물가, 바닷가 3. 좌초시키다	[1459] string
[strand]		
	DNA is composed of two strands.	

3414 토익		
wallet	지갑	
[WOL-it]		
	I lost my wallet.	

3415 토플		
feather	1. (깃)털 2. 날개처럼 움직이다	
[FETH-er]		
	The baby is as light as a feather.	

3416 공무원 편입		
subsidiary	1. 자회사(의) 2. 부수적인, 보조의 3. 보조자	
[suhb-SID-ee-er-ee]		
	The subsidiary company is more famous than the parent company.	

3417 수능 토플 GRE		
condemn	1. 비난하다, 규탄하다 2. 유죄 판결을 내리다, 선고하다	[5586] denounce
[kuhn-DEM]		
	He was condemned for his violent behavior.	

3418 고등 토익 토플		
ladder	사다리	
[LAD-er]		
	She climbed the ladder.	

3419 편입		
pending	1. 미결정의 2. 기다리는 동안	[625] awaiting
[PEN-ding]		
	The decision on this issue is still pending.	

3420 공무원		
abdominal	1. 복부의 2. 복근	abdomen (복부)
[ab-DOM-uh-nl]		
	He suffered from abdominal pain.	

3421	토익	배지, 표, 증표	[1700] symbol
badge [baj]		You need a badge to get into this building.	

3422	토익 공무원	1. 화물, 적하 2. 짐, 뱃짐	[844] load
cargo [KAHR-goh]		How many passengers are without cargo?	

3423		1. 도매의 2. 대량의, 대대적인 3. 도매하다	[2570] sweeping
wholesale [HOHL-seyl]		His mom prefers to buy wholesale.	

3424	고등 GRE	1. 어색한, 불편한, 곤란한 2. 서투른, 이상한	[5858] clumsy
awkward [AWK-werd]		Don't ask any awkward questions.	

3425	고등	여관, 여인숙, 작은 호텔	
inn [in]		We are spending the night at an inn.	

3426	토익 공무원 토플	1. 성형의 2. 화장품 3. 화장용의	[542] beauty
cosmetic [koz-MET-ik]		I don't advocate cosmetic surgery.	

3427		1. (장기)이식 2. 옮겨 심다	[4947] graft
transplant [trans-PLANT]		He needs a heart transplant.	

3428	공무원 편입	1. 흐려지다, 희미하게 하다 2. 얼룩	blurry (흐릿한) [6399] smudge
blur [blur]		Tears made my vision blur.	

3429	토플	막, 세포막	[749] skin
membrane [MEM-breyn]		Fine dusts can penetrate our mucus membrane.	

3430	수능	1. 대도시의, 수도권의 2. 교구의	metropolis (대도시) [2765] municipal
metropolitan [me-truh-POL-i-tn]		She loves living in a metropolitan area.	

3431	공무원	1. 은닉처 2. 저장소 3. 감추다, 숨기다	[322] store
cache [kash]		He has a cache of gold bars.	

3432	수능	1. 첨벙대다 2. 튀다 3. 방울, 얼룩	
splash [splash]		I splashed my face with cold water.	

3433	공무원 편입	1. 순전히 2. 속이 비치는, 얇은	[1549] pure
sheer [sheer]		She won that prize out of sheer luck.	

3434	수능	1. 적자 2. 부족액	[443] shortage
deficit [DEF-uh-sit]		The company has a huge deficit.	

3435	고등 토플	1. 줄어들다, 감소하다 2. 완화하다 3. 깎아내리다	diminishing (줄어드는) [509] reduce
diminish [dih-MIN-ish]		The value of this car will diminish over time.	

3436		1. 중간값(의) 2. 중간에 위치한, 중앙에 있는	medial (중간의) [1047] middle
median [MEE-dee-uhn]		The median age of the workers is 30.	

3437	고등 토플	1. 대립하다, 충돌하다 2. 충돌, 불일치, 언쟁 3. (색의)부조화	[1717] conflict
clash [klash]		Their opinions often clash.	

3438		놈, 녀석, 친구, 자식	[3510] buddy
dude [dood]		He is a cool dude.	

3439	수능 토플	중세의	
medieval [mee-DEE-vuhl]		I study medieval history.	

3440	토익 공무원	배관, 배관설비, 배관공사	plumber (배관공)
plumbing [PLUHM-ing]		He helped us fix the plumbing.	

3441		1. 반짝이다, 빛나다 2. 반짝임, 광채	sparkling (반짝이는) [6365] twinkle
sparkle [SPAHR-kuhl]		Her eyes were sparkling with excitement.	

3442		1. 끌다, 운반하다 2. 잡아당기다 3. 많은 양	[2074] drag
haul [hawl]		He couldn't haul the heavy luggage by himself.	

3443	고등	1. 국한되다, 제한되다, 가두다 2. 꽉 막힌, 밀폐된	confines (경계) confinement (감금) [402] limit
confine [kuhn-FAHYN]		She hates to be confined in an office all day.	

3444	토익	독감, 유행성 감기, 인플루엔자	influenza (=flu)
flu [floo]		He caught the flu last week.	

3445		직사각형	
rectangle [REK-tang-guhl]		Do you know how to draw a rectangle?	

3446		단풍나무	
maple [MEY-puhl]		I love eating pancakes with maple syrup.	

3447	고등	1. 산들바람, 순풍 2. 쉬운 일 3. 나아가다, 움직이다	[1218] wind
breeze [breez]		She enjoys a cool breeze in the evening.	

3448	수능 GRE	1. 막대한, 엄청난 2. 거대한	[2777] enormous
immense [ih-MENS]		Dictators have immense power and authority.	

3449	수능 GRE	1. 규제, 금지, 제한 2. 자제, 억제 3. 구속, 감금	restrain (제한하다) [273] control

restraint
[ri-STREYNT]

Prices kept on rising without any restraint.

3450		(공동)묘지, 무덤	

cemetery
[SEM-i-ter-ee]

His body will be buried in a cemetery.

3451	공무원	1. 호흡의 2. 호흡 기관의	respirator (마스크)

respiratory
[RES-per-uh-tawr-ee]

Air pollution can cause respiratory infection.

3452	고등 토플	1. 천박한, 깊이가 없는 2. 얄팍한, 피상적인	[4931] superficial

shallow
[SHAL-oh]

He hated her shallow personality.

3453		1. 햇볕에 타다 2. 태닝	

tan
[tan]

She got a nice tan.

3454	공무원	1. 조달 2. 획득, 확보 3. 구매	[483] purchase

procurement
[proh-KYOOR-muhnt]

Public procurement projects transformed how a government buys goods and services.

3455	공무원 편입	1. 조상, 선조 2. 시조 3. 전신	ancestry (조상) [3894] predecessor

ancestor
[AN-ses-ter]

Where are your ancestors from?

3456	공무원	1. 산책(하다) 2. 걷다	stroller (산책하는 사람, 유모차) [533] walk

stroll
[strohl]

I like strolling down the street.

3457	수능	1. 더러운, 역겨운, 추잡한 2. 난처한, 귀찮은	[3788] foul

nasty
[NAS-tee]

That food looks nasty.

3458	토익 공무원 토플	1. 주된, 중요한 2. 주요 산물, 주식 3. 철사 심	stapler (호치키스) [541] main

staple
[STEY-puhl]

Rice is the staple crop in Asian countries.

3459	토익	1. 자동차의 2. 자동인	[1775] automobile

automotive
[aw-tuh-MOH-tiv]

The country's automotive industry is on the rise.

3460	토익 공무원 편입	1. 후원자 2. 단골 손님, 고객	patronize (후원하다)

patron
[PEY-truhn]

The young entrepreneur is a patron of many artists.

3461	토익	1. 쓰레기 2. 쓸데없는 물건	[3087] trash

junk
[juhngk]

Children should not be consuming junk food.

3462	수능	1. 환영, 환상 2. 오해, 착각	illusory (환상의, 착각의) [1073] dream

illusion
[ih-LOO-zhuhn]

Her marriage was an illusion.

3463			
benchmark	1. 기준점 2. 기준점으로 삼다		[450] standard
[BENCH-mahrk]	His outstanding performance set a new benchmark.		

3464			
worm	지렁이		
[wurm]	She accidentally stepped on a worm.		

3465	토익 공무원 토플 편입		
streamline	1. 능률적으로 하다, 간소화하다 2. 유선형으로 하다		
[STREEM-lahyn]	Shoemaking has been streamlined with the help of machines.		

3466			
elbow	1. 팔꿈치 2. 팔꿈치로 찌르다, 밀치다		[1013] push
[EL-boh]	I hurt my elbow.		

3467	토익		
earthquake	1. 지진 2. 대변동		quake (떨다, 진동)
[URTH-kweyk]	There was an earthquake last night.		

3468	토익 공무원 편입 GRE		
recession	1. 경기 후퇴, 불황, 침체 2. 위기, 퇴거, 후퇴 3. 쑥 들어간 곳		recede (뒤로가다) recessive (후퇴하는) [4333] regression
[ri-SESH-uhn]	The global economy is facing a recession.		

3469			
in-depth	심도있는, 심층적인, 상세한		[2139] thorough
[IN-depth]	We need an in-depth discussion about the matter.		

3470	고등 토플		
cruel	잔인한, 잔혹한, 무참한		cruelty (잔인함) [3041] brutal
[KROO-uhl]	He was so cruel to her.		

3471	공무원 편입		
sibling	형제자매		[1189] brother
[SIB-ling]	I have two siblings.		

3472	초등 토익		
clerk	1. 점원 2. 서기 3. 사무원, 행원, 사원 4. (영국 국교회의)목사		[2095] secretary
[klurk]	She works as a clerk.		

3473			
premiere	1. 개봉(하다), 최초 상영(하다) 2. 첫날, 초연		[2199] premier
[pri-MEER]	Many actors showed up at the film premiere.		

3474	공무원 편입		
sturdy	1. 튼튼한, 견고한, 단단한 2. 완강한		[498] strong
[STUR-dee]	Denim fabrics tend to be very sturdy.		

3475	토익 공무원		
dispatch	1. 보내다, 급송하다 2. 파견(하다) 3. 배치		[396] send
[dih-SPACH]	All the parcels have been dispatched.		

3476	토플		
rib	갈비(뼈)		
[rib]	He has a broken rib.		

3477		허리, 요부	
waist			
[weyst]		What is your waist size?	

3478	공무원	1. 감시, 감독 2. 추적	[476] watch
surveillance			
[ser-VEY-luh ns]		She works under thorough surveillance.	

3479	공무원	1. 소아과의 2. 소아과학의	
pediatric			
[pee-dee-A-trik]		He is completing his pediatric residency.	

3480	공무원 편입	1. 제재(하다) 2. 허가, 인가(하다)	[2864] endorse
sanction			
[SANGK-shuhn]		The UN is imposing heavy sanctions on North Korea.	

3481	토플	터빈, 터보차저가 달린 엔진	turbine (터빈)
turbo			
[TUR-boh]		I drive the turbo version of the model.	

3482	공무원 토플 편입	요새, 보루, 성채	fortify (요새화하다) [2454] castle
fort			
[fawrt]		The fort was occupied by the enemy.	

3483	편입	1. 음모, 모의 2. (불법)공모	conspire (음모를 계획하다) [2079] plot
conspiracy			
[kuhn-SPIR-uh-see]		She was charged with conspiracy.	

3484		1. 요정 2. 선녀	
fairy			
[FAIR-ee]		I don't believe in fairies.	

3485		1. 자격, 증명서 2. 신임장	[885] certificate
credential			
[kri-DEN-shuh l]		He didn't have enough credentials for the job.	

3486		1. 공연 2. 일 3. 기가바이트	
gig			
[gig]		He is going to perform at a small pub gig.	

3487		1. (아이스크림 끝부분)콘 2. 원뿔(의) 3. 솔방울	
cone			
[kohn]		She loves eating ice cream cones.	

3488	수능 토익 토플 GRE	1. 모순되다, 반대되다 2. 반박하다, 부정하다	contradiction (모순) [1655] deny
contradict			
[kon-truh-DIKT]		His actions contradict his words.	

3489		황제	[914] king
emperor			
[EM-per-er]		The emperor eventually lost his power.	

3490	토익	1. 쓰레기(통) 2. 형편없는	[4865] rubbish
garbage			
[GAHR-bij]		He took out the garbage.	

3491	고등 토플	외교의, 외교적	diplomat (외교관)
diplomatic			diplomacy (외교)
[dip-luh-MAT-ik]		She stressed the importance of diplomatic ties.	[747] politic

3492		권총	
pistol			
[PIS-tl]		He had a loaded pistol.	

3493	고등 토플	1. 털 2. 모피, 가죽	[1587] coat
fur			
[fur]		That dog has a beautiful fur.	

3494	공무원 편입	1. 휘청거리다, 비틀거리다 2. 헛디디다 3. 더듬거리다, 실수하다	[945] trip
stumble			
[STUHM-buhl]		She stumbled and fell.	

3495	고등	1. 겹치다 2. 공통부분, 중복(되다)	
overlap			
[oh-ver-LAP]		She loves talking to people with overlapping interests.	

3496	수능 토플	1. 자세히 설명하다 2. 정교한, 면밀한	[3983] intricate
elaborate			
[ih-LAB-er-it]		Can you elaborate on your plan?	

3497	공무원 토플 편입	1. 비참한, 초라한 2. 소량의	misery (고통)
miserable			[594] unhappy
[MIZ-er-uh-buhl]		She felt miserable after he left her.	

3498	토플	1. 음향의 2. 청각의, 보청의	
acoustic			
[uh-KOO-stik]		The acoustic quality of the concert hall has been improved.	

3499		1. 스파이, 첩자 2. 스파이 활동을 하다	[3690] glimpse
spy			
[spahy]		He will make a good spy.	

3500	고등	1. 승리를 기뻐하다, 의기양양하다 2. 이기다, 승리하다 3. 업적, 성공	triumphant (승리를 기뻐하는)
triumph			[1795] victory
[TRAHY-uhmf]		The victorious team returned in triumph.	

3501	수능	정복하다, 승리를 얻다, 제패하다	[2401] overcome
conquer			
[KONG-ker]		Our allies conquered the enemy.	

3502	토익 공무원 편입	1. 빈 방, 빈 객실 2. 공석, 결원 3. 공허	vacant (비어 있는)
vacancy			
[VEY-kuhn-see]		There are no vacancies at this hotel.	

3503		매우 작은, 극소의	[1869] tiny
micro			
[MAHY-kroh]		I studied microbiology.	

3504	토플	1. 동맥 2. 중추	[3268] vein
artery			
[AHR-tuh-ree]		His artery was severed with a knife.	

3505		상당한	[1432] substantial
considerable			
[kuhn-SID-er-uh-buhl]		I have saved a considerable amount of money.	

3506	토익	1. 스테레오, 입체 음향 2. 전축	
stereo			
[STER-ee-oh]		I bought a new stereo for my car.	

3507		아름다운, 훌륭한	
wonderful			
[WUHN-der-fuhl]		Your idea sounds wonderful.	

3508	고등 토익 GRE	1. 동떨어져 있는 2. 공정한, 사적인 감정이 없는 3. 무심한, 냉소적인	[7215] aloof
detached			
[dih-TACHT]		He detached himself from the world.	

3509		상징적으로, 비유적으로	[4076] metaphorically
figuratively			
[FIG-yer-uh-tiv-lee]		When I met Jane, figuratively speaking, had a heart attack.	

3510		(친한) 친구	[288] friend
buddy			
[BUHD-ee]		He is a good buddy.	

3511	공무원 편입	1. 애원하다 2. (법정에서 피고가) 답변하다, 변호하다, 주장하다	plea (탄원) [6931] implore
plead			
[pleed]		Fearing his life, he pleaded the gunman for mercy.	

3512		문법	grammatical (문법적인) [880] language
grammar			
[GRAM-er]		You need to study grammar.	

3513	공무원	대리(로서), 대리인, 대용물	[2386] substitute
proxy			
[PROK-see]		The government initiated a proxy war.	

3514	공무원	1. 화석 2. 시대에 뒤쳐진	[3286] antique
fossil			
[FOS-uhl]		Fossil fuels can be used to generate electricity.	

3515	공무원	1. (용기 따위를)불러 일으키다 2. 부르다, 소집하다, 소환하다	
summon			
[SUHM-uhn]		She had to summon the energy to finish the assignment.	

3516	고등	돼지고기	[6651] swine
pork			
[pawrk]		He doesn't eat pork.	

3517		위젯, 소형 장치, 도구	[7104] gizmo
widget			
[WIJ-it]		Apps are different from widgets.	

3518	편입 GRE	1. 변동성, 변덕 2. 휘발성	volatile (휘발성의) [1305] instability
volatility			
[VOL-uh-tl-i-tee]		Volatility in financial markets is low at this point in time.	

288

3519 **paradise** [PAR-uh-dahys]	지상 낙원, 천국, 극락	[1994] heaven
	This beach looks like a paradise.	
3520 **villa** [VIL-uh]	1. 별장 2. 시골 저택	[4099] mansion
	I want to buy a villa in France.	
3521 **scar** [skahr]	상처, 흉터, 상흔	[837] mark
	Where did you get that scar?	
3522 공무원 GRE **pivot** [PIV-uh t]	1. 중심축, 중심점 2. 회전하다, 돌리다	pivotal (중요한) [5455] swivel
	Her teaching has been the pivot of my life.	
3523 토플 편입 **immerse** [ih-MURS]	1. 열중시키다, 몰두하다 2. 담그다, 적시다	immersion (몰두) [5278] submerge
	Immersing yourself in nature helps you restore balance.	
3524 공무원 토플 편입 GRE **spur** [spur]	1. 원동력이 되다, 자극하다 2. 박차를 가하다 3. 자극제	
	Investing in education will spur economic growth.	
3525 수능 토플 GRE **haunt** [hawnt]	1. (유령이)나오다, 출몰하다 2. 계속 떠오르다 3. 자주가는 장소	[2546] ghost
	He used to live in a haunted house.	
3526 토익 **freelance** [FREE-lans]	프리랜서로서 일하다, 자유계약으로 일하다	freelancer (프리랜서) [386] independent
	She works as a freelance interpreter.	
3527 **turtle** [TUR-tl]	(바다)거북	[5891] tortoise
	They went to see some turtles on the beach.	
3528 고등 GRE **instinct** [IN-stingkt]	1. 본능, 타고난 성질, 천성 2. 직관, 직감	instinctively (본능적으로)
	She tends to follow her instincts.	
3529 고등 **tin** [tin]	1. 주석 2. 통, 양철 깡통 3. 통조림	[503] container
	This little box is made of tin.	
3530 수능 **torture** [TAWR-cher]	고문(하다), 괴롭히다	[5104] torment
	He confessed everything under torture.	
3531 공무원 토플 **cuisine** [kwi-ZEEN]	요리, 요리법	[332] food
	I don't like French cuisine.	
3532 **streak** [streek]	1. 줄무늬(지다), 줄(이 지다) 2. 연속	[3145] stripe
	There was a streak of tear on her face.	

3533	고등 토플	1. 삼키다 2. (나쁜 감정을)참다, 억누르다 3. 받아들이다	[6577] gulp
swallow [SWOL-oh]		He accidentally swallowed a bug.	

3534		1. 버팀대, 보조기 2. 치아 교정기 3. 대비하다 4. 힘을 주다, 버티다	
brace [breys]		He had to wear a brace after the accident.	

3535	공무원 토플	고고학의	
archaeological [ahr-kee-uh-LOJ-i-kuhl]		Historians often visit archaeological sites.	

3536	토플	나트륨	
sodium [SOH-dee-uhm]		We should avoid consuming too much sodium.	

3537	수능	1. 문질러서 씻어내다, 청소하다 2. 관목(지대)	[1357] wash
scrub [skruhb]		I scrubbed my body with a brush.	

3538	수능	1. 합의, 일치 2. 여론	[427] agreement
consensus [kuhn-SEN-suhs]		The two parties finally reached a consensus.	

3539	공무원 토플	1. (찻잎을)우리다, 우려내다 2. 주입하다, 불어넣다	[5056] permeate
infuse [in-FYOOZ]		Let the tea infuse for ten minutes.	

3540		1. 도자기, 요업 2. 세라믹	
ceramic [suh-RAM-ik]		She enjoys collecting ceramic bowls.	

3541		1. 암살자, 자객 2. 살인청부업자	assassination (암살) [682] killer
assassin [uh-SAS-in]		He hired an assassin to kill his enemy.	

3542	공무원 편입	소송, 법정 공방	litigate (소송하다)
litigation [lit-i-GEY-shuhn]		The politician engaged in litigation against media.	

3543	공무원 편입	천문학	astronomer (천문학자)
astronomy [uh-STRON-uh-mee]		He owns a lot of books about astronomy.	

3544		아장아장 걷는 아이, 유아	
toddler [TOD-ler]		Her daughter is a two-year-old toddler.	

3545		1. 쾅(하고 닫다) 2. 세게 내던지다, 놓다 3. 강타하다	
slam [slam]		Don't slam the door.	

3546	고등	1. 관목 2. 무성하게 자란 머리털	
bush [boosh]		She was hiding behind a bush.	

3547	공무원 편입	~하기 쉬운, ~당하기 쉬운	
prone			
[prohn]		He is prone to headaches.	

3548		섬(보통 고유명사인 이름과 함께 쓰임)	[976] island
isle			
[ahyl]		The Isle of Capri is one of the best places to visit in Italy.	

3549		1. 가렵다, 근질근질하다 2. 욕구, 욕망, 갈망	[1100] desire
itch			
[ich]		My whole body itches.	

3550	토익	1. 급여 명단 2. 급여 총액	[2123] salary
payroll			
[PEY-rohl]		The company has 200 employees on the payroll.	

3551	공무원 토플 편입	추진하다, 몰고가다, 나아가게 하다	propeller (프로펠러)
propel			
[pruh-PEL]		He propelled the project with determination.	

3552	공무원 편입	1. 화해 2. 조화, 화합	reconcile (화해하다) [2434] compromise
reconciliation			
[rek-uhn-sil-ee-EY-shuhn]		The president hoped to secure a lasting reconciliation between the two countries.	

3553		만화	[3085] sketch
cartoon			
[kahr-TOON]		What's your favorite cartoon?	

3554	토플	1. 탐험, 탐사 2. 여행	[1484] journey
expedition			
[ek-spi-DISH-uhn]		They left on an expedition to the Antarctic.	

3555	토익	콘도미니엄, 아파트	
condominium			
[kon-duh-MIN-ee-uhm]		I have a condominium in Upper West Side New York.	

3556	토익 공무원 편입	1. 변제, 배상 2. 상환, 환급	[441] refund
reimbursement			
[ree-im-BURS-muhnt]		She received reimbursement for her medical expenses.	

3557	토플 편입	1. 식욕 2. 욕구	[2470] hunger
appetite			
[AP-i-tahyt]		I lost all my appetite.	

3558	고등	댐, 둑	[849] block
dam			
[dam]		A new dam is under construction.	

3559	토익 편입	아치(의), 호, 활 모양	[1954] curve
arc			
[AHRk]		The ball was thrown in an arc shape.	

3560	공무원 편입 GRE	1. 표현하다, 설명하다 2. 발음하다 3. 또렷한, 분명한, 정확히 표현하는	
articulate			
[ahr-TIK-yuh-lit]		I always have a hard time articulating my own thoughts.	

3561	수능 토플	1. 두려워하다, 걱정하다 2. 공포, 두려움	[1198] fear
dread [dred]		He dreads going to work every morning.	

3562	토익 공무원 토플	옷, 의복	[1190] dress
garment [GAHR-muhnt]		This garment should be dry-cleaned.	

3563	고등 토플	1. 창백한 2. 엷은, 연한, 흐릿한	[617] white
pale [peyl]		She always looks pale.	

3564	고등	껴안다, 끌어안다, 포옹(하다)	[2339] embrace
hug [huhg]		He hugged me.	

3565	토플	누비 이불, 퀼트, 덮개	
quilt [kwilt]		I like sleeping under the quilt my grandmother gave me.	

3566	고등 토플	(해안가의)낭떠러지, 절벽, 벼랑	
cliff [klif]		She fell off the cliff by accident.	

3567	GRE	1. 우회하다, 건너뛰다 2. 보조도로	[6059] circumvent
bypass [BAHY-pas]		We were able to bypass the hectic city center by taking side-streets.	

3568	고등	소, 축우	[1149] livestock
cattle [KAT-l]		They raise horses and cattle.	

3569	고등 토익 토플 GRE	1. 이국적인, 희한한 2. 외국의, 외래의	[6982] outlandish
exotic [ig-ZOT-ik]		I hate exotic flavors.	

3570	고등	애정, 애착심	affectionate (애정어린)
affection [uh-FEK-shuhn]		He has no affection for her.	

3571	공무원 편입	1. 쓰레기, 먼지 2. 파괴의 자취, 잔해	[4865] rubbish
debris [duh-BREE]		She cleared debris on the street.	

3572	공무원 토플 편입	1. 일관된 2. 논리있는, 조리있는	incoherent (일관되지 못한) [1337] consistent
coherent [koh-HEER-uhnt]		Our company needs a coherent plan.	

3573	토플	1. 암초 2. 장애물	[628] bank
reef [reef]		Coral reef bleaching is a serious environmental problem.	

3574	공무원	1. 합성의, 혼성의, 복합의 2. 합성물, 복합물	composition (구성, 합성) [2252] compound
composite [kuhm-POZ-it]		The team conducted a composite study across different fields.	

3575	공무원	1. 부활 2. 부흥, 재유행	[3215] revival
resurrection [rez-uh-REK-shuhn]		There was a resurrection of her dead feelings.	

3576	수능	격노, 격분	furious (격노한) [1494] violence
fury [FYOOR-ee]		She wasn't able to contain her fury.	

3577	공무원 편입	1. 회전하다, 공전하다, 돌다 2. 주기적으로 일어나다, 순환하다	[1945] rotate
revolve [ri-VOLV]		He thinks the world revolves around him.	

3578		1. 축제, 잔치 2. 포식하다	[462] party
feast [feest]		The feast lasted all night long.	

3579	편입	1. 신호, 큐 2. 단서 3. 암시	[1890] prompt
cue [kyoo]		He stood still, waiting for the cue from his boss.	

3580	고등	1. 숨기다, 감추다, 비밀로 하다 2. 내색 안 하다	[1262] hide
conceal [kuhn-SEEL]		She is good at concealing her feelings.	

3581		안뜰, 파티오	[외래어] terrace
patio [PAT-ee-oh]		Let's go sit at the table on the patio.	

3582	공무원 편입	1. 학위 논문 2. 논제, 주제	[1279] theme
thesis [THEE-sis]		What's your thesis topic?	

3583		포르노물, 외설물	pornography (=porn)
porn [pawrn]		He was watching porn.	

3584		1. 2인조, 콤비 2. 이중주	[기타] twosome
duo [DOO-oh]		They played violin together as a duo.	

3585		1. 울타리, 장벽 2. 대비책	
hedge [hej]		He parked his bicycle behind the hedge.	

3586	공무원 편입	생태학의, 생태계의	[532] environmental
ecological [ih-KOL-uh-ji-kuhl]		The ecological consequences of climate change are incalculable.	

3587		1. 산호(의) 2. 산호빛의, 옅은 주황색의	
coral [KAWR-uhl]		She bought a coral necklace.	

3588	편입	1. 가까움, 근접 2. 접근	[5099] vicinity
proximity [prok-SIM-i-tee]		The school is in close proximity to our house.	

3589	공무원	1. 자주의, 독립의, 주권 있는 2. 군주 3. 주권자	sovereignty (주권)
sovereign			[914] king
[SOV-rin]		Can you name a sovereign state?	

3590	고등 토익 GRE	1. 금하다, 금지하다 2. 방해하다, 어렵게 만들다 3. 용납 안 하다	forbidden (금지된)
forbid			[2343] prohibit
[fer-BID]		Smoking is forbidden here.	

3591		1. 괴짜, 변덕쟁이 2. (기계의) 크랭크 (를 돌리다)	
crank			
[krangk]		My boss is an old crank.	

3592	공무원 토플 편입	1. 충족하다, 채우다 2. 마음대로 하다, 제멋대로 하다 3. 빠지다	indulgence (즐거움을 위해 마음대로 함)
indulge			[5435] pamper
[in-DUHLJ]		She often indulges in a glass of wine.	

3593	편입	1. (신체의) 관 또는 계 2. 넓은 땅, 지역	
tract			
[trakt]		He has a urinary tract infection.	

3594	고등	1. 무서운, 소름끼치는 2. 놀라운 3. 위급한	[1961] scary
frightening			
[FRAHYT-n-ing]		Dogs can be quite frightening when they are angry.	

3595		1. 푸다, 뜨다 2. 숟갈, 국자	
scoop			
[skoop]		It is difficult to scoop the pumpkin seeds and fibers out.	

3596	토플	1. 실 2. 뜨개질 3. 이야기, 허풍	[1444] thread
yarn			
[yahrn]		My cat likes to play with the yarn on the floor.	

3597		1. 시민(공민)의 2. 도시의, 시의 3. 민간	[1284] civil
civic			
[SIV-ik]		It is our civic duty to vote.	

3598	고등 토플	염소	
goat			
[goht]		Goat cheese tastes amazing.	

3599		연어	
salmon			
[SAM-uhn]		He loves smoked salmon.	

3600	공무원 편입	1. 시작하다, 출범하다 2. 배를 타다, 승선하다, 탑승하다	[515] board
embark			
[em-BAHRK]		I am about to embark on a new journey.	

3601		1. 게임방식 2. 작전, 전략	
gameplay			
[GEYM-pley]		This particular gameplay is more fun with a greater number of players.	

3602		1. 정의, 정직, 공정 2. 고결, 고결한 행위	[1980] morality
righteousness			
[RAHY-chuh s-nis]		She values moral righteousness.	

3603	수능 토플 GRE	1. 적대적인, 호전적인 2. 완강히 반대하는, 강경한 3. 적군의	hostility (적대심)
hostile			[288] unfriendly
[HOS-tl]		I don't know why she is hostile to me.	

3604	편입	1. 향기, 방향 2. 기품, 품격	[1836] smell
aroma			
[uh-ROH-muh]		My room is filled with the aroma of coffee.	

3605	공무원 토플 GRE	양조장, 증류수 제조장	
distillery			
[dih-STIL-uh-ree]		Our family owns a distillery where we produce rum and whiskey.	

3606	공무원 토플 편입	1. 돌연변이, 변종 2. 변화	mutant (돌연변이의)
mutation			
[myoo-TEY-shuhn]		Genetic mutations often lead to many severe impairments.	

3607		수족관	auqa (물)
aquarium			
[uh-KWAIR-ee-uhm]		He took her to the aquarium on their first date.	

3608	토플	1. (빵)껍질 2. 표면 3. 겉	
crust			
[kruhst]		I love the golden crust of the bread.	

3609	공무원 GRE	1. 약한 2. 미약한, 미미한	[1445] weak
feeble			
[FEE-buhl]		He was too feeble to leave the house.	

3610	공무원	1. 아늑한, 안락한 2. 친밀한, 친해지기 쉬운	[694] comfy
cozy			
[KOH-zee]		We live in a cozy little house.	

3611	공무원 토플 GRE	1. 선언하다, 선포하다, 공표하다 2. 나타내다	proclamation (선언)
proclaim			[899] announce
[proh-KLEYM]		The company's CEO proclaimed the need for new ideas.	

3612	고등 토플	1. 턱 2. 잔소리하다, 군소리하다	[2045] chatter
jaw			
[jaw]		She punched him on the jaw.	

3613		정글, 밀림	[1627] forest
jungle			
[JUHNG-guhl]		Which animal is considered the king of the jungle?	

3614	고등 토플	1. 볼, 뺨 2. 건방진 말, 뻔뻔함	
cheek			
[cheek]		He kissed her on the cheek.	

3615	공무원 편입	1. 증가, 증대 2. 임금 인상 3. 이익, 이득	incremental (일정 간격으로 증가하는)
increment			[280] increase
[IN-kruh-muhnt]		Even a small increment of vitamin intake can be helpful.	

3616	토플	1. 두개골 2. 머리, 두뇌	[301] head
skull			
[skuhl]		He fractured his skull when he fell down.	

3617	고등	소파, 긴 의자	[외래어] sofa
couch [kouch]		I fell asleep on the couch last night.	

3618	편입	1. 반지름 2. 활동 범위, 반경	[440] spoke
radius [REY-dee-uh s]		Can you measure the radius of this circle?	

3619	토익 공무원 토플 GRE	1. 예비의 2. 준비의 3. 예선, 예비 단계	[1105] initial
preliminary [pri-LIM-uh-ner-ee]		The company conducted a preliminary study before deciding to enter a new market.	

3620	고등	기침(하다)	
cough [kawf]		He coughed loudly.	

3621	수능 토플	1. 꼿꼿이 선 2. 세우다 3. 건설하다 4. 만들다	[842] construct
erect [ih-REKT]		She stood erect on the street.	

3622		(본인의 경험에 대해) 자세히 하나하나 얘기하다	
recount [ri-KOUNT]		The witness was asked to recount the details.	

3623	공무원 편입	1. 희석하다, 묽게 하다 2. 약하게 하다	dilution (희석) [1445] weaken
dilute [dih-LOOT]		You need to dilute the juice before you drink it.	

3624	토익 공무원 토플 편입	1. 보조금, 지원금, 장려금 2. 보상금	subsidize (원조하다) [1237] grant
subsidy [SUHB-si-dee]		The company applied for a government subsidy.	

3625	토플	1. 해부학(구조) 2. 분석	[1120] frame
anatomy [uh-NAT-uh-mee]		Doctors are familiar with human anatomy.	

3626		1. 기념비 2. 기념의, 추도의	[622] remembrance
memorial [muh-MAWR-ee-uh l]		Our class visited the war memorial.	

3627		1. 쿼터백(으로 뛰다) 2. 센터의 후방 3. 지휘하다	
quarterback [KWAWR-ter-bak]		He plays quarterback on his school's football team.	

3628		1. 판으로 된, 슬레이트 2. 후보자 명부 3. 예정하다, 계획하다 4. 혹평하다	[913] schedule
slate [sleyt]		The house has a slate roof.	

3629	고등 토익	1. 그동안, ~하는 동안에 2. 한편 3. 당분간	[2325] meanwhile
meantime [MEEN-tahym]		What are you going to do in the meantime?	

3630	공무원 편입 GRE	1. 겁주는, 겁나게 하는 2. 협박하는	intimidate (겁을 주다) [1961] scary
intimidating [in-TIM-i-dey-ting]		He can be very intimidating when he is angry.	

3631 **tuck** [tuhk]	1. 접다, 집어넣다 2. 감싸다 3. 주름	[1502] gather
	Tuck your shirt in.	
3632 **crunch** [kruhnch]	1. 오독오독 씹다 2. 중요한 상황(정보) 3. 저벅저벅 밟다	[2560] grind
	She was crunching on a cucumber.	
3633　　고등 토플 **ash** [ash]	1. 재, 잿더미 2. 유골	
	Korea rose from the ashes of war.	
3634　　고등 토익 GRE **amusement** [uh-MYOOZ-muhnt]	1. 재미, 즐거움 2. 오락, 놀이	[1412] entertainment
	Dancing is his amusement.	
3635　　토익 공무원 편입 **remainder** [ri-MEYN-der]	1. 나머지, 잔여 2. 재고	[714] rest
	We spent the remainder of the day at the hotel.	
3636 **covenant** [KUHV-uh-nuhnt]	1. 계약 2. 약속, 서약	[738] contract
	The covenant must be signed to be legally effective.	
3637　　공무원 **beneficiary** [ben-uh-FISH-ee-er-ee]	1. 수혜자 2. 수취인, 수령인	
	Korea used to be a beneficiary of U.S. foreign assistance.	
3638　　수능 토플 GRE **provoke** [pruh-VOHK]	자극하다, 유발하다, 도발하다, 성나게 하다	provocative (도발적인) [5780] incite
	Don't provoke her.	
3639 **viral** [VAHY-ruhl]	1. 바이러스성의 2. 퍼지다	[외래어] virus
	He is suffering from a viral disease.	
3640　　공무원 토플 편입 **odor** [OH-der]	1. 냄새, 향기 2. 악취	deodorant (냄새 제거제) [1836] smell
	Newly painted walls have a strong odor.	
3641　　수능 **cathedral** [kuh-THEE-druhl]	1. 대성당 2. 큰 예배당	[867] church
	This cathedral was built a century ago.	
3642　　수능 **ideology** [ahy-dee-OL-uh-jee]	이데올로기, 이념, 사상, 관념	[1837] philosophy
	Terrorists promote evil ideology.	
3643　　공무원 **probation** [proh-BEY-shuhn]	1. 집행유예 2. 보호 관찰 3. 수습기간	[4936] parole
	He was put on probation for two years.	
3644　　토플 **artifact** [AHR-tuh-fakt]	1. 유물, 인공물 2. 공예품, 가공품	[4760] relic
	The exhibition will showcase two hundred artifacts.	

3645	공무원 토플 편입	1. 응결하다 2. 농축하다, 응축하다, 압축되다	[443] shorten
condense [kuhn-DENS]		Water vapor in the air can condense to water droplets early in the morning.	

3646		(법을) 규정하다, 제정하다	[448] pass
enact [en-AKT]		The law was enacted today.	

3647	공무원 편입 GRE	모방하다, 따라하다	[4095] imitate
emulate [EM-yuh-leyt]		He was a leader that everyone wanted to emulate.	

3648		사전 행동을 취하는, 적극적인, 주도적인	
proactive [proh-AK-tiv]		The company came up with proactive measures.	

3649		1. 귀찮은(일), 성가시게 하는 2. 재촉하다, 들들 볶다	[2451] bother
hassle [HAS-uhl]		You can take the shuttle without the hassle of driving.	

3650		광대역(의)	
broadband [BRAWD-band]		Broadband service isn't available in this region.	

3651	공무원 편입 GRE	1. 늦추다, 연기하다 2. 결정을 맡기다 3. 경의를 표하다	deference (존중) deferral (집행 연기) [4705] postpone
defer [dih-FUR]		He deferred the decision for a few weeks.	

3652	GRE	1. 기울다, 젖히다 2. 기울기, 경사	[3341] incline
tilt [tilt]		She tilted her head towards him.	

3653	공무원 토플 편입	1. 자주적인, 자율적인, 독립된 2. 자치의	autonomy (자치권) [386] independent
autonomous [aw-TON-uh-muhs]		It is ideal for students to become autonomous learners.	

3654	공무원	1. 영연방 2. 연방국 3. (공통의 이해 관계를 가진)단체, 사회	
commonwealth [KOM-uhn-welth]		The constitution of the commonwealth has gone through multiple revisions.	

3655	토익 공무원 편입	1. 소포, 꾸러미 2. 한 구획, 일부분	[484] package
parcel [PAHR-suhl]		This parcel doesn't have an address on it.	

3656		1. 고정하다, 물리다 2. 쇠집게	[1866] clip
clamp [klamp]		The microphone needs to be clamped to the stand.	

3657	편입	1. (예수의)제자 2. 사도 3. 신봉자	
disciple [dih-SAHY-puhl]		She was his favorite disciple.	

3658	공무원 토플	1. 긁다, 긁어모으다 2. 찰과상(을 내다) 3. 문지르다	[2247] scratch
scrape [skreyp]		Don't scrape your feet on the floor.	

3659	공무원	1. 멍청한 2. 벙어리의, 말못하는 3. 우둔한	[2459] stupid
dumb [duhm]		I hate dumb people.	
3660		1. 이진법의 2. 둘의	[2396] dual
binary [BAHY-nuh-ree]		Computers use binary numbers.	
3661	토플	1. 황야, 황무지, 사람이 살지 않는 땅 2. 자연	[1547] wild
wilderness [WIL-der-nis]		Without him, this world is a wilderness to me.	
3662	공무원 편입	낙담시키다, 용기를 잃게 하다, 좌절시키다	discouraging (낙담시키는) [3923] deter
discourage [dih-SKUR-ij]		He was discouraged by the criticism.	
3663	고등	도둑, 절도(범)	[4498] burglar
thief [theef]		She captured the thief.	
3664	수능	1. 썩다, 부식(하다), 부패(하다) 2. 타락, 퇴폐 3. 악화된 상황	[3808] decay
rot [rot]		These apples have begun to rot.	
3665	토플	(내분비계의)선 또는 샘	
gland [gland]		Some glands produce oil.	
3666		바보, 멍청이	[2644] fool
idiot [ID-ee-uht]		Are you an idiot?	
3667	공무원 편입	1. 탄력있는, 신축성 있는 2. 융통성 있는 3. 고무줄	elasticity (탄력성) [1309] flexible
elastic [ih-LAS-tik]		A rubber band is elastic.	
3668	공무원	1. 조끼, 내의 2. 권리를 부여하다	vested (소유가 확정된)
vest [vest]		He wore a vest.	
3669	고등	1. 베리, 산딸기 종류의 과일 2. 열매	[1364] fruit
berry [BER-ee]		This jam is made with some berries.	
3670		1. 옷장 2. 옷, 의류	[3169] closet
wardrobe [WAWR-drohb]		She picked out a black dress from the wardrobe.	
3671	고등	1. (머리를)끄덕이다 2. 졸다 3. 턱을 들어 가리키다	[1416] signal
nod [nod]		He nodded in agreement.	
3672		1. 중재인, 중재자 2. 결정권자	arbitration (중재) [993] judge
arbiter [AHR-bi-ter]		He was a moderate arbiter.	

3673	공무원	1. 엄격한 2. 엄숙한 3. 융통성 없는 4. 굳은, 단단한, 뻣뻣한	[3034] stiff
rigid [RIJ-id]		She is following a rigid routine.	

3674		1. 축제의, 축제다운 2. 즐거운, 명랑한	festivity (축제 분위기)
festive [FES-tiv]		They were in a festive mood.	

3675	공무원 편입	1. 자만심, 허영심 2. 헛됨, 무익, 무가치	vain (헛된)
vanity [VAN-i-tee]		She is full of vanity.	

3676	공무원	1. 신랑 2. 손질하다, 깔끔하게 다듬다 3. 대비하다, 훈련하다 4. 마부	bridegroom (신랑)
groom [groom]		The bride and the groom held hands together.	

3677		1. 목을 조르다, 질식시키다 2. 조절판	
throttle [THROT-l]		He throttled his wife.	

3678		1. 추기경 2. 가장 기본적인, 주요한 3. 새빨간	
cardinal [KAHR-dn-l]		Three new cardinals have been appointed this year.	

3679		믿고 맡기다, 신탁 받는 곳/사람, 전문가	
oracle [AWR-uh-kuhl]		The oracle thinks it's time to make a decision	

3680	공무원 편입	1. 오랫동안 계속되는, 장기적인 2. 연장하는, 늘리는	prolongation (연장) [608] extended
prolonged [pruh-LAWNG d]		The world economy is undergoing a prolonged depression.	

3681	수능 토플	1. 매우 충격적인 2. 엄청난, 심한, 지나친	outrage (분노) [1728] shocking
outrageous [out-REY-juh s]		She apologized for her outrageous behavior.	

3682	수능 토플	1. 항복(하다), 굴복(하다) 2. 포기하다 3. 인도(하다), 양도(하다)	
surrender [suh-REN-der]		They refused to surrender.	

3683		마녀	
witch [wich]		A witch turned the princess into a monster.	

3684	수능	1. 덩어리 2. 많음 3. 혹 4. 함께 묶이다	[3037] chunk
lump [luhmp]		I usually put a lump of sugar in my coffee.	

3685	수능 토익	꺼리는, 주저하는, 달갑지 않은	reluctance (주저함)
reluctant [ri-LUHK-tuhnt]		He was reluctant to talk to her.	

3686	공무원	1. 촉발하다, 일으키다 2. 속박을 풀다, 해방하다	leash (강아지 목줄) [438] release
unleash [uhn-LEESH]		It is important to unleash our imaginations.	

3687	토플	1. 시료 2. 견본, 표본	[1196] sample
specimen [SPES-uh-muhn]		We examined the specimen under a microscope.	

3688	수능 토플	1. 수목, 산림 2. 목재	[1179] wood
timber [TIM-ber]		The country is famous for its timber export.	

3689	고등	1. 청소년 2. 청년기의	adolescence (청소년기) [3896] juvenile
adolescent [ad-l-ES-uhnt]		I can't remember my adolescent years.	

3690	수능	1. 흘긋 봄, 잠깐 봄 2. 짧은 경험 3. 깨닫다, 알아차리다	[3315] glance
glimpse [glimps]		She caught a glimpse of him.	

3691	편입	1. 뒤처지다 2. 느릿느릿 걷다 3. 지연, 지체	[2074] drag
lag [lag]		We should never let any of our team members lag behind.	

3692	토플	1. 협회, 조합 2. 길드(중세의 동업 조합)	[1403] union
guild [GILD]		He is a member of the translator guild.	

3693	공무원	1. 빗발치듯 쏟아지다, 퍼붓다 2. 환영하다 3. 묘사하다 4. 우박	[4946] salute
hail [heyl]		His new novel met with a hail of criticism.	

3694		1. 천둥(같은 소리) 2. 천둥 치다 3. 질주하다	[4320] roar
thunder [THUHN-der]		Thunder and lightning go hand in hand.	

3695	토익 공무원 편입	버리다, 폐기(하다)	[2645] dump
discard [dih-SKAHRD]		It is time to discard old clothes.	

3696	공무원 편입	의심하는, 회의적인, 비관적인	skepticism (회의) skeptic (회의론자) [1464] suspicious
skeptical [SKEP-ti-kuhl]		He was skeptical about her intention.	

3697	공무원 편입	1. 생각하다, 고려하다 2. 예상하다 3. 응시하다	[282] consider
contemplate [KON-tuhm-pleyt]		She is contemplating a trip to Barcelona.	

3698		저장소, 보관소, 창고	[322] store
repository [ri-POZ-i-tawr-ee]		He is a repository of useless knowledge.	

3699	토플	인구 조사(하다), 공적 조사	
census [SEN-suhs]		According to the national census of 2000, the population was two million.	

3700		1. 노(를 젓다), 패들 2. 주걱 3. 물장난하다, 첨벙거리다	[1570] rowing
paddle [PAD-l]		She kept on paddling the boat.	

3701	공무원 편입	성실한, 부지런한, 근면한	diligence (성실함)
diligent		He is a diligent student.	
[DIL-i-juhnt]			

3702	고등	사전	[3816] glossary
dictionary		Can I borrow your dictionary?	
[DIK-shuh-ner-ee]			

3703	토플	1. 똑똑 흐르다, 물이 새다 2. (물)방울	[676] drop
drip		Water is dripping from the wet swimsuits.	
[drip]			

3704	토플	1. 홈 2. 리듬 3. 최고조	groovy (근사한) [1185] channel
groove		Can you cut a groove for me?	
[groov]			

3705	토플	장, 창자, 내장	
intestine		He had an infection in his small intestine.	
[in-TES-tin]			

3706	토익 공무원 토플 편입	1. 극단적으로, 과감하게 2. 철저하게	[1509] dramatically
drastically		The temperature dropped drastically.	
[DRAS-tik-lee]			

3707		1.설립하다, 창립하다 2. 찾았다	founder (창립자) foundation (기반) foundational (기본의)
found		Harvard College was founded in 1636.	
[found]			

3708	공무원	1. 손잡이 2. 마디, 혹	doorknoh (문 손잡이) [850] handle
knob		I couldn't turn the knob.	
[nob]			

3709	수능	1. 꼬집다 2. 움츠러들게 하다 3. 꼬집어 집어든 만큼 소량의	
pinch		He pinched her.	
[pinch]			

3710	토익	숙달, 능숙, 유창	proficient (능숙한) [520] skill
proficiency		We admire her proficiency in English.	
[pruh-FISH-uhn-see]			

3711	토익 토플	화물(수송)	[3422] cargo
freight		There is a separate elevator for freight.	
[freyt]			

3712	고등	수염	
beard		He has a long beard.	
[beerd]			

3713	토플 편입	1. 낚싯대 얼레(를 당기다, 풀다) 2. 필름 롤 3. 비틀대다, 휘청대다	[981] roll
reel		He reeled in his fish.	
[reel]			

3714	수능	이슬(방울)	[3279] humidity
dew		There are dew drops on the leaves.	
[doo]			

3715 **platinum** [PLAT-n-uhm]		백금	
		He gave her a platinum ring.	

3716 **cab** [KAB]	고등 토익	택시	[외래어] taxi
		We took a cab.	

3717 **aboriginal** [ab-uh-RIJ-uh-nl]		1. 원주민의, 토착민의 2. 토착의 동식물	[3278] indigenous
		He had a hard time getting along with aboriginal people in the region.	

3718 **yell** [yel]	고등	소리지르다, 외치다	[3172] shout
		She yelled at her son.	

3719 **knight** [nahyt]	고등	(중세) 기사	[5386] cavalier
		A knight fell off his horse.	

3720 **boutique** [boo-TEEK]		1. 부티크, 양품점 2. 명품 상점 3. 가게	
		She bought a dress from the new boutique.	

3721 **calibration** [KAL-uh-brey-shuh n]		눈금 매기기, 측정하다	calibrate (눈금을 긋다) [1157] scale
		Calibration is required for the thermometer.	

3722 **foil** [foil]	편입	1. 은박지 2. 포장지	
		She wrapped her sandwich in kitchen foil.	

3723 **gesture** [JES-cher]	초등	1. 몸짓, 손짓, 제스처 2. 표시 3. 손짓하다	[1688] motion
		Gestures are important for communication.	

3724 **acclaimed** [uh-KLEYM d]	토익 공무원 편입 GRE	칭찬받고 있는, 좋은 평을 받는	acclamation (환호성) [1159] famous
		The film was acclaimed as a masterpiece.	

3725 **scandal** [SKAN-dl]	고등	1. 스캔들, 추문, 치욕(이 되는 물건, 일) 2. 사건	foggy (안개가 낀) [2621] shame
		He was involved in a sexual scandal.	

3726 **fungus** [FUHNG-guh s]	토플	1. 균류 2. 곰팡이 3. 버섯	[3397] mushroom
		This fungus is harmless.	

3727 **tee** [tee]		티(골프공의 위치)	
		It was a difficult tee shot.	

3728 **limb** [lim]	토플 편입	1. 팔다리, 수족 2. 의족 3. 나뭇가지	[1686] branch
		He broke his limb when he fell.	

3729 **bark** [bahrk]	고등 토플	1. 짖다 2. 소리를 지르다 3. 나무껍질 I heard the dog barking.	[3014] peel
3730 **foremost** [FAWR-mohst]	공무원 토플	1. 가장 중요한, 최우선 2. 맨 앞의 First and foremost, climate change affects people.	
3731 **dull** [duhl]	고등 토익	1. 따분한, 지루한, 재미없는 2. 무딘, 둔감한 This movie is dull and boring.	[1109] boring
3732 **wreck** [rek]	수능	1. 난파(시키다), 난파선 2. 잔해 3. 망가뜨리다, 파괴하다 People were safely rescued from the wreck.	wreckage (사고 잔해) [2431] ruin
3733 **invoke** [in-VOHK]	공무원 편입	1. 불러내다 2. (법, 규칙을)적용하다 3. (법에)호소하다 4. 연상시키다, 떠오르게 하다 The witch invoked evil spirits.	[5345] conjure
3734 **communist** [KOM-yuh-nist]	고등 토플	1. 공산주의자(의) 2. 공산당원 She rejected communist ideology.	communism (공산주의)
3735 **hierarchy** [HAHY-uh-rahr-kee]	공무원 GRE	1. 계층(제도) 2. 지배층 3. 성직자 계급 He was always at the top of the hierarchy of power.	
3736 **congregation** [kong-gri-GEY-shuhn]	공무원 편입	1. 신도 2. 모임, 집회 The congregation knelt to pray.	
3737 **majesty** [MAJ-uh-stee]	편입	1. 장엄함, 웅장함, 위엄있는 2. 폐하 We were shocked by the majesty of the building.	majestic (장엄한)
3738 **nonetheless** [nuhn-thuh-LES]	수능	그럼에도 불구하고 Though he is ugly, I like him nonetheless.	
3739 **choir** [kwahyuhr]	고등	1. 합창대, 성가대 2. 합창하다 She sings in a church choir.	
3740 **sleek** [sleek]	토플	1. 윤기가 나는 2. 매끈한 He took a ride in that sleek limousine.	[1410] smooth
3741 **junction** [JUHNGK-shuhn]	편입	1. 교차점, 교차로 2. 합류점, 접합점 Make a left turn at the junction.	[1488] joint
3742 **ballot** [BAL-uht]	토플	1. 투표(하다) 2. 비밀 투표 3. 투표용지 You should cast a ballot as a citizen.	[936] vote

3743	고등	1. 모욕(하다) 2. 무례	
insult			
[in-SUHLT]		I didn't mean to insult you.	

3744		1. 양육(하다), 육성(하다), 양성하다 2. 영양을 공급하다	[2680] foster
nurture			
[NUR-cher]		She chose to stay at home to nurture her child.	

3745	수능 토플	1. 비하(하다) 2. 떨어뜨리다, 타락시키다 3. 훼손	degradation (비하)
degrade			
[dih-GREYD]		I won't let anyone degrade me.	

3746		1. (조직이) 단합된 2. 접착성의	cohesive (결합)
cohesive			[3572] coherent
[koh-HEE-siv]		We should work together as a cohesive group.	

3747		어떠한 것도(whatever의 강조형)	
whatsoever			
[hwuht-soh-EV-er]		You make no sense whatsoever	

3748		쓰레기(를 버리다)	[3490] garbage
litter			
[LIT-er]		Littering is strictly prohibited.	

3749		1. 봉사활동 2. ~의 앞까지 도달하다, 뻗치다	
outreach			
[out-REECH]		She pursues outreach work to contribute to society.	

3750		1. 쭈그리고 앉다 2. 스쿼트, 쭈그린 자세 3. 불법 거주 건물	[5971] crouch
squat			
[skwot]		She squatted down to talk to a baby.	

3751	공무원 편입 GRE	1. 모호한, 이해하기 어려운 2. 잘 알려져 있지 않은 3. 어렵게 하다	[372] unclear
obscure			
[uhb-SKYOOR]		The meaning of the poem is very obscure.	

3752	토익	1. 객실 2. 칸	[2349] chamber
compartment			
[kuhm-PAHRT-muhnt]		Our father reserved a private compartment for us.	

3753		1. 초보자 2. 신인 선수	[4392] novice
rookie			
[ROOK-ee]		The rookie cop didn't have a clue.	

3754	공무원	1. 자존심, 자부심 2. 자아	[2436] pride
ego			
[EE-goh]		She has a huge ego.	

3755		1. 대리석 2. 구슬	[1434] stone
marble			
[MAHR-buhl]		Marble floors are beautiful and luxurious.	

3756	고등 토익	1. 분수 2. 식수대 3. 원천	[1025] spring
fountain			
[FOUN-tn]		We took a photo in front of that famous fountain.	

3757 **shortcut** [SHAWRT-kuht]		1. 지름길, 최단 노선 2. 쉬운 방법	
		There's no shortcut to the place.	
3758 **vocabulary** [voh-KAB-yuh-ler-ee]	고등	어휘, 단어, 용어	
		Students are trying hard to build up their vocabulary.	
3759 **stance** [stans]	공무원 토플	1. 입장, 태도 3. 선 자세 4. 위치	[487] position
		What is your stance on capital punishment?	
3760 **nowadays** [NOU-uh-deyz]	고등	1. 요즘에는, 최근 2. 오늘날에는	[362] today
		Assessing the internet is so easy nowadays.	
3761 **hilarious** [hi-LAIR-ee-uhs]	공무원	1. 매우 재미있는, 우스운 2. 법석대는	[514] funny
		His joke was hilarious.	
3762 **pest** [pest]	공무원	1. 해충, 유해물 2. 성가신 사람	pester (성가시게 하다) [3766] plague
		Pest control tends to be unsafe for humans.	
3763 **salon** [suh-LON]	수능 토익	1. 미용실 2. 응접실 3. 살롱	
		I made a reservation at the salon this afternoon.	
3764 **fermentation** [fur-men-TEY-shuhn]		1. 발효 2. 소동, 흥분, 동요	
		Cheese is the product of milk fermentation.	
3765 **disclaimer** [dis-KLEY-mer]	공무원 편입	1. 권리 포기, 포기 성명 2. 부인 3. 포기자, 부인자	[1655] denial
		He issued a disclaimer.	
3766 **plague** [pleyg]	공무원 토플 편입	1. 전염병, 역병 2. 시달리다, 골치를 앓다	[5104] torment
		Plagues kill many people in no time.	
3767 **glaze** [gleyz]		1. (눈이)게슴츠레하다 2. 윤이 나게 하다 3. 유약	
		My eyes glaze over when my boss starts talking.	
3768 **cult** [kuhlt]	공무원 편입	1. 광신적 교단 2. 추종, 숭배 3. 제례의식	[1240] religion
		Scientology is a cult.	
3769 **mob** [mob]	편입	1. 떼 지어 몰려들다 2. 군중, 집단, 무리 3. 조직 폭력배	[1635] crowd
		He was mobbed by reporters.	
3770 **pore** [pawr]	공무원	1. 구멍 2. 생각하다	
		Oil was seeping out of pores on his face.	

3771 **numerical** [noo-MER-i-kuhl]		1. 수의 2. 숫자로 나타낸	numerate (열거하다)
		We need to convert numerical variables to a string.	
3772 **tease** [teez]	수능	놀리다, 장난(치다), 괴롭히다	teaser (예고편) [5871] taunt
		She was fed up with constant teasing.	
3773 **doom** [doom]		1. 불행한 운명을 맞다 2. 파멸, 죽음 3. 비운	[3007] fate
		This project was doomed from the beginning.	
3774 **embody** [em-BOD-ee]	토플 편입	1. 구현하다 2. 상징하다 3. 포함하다	embodiment (형상화)
		This book embodies my beliefs.	
3775 **intercept** [in-ter-SEPT]	편입	1. 가로막다, 가로채다 2. 요격하다 3. 방해하다	interception (가로채기) [439] stop
		The ball was intercepted by the other team.	
3776 **clan** [klan]	토플	1. 집단 2. 씨족 3. 대가족	[2453] tribe
		Each clan in the village has its own tradition.	
3777 **chassis** [CHAS-ee]		1. 차대, 섀시 2. (특히 여성의)몸체	[1120] frame
		The accident was so severe that her car's chassis was damaged.	
3778 **thereof** [thair-UHV]	공무원	앞에 언급된 그것의, 그것에 관하여	
		Drinking, smoking, or a combination thereof can cause serious health issues.	
3779 **turnover** [TURN-oh-ver]	수능 토익	1. 매출량 2. 이직률 3. 투자 자본 회전율	overturn (뒤엎다)
		Our company had a great turnover this year.	
3780 **mock** [mok]	수능 GRE	1. 놀리다, 우롱하다, 무시하다 2. 가짜의, 모조의 3. 모의의	mockery (우롱) [2708] ridicule
		You shouldn't mock your friends.	
3781 **sip** [sip]		1. 홀짝홀짝 마시다, 조금씩 마시다 2. 한 모금	[1065] taste
		Please sip your wine instead of gulping it down.	
3782 **cement** [si-MENT]		1. 시멘트 2. ~와 ~를 접합시키다 3. 강화하다	[2437] glue
		This building was built without using cement.	
3783 **obstruction** [uhb-STRUHK-shuhn]	공무원 토플	1. 방해(물), 장애(물) 2. 차단	[4133] hindrance
		Please watch out for the obstruction ahead.	
3784 **ginger** [JIN-jer]	공무원	1. 생강 2. 연한 갈색(의)	
		Ginger juice is good for your immunity.	

3785		여드름	
acne			
[AK-nee]		Wash your face regularly to keep acne away.	

3786		1. 효모, 이스트 2. 누룩	
yeast			
[yeest]		This dough has too much yeast in it.	

3787	공무원 토플	1. 회복력, 복원력 2. 탄력, 탄성	resilient (회복력 있는)
resilience			
[ri-ZIL-yuhns]		She showed her resilience by never giving up on her job.	

3788	공무원 편입	1. 더러운, 악취가 있는 2. 성격이 안 좋은 3. 파울, 반칙(하다)	
foul			
[foul]		His bathroom was filled with a foul stench.	

3789	공무원 토플 편입 GRE	1. 무효의, 존재하지 않는 2. 가치 없는	nullify (무효화하다)
null			
[nuhl]		The contract is null and void.	

3790	토익 공무원 토플 편입	현미경	microscopic (미세한)
microscope			
[MAHY-kruh-skohp]		He was looking through a microscope.	

3791	수능	1. 심술궂은, 장난이 심한 2. 사악한, 나쁜, 위험한	[1930] evil
wicked			
[WIK-id]		She played such a wicked prank on him.	

3792		1. 출입구 2. 부화하다 3. 만들어내다, 계획을 세우다	[4318] devise
hatch			
[hach]		The crew has to open the hatch in case of an emergency.	

3793	고등	1. 헛간, 외양간 2. 차고	[2481] shed
barn			
[bahrn]		Ten horses escaped the barn.	

3794	토플	1. 중심의, 중요한 2. 초점의	
focal			
[FOH-kuhl]		This slide is the focal point of our presentation.	

3795		1. (콩이 있는)꼬투리 2. 비행기 본체 밑의 유선형 공간	[3120] capsule
pod			
[pod]		The couple is like two peas in a pod.	

3796	토플	고도, 높이, 고지	[2053] elevation
altitude			
[AL-ti-tood]		It was fun to be riding in a helicopter at such low altitude.	

3797	공무원	천식	
asthma			
[AZ-muh]		I carry around my asthma pump with me everywhere.	

3798	공무원 GRE	1. 자존감, 자긍심 2. 자존심	esteem (존중) [2436] pride
self-esteem			
[SELF-i-steem]		She raises her child to have high self-esteem.	

3799 **millennium** [mi-LEN-ee-uhm]	천년(의 기간) She was born on the first day of the new millennium.	millennial (천년의)
3800　　　　수능 **gulf** [guhlf]	1. 만　2. 큰 간격　3. 깊은 구멍 Where is the Gulf of Mexico?	engulf (휩싸다) [5962] abyss
3801　　　　편입 **faction** [FAK-shuhn]	1. 파벌, 당파　2. 파벌 싸움, 알력 The faction was never able to win a majority.	[3218] coalition
3802　토익 공무원 토플 **appraise** [uh-PREYZ]	1. 평가하다, 감정하다　2. 살피다 His house was appraised for a very high price.	appraisal (감정, 평가) [1283] evaluate
3803　　　　공무원 **tomb** [toom]	1. 무덤　2. 매장하다 Zombies rose from their tombs.	tombstone (묘석) [2092] grave
3804　　토플 편입 **maternity** [muh-TUR-ni-tee]	1. 어머니인 상태　2. 모성 She is on maternity leave after giving birth to a triplet.	maternal (어머니의) [952] motherhood
3805　　　　공무원 **penny** [PEN-ee]	페니(미국 1센트 동전) 100 pennies make a dollar.	penniless (무일푼의) [1443] cent
3806 **dome** [dohm]	1. 돔　2. 반구형(둥근) 지붕 They are building a new dome stadium.	
3807　공무원 토플 편입 **tangible** [TAN-juh-buhl]	1. 확실(명백)한　2. 만질 수 있는　3. 유형의 There is a piece of tangible evidence that he is the killer.	intangible (무형의) [6030] palpable
3808　　고등 토플 **decay** [dih-KEY]	1. 부패(하다), 부식(되다), 썩다　2. 쇠퇴(하다) Bananas will start to decay after a few days.	[1792] decline
3809 **chronicle** [KRON-i-kuhl]	1. 연대기(에 싣다)　2. 연대순으로 기록하다 The author wrote a book on the chronicle of his life.	[342] record
3810　　　　수능 **sack** [sak]	1. 부대, 자루　2. 봉지　3. 해고(되다)　4. 약탈하다 I need to deliver a sack of potatoes to the restaurant.	[2703] dismiss
3811　토익 공무원 토플 편입 **ample** [AM-puhl]	1. 충분한, 풍부한　2. 넓은, 광대한 There is an ample amount of food for everyone.	
3812　　　수능 토플 **vague** [veyg]	1. 모호(막연)한, 분명치 않은　2. 희미한 He gave her a vague answer.	[372] unclear

3813 **vault** [vawlt]	편입	1. 금고 2. 뛰어넘다, 도약하다	
		Diamonds are locked behind the heavy vault door.	
3814 **stab** [stab]		1. 찌름 2. (푹)찌르다 3. 덤벼들다 4. 시도(하다)	[3818] pierce
		You need to keep the stab wounds clean.	
3815 **oppression** [uh-PRESH-uhn]	공무원 토플 편입	1. 압박, 억압, 탄압 2. 압제	[4779] repression
		Prisoners of war went through such harsh oppression.	
3816 **gloss** [glos]		1. 윤, 광택 2. 겉치레 3. 주석, 해설(을 달다)	[1962] shine
		She used gel to add gloss to her hair.	
3817 **villain** [VIL-uhn]	공무원 편입	1. 악당, 악한 사람 2. 악역	[7337] scoundrel
		The man was such a powerful villain.	
3818 **pierce** [peers]	토플	1. 뚫다 2. 찢다 3. 관통하다	[5499] puncture
		She pierced her ears.	
3819 **plaintiff** [PLEYN-tif]		원고, 고소인, 소송을 제기한 사람	[1782] complainant
		The plaintiff was very angry with the defendant.	
3820 **ace** [eys]		1. 성공적으로 수행하다 2. 고수, 에이스	
		I aced that exam.	
3821 **commemorate** [kuh-MEM-uh-reyt]		1. 기념하다 2. 기리다 3. 축하하다	[1134] celebrate
		Let's have a drink to commemorate this occasion.	
3822 **shred** [shred]	공무원	1. 조각 2. 찢다, 완전히 썰다	shredder (파쇄기) [3269] scrap
		Not a shred of evidence was found in the crime scene.	
3823 **dim** [dim]		1. 조명을 낮추다, 빛을 줄이다 2. 어두운, 어둑한 3. 흐릿한, 희미한	[3751] obscure
		I like to dim the light at night when I read.	
3824 **polite** [puh-LAHYT]	고등 토익	1. 예의 바른, 공손한 2. 품위있는, 세련된	politely (공손하게) impolite (무례한) [2891] courteous
		Her son was such a polite boy.	
3825 **synchronize** [SING-kruh-nahyz]	토플	동시에 일어나다	synchronous (동시의) asynchronous (따로 일 어나는) sync (동기화)
		Her dancing was perfectly synchronized with the music.	
3826 **dodge** [doj]	공무원	1. 피하다, 회피하다 2. 빠르게 움직이다	[848] avoid
		He attempted to dodge paying his taxes.	

3827	수능 토플	멈춤, 중단(하다), 정지(하다)	halter (고삐) [439] stop
halt [hawlt]		I've put a halt to this project to take a break.	

3828	공무원	망원경	
telescope [TEL-uh-skohp]		You can see the moon through this telescope.	

3829	토익 공무원 토플 편입	1. 보행자(의) 2. 진부한, 단조로운	[533] walker
pedestrian [puh-DES-tree-uhn]		A pedestrian was hit by a bus.	

3830	고등 GRE	양심, 도덕심	conscientious (양심적 인) [1980] morals
conscience [KON-shuhns]		His conscience didn't allow him to steal.	

3831		(월급 이외의)특전, 혜택	[1884] bonus
perk [purk]		There are many perks to being self-employed.	

3832	토플	1. 유역 2. 분지 3. 세면기	[1557] bowl
basin [BEY-suhn]		Houses located near the river basin are expensive.	

3833	공무원 토플	1. 부식, 녹 2. (근심이) 마음을 좀먹기	
corrosion [kuh-ROH-zhuhn]		Corrosion on the fence was so bad that it crumbled.	

3834	공무원	관절염	
arthritis [ahr-THRAHY-tis]		My grandmother is taking arthritis supplements.	

3835		바라보다, 주시하다	
behold [bih-HOHLD]		She beholds the universe just by looking out the window.	

3836	토플	1. 저수지 2. 매장량, 비축	[322] store
reservoir [REZ-er-vwahr]		Let's run a lap around the reservoir.	

3837	고등	1. 기지, 재치 2. 지혜 3. 분별력	[1588] intelligence
wit [wit]		His speech was full of wit.	

3838		1. 기둥, 지주 2. 기념비 3. 원칙	[1604] column
pillar [PIL-er]		This house is supported by solid pillars.	

3839	토익 토플 편입	메신저, 전달자	[4852] courier
messenger [MES-uhn-jer]		This messenger is here on behalf of the king.	

3840	공무원	경첩(을 달다)	[493] link
hinge [hinj]		The door didn't close because the hinge was broken.	

3841	공무원	1. 튀기다, 튕기다 2. 빠르게 움직이다 3. 넘겨봄	
flick [flik]		She flicked off the mosquito.	

3842	토익	1. 요리의, 조리의 2. 부엌용의	[1058] cook
culinary [KYOO-luh-ner-ee]		I've been working on my culinary skills for a long time.	

3843		1. 질투하는, 샘내는, 부러워하는 2. 경계하는, 견제하는	[4134] envious
jealous [JEL-uhs]		He is jealous of her fame.	

3844		1. 일식, 월식 2. 가리다 3. ~의 명성을 능가하여 무색하게 하다	[1963] overshadow
eclipse [ih-KLIPS]		He was fascinated by the lunar eclipse.	

3845		1. 유니폼, 저지 2. 부드러운 천	[외래어] shirt
jersey [JUR-zee]		She signed her fan's basketball jersey.	

3846		1. 진주 2. 매우 귀중한 것	[2963] gem
pearl [purl]		He found a pearl in an oyster he was about to eat.	

3847	토플 편입	1. 공존하는, 동시 발생의, 병행의 2. 의견이 같은	concur (동의하다, 동시발생하다) [2764] simultaneous
concurrent [kuhn-KUR-uhnt]		He will serve concurrent sentences for his crimes.	

3848	수능	1. 자막 2. 표제, 제목	[663] subtitle
caption [KAP-shuhn]		The movie had an erroneous caption.	

3849	토플	송진, (합성)수지	
resin [REZ-in]		You can make glue out of pine resin.	

3850	공무원 편입	중앙, 가운데	[1047] middle
midst [midst]		He interrupted her in the midst of her sentence.	

3851	고등 토플	운명, 숙명, 천명	destined (운명의) [3007] fate
destiny [DES-tuh-nee]		He believed it is his destiny to be a world champion.	

3852	고등	지질학의, 지질의	geology (지질학)
geological [jee-uh-LOJ-i-kuhl]		He studies geological evolution.	

3853	고등	1. 크리켓(영국의 대표적인 스포츠) 2. 귀뚜라미	[7035] grasshopper
cricket [KRIK-it]		Cricket is a famous sport that no one knows in the US.	

3854		1. 끌기, 견인(력) 2. 마찰	
traction [TRAK-shuhn]		Old tires have no traction and need to be replaced.	

3855		
waterproof	방수, 방수복	
[WAW-ter-proof]	On a rainy day, I always wear waterproof boots.	

3856	수능	
fond	1. 애정있는, 다정한 2. 좋아하는, 즐기는	
[fond]	She is so fond of her daughter for being kind.	

3857		
warfare	싸움, 전쟁, 교전	
[WAWR-fair]	She engaged in psychological warfare with him.	

3858		glamor (매력)
glamorous	1. 화려한 2. 매력적인, 매혹적인	
[GLAM-er-uhs]	Her life seemed glamorous on the surface.	

3859	토플	
vibe	1. 분위기, 느낌 2. 발산하다, 영향을 주다	
[vahyb]	This restaurant has a good vibe.	

3860	수능 토플	[421] quick
swift	1. 빠른, 신속한 2. 즉석의	
[swift]	He made a swift adjustment to her requests.	

3861		[3966] lure
bait	1. 미끼(를 달다), 유혹(하다) 2. (일부러)화나게 하다	
[beyt]	I was using earthworms as bait for fishing.	

3862	공무원 토플 편입 GRE	defiant (반항하는)
defy	1. 반항하다, 저항하다, 거부하다 2. 도전하다 3. 믿기, 묘사하기 어려운 4. 견디다	[602] challenge
[dih-FAHY]	They were sent to prison for defying the law.	

3863	공무원 토플	[4802] coarse
crude	1. 천연의, 가공하지 않은 2. 대충 만들어진, 조잡한	
[krood]	Crude diamonds need to be carved.	

3864	토익 토플	[외래어] carpeting
rug	(방바닥에 까는) 깔개, 양탄자	
[ruhg]	Rugs increase the temperature of the house.	

3865	공무원 편입	[487] position
posture	(사람의 신체적) 자세	
[POS-cher]	Good posture is important for your health.	

3866	토익	[3404] vegan
vegetarian	채식주의자	
[vej-i-TAIR-ee-uhn]	Vegetarians support animal rights.	

3867	고등	fiercely (치열하게)
fierce	1. 사나운, 흉포한 2. 지독한, 거센	[4762] savage
[feers]	Tigers will become fierce if you enter their territory.	

3868	고등 토플	[1518] victim
prey	먹이(로 하다), 사냥감(으로 삼다)	
[prey]	Lions prey on deer.	

3869	수능	(건물의) 복도	[1405] hall
corridor			
[KAWR-i-der]		The corridor curves to the left.	

3870		(수학적 개념의) 정수	[159] number
integer			
[IN-ti-jer]		Every integer can be divided by 1.	

3871	공무원 편입	장식품	[1667] decorate
ornament			
[AWR-nuh-muhnt]		The children are decorating the Christmas tree with ornaments.	

3872	공무원 토플 편입	손상되지 않은, 완전한	[3203] integral
intact			
[in-TAKT]		The vase remained intact despite rough handling.	

3873	편입	활기있는, 쾌활한	[2031] animated
lively			
[LAHYV-lee]		After a long nap, the children were lively.	

3874	공무원 토플 편입 GRE	분산하다, 퍼뜨리다	[1373] spread
diffuse			
[dih-FYOOZ]		Diffusing investments is safer.	

3875	공무원 편입	얼쩡거리다, 맴돌다	[2143] float
hover			
[HUHV-er]		The shy student hovered near the teacher.	

3876	공무원 토플 편입 GRE	(마음의) 충동	Impulsive (충동적인) [1935] urge
impulse			
[IM-puhls]		I had a strong impulse to buy a new laptop.	

3877		소규모의 숲	[1179] wood
grove			
[grohv]		Many small animals live in the grove.	

3878	공무원	심혈관의	cardiac (심장의) vascular (혈관의)
cardiovascular			
[kahr-dee-oh-VAS-kyuh-ler]		Exercise boosts cardiovascular health.	

3879	고등 토익	굉장한, 뛰어난	[605] wonderful
terrific			
[tuh-RIF-ik]		He is a terrific teacher who is loved by all students.	

3880	수능 토플	빼앗다, 박탈하다	[1848] strip
deprive			
[dih-PRAHYV]		The prisoners were deprived of food and water.	

3881	공무원	(병원, 교도소 등의) 피수용자, 입소자	[1561] prisoner
inmate			
[IN-meyt]		This prison has 100 inmates.	

3882		반도	
peninsula			
[puh-NIN-suh-luh]		The Korean peninsula is close to China.	

3883	수능 토익	1. 원한, 악의 2. ~에도 불구하고	spiteful (앙심 깊은)
spite			[3963] malice
[spahyt]		I put worms in her shoe out of spite.	

3884		1. (거센) 불길, 불꽃 2. 타오르다	[1670] flash
flare			
[flair]		The flare became bigger once we put more wood.	

3885		1. 점화하다, 불을 붙이다 2. (식었던 감정을) 되살리다	[5094] arouse
kindle			
[KIN-dl]		Dry grass can kindle a dying fire.	

3886	토플	1. 끈기 2. 모래, 티끌	
grit			
[grit]		Students with grit have higher grades.	

3887	고등	비탄, 비통, 큰 슬픔	grieve (슬퍼하다)
grief			grievous (슬픈)
[greef]		Her death was a great grief to John.	[4508] sorrow

3888	토익 공무원 토플 GRE	변동, 오르내림	fluctuate (오르내리며 변 동하다)
fluctuation			[604] variation
[fluhk-choo-EY-shuhn]		There were large fluctuations in stock prices.	

3889		식물학의	botanic (식물의)
botanical			
[buh-TAN-i-kuhl]		Botanical researchers collect rare plants.	

3890	토플	구문론, 문장론	
syntax			
[SIN-taks]		Syntax errors can be detected through this word processor.	

3891		합창(단), 합주(단)	[2526] outfit
ensemble			
[ahn-SAHM-buhl]		There is a string instrument ensemble today.	

3892	고등	어린 양	[3283] sheep
lamb			
[lam]		Children wanted to pet the lamb.	

3893	공무원	1. 강건한, 튼튼한 2. 세련되지 못한, 억센	[1719] rough
rugged			
[RUHG-id]		He is a rugged man.	

3894	공무원 토플 GRE	전임자	[5315] precursor
predecessor			
[PRED-uh-ses-er]		My predecessor taught me how to do the work.	

3895	수능 토익	대피시키다, 비우다	evacuation (대피)
evacuate			[1889] empty
[ih-VAK-yoo-eyt]		This building is on fire. We need to evacuate everyone.	

3896	공무원	1. 청소년의 2. 유치한, 아이같은	[399] youth
juvenile			
[JOO-vuh-nl]		Recently, there has been an increase in juvenile crime rates.	

3897	수능 토플	존엄, 위엄	indignity (치욕)
dignity			dignified (위엄있는)
[DIG-ni-tee]		It was beneath his dignity to cheat.	[2436] pride

3898	고등	금발의	
blonde			
[blond]		The girl with blonde hair is staring at me.	

3899		잠시, 일시	
awhile			
[uh-HWAHYL]		I might be gone awhile. Don't wait for me.	

3900	토플	안개, 흐릿함	[4874] haze
mist			
[mist]		It is difficult to drive because there is a lot of mist.	

3901	토플	문의, 수사	[2390] inquiry
enquiry			
[en-KWAHYUHR-ee]		The police conducted an enquiry to find the murderer.	

3902	공무원	악명 높은, (나쁜 의미로) 이름난	notoriety (악명)
notorious			[4144] infamous
[noh-TAWR-ee-uhs]		This restaurant is notorious for ignoring health regulations.	

3903	고등 토익	(배, 비행기 등에) 탑승한	
aboard			
[uh-BAWRD]		All passengers should come aboard.	

3904	토플 GRE	관심을 다른 곳으로 돌리다, 전환하다	diversion (다른 곳으로 돌
divert			리는 것)
[dih-VURT]		The child tried to divert his parent's attention from his report card.	

3905		허벅지, 넓적다리	
thigh			
[thahy]		My thighs don't fit into these pants.	

3906		(자동차 바퀴의) 차축	
axle			
[AK-suhl]		If we want the wheels to move smoothly, we need to grease the axles.	

3907	토플	1. 뺄셈, 빼기 2. ~을 뺀 3. 영하의	
minus			
[MAHY-nuhs]		What is 4 minus 2?	

3908	공무원 토플	가능한, 현실적인, 실현 가능한	
feasible			
[FEE-zuh-buhl]		I like your plan, but is it feasible?	

3909	고등 토플	심포니, 교향곡, 음의 조화	
symphony			
[SIM-fuh-nee]		Beethoven's 9th symphony is very popular.	

3910	공무원 토플	빗나가다, 벗어나가	deviation (편차)
deviate			deviant (벗어난)
[DEE-vee-eyt]		The car deviated from the road.	[4854] diverge

3911		던전, 지하 감옥	[833] cell
dungeon			
[DUHN-juhn]		There are monsters in the dungeon.	

3912	토플	(도시의) 광장	[1278] square
plaza			
[PLAH-zuh]		There are many shops and restaurants in the plaza.	

3913	공무원 토플 GRE	부식, 침식	[3833] corrosion
erosion			
[ih-ROH-zhuhn]		Acid rain causes erosion of cultural artifacts.	

3914	공무원	1. 주위의, 주변환경의 2. 잔잔한, 은은한	[532] environment
ambient			
[AM-bee-uhnt]		The ambient air smells like smoke.	

3915	수능 토플 GRE	드문, 부족한	scarcity (결핍) [5426] sparse
scarce			
[skairs]		Diamonds are scarce.	

3916	토플	원고, (발표하기 위해 작성한) 문서	[606] document
manuscript			
[MAN-yuh-skript]		The writer gave her manuscript to the publishers.	

3917	공무원	무르익은, 탐스러운	[2155] mature
ripe			
[rahyp]		Is this peach ripe?	

3918		1. 입학, 입장 2. 인정	[365] entry
admission			
[ad-MISH-uhn]		There will be free admission for students.	

3919	토플	1. 나선형의 2. 나선형으로 움직이다 3. 급증하다	[2517] coil
spiral			
[SPAHY-ruhl]		I walked up the spiral stairway.	

3920		비밀의	confide (비밀을 털어놓다) confidant (비밀을 털어놓을 수 있는 친구) [1334] secret
confidential			
[kon-fi-DEN-shuhl]		I consider everything discussed today to be strictly confidential.	

3921	공무원 토플	1. 침입, 침해 2. 방해	intruder (침입자) [2639] interference
intrusion			
[in-TROO-zhuhn]		Intrusion into my private life makes me angry.	

3922	토플	윤활유, 윤활제	[3256] grease
lubricant			
[LOO-bri-kuhnt]		Oil is a lubricant that can be used to reduce friction.	

3923	공무원 GRE	단념시키다, 포기하게 하다	deterrent (억제제) deterrence (억제) [3662] discourage
deter			
[dih-TUR]		Selfish actions need to be deterred.	

3924	토플	1. 마찰(력) 2. 부조화, 다툼	[1717] conflict
friction			
[FRIK-shuhn]		Good shoes increase friction between your feet and the ground.	

3925 **impersonate** [im-PUR-suh-neyt]		다른 사람인 척하다	impersonation (위장) [4095] imitate
		The old man was caught impersonating the president.	
3926 **soothing** [SOO-th ing]	공무원	달래는, 가라앉히는	soothe (달래다) [2260] calming
		He applied a soothing lotion for his sunburn.	
3927 **trio** [TREE-oh]		삼인조, 삼중창	[기타] threesome
		The trio became famous.	
3928 **yummy** [YUHM-ee]		맛있는	[1065] tasty
		This cake is yummy.	
3929 **co-op** [KOH-op]		1. 협동 조합 2. 협력하는, 협조하는	[2147] cooperative
		Farmers and fishers often create co-ops.	
3930 **fireworks** [FAHYUH R-wurks]	토익	1. 불꽃놀이 2. 폭발, 번뜩임	
		The fireworks are beautiful.	
3931 **sequel** [SEE-kwuhl]		후속편	prequel (속편) [1746] consequence
		Many readers wanted the author to write a sequel.	
3932 **dawn** [dawn]	고등 토플	1. 새벽, 동틀녘 2. 동이 트다, 밝아지다	[955] sunrise
		We got up before dawn.	
3933 **nucleus** [NOO-klee-uhs]	토플	1. 핵심, 중축 2. 원자핵	nucleic (핵의) [1248] core
		Hollywood is the nucleus of the film industry.	
3934 **magnitude** [MAG-ni-tood]	공무원 토플	1. 크기, 규모 2. 중요도	[417] size
		The earthquake had a large magnitude.	
3935 **bleach** [bleech]		1. 표백하다, 미백하다 2. 표백제	[617] whiten
		He bleached his hair to dye it green.	
3936 **pathology** [puh-THOL-uh-jee]	공무원 토플	병리학, 병상	[2113] illness
		Pathology is the science of studying diseases.	
3937 **vivid** [VIV-id]	수능 토플	1. (색감이) 선명한 2. (기억이, 감정이) 생생한	[1397] bright
		The painter uses vivid colors in her painting.	
3938 **alloy** [AL-oi]	토플	합금(하다)	[1620] blend
		The alloy contains 15% steel and 20% copper.	

3939 공무원 토플		
porch	1. 베란다 2. 현관	[외래어] veranda
[pawrch]	They grow flowers on the porch.	

3940 공무원 토플 GRE		
susceptible	민감한, 예민한, ~의 영향을 많이 받는	[2192] vulnerable
[suh-SEP-tuh-buhl]	Babies are susceptible to diseases.	

3941 공무원 토플 GRE		
mimic	흉내내다, 모방하다	[4095] imitate
[MIM-ik]	The ducklings mimicked their mother.	

3942 토플		
bladder	1. 방광 2. (물고기의) 부레, 공기 주머니	
[BLAD-er]	He had a full bladder and needed to use the restroom.	

3943 수능 토플 GRE		
undermine	1. 얕잡아보다 2. (서서히) 손상시키다, 약화하다	[1445] weaken
[uhn-der-MAHYN]	She undermines my capabilities.	

3944		
sage	현명한, 지혜로운	
[seyj]	He is a sage old man.	

3945 고등 토플		
flourish	번영하다, 번성하다	
[FLUR-ish]	I hope your business flourishes.	

3946		
trek	여행(을 하다), 여정(을 떠나다)	
[trek]	They trekked towards the North Pole.	

3947 고등		
flock	1. 무리 2. 모이다, 무리 짓다	
[flok]	Birds flocked together.	

3948 공무원 토플 GRE		
disguise	1. 변장하다, 감추다, 위장하다 2. 변장, 위장	
[dis-GAHYZ]	The wizard disguised himself as a cat.	

3949 고등 토플		
straw	1. 빨대 2. 짚	
[straw]	Can I have a straw for my drink?	

3950		
gadget	1. 도구, 장치2. (기계의) 부속품	[562] device
[GAJ-it]	This kitchen gadget automatically peels potatoes.	

3951		
feat	위업, 성과	[1760] achievement
[feet]	Writing a book is her greatest feat in life.	

3952 토익 공무원		
underway	1. (계획 등이) 진행 중인 2. 여행 중인	[2027] ongoing
[UHN-der-wey]	Plans to develop the region are underway.	

3953		1. 비료, 퇴비 2. 혼합물	[2512] fertilizer
compost			
[KOM-pohst]		Compost helps plants grow quicker.	

3954	공무원	주지 않다, 보류하다	[1655] deny
withhold			
[with-HOHLD]		The father is withholding his son's allowance.	

3955	토플	1. 혈청 (피가 굳을 때 분리되는 액체) 2. 장액	
serum			
[SEER-uhm]		When a wound starts to heal you can see serum form.	

3956	공무원 토플 GRE	정교의, 정통의	[736] traditional
orthodox			
[AWR-thuh-doks]		Orthodox Christians did not want any change in their religion.	

3957	공무원 토플 GRE	1. 주위의, 주변적의 2. 말초의 3. 중요하지 않은	periphery (주변)
peripheral			
[puh-RIF-er-uhl]		The peripheral environment was safe.	

3958		1. 임시의, 잠정조치의 2. 중간의	[1648] temporary
interim			
[IN-ter-uhm]		An interim president was nominated.	

3959		1. 피난처, 안전한 보호 구역 2. 성소, 신전, 성당	[2464] shelter
sanctuary			
[SANGK-choo-er-ee]		The church became a sanctuary for citizens escaping from the flood.	

3960	GRE	철회하다, 취소하다, 무효화하다	[1713] cancel
revoke			
[ri-VOHK]		The president revoked the ban on smoking.	

3961		1. 편향되지 않은 2. 무관심한, 흔들리지 않은	[6417] apathetic
indifferent			
[in-DIF-er-uhnt]		The man was indifferent to his 2 sons.	

3962	토익 공무원	파괴하다, 철거하다	demolition (파괴) [1255] destroy
demolish			
[dih-MOL-ish]		The old building was demolished.	

3963	공무원	악의 있는, 나쁜 의도를 가진	malice (악의) [7157] malevolent
malicious			
[muh-LISH-uhs]		He doesn't have malicious intent.	

3964		1. 토(하다) 2. (용암 등을) 분출하다	
vomit			
[VOM-it]		After drinking too much, he vomited	

3965	공무원	북극(의)	antarctic (남극) [1579] freezing
arctic			
[AHRK-tik]		Polar bears live in the arctic pole.	

3966	공무원 GRE	1. 꾀어들이다, 유혹하다 2. 유혹	[1069] attract
lure			
[loor]		Flowers lure in bees.	

3967 superintendent [soo-per-in-TEN-duhnt]		감독관, 관리자, 지도자	[1291] chief
		Each superintendent takes care of 10 students.	
3968 whisper [HWIS-per]	고등	1. 속삭이다, 조용히 말하다 2. 속삭임	[6428] murmur
		The students were whispering in class.	
3969 cardboard [KAHRD-bawrd]		카드보드, 보드지	[418] card
		Cardboard should be recycled as paper.	
3970 surpass [ser-PAS]	공무원	~를 능가하다, ~보다 낫다	[1983] exceed
		The student surpassed her teacher.	
3971 bunker [BUHNG-ker]	토플 GRE	벙커, 지하 엄폐호	[2464] shelter
		Some people build a bunker in their homes to prepare for earthquakes.	
3972 riot [RAHY-uht]	수능	1. 폭동, 소동 2. 폭동을 일으키다	[2665] disturbance
		The increased oil prices caused citizens to riot.	
3973 psychic [SAHY-kik]	공무원	1. 심령의, 정신의 2. 무당과 관련된	[7321] clairvoyant
		Psychic trauma should be treated with medication.	
3974 multitude [MUHL-ti-tood]	공무원 토플	1. 다수, 큰 수 2. 군중	[1500] mass
		This charity organizes a multitude of kind actions.	
3975 upright [UHP-rahyt]	토플 GRE	1. 곧은, 똑바른 2. 올바른, 정직한	[3602] righteous
		After waking up, she sat upright in bed.	
3976 contingent [kuhn-TIN-juhnt]	토플 GRE	1. ~에 따라 변하는, ~에 부수하는, ~에 의존하는 2. (행사 파견) 대표단	contingency (비상시의) [446] conditional
		Free trade agreements are contingent on the approval of parliament.	
3977 starve [stahrv]	수능 토플	1. 굶주리다, 아사하다 2. 굶기다, 굶주리게 하다	starvation (굶주림) [2470] hunger
		Children in Africa are starving to death.	
3978 saddle [SAD-l]		1. (말이나 자전거의) 안장 2. ~에 올라타다	
		My bike saddle needs to be replaced.	
3979 sophomore [SOF-uh-mawr]		대학교 2학년생	
		He is a sophomore at Iowa state university.	
3980 chorus [KAWR-uhs]	고등	1. 합창, 일제히 내는 소리 2. 코러스, 후렴	[3739] choir
		The comedian received a chorus of boos for his racist joke.	

3981		1. (특히 과거 로마의) 군단 2. 여럿의, 큰 무리의	[855] host
legion			
[LEE-juhn]		The American legions attacked Iraq.	

3982	토익 공무원	1. 잔디/풀 깎는 기계 2. 잔디 베는 사람	mow (베다)
mower			
[MOH-er]		Before the invention of the mower, it took a long time to trim the lawn.	

3983	공무원 토플 GRE	1. 복잡한, 난해한 2. 정교한	intricacy (복잡함) [1088] complex
intricate			
[IN-tri-kit]		The police had a hard time trying the solve the intricate crime.	

3984	공무원	방황하다, 배회하다, (정처없이) 걸어다니다	[3039] wander
roam			
[rohm]		Who is this person roaming around the streets?	

3985		팔찌	
bracelet			
[BREYS-lit]		My favorite bracelet has pink seashells.	

3986	공무원 토플	1. 발진, 뾰루지 2. 무모한, 경솔한, 성급한	[4864] reckless
rash			
[rash]		If he eats peaches, he will get a rash.	

3987		1. 장식 못, 단추 모양의 보석 2. 종마	[944] button
stud			
[stuhd]		The bag is decorated with studs.	

3988	공무원	군주, 왕	monarchy (군주제) [914] king
monarch			
[MON-erk]		England still has a monarch.	

3989		1. 과장된 광고, 과대광고 2. 흥분시키다, 자극하다	
hype			
[hahyp]		The hype surrounding this medicine turned out to be false.	

3990		(숨, 공기, 가스 등을) 들이쉬다	[964] inspire
inhale			
[in-HEYL]		The hikers inhaled the fresh mountain air.	

3991		여성스러운, 여자같은	[1438] female
feminine			
[FEM-uh-nin]		Her voice was soft and feminine.	

3992	토플	1. 질식하다, 숨이 막히다 2. 숨막히게 하다, 질식시키다	[6303] suffocate
choke			
[chohk]		This neckband is choking the cat.	

3993	공무원	1. 우묵한, 속이 텅 빈 2. 도려내다, 우묵하게 하다	[1889] empty
hollow			
[HOL-oh]		Bird nests are hollow.	

3994		~임에도 불구하고, 비록 ~이지만	[570] although
albeit			
[awl-BEE-it]		She is beautiful, albeit selfish.	

3995 **vow** [vou]	공무원	1. 맹세, 다짐 2. 서약하다, 맹세하다	[3242] pledge
		The couple vowed to never break up.	
3996 **redundant** [ri-DUHN-duhnt]	공무원 토플	1. 중복되는, 말이 많은 2. 여분의, 과다한	redundancy (중복, 과잉) [6940] superfluous
		Nobody is listening to the principal's redundant speech.	
3997 **calf** [kaf]	공무원	1. 송아지 2. 종아리	calve (새끼를 낳다)
		The calf is drinking milk from its mother.	
3998 **enchanting** [en-CHAN-ting]	공무원 토플	매혹적인, 마음을 사로잡는	disenchantment (꿈에 서 깨는, 각성) [2312] charming
		She had an enchanting personality.	
3999 **pigment** [PIG-muh nt]		색소, 물감	[330] color
		Artists used to collect pigment from flower petals.	
4000 **slash** [slash]	토플	1. 삭감하다, 깎다 2. 내려치다, 베다, 난도질하다	slashing (맹렬한)
		After the big mistake, his salary was slashed.	

외래어 및 기타 표현

| 외래어 및 기타 표현

무료 MP3 파일 제공 | Allvoca.com

외래어	
Accordion	아코디언
Adrenalin	아드레날린
Album	앨범
Algorithm	알고리즘
Alibi	알리바이
Almond	아몬드
Alphabet	알파벳
Alps	알프스
Aluminum	알루미늄
Amateur	아마추어
Amen	아멘
Ammonia	암모니아
Antenna	안테나
Asparagus	아스파라거스
Asphalt	아스팔트
Aspirin	아스프린
Audition	오디션
Avocado	아보카도
Bacon	베이컨
Bacteria	박테리아
Badminton	배드민턴
Bagel	베이글
Balcony	발코니
Ballad	발라드
Ballet	발레
Banana	바나나
Banner	배너
Barbecue	바비큐
Barbell	바벨
Barricade	바리케이드
Bartender	바텐더
Basil	바질
Bazaar	바자회
Beaver	비버
Beige	베이지
Bench	벤치
Bikini	비키니
Biorhythm	바이오리듬
Biscuit	비스킷

Blog	블로그
Blouse	블라우스
Blu-Ray	블루레이
Bonnet	자동차 본넷
Bouquet	부케
Bourgeois	부르주아
Brassiere	브래지어
Broccoli	브로콜리
Brownie	브라우니
Brunch	브런치
Bulldog	불도그
Bulldozer	불도저
Burger	햄버거
Burrito	브리또
Bus	버스
Cafe	카페
Caffeine	카페인
Cake	케이크
Calcium	칼슘
Calorie	칼로리
Camcorder	캠코더
Cameo	까메오
Camera	카메라
Campus	캠퍼스
Canoe	카누
Caramel	카라멜
Cardigan	가디건
Carol	캐럴
Carpet	카펫
Cashmere	캐시미어
Casino	카지노
Catholic	가톨릭
Cauliflower	콜리플라워
Celery	셀러리
Cello	첼로
Cellphone	핸드폰
Centimeter	센티미터
Cereal	시리얼
Chameleon	카멜레온
Champagne	샴페인

Chandelier	샹들리에
Checkout	체크아웃
Cheetah	치타
Chef	셰프
Cherry	체리
Chess	체스
Chilli	칠리
Chimpanzee	침팬지
Chiropractic	카이로프랙틱
Chocolate	초콜릿
Cholesterol	콜레스테롤
Christmas	크리스마스
Cigar	시가
Circus	서커스
Clarinet	클라리넷
Clover	클로버
Cobalt	코발트색 (푸른)
Cobra	코브라
Cocaine	코카인
Cocktail	칵테일
Cocoa	코코아
Coconut	코코넛
Codec	코덱
Coffee	커피
Coke	콜라
Cola	콜라
Colon	콜론 (:)
Colosseum	콜로세움
Condom	콘돔
Cookie	쿠키
Copywriter	카피라이터
Cork	코르크
Corset	코르셋
Coupe	쿠페
Coupon	쿠폰
Cowboy	카우보이
Coyote	코요테
Cranberry	크랜베리
Crayon	크레용
Cream	크림

Crowdfunding	크라우드펀딩		Freestyle	프리스타일		Internet	인터넷
Curry	카레		Gallon	갤런		Ipod	아이팟
Cursor	커서		Gamma	감마		Italics	이탤릭체
Curtain	커튼		Gel	젤		Jab	잽
Custard	커스터드		Genie	지니		Jacket	자켓
Cuticle	큐티클		Genome	게놈		Jaguar	재규어
Cyber	사이버		Genre	장르		Jazz	재즈
Cymbal	심벌즈		Golf	골프		Jeep	지프
Database	데이터베이스		Gondola	곤돌라		Jelly	젤리
Debut	데뷔		Gorilla	고릴라		Kale	케일
Denim	데님		Gradation	그라데이션		Kangaroo	캥거루
Dessert	디저트		Graffiti	그래피티		Karate	가라테
Diamond	다이아몬드		Gram	그램		Kayak	카약
Diesel	디젤		Graph	그래프		Ketchup	케첩
Disco	디스코		Greenhouse	그린하우스		Keyboard	키보드
Dna	DNA		Guitar	기타		Khaki	카키색
Dollar	달러		Gypsy	집시		Kilogram	킬로그램
Domino	도미노		Halloween	할로윈		Kilometer	킬로미터
Donut	도넛		Ham	햄		Kiss	키스
Dopamine	도파민		Hammock	해먹 침대		Kiwi	키위
Download	다운로드		Hamster	햄스터		Koala	코알라
Drone	드론		Hardware	하드웨어		Koran	코란
Drum	드럼		Harp	하프		Lavender	라벤더
Dynamite	다이나마이트		Hectare	헥타르		Lasagna	라자냐
Email	이메일		Helicopter	헬리콥터		Laser	레이저
Emerald	에메랄드		Helmet	헬멧		Latex	라텍스
Emulsion	에멀션		Heroin	헤로인		Latin	라틴
Encore	앙코르		Herpes	헤르페스		Latte	라떼
Engine	엔진		Hippie	히피		League	리그
Epoxy	에폭시		Hipster	힙스터		Lemon	레몬
Escalator	에스컬레이터		Hobbit	호빗		Lemonade	레몬에이드
Espresso	에스프레소		Hockey	하키		Lens	렌즈
Estrogen	에스트로겐		Homo Sapiens	호모사피엔스		Lesbian	레즈비언
Etiquette	에티켓		Hormone	호르몬		Lifeguard	라이프가드
Eureka	유레카		Hose	호스		Lifestyle	라이프스타일
Euro	유로		Hotel	호텔		Lime	라임
Fax	팩스		Humor	유머		Limousine	리무진
Feminism	페미니즘		Hyphen	하이픈		Linen	리넨
Fender	펜더		Igloo	이글루		Lingerie	란제리
Flute	플룻		Inch	인치		Lipstick	립스틱
Font	폰트		Ink	잉크		Liter	리터
Franc	프랑		Inning	이닝		Lithium	리튬
Franchise	프랜차이즈		Insulin	인슐린		Lobster	랍스터

Logo	로고	Neanderthal	네안데르탈인	Pickle	피클
Lotion	로션	Network	네트워크	Picnic	피크닉
Macaroni	마카로니	Neuron	뉴런	Pie	파이
Mafia	마피아	News	뉴스	Pineapple	파인애플
Mahogany	마호가니	Newsletter	뉴스레터	Pink	핑크
Makeup	메이크업	Nicotine	니코틴	Pint	파인트
Malaria	말라리아	Nightclub	나이트클럽	Pizza	피자
Mango	망고	Ninja	닌자	Placebo	플라시보
Manicure	매니큐어	Notebook	노트북	Playoff	플레이오프
Marathon	마라톤	Nylon	나일론	Podcast	포드캐스트
Marshmallow	마시멜로	Oasis	오아시스	Polo	폴로
Martini	마티니	Octave	옥타브	Polyester	폴리에스터
Mascara	마스카라	Ok	오케이	Popcorn	팝콘
Mascot	마스콧	Olive	올리브	Pretzel	프레젤
Massage	마사지	Omega	오메가	Pudding	푸딩
Mayonnaise	마요네즈	Omelette	오믈렛	Puma	퓨마
Mediterranean	지중해(의)	Online	온라인	Pump	펌프
Megaphone	메가폰	Opera	오페라	Putt	퍼트
Melody	멜로디	Opioid	오피오이드	Pyramid	피라미드
Melon	멜론	Orange	오렌지	Quinoa	퀴노아
Memo	메모	Orchestra	오케스트라	Quiz	퀴즈
Mentor	멘토	Orgasm	오르가즘	Rabbi	라비
Menu	메뉴	Oven	오븐	Radio	라디오
Message	메시지	Page	페이지	Ramadan	라마단
Methane	메탄	Pajamas	파자마	Rap	랩
Microphone	마이크	Palette	팔레트	Raspberry	래스베리
Milligram	밀리그램	Pamphlet	팜플렛	Rehearsal	리허설
Millimeter	밀리미터	Panda	팬더	Repertoire	레퍼토리
Mini	미니	Panty	팬티	Rhythm	리듬
Missile	미사일	Paprika	파프리카	Ribbon	리본
Mocha	모카	Parody	패러디	Robin	로빈
Modem	모뎀	Pasta	파스타	Robot	로봇
Montage	몽타주	Pecan	피칸	Rodeo	로데오
Mosaic	모자이크	Pedal	페달	Roommate	룸메이트
Mosque	모스크	Pedicure	페디큐어	Ruby	루비
Motel	모텔	Pelican	펠리칸	Rugby	럭비
Moto	모토	Pen	펜더	Rupee	루피
Mozzarella	모짜렐라	Penguin	펜귄	Sadism	사디즘
Muffin	머핀	Penthouse	펜트하우스	Safari	사파리
Mustang	머스탱	Percent	퍼센트	Salad	샐러드
Mustard	머스터드	Percentage	퍼센트	Samurai	사무라이
Nano	나노	Pharaoh	파라오	Sandal	샌들
Napkin	냅킨	Piano	피아노	Sandwich	샌드위치

Satan	사탄	Storytelling	스토리텔링	Url	유알엘
Sauna	사우나	Strawberry	스트로베리	Vaccine	백신
Sausage	소시지	Studio	스튜디오	Valentine	발렌타인
Saxophone	색소폰	Suede	스웨이드	Vampire	뱀파이어
Scarf	스카프	Suite	스위트룸	Vanilla	바닐라
Scenario	시나리오	Sunscreen	썬스크린	Velvet	벨벳
Scooter	스쿠터	Supermarket	슈퍼마켓	Veranda	베란다
Scrum	스크럼	Superstar	슈퍼스타	Video	비디오
Scuba	스쿠버	Sushi	초밥	Violin	바이올린
Sedan	세단	Sweater	스웨터	Virus	바이러스
Semicolon	세미콜론	Sweatshirt	스웨트 셔츠	Visa	비자
Seminar	세미나	Syrup	시럽	Vitamin	비타민
Shale	셰일	Taco	타코	Vodka	보드카
Shampoo	샴푸	Taliban	탈레반	Waffle	와플
Shirt	셔츠	Tampon	탐폰	Waltz	왈츠
Sigma	시그마	Tango	탱코	Watt	와트
Silicon	실리콘	Tar	타르	Website	웹사이트
Siren	사이렌	Tarot	타로카드	Wheelchair	휠체어
Sitcom	시트콤	Tart	타르트	Whiskey	위스키
Ski	스키	Tattoo	문신	Wine	와인
Skirt	스커트	Taxi	택시	Wink	윙크
Skunk	스컹크	Telepathy	텔레파시	Workshop	워크샵
Slipper	슬리퍼	Tennis	테니스	X-Ray	엑스레이
Slogan	슬로건	Tent	텐트	Yacht	요트
Smartphone	스마트폰	Tequila	데킬라	Yen	엔화
Smog	스모그	Terrace	테라스	Yoga	요가
Smoothie	스무디	Terrier	테리어	Yogurt	요거트
Sneakers	스피커즈	Tomato	토마토	Yuan	위안
Snorkeling	스노클링	Tractor	트랙터	Zombie	좀비
Soda	소다	Trademark	트레이드마크		
Sofa	소파	Tram	트램		
Software	소프트웨어	Trauma	트라우마		
Sonata	소나타	Truck	트럭		
Soprano	소프라노	Truffle	트러플		
Spa	스파	Tsunami	쓰나미		
Spaghetti	스파게티	Tulip	튤립		
Spam	스팸	Tunnel	터널		
Sponge	스폰지	Tumbler	텀블러		
Sport	스포츠	Tuxedo	턱시도		
Spotlight	스포트라이트	Tv	텔레비전		
Spreadsheet	스프레드시트	Ukulele	우쿨렐레		
Steak	스테이크	Unicorn	유니콘		
Steroids	스테로이드	Upload	업로드		

Monday	월요일
Tuesday	화요일
Wednesday	수요일
Thursday	목요일
Friday	금요일
Saturday	토요일
Sunday	일요일
January	1월
February	2월
March	3월
April	4월
May	5월
June	6월
July	7월
August	8월
September	9월
October	10월
November	11월
December	12월
P.M.	오후
A.M.	오전
Zero	0
One	1
Two	2
Three	3
Four	4
Five	5
Six	6
Seven	7
Eight	8
Nine	9
Ten	10
Eleven	11
Twelve	12
Thirteen	13
Fourteen	14
Fifteen	15
Sixteen	16
Seventeen	17
Eighteen	18
Nineteen	19
Twenty	20

Thirty	30
Forty	40
Fifty	50
Sixty	60
Seventy	70
Eighty	80
Ninety	90
Hundred	100
United States	미국
European Union	유럽 연합
China	중국
Japan	일본
United Kingdom	영국
Germany	독일
France	프랑스
India	인도
Italy	이탈리아
Brazil	브라질
Canada	캐나다
Russia	러시아
Korea	한국
Spain	스페인
Australia	호주
Mexico	멕시코
Indonesia	인도네시아
Saudia Arabia	사우디아라비아
Netherlands	네덜란드
Turkey	터키
Switzerland	스위스
Taiwan	타이완
Poland	폴란드
Sweden	스웨덴
Belgium	벨기에
Argentina	아르헨티나
Thailand	태국
Iran	이란
Norway	노르웨이
Nigeria	나이지리아
Ireland	아일랜드
Israel	이스라엘
Hong Kong	홍콩
Singapore	싱가포르
Malaysia	말레이시아

Denmark	덴마크
Columbia	컬럼비아
Philippines	필리핀
Pakistan	파키스탄
Chile	칠리
Bangladesh	방글라데시
Finland	핀란드
Egypt	이집트
Vietnam	베트남
Portugal	포르투갈
Iraq	이라크
Peru	페루
Greece	그리스
New Zealand	뉴질랜드
Scotland	스코틀랜드
Nepal	네팔
Europe	유럽
Asia	아시아
Africa	아프리카
Atlantic	대서양
Pacific	태평양

INDEX

| INDEX

bike	1239	booth	3373	brother	1189	cage	783
bill	1057	border	1823	brown	1858	calculate	1282
billion	1390	boring	2460	browse	1413	calendar	1972
bin	1614	born	1270	brush	1799	calf	3997
binary	3660	borrow	2210	brutal	3041	calibration	3721
bind	1507	boss	2085	bubble	2535	call	129
biography	2850	botanical	3889	buck	2875	calm	2260
biological	1970	both	151	bucket	2959	camp	1275
bird	1598	bother	2451	bud	3277	campaign	1006
birth	1619	bottle	1451	buddy	3510	can	24
bishop	2831	bottom	999	budget	1192	canal	3229
bit	409	bounce	2689	buffer	2521	cancel	1713
bite	2061	bound	1881	bug	1642	cancer	1074
bitter	3130	boutique	3720	build	139	candidate	1353
bittersweet	3309	bow	2702	bulb	2726	candle	3125
black	556	bowl	1557	bulk	2490	candy	2694
bladder	3942	box	569	bull	2942	cannabis	3255
blade	2010	boy	1093	bullet	2677	canvas	3092
blame	2316	brace	3534	bully	3097	cap	1592
blank	2681	bracelet	3985	bump	2332	capability	1195
blanket	3142	bracket	2881	bunch	2070	capacity	1457
blast	2572	brain	1286	bundle	2757	capital	1056
bleach	3935	brake	2128	bunker	3971	capsule	3120
bleed	2707	branch	1686	burden	2760	captain	2048
blend	1620	brand	702	bureau	2811	caption	3848
bless	1918	brass	3235	burn	1224	captive	3366
blind	2191	brave	2865	burst	2828	capture	1344
block	849	breach	2628	bury	2393	car	346
blonde	3898	bread	2134	bush	3546	carbohydrate	2670
blood	860	break	445	business	1657	carbon	1834
bloom	3252	breakfast	1957	bust	3329	card	418
blow	1568	breakthrough	3074	busy	135	cardboard	3969
blue	934	breast	2077	but	29	cardinal	3678
blur	3428	breathe	2018	butter	1774	cardiovascular	3878
board	515	breed	1912	butterfly	799	care	256
boast	2650	breeze	3447	button	944	career	706
boat	1414	brew	2234	buy	274	cargo	3422
body	335	brick	2778	buyout	3304	carrot	804
boil	2156	bride	3012	by	28	carry	553
bold	2591	bridge	1525	bypass	3567	cart	2717
bolt	2284	brief	1671	bystander	3305	cartoon	3553
bomb	2059	bright	1397			cartridge	3154
bond	1707	brilliant	2178	**C**		carve	3140
bone	1646	bring	293			case	218
bonus	1884	broad	1630	cab	3716	cash	1247
book	240	broadband	3650	cabin	2642	cast	1427
boom	2858	broadcast	2132	cabinet	2372	castle	2454
boost	1566	broker	2654	cable	1436	casual	2571
boot	1562	bronze	3314	cache	3431	cat	1361

catalog	2610	cheese	1966	cliff	3566	commercial	1011
catch	965	chemical	1576	climate	1706	commission	1180
category	1122	chemistry	2630	climb	1681	commit	530
cater	2844	chest	2173	clinic	1154	committee	2499
cathedral	3641	chew	3328	clip	1866	commodity	3320
cattle	3568	chicken	1640	clock	2238	common	485
cause	323	chief	1291	clone	3311	commonwealth	3654
caution	2149	child	170	close	247	communicate	698
cave	2886	chill	2763	closet	3169	communist	3734
cease	3025	chip	1853	cloth	2833	community	320
ceiling	2567	choice	666	clothes	1392	commute	3173
celebrate	1134	choir	3739	cloud	1363	compact	2421
celebrity	2722	choke	3992	club	765	companion	2713
cell	833	choose	387	clue	2736	company	148
cement	3782	chop	2626	cluster	2598	compare	572
cemetery	3450	chord	3010	clutch	3233	compartment	3752
census	3699	chorus	3980	coach	961	compassion	3146
cent	1443	chronic	2463	coal	2925	compatible	1964
center	214	chronicle	3809	coalition	3218	compelling	2602
century	1171	chunk	3037	coast	1327	compensation	1991
ceramic	3540	church	867	coat	1587	compete	583
ceremony	2190	cigarette	3296	code	490	competent	2388
certain	385	cinema	2848	cognitive	3197	compile	2224
certificate	885	circle	1241	coherent	3572	complaint	1782
chain	1529	circuit	1908	cohesive	3746	complement	2660
chair	1544	circumstance	1735	coil	2517	complete	207
chairman	2327	cite	2142	coin	2122	complex	1088
challenge	602	citizen	1496	coincide	3224	compliance	1469
chamber	2349	city	261	cold	1163	complicated	1817
champion	1082	civic	3597	collaboration	1441	compliment	2646
chance	733	civil	1284	collapse	2604	compose	775
change	123	civilize	1615	collar	3322	composite	3574
channel	1185	claim	588	colleague	2218	compost	3953
chaos	2962	clamp	3656	collect	420	compound	2252
chapter	1422	clan	3776	college	519	comprehensive	1546
character	466	clap	825	collision	3082	compression	1959
charge	415	clarity	2184	colony	2244	comprise	2479
charity	1840	clash	3437	color	330	compromise	2434
charm	2312	class	353	column	1604	compute	575
chart	1273	classic	1106	combat	2087	con	2647
charter	2575	clause	3046	combine	613	conceal	3580
chase	2251	clay	3065	combo	3094	concentration	1617
chassis	3777	clean	559	come	81	concept	963
chat	2045	cleanse	3028	comfortable	694	concern	705
cheap	1230	clear	372	comic	1594	concert	2217
cheat	2774	clerk	3472	command	1012	concession	3407
check	304	clever	3031	commemorate	3821	conclusion	1304
cheek	3614	click	480	commence	3051	concrete	2409
cheer	2488	client	593	comment	525	concurrent	3847

express	977	fatigue	3144	first	73	forecast	2429
extend	608	fault	2138	fish	983	foreign	1442
extent	2124	favor	1571	fit	452	foremost	3730
exterior	3006	favorite	723	fix	769	forest	1627
external	1660	fear	1198	flag	1916	forever	1141
extra	869	feasible	3908	flame	1860	forge	3190
extract	1968	feast	3578	flare	3884	forget	1095
extraordinary	2704	feat	3951	flash	1670	forgive	2532
extremely	893	feather	3415	flat	1398	fork	2996
eye	620	feature	266	flavor	1471	form	220
eyebrow	1921	federal	1023	flaw	2643	formal	1747
		fee	884	flee	3148	format	1232

F

		feeble	3609	fleet	2554	former	916
		feed	1033	flesh	2997	formula	1559
fable	2275	feedback	1137	flexible	1309	fort	3482
fabric	1711	feel	144	flick	3841	forth	2107
fabulous	2547	fellow	1580	flight	1263	fortune	992
face	404	female	1438	flip	2432	forum	1531
facilitate	2235	feminine	3991	float	2143	forward	713
facility	1003	fence	2584	flock	3947	fossil	3514
fact	407	fermentation	3764	flood	2126	foster	2680
faction	3801	ferry	3411	floor	975	foul	3788
factor	930	fertility	2512	floral	3265	found	3707
factory	1911	festival	1517	flour	2739	fountain	3756
faculty	1847	festive	3674	flourish	3945	fox	816
fade	2802	fever	788	flow	1178	fraction	2936
fail	621	few	181	flower	1418	fracture	3333
faint	2574	fiber	1993	flu	3444	fragment	3352
fair	886	fiction	2315	fluctuation	3888	fragrance	3363
fairy	3484	field	482	fluid	2106	frame	1120
faith	1380	fierce	3867	flush	3115	framework	2187
fake	2552	fight	697	fly	986	frankly	2168
fall	454	figuratively	3509	foam	2559	fraud	2439
familiar	1560	figure	618	focal	3794	freak	3350
family	203	file	294	focus	447	free	216
famous	1159	fill	685	fog	805	freelance	3526
fan	725	film	629	foil	3722	freeze	1579
fancy	2667	filter	1221	fold	1182	freight	3711
fantasy	1277	final	360	folk	1821	frequently	1017
far	211	finance	433	follow	155	fresh	1103
fare	2930	find	64	fond	3856	freshman	3117
farm	1050	fine	716	food	332	friction	3924
fascinating	2469	finger	1725	fool	2644	fridge	2197
fashion	1417	finish	592	foot	657	friend	288
fast	585	fire	655	footage	3035	frightening	3594
fat	1328	firearm	3163	football	1456	frog	811
fatal	3043	firefly	3303	for	12	from	26
fate	3007	fireworks	3930	forbid	3590	front	552
father	980	firm	1036	force	395	frost	3249

frown	826	generous	2507	grammar	3512	H	
fruit	1364	genius	3360	grand	1677		
frustration	1977	gentle	2065	grandmother	1693	habit	1979
fry	2648	gentleman	793	grant	1237	habitat	2960
fuel	1292	genuine	2303	grape	803	hack	2174
fulfill	2056	geography	2417	graphic	1606	hail	3693
full	228	geological	3852	grasp	3371	hair	891
fun	514	geometry	3180	grass	2351	half	661
function	495	gesture	3723	grateful	2496	hall	1405
fund	441	get	38	grave	2092	halt	3827
fundamental	2042	ghost	2546	gravity	2277	hammer	2867
funeral	2839	giant	1828	gray	2154	hand	291
fungus	3726	gift	984	grease	3256	handle	850
fur	3493	gig	3486	great	101	handsome	818
furnish	3174	gill	3308	green	859	handy	2530
furniture	2175	ginger	3784	greet	2800	hang	1331
furthermore	2749	giraffe	828	grid	2540	happen	370
fury	3576	girl	744	grief	3887	happy	594
fuse	2582	give	91	grill	2508	harassment	3275
future	488	glad	1886	grind	2560	harbor	2595
		glamorous	3858	grip	2200	hard	308
		glance	3315	grit	3886	harm	1708
G		gland	3665	grocery	2638	harmony	2723
		glass	1215	groom	3676	harness	3212
gadget	3950	glaze	3767	groove	3704	harsh	2939
gain	834	glimpse	3690	gross	2622	harvest	2515
galaxy	2363	global	721	ground	766	hassle	3649
gallery	2023	glory	2133	groundbreaking	3073	hat	2150
gambling	3370	gloss	3816	group	223	hatch	3792
game	132	glove	2746	grove	3877	hate	1599
gameplay	3601	glow	2945	grow	239	haul	3442
gang	2827	glue	2437	guarantee	1447	haunt	3525
gap	1871	go	55	guard	1661	have	13
garage	2311	goal	560	guardian	2617	hazard	2553
garbage	3490	goat	3598	guess	1216	he	21
garden	1068	god	1393	guest	1125	head	301
garlic	2961	gold	847	guide	609	headline	3066
garment	3562	good	42	guideline	1971	headquarters	2159
gas	1128	goodbye	817	guild	3692	heal	1631
gate	2072	goodwill	2160	guilty	2118	health	185
gather	1502	gorgeous	2513	gulf	3800	hear	379
gauge	2825	gospel	2744	gum	3380	heart	619
gay	2743	government	349	gun	1330	heat	710
gear	1406	grab	1757	gut	2718	heaven	1994
gem	2963	grace	2097	guy	660	heavy	1002
gender	2331	grade	971	gymnasium	2292	hedge	3585
gene	1524	gradual	2276			heel	2669
general	329	graduate	866			hell	1842
generate	603	grain	2206			help	85
generation	1585						

moreover	2862	necessity	2950	nucleus	3933	onion	2854
morning	957	neck	1978	null	3789	only	69
mortality	2721	need	63	number	159	open	186
mortgage	1943	needle	2809	numerical	3771	operation	351
most	72	negative	1315	numerous	1718	opinion	1234
mother	952	neglect	3188	nurse	1217	opponent	1169
motion	1688	negotiation	1929	nurture	3744	opportunity	465
motivate	1591	neighborhood	1246	nut	2208	opposite	2026
motor	1356	neither	1913	nutrition	1466	oppression	3815
motorcycle	1483	nerve	1833			optical	2527
mount	1272	nest	2727	**O**		optimal	2883
mountain	1211	net	1465			optimistic	3355
mouse	2098	neutral	2495	oak	2810	optimize	1862
mouth	1773	never	242	obedient	2691	option	272
move	175	nevertheless	3048	obesity	3351	or	23
movie	924	new	60	obey	2988	oracle	3679
mower	3982	newspaper	2179	object	925	oral	2474
much	110	next	232	objective	1679	orbit	3219
mud	3131	nice	664	obligation	1938	order	290
multiple	763	niche	3164	obscure	3751	ordinary	2503
multitude	3974	night	388	observe	1175	organ	1905
municipal	2765	nightmare	3334	obsessed	2876	organic	1269
murder	1741	no	67	obstacle	3084	organization	1658
muscle	1329	noble	3222	obstruction	3783	organize	350
museum	1424	nobody	2242	obtain	1250	oriental	2281
mushroom	3397	nod	3671	obvious	1079	orientation	2314
music	394	node	2410	occasion	1326	origin	1729
must	194	noise	1673	occupation	2036	original	510
mutation	3606	nominate	2237	occupy	1573	ornament	3871
mutual	2730	none	1489	occur	874	orthodox	3956
mystery	1926	nonetheless	3738	ocean	1829	other	59
myth	2724	noon	808	odd	1843	otherwise	1231
		nor	1522	odor	3640	ought	996
N		norm	3394	of	6	ounce	2616
		normal	649	off	153	out	43
nail	2204	north	550	offender	2661	outcome	1726
naked	3402	nose	2309	offensive	1584	outfit	2526
name	176	not	27	offer	164	outgoing	1150
narrative	2295	notch	3217	office	179	outlet	2539
narrow	2043	note	299	official	1895	outline	2119
nasty	3457	nothing	589	offset	2841	outlook	2770
nation	154	notice	481	often	340	output	1437
native	1602	notion	2917	oil	616	outrageous	3681
nature	339	notorious	3902	old	243	outreach	3749
navigate	1762	novel	1873	omit	3410	outstanding	1140
navy	2151	now	89	on	15	over	84
near	389	nowadays	3760	once	283	overall	978
neat	2920	nowhere	3141	one	34	overcome	2401
necessary	658	nuclear	2264	ongoing	2027	overlap	3495

smart	1486	spare	2504	stadium	2406	straightforward	3384
smash	3347	spark	2522	staff	634	strain	2286
smell	1836	sparkle	3441	stage	852	strand	3413
smile	1931	spawn	3379	stain	1896	strange	1659
smoke	1421	speak	440	stair	3175	strap	2477
smooth	1410	special	312	stake	2889	strategy	679
snack	2505	species	1519	stall	3274	straw	3949
snake	3001	specific	434	stamp	2609	streak	3532
snap	2285	specimen	3687	stance	3759	stream	1470
sneak	2894	spectacular	1925	stand	524	streamline	3465
snooze	2501	spectrum	2606	standard	450	street	684
snow	1898	speculate	2822	staple	3458	strength	1007
so	37	speech	1813	star	669	stress	1243
soak	2733	speed	728	stare	3184	stretch	1605
soap	2528	spell	1797	start	106	strict	2287
soccer	2755	spend	424	starve	3977	strike	1226
social	405	sperm	2980	stat	2837	string	1459
sock	3038	sphere	3317	state	124	strip	1848
socket	3267	spice	2353	static	2916	stripe	3145
sodium	3536	spider	3412	station	1102	strive	2682
soft	1245	spike	3057	statistics	1712	stroke	2340
soil	1830	spill	3216	statue	3101	stroll	3456
solar	1856	spin	1960	status	1253	strong	498
soldier	2015	spine	2615	statute	2651	structure	854
sole	1902	spiral	3919	stay	521	struggle	1333
solid	1307	spirit	923	steady	2483	stud	3987
solo	2397	spite	3883	steal	1736	student	92
solution	577	splash	3432	steam	2211	study	1383
solve	1313	split	1800	steel	1577	stuff	919
some	33	spoil	2896	steep	2934	stumble	3494
somewhat	1992	spokesperson	2978	steer	2578	stun	1958
son	928	sponsor	1621	stem	2110	stupid	2459
song	989	spoon	795	step	381	sturdy	3474
soon	726	spot	940	stereo	3506	style	529
soothing	3926	spouse	2742	stick	915	subdued	2273
sophisticated	2627	spray	1997	stiff	3034	subject	720
sophomore	3979	spread	1373	still	142	submit	969
sore	3116	spring	1025	stimulate	2297	subscribe	1487
sorry	1682	sprinkle	3182	stir	2491	subsequent	2078
sort	1098	sprint	3153	stitch	2618	subsidiary	3416
soul	1643	spur	3524	stock	868	subsidy	3624
sound	444	spy	3499	stomach	2525	substance	1432
soup	2738	squad	2632	stone	1434	substantial	2714
sour	813	square	1278	stop	439	substitute	2386
source	534	squat	3750	store	322	subtle	2569
south	680	squeeze	2967	storm	1878	suburb	3044
sovereign	3589	stab	3814	story	377	subway	822
space	403	stable	1305	stove	3387	succeed	1649
span	2587	stack	2130	straight	1233	success	393

tone	1590	treasure	2040	ultra	3335	value	253
tongue	2863	treat	366	umbrella	814	valve	2223
tonight	2415	treaty	3266	uncle	791	van	3089
too	173	tree	958	under	236	vanity	3675
tool	505	trek	3946	undergo	2673	vapor	3339
tooth	1805	tremendous	2758	undermine	3943	various	762
top	244	trend	1379	underneath	3027	vary	604
topic	1126	triangle	2951	understand	317	vast	2019
torque	3313	tribe	2453	undertake	2364	vault	3813
torture	3530	tribute	3104	underway	3952	vector	3260
toss	2890	trick	1595	uniform	2420	vegan	3404
total	508	trigger	1763	unify	2561	vegetable	1731
touch	966	trim	2263	union	1403	vegetarian	3866
tough	1543	trio	3927	unique	754	vehicle	751
tour	835	trip	945	unit	633	vein	3268
tournament	1920	triple	2912	united	1409	velocity	3273
tow	1639	triumph	3500	universe	1462	vendor	1990
towards	722	troops	2394	university	376	ventilation	2414
towel	2791	trophy	3262	unleash	3686	venture	2317
town	846	tropical	2857	unless	1083	venue	2148
toxic	2473	trouble	1446	unprecedented	2306	verbal	2671
toy	2047	true	1285	until	331	verify	1778
trace	2226	trunk	3399	unto	3058	versatile	2533
track	561	trust	882	unveil	2990	verse	2468
tract	3593	try	122	up	49	version	517
traction	3854	tub	3223	upcoming	2232	versus	1534
trade	667	tube	1652	update	568	vertical	2302
traditional	736	tuck	3631	upgrade	1325	very	90
traffic	1236	tuition	2786	upon	687	vessel	2326
tragedy	2636	tumor	2794	upper	1611	vest	3668
trail	1090	tune	1680	upright	3975	veteran	1915
train	311	turbo	3481	upset	2705	veterinarian	2255
trait	3002	turn	278	upward	3185	via	894
transaction	1473	turnout	2166	urban	2100	viable	2948
transcript	2659	turnover	3779	urge	1935	vibe	3859
transfer	922	turtle	3527	urine	2737	vibrant	2932
transform	1453	tutor	1723	use	30	vibration	3024
transition	1463	tweak	3105	usual	426	vice	2105
translate	1593	tweet	2611	utilize	1202	victim	1518
transmit	1625	twice	1613	utter	3013	victory	1795
transparent	2413	twin	2411			view	116
transplant	3427	twist	2202		**V**	viewpoint	2982
transport	1188	type	281			villa	3520
trap	2067	typical	972	vacancy	3502	village	1691
trapezoid	3067			vacation	1989	villain	3817
trash	3087		**U**	vacuum	2779	vinegar	3245
travel	472			vague	3812	vintage	2623
tray	3060	ugly	785	valid	1345	vinyl	3225
treadmill	2163	ultimate	1256	valley	1784	violation	1835

Allvoca basic

초　판 1쇄 발행일 2020년 7월 20일
초　판 6쇄 발행일 2024년 8월 22일

지은이 송승호
펴낸이 양옥매
디자인 송예린

펴낸곳 도서출판 책과나무
출판등록 제2012-000376
주소 서울특별시 마포구 방울내로 79 이노빌딩 302호
대표전화 02.372.1537 **팩스** 02.372.1538
이메일 booknamu2007@naver.com
홈페이지 www.booknamu.com
ISBN 979-11-5776-913-1 (13740)